The Video Game Theory Reader 2

The Video Game Theory Reader 2 continues the exploration begun in the first *Video Game Theory Reader* (Routledge, 2003) with a group of leading scholars turning their attention to a wide variety of theoretical concerns and approaches, examining and raising new issues in the rapidly expanding field of video games studies. The editors' Introduction picks up where the Introduction in the first *Video Game Theory Reader* left off, considering the growth of the field and setting challenges for the future. The volume concludes with an appendix presenting over 40 theories and disciplines that can be usefully and insightfully applied to the study of video games.

Bernard Perron is an Associate Professor of Cinema at the University of Montreal. He has co-edited *The Video Game Theory Reader* (2003), written *Silent Hill: il motore del terrore* (2006), an analysis of the Silent Hill video game series, and is editing *Gaming After Dark: Essays on Horror Video Games* (forthcoming, 2009).

Mark J. P. Wolf is an Associate Professor in the Communication Department at Concordia University Wisconsin. His books include *Abstracting Reality: Art, Communication, and Cognition in the Digital Age* (2000), *The Medium of the Video Game* (2001), *Virtual Morality: Morals, Ethics, and New Media* (2003), *The Video Game Theory Reader* (2003), *The World of the D'ni: Myst and Riven* (2006), *The Video Game Explosion: A History from PONG to PlayStation and Beyond* (2007), and *J. R. R. Tolkien: Of Words and Worlds* (forthcoming, 2009).

The Video Game Theory Reader 2

Edited by **Bernard Perron and Mark J. P. Wolf**

Routledge
Taylor & Francis Group

NEW YORK AND LONDON

First published 2009
by Routledge
270 Madison Ave, New York, NY 10016

Simultaneously published in the UK
by Routledge
2 Park Square, Milton Park, Abingdon, Oxon OX14 4RN

Routledge is an imprint of the Taylor & Francis Group, an informa business

© 2009 Taylor & Francis

Typeset in Minion by
RefineCatch Limited, Bungay, Suffolk
Printed and bound in the United States of America on acid-free paper by
Edwards Brothers, Inc.

Library of Congress Cataloging-in-Publication Data
The video game theory reader 2 / edited by Bernard Perron and Mark J. P. Wolf.
    p. cm.
    Includes bibliographical references and index.
    1. Video games. I. Perron, Bernard.   II. Wolf, Mark J. P.   III. Video game theory
reader.   IV. Title: Video game theory reader 2.
    GV1469.3.V57 2008
    794.8—dc22

ISBN10: 0–415–96282–X (hbk)
ISBN10: 0–415–96283–8 (pbk)
ISBN10: 0–203–88766–2 (ebk)

ISBN13: 978–0–415–96282–7 (hbk)
ISBN13: 978–0–415–96283–4 (pbk)
ISBN13: 978–0–203–88766–0 (ebk)

Contents

Foreword

TIM SKELLY

One of the early innovators working in the video game industry during the 1970s and 1980s, Tim Skelly has a number of notable accomplishments which influenced the growing video game industry. While working at Cinematronics, he designed and wrote vector games, the first of which, Starhawk *(1978) saved the company from going bankrupt (*Starhawk *was also one of the earliest games to breach the boundary between the diegetic and non-diegetic aspects within a video game; see his description below). Skelly's second game,* Sundance *(1979), for which he also designed the cabinet artwork (as he did for all his games), had a switch that could set the display to either English or Japanese, making it one of the first multilingual games produced. Next Skelly wrote* Warrior *(1979), the first one-on-one fighting game which began the fighting genre.* Warrior *featured a top view of two knights sword-fighting, and it was the first game to use inverse kinematics, a computer animation technique which determines the positions of joints based on the endpoints of the jointed figure (in* Warrior, *the points of the swords), rather than requiring the movements to be calculated segment by segment. In addition to inventing the fighting genre, Skelly also designed the first true two-player co-operative game,* Rip Off *(1980). (An earlier two-player game, Atari's* Fire Truck *(1978), came close, but was really a single-player game operated by two players.) After three more vector games for Cinematronics,* Armor Attack *(1980),* Star Castle *(1980), and* War of the Worlds *(1982), Skelly created* Reactor *(1982) for Gottlieb, which became the first video game in which the game company agreed to feature the designer's name onscreen. Skelly would create two more games for Gottlieb (later renamed Mylstar),* Insector *(1982) and* Screw Loose *(1983), before going on to co-found a company, Incredible Technologies, which designed and developed interactive software. After working with clients including Williams*

Electronics, Bally/Midway, and Capcom, Skelly joined the Sega Technical Institute, and later became a member of the Microsoft User Interface Research Group.

There are compelling reasons to play video games, but the most important of these have little to do with the apparent content of the games themselves. For instance, short of watching paint dry, *PONG* has got to be the baseline of entertainment, at least on its surface. In the early years of video games, why was it that *PONG* and its offspring were so outrageously successful and why were bars and restaurants suddenly filled with them? Bars have welcomed pinball games ever since there were pinball games, so it is not surprising that they would welcome video games as well. When the first wave of video games washed over the world, they were suddenly everywhere. Early video games were not just in bars and amusement arcades, their ancestral homes, they were in barber shops and beauty salons and everywhere paper money could be changed for quarters. Why? I have an explanation for this that does not require invoking the paranormal, black ops or alien invasions. Businesses that operate at a level that requires making change (A) have quarters and (B) are usually operating on a shoestring. Early video games were an income supplement, and for as long as the craze lasted they were a friend to small businesses. After the first wave, video arcade games continued (and still continue) to provide support to movie theaters, Ma and Pa arcades, boardwalks, etc. In 1983, I wrote and illustrated a book of cartoons about video games called *Shoot the Robot, Then Shoot Mom* (though I am *not* a sociopath!). In it I had a running gag called "One of fifteen remaining places you haven't seen a video game." One of those places was a jogging path, another was a bathtub. I had a difficult time coming up with fifteen.

That is my economic theory of *PONG* and other early video games, which takes as given that there were hordes of players eager to fill coin boxes with quarters. This tells us nothing about why the hordes wanted to play the game. For all we knew at the time, it was just a fad or fashion like the Wonderbra. (Not exactly like the Wonderbra, of course.) Still, why were such large numbers and varieties of people playing these things, especially the earliest, most primitive machines like *PONG*? Questions like that weighed heavily on me from the moment I was put in the position of inventing a video game that would earn its keep and, by fortunate extension, mine.

Between 1978 and 1982, I designed eight successful video arcade games and programmed all but one myself. The exception was *Star Castle*, which I designed, and Scott Boden programmed. I designed the cabinet art for these games as well. Doing the math, I averaged two successful games a year. What was my secret? What had I learned from my experience that

I could use myself and pass on to others? Almost nothing, I'm ashamed to say. I had been lucky. I credit myself with some good intuitions, but I also worked in an industry that was beginning to burn as bright as the Sun. For the sake of my ego, I will say that there were only a few designers like myself who had such a strong string of hits, but it all came down to intuition, constraints and a few lucky hunches. Looking back, I would have to describe those hunches as successful theories. For instance, I can now tell you why I think *PONG* and its clones were so successful, and I promise to do just that. But first, let us dive into the past.

"A man walks into a bar with an orange box under his arm."

Is this a shaggy dog story or the beginning of a text adventure game? It is neither. It is how I came to be a programmer and designer of video games. One evening in 1977, I was wondering whether to go see the movie *Star Wars* for the fifth time. I worked at the restaurant next door to the bar I just mentioned and the fellow with the orange box had this wacky idea. He wanted to run an arcade featuring computer games, not video games. He had nothing against video games. He just felt that they weren't as multi-purpose as computers. (I would like to insert here that Douglas Pratt, the man with the orange box under his arm, went on to found some seminal game company that you would recognize in a heartbeat, but I cannot. Sometimes people who are ahead of their time are just too far ahead of their time.) Together, Doug and I began the Cyborg Computer Gaming Center in Kansas City, Missouri.

A game program that came with our orange boxes (The PolyMorphic Systems Poly 88 computer) was a version of the classic text game, *Oregon Trail*, created by Don Rawitsch, Bill Heinemann, and Paul Dillengerger. *Oregon Trail* was an exercise in resource management. If not the first, it was certainly one of the forerunners of today's simulation games. The version we had was text-based and like most games of this type, it assumed that the player would find balancing resources to be interesting and perhaps fun. For many, that would be true, but I hated *Oregon Trail*. I really, really, hated it. It was all about trade-offs and the arbitrary nature of life. I especially hated Doc, the game's frontier physician. About every third turn, Doc would inform you that you had contracted some hideous frontier disease. Or, just as bad, you were randomly wounded by arrows or stray shots. Alright, don't shoot the messenger, as they say, but Doc demanded cold hard cash for his services and that was in short supply. Fresh wild game, protection from raiders and indigenous peoples, etc., these should have been enough payment for him, but no, Doc wanted hard cash on the barrelhead.

Of course, "Doc" wanted nothing. "Doc" was a text string attached to some simple branching code and print commands. The game was not capable of changing its mind, nor could it offer me alternatives to the bits of language that were embedded in the game. I had been emotionally aroused by text, but not in the conventional, literary manner. The authors of *Oregon Trail* probably did not intend to negatively arouse the emotions of the game's players. Even so, my frustration was on a par with a man assembling a bicycle from instructions translated into English from Cantonese via the original Tagalog. My intention to live a carefree frontier life had been frustrated, and frustrating the intentions of a computer user was then, and still is, one of the worst things any game or interface designer could be responsible for. I would revisit this scenario many times over the years and it inspired me to coin this catch phrase: "The effect of any interface is to affect the user." I would return often to that phrase as theory.

I will give this to "Doc," he motivated me to write my own games. My first game mod was to alter the code for *Oregon Trail* so that the player could "SHOOT DOC." Oh, sure, the next time I was wounded I died of sepsis because Doc was no more, but I died knowing that the old bastard went before me.

So, back to my question, what made *PONG* and other early video games so popular? Text adventures like *Oregon Trail* were usually displayed on light emitting CRTs, but the text did not move. The functional effect was virtually the same as reading text on paper. But even a non-moving source of direct light attracts the eye with a pull greater than reflected light. Add motion, a survival cue for us mammals, to a light source and you almost have a video game. Does adding motion to a direct source of light explain the popularity of *PONG*? I am tempted to say yes, but if that were the case we would be talking about the theoretical aspects of Lava Lamps. Determining what makes any particular video game successful requires looking at business models (see above), novelty of design, timing (being at the right place at the right time) and yes, gameplay. But, almost as important as those other factors, the "ball" and "paddles" of *PONG* were rendered at a refresh rate of sixty frames per second, fast enough to pass the flicker fusion threshold, fast enough to give the player the impression that the glowing white square was something tangible. Combine that with tightly synchronized interaction between real knobs and virtual paddles, and for a quarter, you could luxuriate in a sense of efficacy. And, if you cared to, you could even play a game of Ping Pong. That was my theory when I was making games at the Cyborg Computer Gaming Center. After that, it held up quite well at the first real game company I worked for, Cinematronics.

In the area of video arcade games, I am best known for those I created at Cinematronics in the late 1970s. Between them, the owners of Cinematronics, Jim Pierce and "Papa" Tom Stroud, had years of experience with a wide range of coin operated devices, many of which were the mechanical forerunners of the video game. These men were long time friends of pinball games, darts, skeeball, and the like, but they were not game players. They were businessmen who, because of the monstrous success of *PONG*, sensed that the future of their families and perhaps their families' families was bound up with video arcade games. Operators ran cash businesses and to them games were games and video games were just another way to fill their home freezers with silver dollars. Suddenly, I was in the Wild West.

Before Cinematronics, I had been working within the constraints of the Polly 88 graphics display which had a pixel resolution of 128 × 48. I often had to use punctuation marks and other built in characters to add detail. Screen refresh cycles were slow enough to be visible, giving me a way to add a sense of animation to the scene. The Cinematronics hardware and display systems, created by Larry Rosenthal, could not have been more different. The Poly 88 was a big brush with a small canvas. The Cinematronics hardware system was ultra fast (compared with the Poly 88), had a huge canvas and a fine line pen that kept running out of ink. Or, put another way, the vector display was a short, stiff string that had two states, floating on or hiding below a sea of black. The cathode ray tubes used by Cinematronics were literally a blank slate. There was no raster. There was nothing but a screaming beam of electrons being shot in the direction I specified in my program. Unlike "real" vector displays, there was no display list. There wasn't even a flag that would tell me that a line had finished drawing. I had to work out a rule-of-thumb algorithm based on line length to tell me when it was safe to move the beam again. I was always refining that code, trying to get just a little more line time on screen, more pointing and moving, relieved by blackness when the beam needed to jump to an area not contiguous with the current visible line. As a game designer, what can you do with that, especially when so little can be displayed?

During the years I worked at Cinematronics, we almost always used the same make and brand of cathode ray tube in every game, even though it was sometimes difficult to obtain. The reason for that was the specific decay time of the phosphor after the beam had moved on. The electron beam left behind a visible motion blur, or more accurately, a motion glow. Other tubes had a decay rate that was too short, causing flickering. Most others, designed for raster scanned devices, had a much longer decay rate which made lines streak in uninteresting ways. In the sweet spot, one particular make of cathode ray tube gave us a perfect motion blur that punched up the sense of reality. With this, added to the fixed frame rate of 60 frames per second, the player had a sense that they were reaching through the looking glass. Today I hear gamers using the words "buttery smooth" to describe the effect of high refresh rates. We have yet to go beyond the glass, but the desire to get there has always been strong.

In the case of Cinematronics, which based its hardware on the MIT mainframe game *Spacewar!*, I could display fine detail and rotations that could not be found in raster games at the time. I made it a point to keep my lines short and close together because that reduced the distance the beam had to travel, thus giving me more time with the lights on, as it were. It was a strategy, a working theory, that had functioned well for *Space War* and it proved to be useful for me. My games *Rip-Off, Warrior*, and *Armor Attack* all benefited from it. Unfortunately, I was not always mindful of this rule. My own game *Sundance* and *War of the Worlds*, for which I designed the screen graphics and animation, both failed partially because I had not taken my own observations into account. The ultimate proof of my theory came when Jim Pierce forced a new programmer to create a vector version of an LED handheld game. It was called *Barrier* and it is perhaps the worst vector game ever made. By negative example, this game confirmed the correctness of my theory. It had no rotations, moves were in discrete jumps and vectors were long and static.

The play action of my first Cinematronics game, *Starhawk*, was informed by its predecessors from the midway. Functionally, *Starhawk* was nothing more than a video version of the shooting gallery games you would find at any carnival. But, rather than emulate the bull's-eyes, ducks, and clay pipes of the midway, I naturally looked to *Star Wars* for my thematic material. (My primary source was Tom DeFanti's computer graphics readout which he created for that movie. Tom was a friend of mine in Chicago and at one point he offered to send me one of his students if I wasn't able to master the Cinematronics hardware I managed.) *Starhawk* featured a background similar to the trench run, with a few different ships that could be targeted and destroyed for various point scores. Unlike what was to become the standard "three tries and you die" method of terminating a game, I gave the player an initial time to play of sixty seconds and awarded additional time when a certain number of points were scored. One particular enemy ship, if not destroyed quickly, would attack the digits displaying the player's time remaining, replacing those with a new, lower number of seconds left. My small way of letting the player know that there was a "man behind the curtain," the game designer. *Starhawk* could be played by one or two players, each represented by a crosshairs on the screen. Few video games had high score tables at that time, so the real goal for the player was longevity, seeing how much enter-tainment could be had for a quarter. Though *Starhawk* was not designed to be played in this manner, a single player could select two-player mode and use both joysticks at once, each stick collecting its own score. Crazy fun, even if it usually meant a very short game. A game designer should keep in mind that the player is a subversive collaborator. There are gamers of every stripe and kind that believe rules are there to be tested, broken, and rebuilt to suit their own idea of fun. This sort of behavior is not always welcomed by designers, but it is understandable.

One of the primary reasons to play games is to gain a sense of being effective in the world, even if that world is on the other side of a window through which we cannot pass. Our need for efficacy is powerful. We crave a sense of tangible effectiveness and we are made anxious if we are denied it. Fortunately, it is quite easy to give game players a feeling of efficacy and a little bit goes a long way. A surprisingly subtle example is the high-score table. As I just mentioned, high score tables were not present when the era of video arcade games began, but many game designers thought it would be a good idea to have them, myself included. Games of all kinds, well before video games, used various ranking systems to establish hierarchies amongst players and to give onlookers something to talk about. Early on we did not add them to our machines simply because memory chips were relatively expensive and game operators, as a rule, were tight with a dollar. When we were finally given enough memory to display top scores, we discovered that the high-score table was an extraordinarily popular feature. Here's my idea of why that was. If you just walk away from an arcade game without setting a high score, the game resets to its original state. It is as though you were never there. But if you get your name on the high-score table, it stays until it is pushed off by higher scores. For some period of time, however short, everybody who can see the game can see your name. You can bring your friends to the machine and show them your score or you could let your friends and competitors find out for themselves. You have made a tangible mark on the world and for the tiniest fraction of eternity you have affirmed your existence.

Speaking of efficacy, what is my all time favorite fun thing to do? First, design a video game that features balls of glowing energy bouncing between two walls. Then, late at night, go down to the factory floor after about 200 of those games have been manufactured, ready to be shipped the next day. Make sure that the "Sound in Attract Mode" switch has been set to "on" for all of them. Hit the coin switches and bask.

I wish everyone could do that.

The game was *Sundance*, my second for Cinematronics. Besides the amazing sound of those bouncing balls of energy, *Sundance* had vectors with variable levels of intensity and a switch that allowed the word "BONUS" to be displayed in Japanese as well as English. Unfortunately, nearly half of all *Sundance* games that were manufactured suffered damage because of faulty parts, so the run was very small. Whatever the fate of the game might have been, that night in the warehouse I enjoyed a powerful sense of efficacy that I never had before or since. I know, it's nothing compared to childbirth, but I'll take it.

Vector graphics were great if you wanted smooth rotation, finely detailed tracings of glowing lines, and a fast refresh rate. I wanted these things very much and I was happy to have them. The big trade-off was what I could not have in my game graphics; that would be anything that wasn't a short, glowing piece of stiff string. When I chose to make a game about two sword-fighting knights, *Warrior*, I knew I had a few design problems to deal with. The player-characters had to be viewed from the top down to help computation speed and simplify hit testing. Although the Vectorbeam system was capable of generating accurate representations of 3-D objects, this was quite expensive computationally. For his game *Speed Freak*, even Larry Rosenthal, the designer of the Cinematronics hardware, made extensive use of restrictions and simplifications to create the first true 3-D views of objects in a video game.

Hit testing was not a simple matter in a vector environment either. Raster games had many fast, simple ways to indicate when objects collided because of their cell-like structure. Whenever a pixel or group of pixels changed state, that information became available to the program, which would then take these changes into account when the next refresh cycle occurred. I had only one method for detecting collisions between objects. I knew the X and Y values of the endpoints of each line because that was the information I used to draw lines. I wrote a very simple, very fast piece of code that determined if two lines crossed. Not all lines had to be tested, so I was able to test just the lines that made up a sword edge or the area around the head of a player's knight

That worked out well, but having concentrated so much of my glowing string in two small areas, what could I do about that big, empty wasteland on the screen? The large number of vectors that made up the knights ate up so much of my string's length that the figures were quite tiny. Not a small thing if you are trying to affect the emotions of your players, or at least give them some eye candy to relieve the grim blackness of the screen. Taking a cue from the multitude of mechanical shooting games that made use of black lights and mirrors, I designed *Warrior* with a half-silvered mirror in mind. It reflected a day-glow top-down view of medieval stairways and pits onto the screen. This was not just for decoration. The reflected art indicated the areas the player should avoid if they were not to fall into a pit, a fall that would give points to your opponent. For this game I relied on the craft and theory of coin-operated amusement device designers, who in turn owed much to stagecraft centuries old.

By now, my theories regarding the Cinematronics hardware were well tested and proven, but each game I designed came embedded with its own need for theory. For instance, how was I to enable the players to engage their opponents? If you have a novel design problem and no one has come up with a solution before you, you have to be inventive. So, I asked myself, "What is the most important point in a sword fight?" "The tip of the sword" was my theory. In fighting games that came years later, like *Street Fighter II*, gameplay would take the form of a slightly complex version of Ro Sham Bo, also known as Rock, Paper, Scissors. That was not a bad idea as it turned out, but much earlier, when I made *Warrior*, I had the opportunity to use vector graphics, which allowed me to do things that could not be done with sprites and character blocks.

My knights and their swords were made up of endpoints that my program would organize within the constraints I assigned to it. Recall that the view of the game was from the top down. If a player moved a single endpoint, the tip of their sword, towards the top of their character's head, the visual effect was to see a sword raised vertically. If the sword tip was pulled away from the body of the player's knight, the sword would extend and rotate based again on the position of the sword tip. This scheme of mine might be described as analogue inverse kinematics. My program saw to it that the lines stayed connected in a meaningful way, and by manipulating just two crucial points, the sword tip and the center of the player's head, the player was able to control all meaningful aspects of

Figure 0.1 For the game *Warrior* (1979), static artwork was reflected over a vector display, an ancient illusion in the service of video games. (Photograph by Archer Maclean.)

the figure. I have to give much credit and thanks to fantasy artist Frank Brunner who made real the great hall of the game. Also to his credit, Frank executed the magnificent art for the side of the cabinet, a feature that helped to flesh out the bits of string. Given the abstract nature of vector graphics, or many early primitive video game graphics for that matter, cabinet artists did us all a great service by illustrating for the player just what the hell we thought they should think they were playing.

Not counting *War of the Worlds*, an exercise I began for new programmer Rob Patton, *Rip-Off*, *Star Castle*, and *Armor Attack* were the vector games I created and completed after *Warrior*. They all had special elements and each was a success. My theories about vector graphics and gameplay were holding up well. Especially successful was *Rip-Off*, my cooperative play game inspired by market research. Not research for any game company, but a tip I got from my girlfriend, a disc jockey at a radio station with a large and broad market. This is what she heard and repeated to me: "People like to cooperate," "people" being listeners to mammoth radio stations, not "people" being arcade game players. Not a sure thing, but a theory worth testing. Because of repeated application and refinement, in all aspects *Rip-Off* was the most true to my own theories. Adding "people like to cooperate" was a bonus. Over the years there has been ample proof that the game and its embedded theories were successful. First, it was fun to play. I would have settled for that alone. Second, it was financially successful, nothing wrong with that either. And third, the proof of theory that still means the most to me, I continue to get e-mails from players who fondly remember the great fun they had playing *Rip-Off* with a friend.

You would think that by this time I knew a few things about what made a great video game. Maybe I did know a few things, but there are always more factors to success and failure than you can imagine, especially in the Wild West atmosphere of arcade games in the 1980s. Before going freelance as a game designer, I briefly worked for Gremlin/SEGA in San Diego. There they were experimenting with color vector graphics, which were not much of an improvement over black and white vector graphics. I did a few experiments with color vectors; simulating interactive light sources was one idea I tried. But color vectors were just as skinny as white ones, black was still black and there was too much of that to make a colorful display. The theories I formulated at Cinematronics still held true and were transferable, but raster graphics were clearly overtaking vectors. The raster hardware at Gremlin/SEGA supported a relatively wide color palette which could be animated by changing values in the color registers. Other hardware helpers were the "sprites," discreet bits of artwork that could move over the primary background image at a motion resolution similar to what I had at Cinematronics. But rotating raster art was clunky at best because raster sprites did not actually rotate. A rough version of rotation could be had by creating multiple sprites of the same object, each pre-rendered at a different angle. If the sprite image was symmetrical, more space could be saved by flipping and flopping the images. With these resources I prototyped a game that featured a scrolling background with a third-person point of view. The player's ship rotated around a central point. One control swung the ship in a circular path. Another moved the ship in and out around the center, decreasing the ship's size as it moved to the center, growing in size as it pulled back. This gave the illusion that the player was moving forward and backwards. That was on the sprite plane. On the background plane I designed a scrolling terrain which shifted from a top-down view to a view looking at the horizon as the game progressed. For the player, it was a shift from bomber to jet fighter. Still, for all the bells and whistles, the game play was essentially a shooting gallery like *Starhawk*.

My explorations at Gremlin/SEGA were cut short when Cinematronics chose to sue me for allegedly passing along trade secrets. It was a nuisance suit which was quickly dismissed, a token of how much they missed me, I like to think. But I felt bad about not being able to finish my game. If I had been farther along it might have been finished by another programmer, but it wasn't. Still, I was able to walk away with the results from my experiments combining vector style motion with bitmap graphics, another useful bit of theory applied. *Reactor, Insector*, and *Screw Loose*, the games I would create for Gottlieb/Mylstar, all benefited from my work at Gremlin/SEGA.

In the early 1980s, almost every video arcade game had its own gameplay and most were running on hardware that had some new and unique method for producing cool graphics. No one was interested in reflection or nostalgia. It was crackling good fun to create new games with new rules. No one in the arcade game business ever said to me, "Maybe game players want to play the same game for a longer time. Maybe they want more familiarity and depth." For those who wanted that, there were home console games. If you wanted to play the games with the coolest sounds and graphics, you had to play the latest arcade games. Arcade games had another unique thing going for them, the allure of the arcade itself, a place where you probably shouldn't be, young man! (And they were, mostly, young men.) What video arcade games in the early 1980s needed was not novelty. There was too much of that already. Players had a wide range of new games to choose from, with even more titles popping up on a regular basis. For a few years I spent a good part of each weekend playing games in arcades and traveling to competitors' testing locations when word came around that there was a new game to check out. Games with novel gameplay weren't scarce and almost without exception weekly coin counts

Figure 0.2 Sales flyer for *Rip-Off* (1980), illustrated by Frank Brunner who had earlier enhanced *Warrior* with his outstanding background and cabinet art.

seemed to favor novelty. That might have been a reflection of how few sequels were being made, or it might have been a warning sign. Were there only a few sequels because few games were able to last longer than a month or so in the coin reports? Or, were players simply happy to enjoy novelty for its own sake? There was no way to know for sure. Within Gottlieb/

Mylstar, designers labored to create unique games, each different than the one the team across the room was developing. It seemed like every game that was introduced enjoyed at least a few moments at or near the top of coin collections, but with the amount of competition that was erupting, how long any game would stay there was unpredictable. It was not a good time for theory. There were too many variables and the data was chaotic. Perhaps it just seemed that way. When asked, a doctor friend of mine used to reply to the question "How are you?" with "I'm too close to the patient to make a diagnosis." That was definitely my situation. It was, I felt, a good time to find a place where I could step back and observe. I joined up with some friends and fellow game designers when they formed Free Radical Software, which became Incredible Technologies. I chose initially to work with them as Art Director, not as a game designer, because I believed that I did not have enough fundamental knowledge about game design. Truthfully, the chaotic times of the 1980s left me a bit scarred, and I was not eager to dive back in. But I kept my promise to myself and eventually formed some solid ideas about what What Makes Games Fun, some of which I have just shared with you.

Today, I look at my game design years as a time of data collection, with me in the role of an Arctic scientist, examining ice samples collected on expeditions taken years earlier. Perhaps some of what I have written here will serve a similar purpose for you.

Tim Skelly
April 7, 2008

Acknowledgments

A sequel like this could only be possible when the first book is successful, so we would first like to thank our audience, those readers and scholars who have helped develop video game theory into a field of study. A big, hearty thanks goes especially to all our contributors, who graciously joined this endeavor: Thomas H. Apperley, Samuel Archibald, Dominic Arsenault, Mark W. Bell, Tom Boellstorff, Brett Camper, Edward Castronova, Mia Consalvo, Robert Cornell, James J. Cummings, Shanly Dixon, Trevor Elkington, Matthew Falk, Richard E. Ferdig, Clara Fernández-Vara, Alida Field, Sébastien Genvo, Eitan Glinert, Garry C. Gray, Andreas Gregersen, Neal Grigsby, Torben Grodal, Carrie Heeter, Aki Järvinen, Henry Jenkins, Jesper Juul, Lars Konzack, Vili Lehdonvirta, Tuukka Lehtiniemi, Lev Manovich, Frans Mäyrä, Michael McGuffin, Sheila C. Murphy, David Myers, Martin Picard, Patrick Poulin, Pierre Poulin, Sarah B. Robbins-Bell, Travis Ross, Guillaume Roux-Girard, Kevin Schut, Michael Seare, Tim Skelly, Philip Tan, Laurie N. Taylor, Carl Therrien, Ragnhild Tronstad, Feichin Ted Tschang, Adrian Vetta, and Eric Zimmerman. Thanks also go to others whose help and support we are grateful for, including Matt Byrnie and Routledge for asking for this anthology and supporting it along the way, and all those who used our first one in the classroom.

Bernard would specially like to thank: Shantal Robert and Léa Elisabeth Perron for their unconditional support; my parents, as always; Simon Niedenthal of the Malmö University Center for Game Studies for his support during the last stretch in Sweden; and last but not the least, Mark with whom it was so agreeable to have collaborated once again.

Mark would specially like to thank: my parents, of course, who let me play video games as a kid long before I knew I was actually doing useful research; my wife Diane Wolf and sons Michael and Christian who were patient with the time taken to work on this book; and I of course must thank my co-editor Bernard who gladly joined me in the making of this anthology, and with whom I enjoyed collaborating. And, as always, thanks be to God.

Introduction

BERNARD PERRON
MARK J. P. WOLF

It need not be said that the field of video game studies is now a healthy and flourishing one. An explosion of new books, periodicals, online venues, and conferences over the past decade has confirmed the popularity, viability, and vitality of the field, in a way that perhaps few outside of it expected. The time has come to ask not only how the field is growing, but in what directions it could or should go.

Looking Back, Looking Ahead

Our "Introduction" in *The Video Game Theory Reader* left off in 2003, and since then, video games have gone through further important developments.[1] Among them, two new handheld video game consoles have been marketed, the Nintendo DS (2004) with a built-in microphone, wireless support, and a stylus used on the bottom touchscreen, and the PlayStation Portable, known as PSP (released in 2005 in North America), with its wireless and multi-media capabilities. A new generation of home video game consoles has also appeared. Microsoft's Xbox 360 (2005) and Sony's PlayStation 3 (PS3, 2006) brought increased engine power to the game industry, along with bigger, richer, and graphically-superior game worlds like the land of Cyrodiil in *The Elder Scrolls IV: Oblivion* (2K Games and

Bethesda Softworks, 2006) or the cities of the Holy Land of *Assassin's Creed* (Ubisoft, 2007). The Nintendo Wii (2006), with its primary handheld pointing device, the Wiimote, has transformed the way people play games.[2] Following in the long line of innovative interfaces from early steering wheels and handlebars to the dance pad of *Dance Dance Revolution* (Konami, 1999 in North America), rhythm games like those of the *Guitar Hero* series (Harmonix/Nerversoft, 2005–2007) have popularized the use of other types of peripherals like the guitar-shaped controller used to simulate guitar playing. Harmonix Music Systems's *Rock Band* (2007) went a step further, combining guitar, drums, and voice inputs into a multi-player music game. Online gaming continues to grow in importance. With the appearance of Microsoft's Xbox LIVE, Sony's PlayStation Network, and Nintendo's Wi-Fi Connection, all the major corporations have con-solidated their online services. Online multiplayer versions and customiza-tion facilities have become common features of first-person shooters, such as *Call of Duty 4: Modern Warfare* (Infinity Ward, 2007) or *Halo 3* (Bungie Studios, 2007). While MMORPGs were already popular, *World of Warcraft* (Blizzard, 2004) found incredible success with its current 10 million sub-scribers worldwide. And today, the average game *player* is now 33 years old and has been playing games for 12 years.[3]

All these changes are worth considering from the outset because video game systems and games themselves are the starting points of theories. They have influenced and will continue to influence the methods of look-ing at video games. Undeniably, the field of video game studies did not undergo quite as much progress; technological revolutions often outstrip and happen more often than intellectual ones. But the field did evolve, and continues to accelerate.

Our approach to this new collection of essays on video game theory reflects these changes. The first *Video Game Theory Reader* was largely concerned with justifying the existence of video game theory in academia. We wanted to establish that there was already a history of writing about video games, from the early writings of computer enthusiasts and hobby-ists, to the trade journals and in-house company journals of the 1970s, and that the video game had begun to be examined more substantially in the 1980s and 1990s, with books like Chris Crawford's *The Art of Computer Game Design* (1982); Marsha Kinder's *Playing With Power: Movies, Televi-sion, and Video Games from Muppet Babies to Teenage Mutant Ninja Turtles* (1991); Leonard Herman's *Phoenix: The Fall and Rise of Home Video Games* (1994); Espen Aarseth's *Cybertext: Perspectives on Ergodic Literature* (1997); Janet Murray's *Hamlet on the Holodeck. The Future of Narrative in Cyberspace* (1997), and others. Perhaps we should have emphasized the work going on in the 1980s even more strongly, for as Jo Bryce and Jason

Rutter point out in *Understanding Digital Games* (2006), this era is often neglected:

> Unfortunately, this resource of digital games analysis is often not fully credited by contemporary authors. For example, Wolf and Perron (2003) suggest that their collection would not have previously been possible because of a lack of academics working on digital games and Newman (2004) suggests that academics have ignored digital games. The trope that digital games have been neglected by researchers and marginalized by the academy is problematic given the lack of substantive evidence provided. There is, of course, a difference between a topic being overlooked and being ignored—there is no malice or intentionality in the former. Suggesting that digital games have not received the academic attention they deserve because they have been framed as "a children's medium" or "mere trifles" (Newman 2004: 5) is difficult to accept without sources for these accusations.[4]

Part of the reason for possible omissions is the multidisciplinary nature of video game studies, even back then. For example, Bryce and Rutter (2006, 1) cite "the case report by McCowan (1981) of 'Space Invader wrist' (a minor ligament strain which we would probably now refer to as repetitive strain injury [RSI])", an essay by medical student Timothy McCowan, which appeared in *New England Journal of Medicine*, and was more concerned with the malady than the game. Thus, the amount of research one finds pertaining to video games depends on the criteria one has for what constitutes "writing about video games," and the degree to which essays refer to games or actually discuss them. But Bryce and Rutter do make the valid point that such broader searches must be made. And there is without a doubt substantive research to conduct on the history of the study of video games, one which would acknowledge its continuities and discontinuities.

In *VGTR1*, our survey of video games studies ended in 2003, the year the book was published (Bryce and Rutter also include, on page 3, a chart following the release of writings on video games, and 2003 is the start of a sharp increase in the number of publications). Since 2003, many scholarly books have appeared, such as *Rules of Play: Game Design Fundamentals* (2003) and *The Game Design Reader: A Rules of Play Anthology* (2005) by Katie Salen and Eric Zimmerman; James Newman's *Videogames* (2004); *Handbook of Computer Game Studies* by Joost Raessens and Jeffrey Goldstein (2005); *Half-Real: Video Games Between Real Rules and Fictional Worlds* by Jesper Juul (2005); *Computer Games. Text, Narrative and Play* by Diane Carr, Andrew Burn, Gareth Schott, and David Buckingham (2006); Jo Bryce and Jason Rutter's *Understanding Digital Games* (2006); and Wolf's *The Video Game Explosion: A History from PONG to PlayStation and*

Beyond (2007), among others. More often than not, these books (including *The Video Game Theory Reader*) begin with an attempt to define what a video game is, and distill its essential features, some (for example, *Rules of Play* and *Half-Real*) with more length and depth than others. Naturally, all these books show an appreciation of the video game as a new medium, a new art form, and a new popular cultural force. They all demonstrate that it is possible to apply existing terms, ideas, concepts, and methods to the video game in a useful and interesting manner, while pointing out that new theoretical tools are needed.

The definition of its object and the vindication of its examination are certainly representative of the first phase in the defining of a new field of research. For the most part, while textbooks with more refined perspectives have appeared (for example, *An Introduction to Game Studies: Games in Culture* by Frans Mäyrä, and *Understanding Video Games* by Simon Egenfeldt-Nielsen, Jonas Heide Smith, and Susana Pajares Tosca), video game studies has passed beyond this phase.[5] Books, such as Edward Castronova's *Synthetic Worlds: The Business and Culture of Online Games* (2005); Geoff King and Tanya Krzywinska's *Tomb Raiders And Space Invaders: Videogame Forms & Contexts* (2006); and Ian Bogost's *Persuasive Games: The Expressive Power of Videogames* (2007) have shed light on the cultural, political, and ideological dimensions of video games. As a list of conferences and their online proceedings, even from just the last five years, would be far too large to include here, suffice it to say that the number of topics, approaches, problems, and questions being considered is staggering.

At this time, video game studies seems to have moved into a second phase, in which, having set its foundations as an academic field of study, it must now attempt to articulate its exact nature and scope, codify its tools and terminology, and organize its findings into a coherent discipline. In a sense, the field has met the conditions set in 2005 by Frans Mäyrä, then president of the Digital Games Research Association (DiGRA). Stressing the overwhelming popularity and societal impact of video games as opposed to their feeble presence in the universities or educational system, Mäyrä highlighted the following essentials:

> Thesis one: There needs to be a dedicated academic discipline for the study of games.
> Thesis two: This new discipline needs to have an active dialogue with, and be building on, existing ones, as well as having its own core identity.
> Thesis three: Both the educational and research practices applied in game studies need to remain true to the core playful or ludic qualities of its subject matter.[6]

There is no doubt that video game studies has formed its own identity apart from other disciplines. While dealing with what Espen Aarseth has called "colonising attempts,"[7] the field has begun to explore its connections with other areas and what it shares in common with them. The richness of abundant theoretical overlaps is described in great detail in the Appendix of this book, which looks at video games through a wide variety of theories and disciplines.

Of course, the consolidation of a new field of research does not come without pitfalls. In the first issue of *Games and Culture*, Tanya Krzywinska, current president of DiGRA, writes:

> What I fear however is that if all game research is done within dedicated departments a kind of new orthodoxy of approach will crystallize. This may be the price of the development of our subject. It might mean blindsiding those who are for example engaged with philosophy or political economy because they are not essential, apparently, to running practical game design programs. There must always be room in the research community for newcomers from whatever background, who may bring ideas that challenge new orthodoxies.
>
> . . . Academia is now industry focused, funding hungry, and biased toward empiricism and entrepreneurialism; as a result, speculative and idiosyncratic work that values intellectual inquiry is becoming an endangered species. If experimental thinking is devalued, academia becomes a less interesting place to work and study. All approaches have their strengths and weaknesses, and each formulate issues and perspectives according to particular rhetorics. Power and pleasure are not therefore simply a dynamic at work in the playing of games. Speculative approaches have their place and are essential components in making game studies a rich, evolving, and multifaceted entity.[8]

Given the current wide variety of approaches, and the inherent playfulness (in both a literal and figurative sense) of the field, it may be hard to imagine a rigid orthodoxy arising and crushing its opposition. But any kind of limited resource, be it university funding, classroom time, page space in a periodical, or book contracts at a publishing house, forces decisions as to the acceptance and rejection of scholarly work and pursuits. At the same time, video game studies is tied closely to, and perhaps the most practiced by, the generations who grew up with video games, and whose outlook differs from that of previous generations. The field, then, may represent the possibility of new approaches that may be taken. As Frans Mäyrä wrote in 2005:

> There is a generation of young academics emerging who have grown up surrounded by digital games, and whose attitudes to life have been formed by simultaneous changes in culture and society. They are part of the post-scarcity experience, where the utilitarian morals of the 20th century generations are

giving way to new priorities in life. Game studies is a discipline that is going to play a part in this change, directing attention also into the ways in which we organise our own work. Only by coordinating the research work and course-work in ways that will keep the qualitative core of games and playing visible to researchers, informants and students alike, will the discipline be the innovative, yet passionately and uncompromisingly pursued field it has every opportunity of becoming.

Through a conscious effort such a vision may be realized. And that will mean walking the line between rigid, uncompromising orthodoxies that seek to crush their opposition, and a collection of loose, vague wide-ranging approaches that operate with little knowledge of each other and fail to cohere into a community of shared ideas and concepts (which at times seems the more likely fate of the field in the absence of meta-theoretical discussions of the field's direction). With collaborative coherence in mind, we present a number of challenges facing video game theory today.

Seven Challenges for Video Game Theory

The concept of challenge is common to almost all video games, and encountered by anyone considering or playing them. It is one of the few objects of study that actively resists analysis by withholding itself from those who do not have skills to keep their avatars alive long enough to see all of a game's areas, states, or levels, and discover all of its secrets. Higher levels and Easter eggs may elude even skilled players who have devoted many hours to a game. And plenty of challenges exist outside of the games themselves, such as the finding of copies of old games and the systems needed to play them, the finding of information on long-defunct companies, attempts to send requests for information or permissions through the convoluted hierarchies of huge corporations, and the tracking down of details and gameplay specifics on individual games, which may vary from one platform to another, or one release to the next. And after these research challenges are met, there are further challenges facing the video game scholar, as so many theoretical issues surrounding the video game are far from being resolved. Seven of these challenges, which we find to be the most pressing, are listed below.

1. Terminology and Accuracy

A set of agreed-upon terms has been slow to develop, even for the name of the subject itself ("video games", "videogames", "computer games", "digital games," etc.).[9] For the field, both "game studies" and "game theory", although often used, are broad enough to include board games, card games, sports, and so on, which they usually do not; at the same time more specific names are less likely to gain consensus, and may be thought to narrow the field as well. Nor is terminology used by gaming communities consistent or rigorous enough for academic application and usage. Other terms like "interaction" are problematic but their persistent usage seems to have made them become standard. The fact that the field is so multidisciplinary may also slow down the codification of terminology, as the variety of approaches slowly converges on definitions and terms. Since terminology is still in flux, current writing must be careful in choosing its wording, not only for clarity and precision, but also to aid the search for acceptable and appropriate terms.

The same is true for journalists who write about games. Authors David Thomas, Kyle Orland, and Scott Steinberg have sought to solve this problem by writing *The Videogame Style Guide and Reference Manual*, which asks for consistent style and vocabulary and accuracy regarding names and terms. In that book's Introduction, Kyle Orland argues that consistent style engenders trust and legitimacy, and is even important in preserving video game history. He also goes on to say:

> It's a reflection of the industry's current state. Has our industry evolved from its component parts of "video" and "game" to become "videogame," a one-word cultural idiom unto itself? What about "interactive entertainment?" Is the term "man"—as in "eat the mushroom to gain an extra man"—sexist? How are "life" and "death" defined in a videogame? Is "karaoke simulation" its own genre? As the industry evolves, these and other questions about self-perception deserve consideration and meaningful attempts at answers.
>
> Finally, with the proliferation of the Internet, it's more important than ever to hold all videogame writers—yes, even FAQ writers—to a higher standard. With website message boards that drip with egregious violations of the English language and videogame FAQs that practically require a translator, flaunting one's ignorance is dangerously close to becoming fashionable on the Internet. Writing well, even in informal forums like Internet message boards, should be celebrated and valued.
>
> Bearing all of this in mind, we have one more principle to add: This guide is by no means written in stone. As the title implies, this volume is simply a suggested guide to navigating previously uncharted waters. No rule featured here is without exception, and we don't expect readers to agree with all our decisions.[10]

As much as one can admire what they are trying to do, it is indeed inevitable that disagreements will arise, and despite its usefulness, parts of the guide could have been thought out a bit more. For example, their decision to go with the one-word "videogame" seems to have been arbitrary. The choice seems to run counter to one of their criteria, "Common Usage and

Accuracy": in a March 4, 2008 search on the top three search engines, Yahoo found 207 million hits for "video game" but only 36.1 million for "videogame"; Google found 71.3 million hits for "video game" and only 15.0 million for "videogame"; and on MSN.com there were 43.9 million hits for "video game" and only 9.38 million for "videogame." Clearly, the two-word version appears to be more commonly used!

But the idea behind the style guide is a good one, and both journalistic and academic realms are in need of consistency and accuracy. And admittedly, accuracy involving even names and release dates can be tricky. Different games can have the same names or ones that are close: for example, there is "*Spacewar!*" (the mainframe game from MIT), vs. the arcade games "*Space War*" (by Vectorbeam), "*Space War*" (Sanritsu's bootleg of *Space Invaders*), "*Space War*" (by Leijac/Konami), not to be confused with "*Space Wars*" (by Cinematronics). Names can include capitalized letters and punctuation or other symbols. Some games, like *PONG* and *M.U.L.E.* and *NARC* and *SWAT* are all uppercase, while some, like *Shark JAWS* or *S.T.U.N. Runner*, mix uppercase and lowercase. Some have intercaps, like *HiGeMaru* or capitalize the second half of hyphenated words, like *Pac-Man*. Nintendo's "GameCube" is one word, while "Game Boy" is two words. *SWAT* uses no periods even though it is based on an acronym, while games like *Spacewar!*, *Qwak!*, and *Spaceward Ho!* include exclamation points, and some even have two exclamation points, like *Punch-Out!!*, *Super Punch-Out!!*, and *Whoopee!!*. A few names include other symbols, like *Dead or Alive++*, *Who Shot Johnny Rock?*, or Neo•Geo. *Wolfenstein 3-D* appeared originally with a hyphen, but later sometimes appeared without one. Usually images from the game's packaging or the game itself can clear up uncertainties, but not always; for example, Exidy's *Mousetrap* has the game's name broken into two words ("Mouse Trap") on its game cabinet above the screen, yet the game's title screen has the name as one word ("Mousetrap"); in such a case it seems more prudent to go with the game imagery, since it is an integral part of the game (however, even this can be misleading; the title screen of the arcade game *Tempest* gives a copyright date of 1980, but the game was released in 1981). With the potential for errors to multiply quickly on the Internet, one has to be quite careful when verifying such details. And both academics and journalists will only add to this problem unless their work is able to avoid these errors and correct them where they can.

2. History

Most academic writing about video games tends to be limited to home video games and online games from only the last five years or so. Relatively little is written about handheld games and older home games and their systems, and very little about arcade games. Part of the reason for this is practical; newer games are contemporary, easier to find, known to a wider audience, more detailed and cinematic than earlier games, accessible, and more to the liking and experience of many writers. Yet, knowledge of older games provides a historical context and background from which more recent games have evolved and on which their own forms, genres, and conventions rely. More attention should be paid to older games, and the way in which genres, conventions, franchises, series, and so forth all developed over time, rather than merely on the latest incarnations of these things as though they have no past or predecessors.

While it is true that older games can be harder to find, and there are no institutional archives yet in the most formal sense, there are an increasing number of venues for researchers to find information about them, or even find the games themselves. Keith Feinstein's Videotopia has been around since 1996, although it still has no permanent home where it can be visited by the public. Feinstein also started the Electronics Conservancy, whose mission is described at the Videotopia.com website:

> The Electronics Conservancy is an organization dedicated to the preservation and restoration of artifacts and information detailing the history of the electronic medium, as well as the use of these artifacts in informing and educating. . . . Having witnessed the destruction of the majority of these games and fearing the loss of their historical importance, we have spent years assembling a collection of over 400 rare machines, forming what may be the most complete collection in the world. We have also gained and will continue to seek information and artifacts from many first-hand sources in order to catalogue and preserve the history encompassing this art form. The Electronics Conservancy also maintains a collection of every home system ever released in the United States, as well as classic and important personal and industrial computers, and an extensive library of software.[11]

Several US universities in association with the Library of Congress have begun the Preserving Virtual Worlds project, which will be working to "develop mechanisms and methods for preserving digital games and interactive fiction."[12] Video games are also part of the Internet Archive, a San Francisco-based non-profit institution, which was established in 1996 "with the purpose of offering permanent access for researchers, historians, and scholars to historical collections that exist in digital format."[13] Even on websites like YouTube one can find footage of older games being played, including arcade games. Although such video clips are often limited in their usefulness in regard to gameplay, they do provide some sense of the games' sound and movement that still images cannot convey. Emulators provide even more of a sense of a game and its gameplay, though they must be used with caution, since they often do not recreate games completely and accurately due to technological differences between systems.

Despite all the new opportunities available online, first-hand experience remains essential to video game research. Old home systems and their games can be purchased at on-line auction websites like eBay, and a large collector community exists for all kinds of games. Organizations like VAPS (Video Arcade Preservation Society)[14] provide contact information for hundreds of collectors who have working copies of arcade games, and who can potentially answer questions regarding gameplay. Some even allow visits to their collections.

And there are now fewer hurdles to video game research. Permissions for game screenshots are no longer necessary, thanks to the 2000 landmark case, Sony *v.* Bleem, which established that the use of video game screenshots falls into fair use, even when that use is both *commercial* and *hostile.*[15] There has never been a better time for researching and writing about the history of video games, and even those concerned mainly with theoretical aspects should have some foundation in the medium's history.

3. Methodology

Lacking formal academic studies before the 1960s, film theory took a while to get beyond the exploratory stage exemplified by Arnheim's *Film as Art* (containing essays from 1933 to 1938) and Bazin's *What is Cinema?* duology (with essays from the 1940s and 1950s). This ontological theoretical approach, as Francesco Casetti came to call it,[16] aimed to define its object of study, draw attention to the constitutive elements considered as fundamentals, and reach an all-encompassing knowledge about it. Once the essence of film had been uncovered, a second paradigm "radically" modified the field, a paradigm Casetti called the methodological theory. With it, the attention shifted to the way in which research was planned and conducted; the "correctness" of the methods of inquiry used in the study was at stake. As mentioned earlier, the video game studies field has moved quickly from the ontological to the methodological paradigm.

Of course, video games still need a more thorough and accurate examination. A glance at the Appendix of this book (which itself contains an entry on methodology) demonstrates how methodologies will vary depending on the purpose of the research being conducted, and even on the researchers themselves as gamers. There are still many discussions as to the implications of these variances, or to what degree they undermine the applicability and usefulness of findings. The need here is not for a strict codification of procedures, but rather for more awareness and acknowledgement of the way in which they operate, and the limitations they will inevitably involve.

The video game is really a complex object of study, and one that involves a performance. This has led Espen Aarseth, in his "Playing Research: Methodological approaches to game analysis", to ask:

> should we expect game scholars to excel in the games they analyze? . . . As game scholars, we obviously have an obligation to understand gameplay, and this is best and sometimes only achieved through play. . . . More crucial here than skills, however, is research ethics. If we comment on games or use games in our cultural and aesthetic analysis, we should play those games, to such an extent that the weight we put on our examples at least match the strata we reach in our play.[17]

Before exercising analytical or interpretative skills, one has to draw on one's ability to play a game (or know someone with ability). One has also to ask what exactly is being analyzed, since the video game is such a multi-layered phenomenon.[18] Players can have very different experiences of a game not only due to their own abilities, but because some games, like MMORPGs, are too large for any individual to see in their entirety. And many games remain unfinished by players. Even when games are finished, portions of them may still go unseen or not be experienced. How much of a game is it necessary to see to draw a conclusion? What is being analyzed—the graphics and sound, the interface, interactions, the structure of the game's world, the storyline or lack thereof, the experience of the player, the sociocultural impact of the experience, even the physical impact of the experience? How is analysis affected if one or more of these is left out?

The notion of intertextuality has helped in the understanding of the complex interrelationships between texts and how meanings in a text are affected by them. While intertexual considerations are relevant to video game studies, the textual examination itself is crucial, because analysis "must rely on an intrinsic comparative study of the *in-textual*, that is, from the text in itself."[19] With the multi-linear, open, and emergent dimensions of video games, gameplay rarely occurs without players considering possible alternatives in actions and storylines. In the case of MMORPGs, vast and persistent, textual examination is inevitably incomplete. Without access to development documents or behind-the-scenes access, analysis tends to shift toward methodological approaches centered on the player experience.[20]

As the history of the video game interface (and more recently the Nintendo Wii) demonstrates, one has to consider more than just what is happening on-screen. The space of play has always been beyond the frame, involving the player's body, the proxemics of players, even the social space of the arcade or home. Games themselves have begun monitoring more of this space, with eye tracking and skin conductance and heartbeat monitoring devices that observe the gamer's psychophysiological responses and can allow the game to adapt to them. As games evolve so will methodologies, and an awareness of how they change is necessary.

4. Technology

An understanding of technology and its development is needed to understand why games look and play as they do, and have developed as they have. Graphics, sound, algorithms, processing speed, storage capability, accessing speed, peripherals, and so forth all exert an influence on both hardware and software design, which in turn limit programming and shape game design and gameplay experiences. How artistic decisions are shaped by technological compromises needs to be understood by game researchers before assumptions regarding game design can be made.

These issues also become apparent when one considers games ported across a variety of platforms, and emulators which attempt to simulate arcade games and home games on computers. For example, many arcade games and home video games use NTSC video cathode-ray tubes, which differ from computer monitors due to differences in pixel aspect ratios, color reproduction, sound, and so forth. Vector graphics, which use a vector-scan monitor, cannot be simulated on a raster monitor with complete accuracy. Thus, specific hardware is often necessary for a game to be accurately represented in its original form. For certain kinds of analyses, such details may not be relevant, but without knowing what those details are, and what has been lost in the technological translation between systems, researchers will be unable to determine whether or not the differences are relevant in the first place. A technological context, then, is necessary for understanding games and also for researching them, even for those whose main interests in video games lie elsewhere.

5. Interactivity

The problematic nature of the term "interactive" has been frequently noted, but use of the term has been persistent and it seems to have stuck. Since it is such a broad concept, a comprehensive theory of interactivity is needed to look at how the interaction of a game is designed, and how a game's options and choices are structured. Wolf's essay "Assessing interactivity in video game design", in *Mechademia*, suggests how the synchronic and diachronic nature of interactivity forms a kind of grid which can serve as a starting point of analysis:

In order to compare interactive structures, we can first consider mapping how a player's decisions are related. The smallest unit of interactivity is the choice, which consists of two or more options from which the player chooses. Choices are made in time, which gives us a two-dimensional grid of interactivity that can be drawn for any game. First, in the horizontal direction, we have the number of simultaneous (parallel) options that constitute the choice that a player is confronted with at any given moment. Second, in the vertical direction, we have the number of sequential (serial) choices made by a player over time until the end of the game. Obviously, the choices a player makes will alter the options and choices available later in the game in both of these dimensions, and in most cases a game's complete grid would be enormous. Even board games like Chess and Checkers have huge trees of moves which have never been mapped in their entirety. But one does not need to map the entire tree of a game to get an overall sense of how its interactivity is structured.[21]

Other dimensions of interactivity to be considered include the historical (the hardware, software, and cultural constraints determining what was possible, or at least typical, at the time when the game was made), the physical (the game interface, the player's ability to use it, and other factors such as reaction time and stamina), and the mental (player speed and game familiarity, the ability to recognize affordances (to use J. J. Gibson's term), pattern recognition, puzzle-solving ability, and so forth). Interactivity also occurs within the onscreen game space yet outside of the game's diegetic world; for example, the choosing of avatar attributes or the setting of other customizable factors such as difficulty level. Decision-making can also be influenced by both short-term and long-term goals within a game, as well as the degree of irreversibility that accompanies a choice (for example, consider the differences between arcade games that cost a quarter a play, home games that can be replayed for free, and MMORPGs which are ongoing and cannot be restarted by the player.) The same game can sometimes be played with a variety of input devices (for example, in 2004 the Interaction Design Institute Ivrea used a large ball that the player sat upon as an input device for *Pac-Man*), and in a variety of different contexts as well. As new controllers, like the Wiimote, new screen formats, and new peripherals appear, they will shed new light on the unacknowledged assumptions of older devices, and will change the relationship of players and games, and between players as well. Are there universal statements and claims about interactivity that will hold up in light of all future innovations?

6. Play

Discussions regarding the ludological vs. the narratological aspects of video games have raised interesting questions as to their nature and drawn attention to their constitutive properties. Just as digital cinema has brought about a re-examination of what it means to be cinema, the rapid technological evolution at the core of gaming will also stimulate new insights. With a growing number of platforms and venues, player modifications, and new intersections with other cultural forms, general statements about video games as a whole will be harder to make. As a result, a more developed notion of "play" becomes increasingly important.

Joost Raessens has pointed out that we are experiencing a "ludification of culture" and that many activities are now engaged with a playful attitude.[22] While classical definitions of play like Huizinga's might still have some relevance, play occurs in many new contexts which must be considered. The theme of the DiGRA 2007 Conference in Tokyo was "Situated Play", and the call for papers stressed this clearly:

> Games are not isolated entities that one can effectively study in vitro. Games are situated in culture and society. To truly understand the phenomenon of digital games, it is not enough to merely study the games themselves or short-term impacts as described by laboratory experiments—these are only part of the story. Their context begins when the games are marketed and circulated, and they reach the hands of players.[23]

Though Roger Caillois's division of play into *paidia* and *ludus* are a good start, a theory of play, playing, and players needs further elaboration to account for new contexts. Different styles of play, modes of play, motivations for playing, and the interweaving of play and game with everyday life reconfigure boundaries between person and persona, natural and digital, real and virtual. For instance, pervasive games are interweaving play and game with the everyday life and pushing us to question the blurred boundaries between the real and the virtual. Serious games make us exploit games for more than just pure entertainment. Virtual worlds like *Second Life* have become a great channel for communication between players, and even institutions. Likewise, much of contemporary life has taken on game-like qualities that make theories of play more widely applicable than they were in the past, but at the same time harder to generalize and bring to coherence. Many of the spectra that need to be considered—contemplative reflection vs. reflex action; new players vs. experienced players; competition vs. cooperation; casual vs. serious play; and so on—will have greater relevance when applied to larger contexts.

7. Integration of Interdisciplinary Approaches

Video games are best understood when they are viewed through a multiplicity of perspectives. As Jesper Juul has noted, these perspectives sometimes find themselves becoming divided between the humanities and the social sciences, in an antagonistic relationship.[24] While the achieving of a multidisciplinary outlook may be the easiest challenge to define, it may also be the hardest to achieve. As the field grows and divides into a wide range of subdisciplinary areas, the interconnections with other fields will strengthen and the field as a whole will be enriched. The challenge of bringing all this together into a coherent discipline of its own will take time and effort, but will bear much fruit. Frans Mäyrä's essay in this volume takes up this topic, and the Appendix lists some of the disciplines that have something to contribute to video game studies.

From Philosophical to Practical: The Essays

The essays in this anthology exhibit a wide variety of theoretical approaches, with perspectives ranging from the philosophical to the practical, from disciplinary points of view to an interdisciplinary dialogue, and the combined effect once again underscores the richness of video game studies. From the outset, Eric Zimmerman takes a stand for the whole field in "Gaming Literacy: Game Design as a Model for Literacy in the Twenty-First Century," which extends the notion of literacy (and of being educated in a society) to games. As games grow more important in our complex, playful world, knowing how they work and being able to understand their significance becomes essential. As a cluster of practices, gaming literacy revolves around three interlinked concepts for Zimmerman: systems, play, and design. Whereas *systems* draw attention to the interrelations among elements producing a significant whole, *play* expresses how players engage within and with the systemic structures, and *design* underlines the creative nature in the production of meaning. Lars Konzack also stresses the importance of design in "Philosophical Game Design," and suggests that game designers need to think beyond the creation of immersive experiences, but strive to express philosophical ideas in game systems and their design. Just as game designers need to know the history of ideas and how to present metaphysical ideas through consistent game constructions, game theorists are likewise required to exert an effort to appreciate the attempts, to grasp the manifestations, and to discuss them properly. Konzack does this, giving careful consideration to ethical, political, and philosophical aspects of games, such as the classic *Dungeons & Dragons* pen-and-paper role-playing game; commercial video games, such as *The Sims* and *BioShock*; and propaganda games, such as *Kabul Kaboom* and *Jennifer Government: NationStates*.

Moving a step in the direction of the practical, David Myers examines the concept of play in "The Video Game Aesthetic: Play as Form", which argues for a formalist approach to the study of play. He identifies three categories of characteristic game forms, each with its own set of rules:

physical forms, encompassing the sensory relationship (the interface) between player and game; semiotic forms, encompassing contextual relationships (values) among game signs; and social forms, encompassing interpersonal relationships (communities) among game players. His analysis demonstrates the degree to which play behavior is rooted in cognitive and perceptual mechanisms existing prior to and yet beyond the influence of language and its related significations of culture. In "Embodiment and Interface," Andreas Gregersen and Torben Grodal further explain how play is rooted in our biological embodiment. As one of the most fundamental conditions that govern our experience of the world, embodiment affects the way we influence the environment; the way we are affected by other agents' actions or events unfolding around us; and the way we play games. Gregersen and Grodal discuss how different types of interfaces and different game worlds mold players' embodied experiences. Focusing their attention on the games *Wii Sports, Eyetoy: Kinetic,* and *ICO*, they analyze how the body and player actions are mapped onto or into video game spaces. Aki Järvinen shifts the notion of embodiment to game design for the purpose of studying emotions in "Understanding Video Games as Emotional Experiences." Järvinen suggests that psychological studies in cognition, emotion, and goal-oriented behavior have to be taken into account when trying to understand video game aesthetics. Accordingly, he develops a systematic method for analyzing how so-called eliciting conditions for emotions are embodied into game designs, for example, which game elements and features potentially trigger emotions that are significant in the light of the play experience as a whole. Järvinen pinpoints emotion categories and different variables affecting their intensity, each element shedding light on design techniques which potentially could be used to explore and design more diverse player experiences.

As video games will always be defined by what the player is doing, Dominic Arsenault and Bernard Perron tackle the concept of gameplay in "In the Frame of the Magic Cycle: The Circle(s) of Gameplay." Opposed to the spatial metaphor of Huizinga's "magic circle" of gameplay, they conceptualize the partaking in a game as a cognitive frame, as an ongoing process. To cast off the implications of redundancy or stagnation contained in a circle, they resort instead to the figure of the spiral, which accounts for the gamer's progression through the game. Their gamer- and gameplay-centric model features three interconnected spirals which represent the cycles gamers have to go through in order to answer gameplay, narrative, and interpretative questions, in both heuristic and hermeneutic fashion. They also underscore the fact that gamers cannot access a game's algorithms directly and must instead construct an image of the game system, whose degree of fidelity towards the actual rules of the game may greatly vary (depending, for instance, if the gamer is playing to progress through the game, as opposed to playing to master the game mechanics). In "Understanding Digital Playability", Sébastien Genvo examines how a player is brought to play a game and engaged in it. By first considering the ludic attitude required to play a game, Genvo defines the notion of "ludic mediation," that is, the process of transmitting the will-to-play to an individual. Based on elements of narrative semiotics introduced by Algirdas Julien Greimas, such as the Canonical Narrative Schema, he proposes a semiotic model of gameplay which looks at both the paradigmatic axis and the syntagmatic axis of a digital playable structure. Taking into account the conditions of meaning production set during a game, and illustrating it with an analysis of *Tetris*, his model also exposes the circularity at the core of gameplay.

Unlike the images found in other media, such as painting, photography, or cinema, the video game image contains an interactivity that brings new challenges to the development of audiovisual representations. Mark J. P. Wolf's "Z-axis Development in the Video Game" traces how technical and graphical limitations were overcome in regard to depiction of an implied z-axis (that is, the dimension of visual depth in an image), and the different methods used to construct it. The essay discusses the relationship of the z-axis to the x-axis and y-axis, as well as its relationship to color resolution, perspective, and the game world itself. In addition to examining the z-axis's development, Wolf considers how games used the z-axis, and how game design was affected by the availability of greater depth in the video game image, and the effect this has on the player. Graphical limitations are also discussed in Brett Camper's essay "Retro Reflexivity: *La-Mulana*, an 8-Bit Period Piece," but he looks at them as self-imposed restrictions in the making of a retro game. To introduce the work of independent developers outside of the traditional commercial industry and emphasize how such indie retro game design helps the medium of video games to mature, Camper takes an in-depth look at *La-Mulana*, a puzzle-centric platform-adventure, which was created by a Japanese amateur development team called the GR3 Project and released in 2005 for Windows PC, but which was designed to look, play, and feel like a game for an older system, specifically the MSX, a Japanese hybrid console-computer from the 1980s. He describes the recognizable "8-bit" retro visual style of the game, analyzes its aesthetic and cultural references, and discusses how the game's visual style and paratextual markers relate to the MSX and its games.

Issues related to home video game systems are also addressed by Sheila C. Murphy in " 'This is Intelligent Television': Early Video Games and Television in the Emergence of the Personal Computer." Using the promotional campaign of Mattel's Intellivision system, she places the history of video games into the context of digital media theory and the histories of computers and television. Murphy traces the connections between television sets, video games, and personal computers during the first home video game craze in the late 1970s, and investigates the ways in which these new technologies promise to remake and reframe TV. In doing so, she questions how productive the rhetorics of convergence, change, emergence, novelty, and innovation are for video game theory and new media studies. Moving the discussion to contemporary corporate practices, Trevor Elkington explains the complexities of licensed adaptations in "Too Many Cooks: Media Convergence and Self-Defeating Adaptations." He differentiates three different forms of adaptations: direct ones like *Van Helsing*, ones integrated into existing franchise storylines like *Enter the Matrix* and *The Lord of the Rings: The Third Age*, and ones pursuing a separate narrative not directly reliant upon film events like *The Chronicles of Riddick: Escape from Butcher Bay*. Analyzing comments about the games and review statistics compiled on Metacritic, Elkington elucidates and explains the bad critical reception of film-to-game adaptations. While he points out the problems in the licensed-game production cycle and in its procedural issues, he also ends by suggesting a solution, which is the creation of central project management.

Failure of a different sort is explored in the next essay, Jesper Juul's "Fear of Failing? The Many Meanings of Difficulty in Video Games," which examines the role of failure and punishment in single-player games, and the paradox of how the potential for failure makes players enjoy a game more. Juul distinguishes between different types of punishment and two separate perspectives players can have on games: a goal-oriented perspective wherein the players want to win, and an aesthetic perspective wherein players prefer games with the right amount of challenge and variation. Moving into the arena of the practical, Juul describes a game prototype he has designed (which contains two different game modes, one with *energy punishment* and one with *life punishment*) in order to test his hypothesis, to gather data on how players perceive failure, and to illuminate his thoughts and theories. Along the way, Juul demonstrates the efficacy of exploring video game theory through the building of game prototypes and the usefulness of an increased interaction between game studies and game development. The goal of designing games which apply, test, and illustrate concepts from video game theory animates the work of the Singapore-MIT GAMBIT Game Lab, which is presented in "Between Theory and Practice: The GAMBIT Experience" by Clara Fernández-Vara, Neal Grigsby, Eitan Glinert, Philip Tan, and Henry Jenkins. The authors describe how this five-year project is trying to erase the line between theory and practice, and to engage more directly with the game industry. Referring throughout to games designed at the lab, the essay is a fascinating analysis of the methods used by student and faculty researchers to build games in an academic context.

Another academic group working on game development is the Synthetic Worlds Initiative, whose work is described in the next essay, "Synthetic Worlds as Experimental Instruments" by Edward Castronova, Mark W. Bell, Robert Cornell, James J. Cummings, Matthew Falk, Travis Ross, Sarah B. Robbins-Bell, and Alida Field. Making reference to the Petri dish, the shallow circular dish used to culture bacteria or other microorganisms, the authors methodically demonstrate the value of conducting research in virtual worlds. Their essay provides concrete examples of how synthetic worlds are being and could be used as social studies laboratories. Also concerned with the social aspects of video games, Mia Consalvo turns to Massively Multiplayer Online games (MMOG) in her essay "Lag, Language, and Lingo: Theorizing Noise in Online Game Spaces." At first, aside from structuralist and formalist approaches, Consalvo calls for the use and adaptation of other theoretical lenses from established fields and disciplines in order to better understand the multifaceted nature of games, and their production and reception. Consequently, she revisits classical and more contemporary communication theory with the goal of theorizing the concept of "noise" as a critical component of online game communication. Drawing on data from an extended virtual ethnography of *Final Fantasy XI Online*, Consalvo explores three types of noise that emerged through extended gameplay and experience with the player community: a technical form (lag) and two cultural/semantic forms (language and lingo).

The need for theoretical lenses and tools from other fields and disciplines is the topic of the last essay in the collection, as well as the Appendix that follows. From his experience as the leader or partner in over twenty different research projects into games and digital culture at the University of Tampere, Frans Mäyrä maps out the benefits and pitfalls of interdisciplinary research in "Getting into the Game: Doing Multidisciplinary Game Studies." Through practical examples, he emphasizes judiciously the potential of game studies as a radical, transformative form of scholarly practice. Finally, our Appendix at the end of the book, compiled from the work of many contributors, looks at video games through a wide variety of theories and disciplines, with entries discussing some of the conceptual tools each field has to offer video game researchers.

Video game studies has proven to be an exciting and thought-provoking new field of research, and a challenging one as well—and one that is fun—and while this fact may cause outsiders to question the seriousness of the field or its validity, it certainly has not discouraged a wide range of scholarship and scholars from taking part in it. The field has proven itself, and as it expands and reflects upon itself, it will continue to grow in relevance, significançe, and excellence. In some ways, the field is also anticipating a third phase in which video games studies' research and findings will provide new insights that will be usefully applied in other fields and contribute to other disciplines, rather than merely taking from them. Though it is probably foolhardy to prognosticate about the advent of such a phase, it will suffice just to suggest that it may be sooner than we might expect.

Notes

1. Mark J. P. Wolf and Bernard Perron, eds. *The Video Game Theory Reader* (New York: Routledge, 2003); hereafter cited as *VGTR1*.
2. A list of home video game systems appears in the Appendix of the *VGTR1*.
3. According to the Entertainment Software Association. See <http://www.theesa.com/facts/>.
4. Jo Bryce and Jason Rutter, "An Introduction to Understanding Digital Games," in *Understanding Digital Games* (London: Sage, 2006), 1–2; hereafter cited as Bryce and Rutter. Bryce and Rutter refer to James Newman, *Videogames* (London: Routledge, 2004).
5. However, discussions are still continuing. An interesting exchange of views on "What is a computer game?" appeared in November 2007 on the Games Research Network.
6. Frans Mäyrä, "The Quiet Revolution: Three Theses for the Future of Game Studies (Hard Core Columns 4)," *DiGRA.org* (2005). Available online at <http://www.digra.org/hardcore/hc4/>; hereafter cited as Mäyrä.
7. "Games are not a kind of cinema, or literature, but colonising attempts from both these fields have already happened, and no doubt will happen again. And again, until computer game studies emerges as a clearly self-sustained academic field." From Espen Aarseth, "Computer Games Studies, Year One," *Game Studies* 1, no. 1 (July 2001). Available online at <http://www.gamestudies.org/0101/editorial.html>. In 2000, Jesper Juul made a peer-reviewed game about defending games against "the imperialism of a thousand theories," which is available online at <http://www.jesperjuul.net/gameliberation/>.
8. Tanya Krzywinska, "The Pleasures and Dangers of the Game. Up Close and Personal," *Games and Culture* 1, no. 1 (January 2006), 120.
9. As many authors have noted (including Perron in *VGTR1* and Wolf in *The Video Game Explosion*), the field needs to come to terms with its terminology before common understanding and discussion are possible.
10. David Thomas, Kyle Orland, and Scott Steinberg, *The Videogame Style Guide and Reference Manual* (London: Power Play Publishing, 2007), 5–6. Also available online at <http://www.gamestyleguide.com> (accessed November 13, 2007).
11. See <http://www.videotopia.com/ec.htm>.
12. See Preserving Creative America: Preserving Virtual Worlds. Available online at <http://www.ndiipp.uiuc.edu/pca/?Home%3A_Preserving_Virtual_Worlds>.
13. See <http://www.archive.org/about/about.php>.
14. See <http://www.vaps.org/>.
15. See <http://caselaw.lp.findlaw.com/scripts/getcase.pl?court=9th&navby=case&no=9917137&exact=1> for a summary of the case.
16. Franceso Casetti, *Theories of Cinema, 1945–1995*, translated by Francesca Chiostri and Elizabeth Gard Bartolini-Salimbeni, with Thomas Kelso (Austin, TX: University of Texas Press, 1999).
17. Espen Aarseth, "Playing Research: Methodological Approaches to Game Analysis," in *Proceedings of the Digital Arts and Culture Conference*, Melbourne, Australia, 2003. Available online at <http://www.spilforskning.dk/gameapproaches/GameApproaches2.pdf>.

18. For instance, Lars Konzack writes about his analytical method that: "The method is based on seven different layers of the computer game: hardware, program code, functionality, game play, meaning, referentiality, and socio-culture. Each of these layers may be analysed individually, but an entire analysis of any computer game must be analysed from every angle. Thereby we are analysing both technical, aesthetic and socio-cultural perspectives." From "Computer Game Criticism: A Method for Computer Game Analysis," in *CGDC Conference Proceedings*, ed. Frans Mäyrä (Tampere: Tampere University Press, 2002), 89–100. Available online at <http://www.digra.org/dl/db/05164.32231>.
19. Dominic Arsenault, Bernard Perron, Martin Picard, and Carl Therrien, "Methodological Questions in Interactive Film Studies," forthcoming in *New Review of Film & Television Studies*, 2008.
20. This is why Arsenault, Perron, Picard and Therrien have introduced the notion of "actional modalities" as opposed to the structures of interactivity usually studied. Actional modalities are "the principal frames of action envisioned by the gamer or player from the conditions of performance, progression, and exploration he is experiencing. These actional modalities are defined by three parameters: sequence of actions, frame of actions, and skills." See Dominic Arsenault, Bernard Perron, Martin Picard, and Carl Therrien, "Methodological Questions," in "*Interactive* Film Studies," forthcoming in *New Review of Film & Television Studies*, 2008.
21. See "Assessing Interactivity in Video Game Design," *Mechademia 1: Emerging Worlds of Anime and Manga*, of the series *Mechademia: An Annual Forum for Anime, Manga and The Fan Arts* (December 2006): 78–85.
22. Joost Raessens, "Playful Identities, or the Ludification of Culture," *Games and Culture* 1, no. 1 (2006): 52–57.
23. See <http://digra2007.jp/Overview.html>.
24. From an e-mail from Jesper Juul to the authors, April 28, 2008.

CHAPTER 1

Gaming Literacy
Game Design as a Model for Literacy in the Twenty-First Century

ERIC ZIMMERMAN

Introduction: Literacy and Games from the Inside-out

Gaming literacy is an approach to literacy based on game design. My argument is that there is an emerging set of skills and competencies, a set of new ideas and practices that are going to be increasingly a part of what it means to be literate in the coming century. This essay's proposal is that game design is a paradigm for understanding what these literacy needs are and how they might be addressed. I look at three main concepts—systems, play, and design—as key components of this new literacy.

Traditional ideas about literacy have centered on reading and writing— the ability to understand, exchange, and create meaning through text, speech, and other forms of language. A younger cousin to literacy studies, *media literacy* extended this thinking to diverse forms of media, from images and music to film, television, and advertising. The emphasis in media literacy as it evolved during the 1980s was an ideological critique of the hidden codes embedded in media. Media studies' scholars ask questions like: Is a given instance of media racist or sexist? Who is creating it and with what agenda? What kinds of intended and unintended messages and meanings do media contain?

Literacy and even media literacy are necessary but not sufficient for one to be fully literate in our world today. There are emerging needs for new kinds of literacy that are simply not being addressed, needs that arise in part from a growing use of computer and communication networks (more about that below). Gaming literacy is one approach to addressing these new sorts of literacies that will become increasingly crucial for work, play, education, and citizenship in the coming century.

Gaming literacy reverses conventional ideas about what games are and how they function. A classical way of understanding games is the "magic circle," a concept that originates with the Dutch historian and philosopher Johann Huizinga.[1] The magic circle represents the idea that games take place within limits of time and space, and are self-contained systems of meaning. A chess king, for example, is just a little figurine sitting on a coffee table. But when a game of chess starts, it suddenly acquires all kinds of very specific strategic, psychological, and even narrative meanings. To consider another example, when a soccer game or *Street Fighter II* (Capcom, 1992) match begins, your friend suddenly becomes your opponent and bitter rival—at least for the duration of the game. While many social and cultural meanings certainly do move in and out of any game (for instance, your in-game rivalry might ultimately affect your friendship outside the game), the magic circle emphasizes those meanings that are intrinsic and interior to games.

Gaming literacy turns this inward-looking focus inside-out. Rather than addressing the meanings that only arise inside the magic circle of a game, it asks how games relate to the world outside the magic circle—how game playing and game design can be seen as models for learning and action in the real world. It asks, in other words, not *What does gaming look like?* but instead: *What does the world look like from the point of view of gaming?*

It is important to be very clear here: gaming literacy is not about just any kind of real-world impact—it is a specific form of literacy. So for the sake of specificity, here are some things that gaming literacy is *not:*

- Gaming literacy is not about "serious games"—games designed to teach you subject matter, such as eighth-grade algebra.
- Gaming literacy is not about "persuasive games" that are designed to impart some kind of message or social agenda to the player.
- Gaming literacy is also not about training professional game designers, or even about the idea that anyone can be a game designer.

Gaming literacy is *literacy*—it is the ability to understand and create specific kinds of meanings. As I describe it here, gaming literacy is based on three concepts: *systems, play,* and *design.* All three are closely tied to game design, and each represents kinds of literacies that are currently not being addressed through traditional education. Each concept also points to a new paradigm for what it will mean to become literate in the coming century. Together they stand for a new set of cognitive, creative, and social skills—a cluster of practices that I call *gaming literacy*.

I like the term "gaming literacy" not only because it references the way that games and game design are closely tied to the emerging literacies I identify, but also because of the mischievous double-meaning of "gaming," which can signify exploiting or taking clever advantage of something. Gaming a system, means finding hidden shortcuts and cheats, and bending and modifying rules in order to move through the system more efficiently— perhaps to misbehave, but perhaps to change that system for the better. We can game the stock market, a university course registration process, or even just a flirtatious conversation. Gaming literacy, in other words, "games" literacy, bending and breaking rules, playing with our notions of what literacy has been and can be.

Systems

To paraphrase contemporary communication theory, a system is a set of parts that interrelates to form a whole. Almost anything can be considered a system, from biological and physical systems to social and cultural systems. Having a systems point of view (being *systems literate*) means understanding the world as dynamic sets of parts with complex, constantly changing interrelationships—seeing the structures that underlie our world, and comprehending how these structures function.

As a key component of gaming literacy, systems can be considered a paradigm for literacy in the coming century. Increasingly, complex information systems are part of how we socialize and date, conduct business and finance, learn and research, and conduct our working lives. Our world is increasingly defined by systems. Being able to successfully understand, navigate, modify, and design systems will become more and more inextricably linked with how we learn, work, play, and live as engaged world citizens.

Systems-based thinking is about process, not answers. It stresses the importance of dynamic relationships, not fixed facts. Getting to know a system requires understanding it on several levels, from the fixed foundational structures of the system to its emergent, unpredictable patterns of behavior. Systems thinking thereby leads to the kinds of improvisational problem-solving skills that will be critical for creative learning and work in the future. In part, the rise of systems as an integral aspect of our lives is related to the increasing prominence of digital technology and networks. But systems literacy is not intrinsically related to computers. The key to systems literacy is about a shift in attitude, not about learning techno-logical skills.

If systems are a paradigm for an emerging form of literacy, what is the connection to games? Games are, in fact, essentially systemic. Every game has a mathematical substratum, a set of rules that lies under its surface. Other kinds of media, art, and entertainment are not so intrinsically struc-tured. Scholars debate, for example, the essential formal core of a film—is it the script? The pattern of the editing over time? The composition of light and shadow in a frame? There is not one correct answer. But with games, there is the clarity of a formal system—the rules of the game. This formal system is the basis of the structures that constitute a game's systems. More than other kinds of culture and media which have been the focus of lit-eracy in the past, then, games are uniquely well-suited to teach systems literacy.

To play, understand, and—especially—design games, one ends up hav-ing to understand them as systems. Any game is a kind of miniature artificial system, bounded and defined by the game rules that create the game's magic circle. Playing a game well to see which strategies are more effective, analyzing the game's rules to see how they ramify into a player's experience, and designing a game by playtesting, modifying the rules, and playtesting again, are all examples of how games naturally and powerfully lend themselves to systems literacy.

Play

Games are systems because at some level, they are mathematical systems of rules. But if games were just math, we would never have the athletic ballet-ics of tennis, the bluffing warfare of poker, or the deep collaboration of *World of Warcraft* (Blizzard, 2004). Play is the human effect of rules set into motion, in its many forms transcending the systems from which it emerges. Just as games are more than their structures of rules, gaming literacy is more than the concept of systems. It is also play.

There is a curious relationship between rules and play. In the classical sense of a game as a magic circle, rules are fixed, rigid, and closed. They are logical, rational, and scientific. Rules really do not seem like much fun at all. But when rules are taken on and adopted by players who enter the magic circle and agree to follow the rules, play happens. Play in many ways is the opposite of rules: as much as rules are closed and fixed, play is improvisational and uncertain. Yet in a game, these two opposites find a common home—gameplay paradoxically occurring only because of game rules.

In *Rules of Play*, Katie Salen and I define play as *free movement within a more rigid structure.*[2] Imagine play as the "free play" of a gear or steering wheel: the loose movement in an otherwise rigid structure of interlocking parts. The free play of a steering wheel is the distance it can move without engaging with the drive shaft, axle, and wheels—the more rigid utilitarian structures of the car. This free play only exists because of the more inflexible, functional structures of the automobile. Yet it also exists *despite* those structures. A joke, for example, is funny because of how it plays with the structures of language, creating subtle ironies, or double-meanings, or vulgar inappropriateness. The free play humor of a joke exists in opposition to the more rigid structures of earnest, ordinary language—yet is utterly dependent on these very structures for its play.

Yet, play is far more than just play *within* a structure. Play can *play with* structures. Players do not just play games; they mod them, engage in metaplay between games, and develop cultures around games. Games are not just about following rules, but also about breaking them, whether it is players creating homebrew rules for *Monopoly* (Charles B. Darrow, 1933), hacking into their favorite deathmatch title, or breaking social norms in classics like "spin the bottle" that create and celebrate taboo behavior.

Although play exists outside of games, games do provide one of the very best platforms for understanding play—from free play within a structure to the transformative play that reconfigures that structure. Any instance of a game is an engine designed to produce play, a miniature laboratory for studying play *qua play.*

So why is play an important paradigm for literacy in this century? Systems are important, but if we limit literacy to structural, systemic literacy, then we are missing part of the equation. When we move from systems to play, we shift focus from the game to the players, from structures of rules to structures of human interaction. Games as play are social ecosystems and personal experience, and these dimensions are key aspects of a well-rounded literacy.

As our lives become more networked, people are engaging more and more with structures. But they are not merely inhabiting these structures—they are playing with them. A social network like Wikipedia is not just a fixed construct like a circuit diagram. It is a fuzzy system, a dynamic system, a social system, a cultural system. Systems only become meaningful as they are inhabited, explored, and manipulated by people. In the coming century, what will become important will not be just systems, but *human* systems.

A literacy based on play is a literacy of innovation and invention. Just as systems literacy is about engendering a systems-based attitude, being literate in play means *being playful*—having a *ludic attitude* that sees the world's structures as opportunities for playful engagement. What does it mean to play with institutional language, with social spaces, or with processes of learning? When these rules are bent, broken, and transformed, what new structures will arise?

Play emerges from more rigid systems, but it does not take those systems for granted. It plays with them, modifying, transgressing, and reinventing. We must learn to approach problem-solving with a spirit of playfulness; not to resist, but to embrace transformation and change. As a paradigm for innovation in the coming century, play will increasingly inform how we learn, work, and create culture.

Design

> The notion of design connects powerfully to the sort of creative intelligence the best practitioners need in order to be able, continually, to redesign their activities in the very act of practice. It connects as well to the idea that learning and productivity are the results of the designs (the structures) of complex systems of people, environments, technology, beliefs, and texts.[3]

If gaming literacy were simply about systems and play, it would be a literacy based on games, not game design. But design, the third component of gaming literacy, is absolutely key, and in many ways helps bring the traditional idea of literacy as understanding and creating meaning back into the mix. There are many definitions of design, but in *Rules of Play* Katie Salen and I describe design as *the process by which a designer creates a context, to be encountered by a participant, from which meaning emerges.*[4]

Design as the creation of meaning invokes the magic circle: designers create contexts that in turn create signification. Although design comes in many forms, from architecture to industrial design, games happen to be incredibly well-suited for studying how meaning is made. Outside the game of rock/paper/scissors, a fist can mean many things. But inside the game, that gesture is assigned a highly specific significance, a defined meaning within the lexicon of the game's language. The creation of meaning through game design is wonderfully complex. A game creates its own meanings (blue means enemy; yellow means power-up), but also traffics with meanings from the outside (horror film music in a shooter means danger is coming; poker means a fun evening with friends).

For a game designer, the creation of meaning is a second-order problem. The game designer creates structures of rules directly, but only indirectly creates the experience of play when the rules are enacted by players. As a game unfolds through play, metaplay, and transformative play, unexpected things happen, patterns that are impossible to completely predict. In this way, design is not about the creation of a fixed object. It is about creating a set of possibilities. The audience is always at least one step removed from the designer. Games embody this aspect of design in a very direct and essential way; even the most straightforward game of chess or *The Sims* (Maxis Software, 2000) is about players exploring the possibilities that they are given by a designed object. In a game, design mediates between structure and play; a game system is designed just so that play will occur.

Over and above game design's affinity for the process of making meaning, it is also radically interdisciplinary. Making a game includes creating a formal system of rules, while also designing a human play experience for a particular cultural and social context. Game design involves math and logic, aesthetics and storytelling, writing and communication, visual and audio design, human psychology and behavior, and understanding culture through art, entertainment, and popular media. For video game design, computer and technological literacy become part of the equation as well.

As an exploration of process, as the rigorous creation of meaning, and as a uniquely interdisciplinary endeavor, game design represents multimodal forms of learning that educators and literacy theorists have been talking about for years, perhaps most significantly in the publications of the New London Group (quoted at the start of this section, above). Game design, as the investigation of the possibility of meaning, truly gets at the heart of gaming literacy, and ties together systems, play, and design into a unified and integrated process.

Conclusion: A Playful World

As we arrive in the early years of the twenty-first century, the world is becoming increasingly transformed by communications, transportation, and information technology that is shrinking our globe, making it a place of cultural exchanges both constructive and destructive. Existing models of literacy simply do not fully address reality in the world today.

Gaming literacy is certainly not the only way to understand the emerging literacy needs I have identified. But games and game design are one promising approach, making use of a cultural form that is wildly popular and wildly varied, both incredibly ancient and strikingly contemporary. And intrinsically playful as well.

So how does one take action to promote gaming literacy? At Gamelab, the independent game development company I founded in 2000 with Peter Lee, we have begun a number of gaming literacy projects. We are building Gamestar Mechanic—funded by the MacArthur Foundation and created in collaboration with the GLS group at the University of Wisconsin-Madison—a computer program that will help youth learn about game design by letting them create and modify simple games. We have also recently created the Institute of Play. With Katie Salen as the Executive Director, the Institute will promote gaming literacy through educational programs and advocacy.

What does gaming literacy mean for game players and game makers? The good news is that games, so often maligned, have much to offer our complex world. And not just so-called "serious games" with explicit educational goals, but *any* game. Gaming literacy can help us feel good about what we do by playing games, making games, studying games, modding games, and taking part in gaming communities. As literacy scholar James Paul Gee likes to say, "video games are good for your soul."

Gaming literacy turns the tables on the usual way we regard games. Rather than focusing on what happens inside the artificial world of a game, gaming literacy asks how playing, understanding, and designing games all embody crucial ways of looking at and being in the world. This way of being embraces the rigor of systems, the creativity of play, and the game design instinct to continually redesign and reinvent meaning.

It is not that games will necessarily make the world a better place. But in the coming century, the way we live and learn, work and relax, communicate and create, will more and more resemble how we play games. While we are not all going to be game designers, game design and gaming literacy offer a valuable model for what it will mean to become literate, educated, and successful in this playful world.

No Essay is an Island

The ideas in this essay are not just my own, but are part of a growing conversation that can be heard across universities, commercial game companies, grade-school classrooms, non-profit foundations, and in other places where game players, game makers, scholars, and educators intersect.

Although I have been a game designer and game design theorist for more than a decade, I began to rigorously connect game design and literacy through my interaction with the GAPPS group (now called GLS), a collection of scholars at the University of Wisconsin-Madison that includes Jim Gee, Rich Halverson, Betty Hayes, David Shaffer, Kurt Squire, and Constance Steinkuehler. I was privileged to be invited to a series of conversations with this stimulating group, about games and literacy, sponsored by the Spencer Foundation. In 2006, during the third of these three meetings, the term "gaming literacy" emerged from our conversations as a concept that could reference growing connections between games, learning, literacy, and design.

I am greatly indebted to game designer, scholar, and educator Katie

Salen for our ongoing collaborations, including the textbook *Rules of Play: Game Design Fundamentals* (Katie also attended that third Spencer meeting). My ideas on game design and learning have also been shaped by my work with the amazing staff at Gamelab, especially my co-founder Peter Lee, and former Gamelab game designers Frank Lantz and Nick Fortugno. Connie Yowell at the MacArthur Foundation also has been instrumental in bringing together scholars, artists, educators, and designers to exchange ideas, including the commission of important foundational research by the polymedia scholar Henry Jenkins. The specific formulations in this book were first instantiated in a talk I gave at Vancouver's Simon Frasier University, in January 2007, and this text received valuable feedback from Jim Gee, Katie Salen, Kurt Squire, and Constance Steinkuehler.

So thanks to everybody. I go to this trouble to highlight some of my sources in order to emphasize the newness of these ideas and the collaborative way that they are emerging from a thick soup of scholarship, debates, and collaborations. This kind of dialog is very much in the spirit of gaming literacy itself, and I encourage you to take part in the conversation as well. Some of the best places to get involved include: the Games, Learning, and Society conference held annually at the University of Wisconsin-Madison (www.glsconference.org); the Serious Games Initiative (www.seriousgames.org); the Education SIG of the International Game Developers Association (www.igda.org/education); and the ongoing dialogs about digital media literacy on the MacArthur Foundation website at http://community.macfound.org/openforum.

Notes

1. Johan Huizinga, *Homo Ludens* (New York: Roy, 1950), 10.
2. Katie Salen and Eric Zimmerman, *Rules of Play* (Cambridge: MIT Press, 2004), 304.
3. The New London Group, "A Pedagogy of Multiliteracies: Designing Social Futures," *Harvard Educational Review* 66, no.1 (Spring 1996): 60–92.
4. Katie Salen and Eric Zimmerman, *Rules of Play* (Cambridge: MIT Press, 2004), 41.

CHAPTER 2

Philosophical Game Design

LARS KONZACK

The challenge of future video games is to design games that go beyond mere entertainment. Not that there is anything wrong with entertainment as such, but video games have more to offer than just entertainment. Video games are able to present worlds and ideas to us in a new way. We should live up to this challenge. Philosophical games, such as *SimCity* (Maxis Software, 1989), *Black & White* (2001), and *BioShock* (2K Games, 2007) attempt to confront us with ideas and how they work in consequential systems.

This way of thinking ought to be applied to other kinds of games. Game worlds should not be simple, fanciful ideas without any real content. On the contrary, game designers need to think of each element of gameplay and each mechanical feature as a part of a consequential philosophical system, a coherent cosmology. They should not think in terms of "this feature would be cool to have" (or something similar), but instead, "this mechanical feature supports the philosophy of the game." Game design should no longer just involve the question of how to create immersive experiences, but instead ask how to express and present philosophical ideas in a game system. Only through such an initiative will it be possible for video games to grow and prosper.

I know, of course, that many games are part of an industry in which philosophical thinking may not be seen as useful and valuable, and there will always be a need for trivial games. That said, I would still like to insist that games with artistic ambitions ought to work with how they convey their philosophy. A game's philosophy may be the philosophy of the game designer, but it might also be a philosophical experiment. There may be multiple philosophies in the game. Still, they should relate to one another, evolve from one another. Even if a game designer does not intentionally control and design the philosophy behind the game, one will exist anyway, just as in film. That's why it is important that game designers consciously establish rational relations to this aspect of the game.

By philosophy in this context, I simply mean the world picture the game springs from, both the fictitious and otherwise. This can be varied, and may even have built-in contradictory propositions. In a well-designed philosophical game, the philosophy of the game is a coherent thought system or even a number of thought systems that interact in conflicting patterns.

To work in such a manner, the game designer needs to know more than the craft of game mechanics; the game designer needs to know the history of ideas, and how to present metaphysical ideas, turning them into consistent game constructions through the creative process. Furthermore, video game theorists need to learn how to appreciate these attempts at expressing ideas and integrating philosophical questions into game systems. To do this, video game theorists need to go beyond discussions of ludology, narratology, and immersive experiences. I am not saying that such discussions are invalid, but rather that in order to grasp the philosophical content of future game design, video game theorists have to be able to grasp these manifestations and discuss them for what they really are.

Strategic Simulations of Philosophical Ideas

SimCity is an example of philosophical game design, not so much because it creates a sandbox in which the player is able to act, or whether the player chooses to play the application either as a game accomplishing a goal or performing a free-play, but because the underlying rules of the game presents a vision of the world. The philosophy of *SimCity* is that of the complexity of modern cities and how social behavior and environmental issues influence city planning. It is a cybernetic philosophy based on feedback relations and game theory.

Another example would be *Sid Meier's Civilization* (MicroProse, 1991). In this game based on the traditional board game *Civilization* (Britain, 1980), the player is asked to build a civilization through the conquering of nations and complex development of social systems, science, and technology. The philosophy behind this game is that of cultural development. Not only that though, it implies that the goal of this development is to reach the stars (building an interstellar spaceship), as in Wellsian[1] science fiction, constantly evolving to adapt to an ever changing world in a modern age.

Will Wright, the designer of *SimCity*, is also famous for his game *The Sims* (2000). This game has been described as a game simulating the ideology of consumerism.[2] The goal of the game is to get rich, get friends, get married, and have a house with lots of consumer goods. But that is not necessarily how the game is played. There are numerous opportunities to play subversive scenarios, using cheat codes, and to explore the limits of the game's simulations. Still, as in *SimCity* and *Civilization*, the main task is to find strategic solutions. In this case, the strategic solutions are about having a career and social life; it is a strategic simulation game of personal life development. Rather than saying the game simulates the ideology of consumerism, the game offers an exploration into consumerism. In that sense, the game is open to interpretation and brings about interactive experiences, rather than merely being simplistic propaganda.

With *SimCity*, Wright was presenting a cybernetic philosophy of urban construction in an aesthetic way, making these feedback relations and game theoretical mechanisms into an experience. The same goes for *Civilization, The Sims*, and many of his other games, too, which are all strategic simulation games presenting interactive, aesthetic experiences based on different emergent philosophical systems. To fully grasp these experiences, the comprehension of immersive gameplay is simply not enough; there is more than flow experience here. The player not only has to open his heart (and reflexes) to the experiences but has to open his mind, too. To engage in this activity, the player has to think about what the game represents and simulates. The player is asked to think about the complex logistics of urban development, cultural development, personal life development, or biological evolutionary development. When investigating these ideas behind the game experiences, only then will the player be able to fully understand and enjoy these kinds of games. Unlike other games in which the player must learn the rules before playing the game, these games are all about the learning of inherent, unstated rules that govern the activities of the game; it is the uncovering of these rules, and learning how to exploit them, that constitutes the heart of gameplay, and which requires the player to actively distill the game philosophy from the embedded worldview. These ideas may be described as theories based on the underlying worldviews that shape the assumptions that the theories make. In this way, the theories and philosophies are layered within the game. More so, it would be difficult to aesthetically and interactively present such philosophies in any other kind of media and genre but strategic simulation computer games. That is not to say it would be impossible, but that the computer as a medium combined with the genre of strategy simulation games has a material and form that is well suited to make these ideas come to life as an interactive, aesthetic experience.

Furthermore, and this is indeed very inspiring, the player is asked to be a part of this philosophical experiment. He is asked to actively take part in investigating and exploring the ideas, creating mental maps of how they work as regards success and failure. What is interesting is that there is not just one way to play these games. Players can explore them from multiple perspectives, try out different strategies, and even use cheat codes and subversive play styles. The games are designed to give consequential feedback based on player input to the system, and that is why they become interesting wonders to explore. They are designed to be interactive, aesthetically expressive experiences of emergent philosophical systems.

Ethical Game Systems

In the classic *Dungeons & Dragons* pen-and-paper role-playing game by Ernest Gary Gygax, there is an ethical system based on two dualisms.[3] The first axis is the choice between having a chaotic, neutral, or lawful character, and the second axis is the choice between having a good, neutral, or evil character. This makes up for an ethical system with nine different possibilities. This system does not only relate to player characters but also to non-player characters, races and creatures in the game world.

This ethical system is based on the philosophical idea that you are born with an alignment and it is very hard if not impossible to change. Races and beings that are born as chaotic evil are for all practical purposes without the possibility of redemption.[4] That is why it makes sense in Gygaxian game design that chaotic evil creatures and races ought to be slain in order to gain experience, gold, and magic items. Needless to say, this ethical game system is closely related to Deterministic and Racist philosophies. Additionally, in Gygaxian role-playing games, the goal is to become an Ubermench, a superman with the highest level of superiority. In some games the maximum level is 60; in others it is 75. Becoming a superior being who is able to kill any opponent is a central part to the game philosophy depicted in *Dungeons & Dragons*.

Gygaxian game design has had, and still has, enormous influence on computer game design. Over the years a large number of games have been directly based on *Dungeons & Dragons* rules, and MMORPGs such as *Ultima Online* (Electronic Arts, 1998), *EverQuest* (Sony, 1999), and *World of Warcraft* (Blizzard, 2004) are all based on Gygaxian principles, having good and evil races fight against each other in dualistic, cosmological battles.

I would like to add that we are in great debt to Ernest Gary Gygax for his particular way of combining game and narrative. His main contribution to gaming was the way in which he quantized everything in the narratives of his games, so that, by representing everything numerically, things such as battles, damage, etc. could be calculated out in an objective way that would allow game events to proceed in a manner agreeable to all the players. This quantization of the game world was, of course, a necessary step in translating a game world into the digital realm, and thus a crucial development needed for video games. Without his vision, computer and video games today would be notably less interesting. He has influenced adventure and role-playing games for the computer for decades. Even more so, his innovation of pen-and-paper role-playing games was a new genre combining game and narrative, and ought to be appreciated in its own right.

That said, role-playing games have been innovated far beyond Gygaxian game design, and computer game designers ought to learn from these experiences. Greg Stafford, for example, (in contrast to the classic *Dungeons & Dragons* game design) created a coherent fantasy game world back in 1978 with his role-playing game *Runequest*. What is even more interesting is that he used a game system based on skill development rather than level increase, creating smoother and more realistic character development. This has, of course, been copied into many variants since then. But the most inspiring game design in this context is Stafford's personality system used in the role-playing game *King Arthur Pendragon* (Chaosium, 1985). One could say this innovation is rather old. Still, modern video game design has not yet been able to reach this level of conceptual game design complexity.

In Greg Stafford's personality system he uses no less than thirteen personality trait dichotomies to represent the ethical values of the character. The dichotomies are represented in a scale from zero to twenty in which zero is the lowest value and twenty is the highest. A neutral character would have 10/10 in a particular trait. If a character has sixteen or more in a trait, the character is influenced by this trait and consequently gets a player character bonus whether this trait is positive or negative as long as the trait is extreme. In this way the system rewards colorful characters with lots of personality. The traits needs to be role-played through character decisions, however, because if the character does not live up to the expectations of a certain trait, then it slowly changes into a more neutral, less colourful character, and consequently the character may lose bonuses earned from character traits.

The personality traits in *King Arthur Pendragon* are as follows:

Chaste vs. Lustful; Energetic vs. Lazy; Forgiving vs. Vengeful; Generous vs. Selfish; Honest vs. Deceitful; Just vs. Arbitrary; Merciful vs. Cruel; Modest vs. Proud;

Pious vs. Worldly; Prudent vs. Reckless; Temperate vs. Indulgent; Trusting vs. Suspicious; Valorous vs. Cowardly.

The traits are, of course, made to represent the genre of Arthurian romantic fantasy. For another genre, the dichotomies might be different. The point is that this game system gives rise to a nuanced understanding of human psychology. A character may indeed be cruel and deceitful but at the same time, be forgiving and generous. The system supports complex characters. What is more, the actions of the player characters influence the character personality. If a character behaves in good or bad manner, the character profile changes as well according to the game rules. Ethical behavior creates ethical characters, instead of the other way around. It is a game system that is able to simulate complex ethical consequences.

Such a consequential ethical system may also be found in video games. For example, in *Black & White* (Electronic Arts, 2001) by Peter Molyneux, the avatar changes towards good or evil based on player behavior. Likewise, a game like *Star Wars: Knights of the Old Republic* (Lucas Arts, 2003) by James Ohlen, is also about player behavior, with the player choosing a path between good and evil. In such games it becomes interesting to try out different modes of moral choice to see how these actions influence the character and the game world. Compared with Greg Stafford's personality system, however, both of these video game systems lack complexity past simplistic dualism, but at least they are both dynamic systems, relating to player decisions. In Greg Stafford's game system it is possible to have a character that is ethically complex, since it is based on more parameters and because the character may be ethically good in certain characteristics but not in others.

Sid Meier once said that *a (good) game is a series of interesting choices.*[5] In a game that has a complex ethical system based on player decision, there is plenty of opportunity to make interesting choices, to try out different strategies, and to follow consequential storylines. In future video games, ethical choices could grow to become far more complex than we are used to today. By actually delving into the philosophical dilemmas of ethical choices, the video game industry could indeed become a mature way to express ethical values. It may even go far beyond that and become a way to seriously experiment with ethical value systems.

Propaganda Shooters

Today, values are expressed in propaganda games. These kinds of games are designed as a persuasive technology, trying to change player attitude and mind-set. The question is whether they are successful, and if they live up to the challenge of philosophical game design.

Simple shooters have been designed that aim to manipulate player opinion towards killings and war. One such an attempt is the racist, violent game *Ethnic Cleansing* (Resistance Records, 2002). In this game, the player-character is portrayed as a man in a Ku Klux Klan outfit or a skinhead, and shoots people of other ethnicity than white. It is difficult to determine whether this game actually changes people's attitude towards ethnic groups. I personally doubt that anyone in their right mind would fall for this simple set-up. However, if a person with racist tendencies plays this needless to say, immoral and tasteless game, he may feel that the game confirms his beliefs. As for any philosophical exploration, there is none; only an empty shell of action and shooting. The game does, on the other hand, state that racism is about murdering innocent people, and in that respect, the game unintentionally serves as a warning against this ideology.

An earlier attempt at creating a propaganda shooting game is *America's Army* (US Army, 2002). In this game the player is a soldier in the US Army. Feeling the tension and excitement of being part of the army, the propaganda may in fact be successful at drafting young people and may even sustain a militaristic attitude. But apart from militarism there is no philosophical exploration here either. In this propaganda game, the players are not asked to think—only to act.[6] Also interesting about *America's Army* is that even when players play against each other, each player-character appears to the player as the US Army, while the enemy is depicted as a terrorist. So when players play each other, each one is actually controlling the terrorist, from the other player's point of view, while controlling a US soldier from their own point of view.

In the vulgar military shooter *Kuma/War* (Kuma Reality Games, 2004), we find an episodic re-creation of real-world missions based on the news, the research of military experts, and Department of Defence records. Most of the missions are based on the war in Iraq, but there have also been re-created missions in Afghanistan and Iran. Just like *America's Army*, the US military was actively involved in creating this game, the player is supposed to act as a soldier, and there is no conscious attempt at philosophical exploration. Certainly, as Aaron Delwiche has illustrated in "From *The Green Berets* to *America's Army: Video Games as a Vehicle for Political Propaganda*," it promotes the military way of life and may accordingly be used to draft young people.[6]

A different approach to propaganda shooters comes from Ken Levine, who designed one of the most exciting shooters ever made; not only from a graphics and gameplay point of view but from an ethical perspective too. I am, of course, referring to *BioShock*. The game is a criticism of Ayn Rand's aesthetic vision of a libertarian utopia based on her so-called objectivist thoughts, which in essence may be interpreted as the decree *greed is good*. In the past, a criticism of such a statement would be based on reductive Marxist ideology or deconstructive mysticism. Since the fall of the Berlin Wall however, such approaches may seem either ethically problematic, downright mistaken, or both. *BioShock* investigates the ethics of *greed is good*. The player is asked to be a part of this investigation, as there are two endings to this story based on player choices made during the game. The player character, Jack, is asked to kill the Little Sisters as his mission in this Ayn Rand-inspired dystopia. If he succeeds in harvesting the girls, Jack will become a dictator and be condemned for his actions, if he chooses not to, the Little Sisters will live full lives under the protection of Jack, ending in a gratifying situation—Jack lying on his deathbed, dying peacefully surrounded by the grown-up Little Sisters. In this manner, the game expresses a plain criticism of Ayn Rand's fantasy as a nightmare in which *greed turns out not to be good*. By re-examining it through ethical criticism based on player actions and asking the player to reflect on his actions, this game stands out from the rest.

However, one has to consider here the player's own calculations, because the game might not be so much about saving (or not) the Little Sisters, than about getting "ADAM rewards." Since the first scene shows a woman asking to spare a girl, the player is prompted at first to go on and save the Little Sisters. But as he will eventually learn (by looking at the game FAQs or by killing one Little Sister to see what happens), he is not getting as much ADAM by not killing the Little Sisters. Therefore, his gameplay might well be influenced by those ADAM rewards. However, even though the player may choose his path based on a non-ethical calculation, the game still provides an ethically interesting choice to the player, and consequently, the ethics of the game remains the same. Of course the player must, in order to grasp the ethics of the game, contemplate on his choices during the game or afterwards. But we know that is true for any ethical choice whether it is in a game or in real life. And as for life, one would not reduce his experience in Rapture to the sole ending of the game.

BioShock is undoubtedly a very different game from *Ethnic Cleansing*, *America's Army*, or *Kuma\War*, because it is a genuinely philosophical game, raising ethical questions, and asking the player to actually think about what he is doing. Such a game may in fact raise awareness of moral values, rather than being just another shooter. Consequently, *BioShock* points towards the future of philosophical games.

Other Political Games

A different approach to propaganda games comes from Gonzalo Frasca. He has made some short and fanciful games that have been readily available on the Internet. The first game to reach attention was *Kabul Kaboom* (2001) in which clip art from the painting *Guernica* by Pablo Picasso shows a child-caring mother who must avoid falling bombs. In addition, there are some falling burgers too, but they have no influence on gameplay. The player does not get any points, and if the player-character (the mother with child) is hit by the bomb, the game ends. It is not possible to win in this scenario. It was intended as a comment on US intervention in Afghanistan when they were not only bombing but also parachuting food boxes to aid the population. The message could be interpreted as: "It does not help to get food boxes if you get hit by a bomb." The game presents a simple idea, but there really is not much thought put into this game frame. It is not possible to explore this dilemma further or to question the premises of the game. If you agree to the statement you might find it amusing to play, if not, then it is a game without any point. Evaluated as propaganda, I do not think it changes the mind-set of the player. Evaluated as art, it is much too simplistic to be interesting. And evaluated as a philosophical game, it does not put the player in a position in which he can try out different scenarios or put real consideration into this ethical dilemma. The game only convinces those that are already convinced. Exploration of the world and the premises of the game are not possible and the players are positioned as an audience experiencing simplistic propaganda rather than intelligent human beings discovering a philosophical worldview.

Frasca's other propaganda game, *September 12th* (2003), is more interesting. The game is set in an Iraqi city and the player is supposed to bomb terrorists among innocent bystanders. When the bomb fires, it takes time to hit its target, and meanwhile the terrorists and innocent citizens move around quickly; so it is only through pure luck that you will hit a terrorist, and even then you will probably hit innocents, too. Even though the dilemma is emphasized, player influence is minimized. Presenting this dilemma in a game, forces the player to deal with it, except there is no way to do this properly within the game frame. Again, the game only convinces those already convinced.

Another attempt at propaganda games comes from Molleindustria. In the *McDonald's Video Game* (Molleindustria, 2006), we find an anti-advergame propaganda simulation that puts the player in charge of the McDonald's industrial complex of making and selling burgers. It is meant as a parody of the business. In order to be successful in the game, the player has to plow the rainforest and demolish villages; feed the cows genetically-altered grains mixed with industrial waste, and also feed the cows with dead cows, later covering up bovine spongiform encephalopathy (BSE) commonly known as mad-cow disease. In addition, the player must try to be cost-effective in the burger restaurant, firing ineffective staff, and rewarding the do-gooders. It is also possible to launch advertising strategies and bring about corruption of public officials with the purpose of counteracting consumer organizations, environmentalists, and radical anti-McDonald's groups. According to McDonald's, this game is a misrepresentation of their people and values.[7]

Whether realistic or not, this game encourages the player to dislike McDonald's and how it symbolizes the effectiveness and strategies of full-fledged capitalism. For that reason, the game may turn out to be useful propaganda. As a philosophical game, however, it lacks opportunities to try out different strategies, exploring the principles further. Moreover, this game does not deal with any real solutions to the problems. It only states that what McDonald's is doing leads to corruption and destruction at many levels, but if one has to be effective and successful, this is the way to do it. In that respect, it may turn out to be counter-productive as an anti-advergame because in a way, the game tells the players that in the real world, corruption works.

As Thessa Lindof and I have already shown, *Jennifer Government: NationStates* by Max Barry (2002) is another kind of political game.[8] The player plays a nation state defined by name, flag, national animal, and motto, and has to make political decisions. Generally, it promotes libertarianism in that player decisions affect political freedom, civil rights, and the economy, and in that equation, libertarianism comes up as one of the most positive solutions. That said, it is much more open than any of the other political games. The player answers several political questions and the nation state changes accordingly between 27 state categories from an Iron Fist Socialist state to a Compulsory Consumerist state, the most common being inoffensive centrist democracy, democratic socialist, and father-knows-best states. The game mechanics do not support conflict between states, but it is possible to declare war on a country or discuss other kinds of international matters through the text-based discussion forum. It is also possible to join the UN and vote on international problems. All of this is done in a tone of satire.

What makes this game different from the previously-mentioned propaganda games is that this game is open-ended and it is possible to explore the consequences of player choices in a frame with several possible outcomes. It is not didactic in the same way, and the player is allowed to try out different solutions to problems, studying the outcomes. In this way, Max Barry's game is open to experimentation and reflection on politics rather than being merely political propaganda. It becomes a philosophical game in which the player is invited to become part of an examination of political ideas. This game takes advantage of the potential in games to truly put the player in control and let him reflect on his own decisions, investigating political theory turned into meaningful game aesthetics.

In general, propaganda games are not that exciting. The player quickly gets a notion of what the game's dogmatic statement has to say about the demonstrative political subject. Players that agree to the political statements may use such games to feel secure in their convictions. Non-believers of the ideologies may find the games boring. The design philosophy behind these games is old-fashioned, because they are designed for a mass audience rather than for individual players. Such an approach to the computer medium does not take into account that contrary to mass media, the player is an individual playing the game on his own premises. A game should be thought of as a dialogue in process with the ideas embodied in the game being played, not as a broadcast monologue. The player is able to reflect and learn from his experience, and accordingly, the player ought to be taken more seriously.

The Future of Philosophical Games

I predict that in the future there will be numerous propaganda games available, but they will not use the video game medium to its fullest potential, because these games limit player influence and how players reflect on political ideas, probably because the people making these kinds of games have a limited understanding of politics in general. Whatever the case, open-ended games based on philosophical ideas and interesting ethical systems are much more exciting to experiment with and explore, turning them into fuller experiences of meaningful play. As for the future of philosophical games, there is the real challenge. I am certainly not saying that every game from now on ought to be a philosophical game. However, if game culture and aesthetics are to develop into mature games beyond teenage power-gaming and simplistic propaganda, designers will have to meet this challenge and create games that expect the players to explore and reflect on game experiences.

One must remember that games are also aesthetic experiences. That is why a flawed philosophical idea may still be interesting to present and explore from an aesthetic perspective as long as it is thought-provoking. This is not to say that we ought to call attention to flawed theories, but to point out that in order to fully understand the truth, we need put the truth into perspective. This also means that philosophies based on imagination are as interesting to experience as any other kind of philosophical theories.

The main thing is that game designers strive towards creating the most mentally-inspiring games.

It is no easy task to design a philosophical game. First of all, game designers must have something to say, some philosophical content to express. Second, the game industry is not always ready to deal with ideas that move beyond mainstream melodrama. Even so, game companies that are bold enough to trust inspired game designers and philosophical game design will be able to stand out from the rest, consequently setting the new milestones of the game industry. They will be remembered as brave game designers (for example, Will Wright and Peter Molyneux) who made a difference.

Notes

1. The term Wellsian science fiction is based on H. G. Wells' science fiction literature.
2. Gonzalo Frasca, "The Sims: Grandmothers are Cooler than Trolls," *Game Studies* 1, no. 1 (July 2001). Available online at <http://www.gamestudies.org/0101/frasca/>.
3. Gary Gygax, *Role-Playing Mastery* (Glasgow: Grafton Books, 1989).
4. Gygaxian game design has often been falsely accused of using Tolkienist ideals. But apart from having orcs and elves in the game world, there is not much of a resemblance. Tolkien, being a Catholic Christian, was indeed open to redemption. In fact *Dungeons & Dragons* is more closely related to *Conan the Barbarian* by Robert E. Howard than *Lord of the Rings* by J. R. R. Tolkien.
5. Andrew Rollings and Dave Morris, *Game Architecture and Design* (Scottsdale, AZ: Coriolis, 2000), 38.
6. Aaron Delwiche, "From the Green Berets to America's Army: Video Games as a Vehicle for Political Propaganda," in *The Player's Realm: Studies on the Culture of Video Games and Gaming*, eds. P. Williams and J. H. Smith (Jefferson, NC: McFarland, 2007), 91–109.
7. Greg Bluestien, "Creators put Politics into Video Games," *The Associated Press* (21 January 2007). Available online at <http://www.sfgate.com/cgi-bin/article.cgi?file=/n/a/2007/01/20/entertainment/e115220S54.DTL>.
8. Lars Konzack and Thessa Lindof, "How Multiplayer Games Create New Media Politics," in *Changing Views: Worlds in Play. Proceedings of DiGRA 2005 Conference*, Vancouver, 2005. Available online at <http://www.digra.org/dl/db/06278.06580.pdf>.

CHAPTER 3

The Video Game Aesthetic
Play as Form

DAVID MYERS

Playing is to games as reading is to books. Sort of. Games are designed to be played, just as books are designed to be read. Both playing a game and reading a book involve transforming a pre-determined set of rules into a more immediate phenomenological experience. And, of course, reading includes a larger set of behaviors than just reading books, just as playing includes a larger set of behaviors than just playing games.

However, there are important differences between the two:

> Reading, for instance, is a learned behavior and, therein, an unnatural behavior—particularly in comparison with play. Literacy is a difficult goal to achieve and, for that reason, remains unachieved by large segments of the human population. Play, on the other hand, is widespread, more analogous to some difficult-to-eradicate weed than the cultivated rose of reading. Play can be motivated and directed by game rules but also appears without evocation by game design; for this reason, the "rules" of play seem, at least in some significant part, pre-formed and hard-wired within human beings.

And, curiously, reading a book—and other forms of related aesthetic experiences, such as viewing a film—demand some measure of solitude and passivity; play, on the other hand, demands some measure of precisely the opposite. While play can certainly be quiet and contemplative, we prototypically describe human play using categories similar to those describing animal play[1]: locomotor play (for example, leaping, soaring, brachiating—or, in general, play with *body*); object play (including play with *conceptual* objects within video games); and social play (play with others).

Each of these categories is an active form of *playing with* something, and it is my contention here that this characteristic form of *playing with* is fundamental to human play, and, further, that this form is similar regardless of who or what is being played with.

If human play conforms to the three categories of play above, then the objects and forms of play can also be one of three sorts: objects and forms involving the manipulation of the interface between our bodies and our environment (during locomotor play); objects and forms involving the transformation of physical sensations into conceptual objects (semiosis); and objects and forms involving the construction, maintenance, and sustenance of relationships with others (during social play).

A Formal Approach

When I refer to "objects" of play, I mean to refer to real-world objects, such as dogs and trees, footballs and joysticks, but also, more importantly, to the values of these objects as those values are determined by representational form. Necessarily intertwined with real-world objects and their in-game representations is then another vital component: the relationship between the two. While objects and representations may vary widely, the relationship between objects and representations has a particular and constant set of forms, which I wish to emphasize here.

For instance, most people are familiar with the game of tic-tac-toe (TTT). Normally, TTT can be recognized by its well-known crosshatch playing field and its conventional playing pieces: Xs and Os. Yet neither of these two game objects—field or pieces—is critical to the formalist. The most fundamental property of any game, according to the formalist, involves relationships among game objects, which determine values.

In part, these relationships are described by the rules of the game, which prioritize and therein value game objects during play; but the rules of the game may be expressed in different languages and in different ways. So, again, the surface appearance of the rules—whether these rules are written in, for instance, French or English—is immaterial. It is the relationships these rules refer to, not the rules themselves, which constitute the form of the game.

Imagine, for instance, another game (we will call it T3) consisting of nine tiles, labeled: a1, a2, a3, b1, b2, b3, c1, c2, and c3. In the game of T3, two players alternate pick tiles, each attempting to select tiles that will create either an a-b-c sequence, a 1–2–3 sequence, or both. Further, imagine a set of rules for T3 that would eliminate from selection any sequences in T3 (such as "a1-c2-b3," or "a3-b1-c1") that would not conform to the winning conditions of TTT. At this point, the game of T3, without a crosshatch playing field, without any Xs or Os, is formally identical to TTT. We might, at this point, say the rules of TTT are more easily understood or, perhaps, more "elegant" than the rules of T3, but both sets of rules point or refer to the same essential form. For the formalist, the elements of TTT and T3 that are dissimilar in content are inconsequential, and the elements of TTT and T3 that are similar in form are fundamental.

One technique of the formalist, then, is to identify and distinguish forms and relationships referenced by game rules and, in that process, to try and find the most efficient or "elegant" way of describing those forms and relationships. However, while game play is guided by game rules, it is not, in all cases, determined by game rules. Game rules can themselves become objects of play, and formal relationships among objects of play within games can be extended to include formal relationships between games and players, and, indeed, between games and play itself. As a consequence, the importance of isolated objects and their values within games is diminished, and the importance of relationships among objects and their values as these are realized during play is increased.

This realization would require the video game formalist be something of a phenomenologist as well: to seek the fundamental form of object-value relationships (if such a form exists) that coincides most closely with the immediate and subjective experience of play.

A Form That is Not

A characteristic form of human play, regardless of the objects being played with, embodies a reference to what is not—or to something other than what is. It is useful to think of this as a "not" or "anti-"form. That is, when we ride a stick horse, it is not a horse, it is something else—something like a horse, but not a horse: an anti-horse, which requires but does not fulfill its reference to a horse. Likewise, during play we might pretend a box is a house, or stacked wooden cylinders are a king, or a finger is a gun.

This anti-form can then be applied, self-referentially, to play itself. Bateson[2] identified this particular form and its peculiar consequences as the single most fundamental characteristic of play in animals and in humans: play as meta-communication. That is, all forms of play transmit a self-referential message: "this is play," or, alternatively, "this is not real."

When we play with objects, for instance, those objects are not what they are; when we play with others, those others are, for the moment, not others. And, when we play with self, that self is something other than what it is: an *anti*-self.

The so-called "magic circle"[3] of play attempts to distinguish between what lies on either side of this anti-form: the real and the make-believe, the necessary and the frivolous. However, the contents of play—those objects and forms that are played with—are, again, less characteristic of the play experience than the formal properties of the boundary condition itself. This boundary condition results from negation, or not-ness, or from what I will call here an *anti*-form.

We begin with play as an embodied mechanism—an anti-form—that acts upon (plays with) objects and their values (that is, their contextual representations) within an organism's natural environment. During this process, these objects and values are transformed—with a variety of consequences—but, assumedly, according to a single and common formal mechanism.

This common mechanic of anti-form is most evident as a self-referential function operating on representations of objects. In fact, the evolution of a human-like cognition is closely associated with—and may depend on—such self-reference. Regardless, however, the three categories of play described earlier—locomotor play, object play, and social play—should then have this peculiar, self-referential anti-form in common and, if so, then these three might be assumed to have common origin in the natural history of our species.

Sutton-Smith has neatly encapsulated these assumptions in his notion of "adaptive variability" as the primary function of human play.

> In looking for what is common to child and adult forms of play, to animal and human forms, to dreams, daydreams, play, games, sports, and festivals, it is not hard to reach the conclusion that what they have in common, even cross culturally, is their amazing diversity and variability. The possibility then arises, that is this variability that is central to the function of play throughout all species.[4]

The analysis I present here is sympathetic to this definition, sharing with it the belief that play is understood best within a naturally evolved biological system.

However, Sutton-Smith positions his definition as inclusive of alternative points of view, particularly those culturally-oriented theories in which human play is subsumed within theories of learning and, even more restrictively, within theories of education. Theories emphasizing the role of play in a particular cultural context tend to distinguish some portion of human play from animal play in order to position human play as an intellectual achievement rather than as a vestigial mechanic. The analysis here is more narrowly focused on those forms of play that have neither allegiance nor debt to cultural values and social norms.

Rules vs. Play

And what do such contentions have to do with video games?

Certainly these claims are relevant to video games insofar as video games are a type of game and playing a game is a type of playing. In order to identify and understand video games and video game play, we would do well to identify and understand the class of object, behavior, and form to which they belong.

Furthermore, these claims are relevant to video games in that much of the common and widespread video game play—particularly play with others—is often classified as aberrant and unruly (for example, as bad or "grief" play[5]) This classification reveals some ambiguity, even conflict, between video game rules and gameplay.

On one hand, game rules are considered fundamental to an understanding of play; and the consequences of gameplay are understood to be guided by the game design and by the game designer who creates, implements, and enforces game rules. On the other hand, interactive video game play commonly avoids, transforms, or contravenes game rules. This tension between game design and game play is most comfortably resolved in favor of the "good" player[6] who adheres to game rules and plays according to the expectations of conventional designs and designers.[7]

What I would like to discuss here is to what extent "bad" play and players—and an anti-form that characterizes both—reveals more of the fundamental than the exceptional nature of video game play.

Locomotor Play

One of the more striking characteristics of video games is the extent to which these depend on and require some mastery of locomotor play prior to engagement with the game as a whole, particularly prior to engagement with game rules governing object and conceptual play. Of course, many generations of games have required similarly physical competencies: mumblety-peg, hopscotch, and virtually all sports. However, few genres of games have maintained such obvious reliance on a ubiquitous mechanical "controller."

The evolution of the dedicated video game controller—much like that of the equally common game interface of keyboard and mouse—has been relatively straightforward, deviating little from the simple toggles and control sticks of the 1970s to the more sophisticated, but otherwise quite similar, hand-held devices of today. Video game controllers have only occasionally employed mechanics beyond the conventional and consensual,[8] or mechanics that strictly and realistically modeled their in-game referents. There are indeed video game interfaces modeled as guns, steering wheels, skateboards, and guitars (for example, for the popular console game *Guitar Hero*, RedOctane, 2005), but these are, by and large, exceptions to the generic controllers used by the majority of games designed for Microsoft's Xbox, Sony's PlayStation, and, until very recently, Nintendo's dedicated game systems.

The innovative Nintendo Wii controller is unique among current controller designs and is characteristic of occasional attempts to broaden the range of body movements used as game commands. Significantly, though, the physical motions allowed by the Wii controller remain abstract and only superficially related to their real-world analogs. For instance, there are several Wii-based golf games[9] in which a golf swing is simulated by an arm swing of the Wii. However, video game players—particularly video game players who are also golfers—quickly learn that the most telling characteristic of these two motions is their dissimilarity. All Wii controller motions—regardless of their reference outside the game system—must be learned in the context of their in-game idiosyncrasies and then, for most successful play, applied with those idiosyncrasies in mind.

All video game controllers—including the Wii and other exceptions to current norms[10]—have at least two common properties: (1) they employ arbitrary and simplified abstractions of the physical actions they reference, and (2) they require some level of habituation of response.

Player actions and choices within video games are delayed, misapplied, and otherwise distorted—to the detriment of successful play—without a thorough and intuitive mastery of the game interface and controller. And, of course, learning to manipulate the video game controller is a necessary but only preliminary stage of video game play.

Habituation of response comes through repetitive play, which video games have in great abundance. This repetitive play integrates increasingly complex controller movements[11] with more strategic and conceptual play. During this process, game instructions are learned so well as to require little conscious attention, and game rules come to dominate player awareness and decision-making. Therein, video game locomotor play is sublimated in service of object (conceptual) play—a difficult and gradual task, which often only willing minds and nimble fingers are able to accomplish.

And, curiously, while basic controller configurations are shared across games,[12] the sequential patterns and manipulations required for advanced levels of video game play are conspicuously unique. That is, while controller buttons have similar configurations patterned after the human hand,[13] new and different games always seem to require that these buttons be pushed in new and different ways. Even within games, there are many and different controller sequences to be mastered for many and different game processes.

For this reason, each new video game tends to evoke at least some portion of the habituation process anew, accompanied by a similar requirement of recurring trials and errors, multiple saves and reloads. This phenomenon seems at first glance a significant barrier to video game play (and therein subject to negative market pressures) and is all the more curious when innovative controller designs have little impact on the subjective experience of video game play.[14]

This requirement of habituation prior to full engagement with video game play is parallel, in part, with requirements for reading. The initial process of controller assimilation and habituation is analogous to the process of learning an alphabet, grammar, and syntax. In both cases, aesthetic pleasures are delayed during a period in which player/reader frustration is more likely than player/reader enjoyment. This analogy is not strict, however. Once literacy has been mastered, there is no recurring requirement of the reader to further understand and access conventional language. For this reason, the video game play experience is perhaps more properly compared to the experience of reading *poetic* language.

The demands of poetic language are more involved than those of conventional language. The poetic language reading experience is, like the video game playing experience, uncertain; and, a successful and pleasurable experience must include some measure of interactivity involving both the knowledge of and the ability to re-evaluate pre-existing linguistic forms (for example, note the capitalization, spelling, and punctuation of poems by e. e. cummings).

Poetic language is therein a counterpoint to existing and conventional language; or, in our earlier terms, a sort of *anti*-language. Correspondingly, the function of poetic language is a direct result of its anti-form: an undermining and questioning of existing linguistic models and a resulting confusion (or, upon occasion, enlightenment) regarding those referents to which conventional language refers.

Poetic language, as Russian formalist Sjklovsky famously observed, serves "to recover the sense of life, in order to feel objects, to make the stone stony" (*Art as technique/design*, 1917).[15]

Formalist claims that poetic language returns us to a pre-linguistic state are based on the function of conventional language as artifice: a virtual representation of real-world objects and sensations. In this function, conventional language distorts our real-world sensations; poetic language, in rebuttal, self-referentially calls our attention to the nature and origin of those distortions. Thus, poetic language is—and is not—part of the language system that contains it.

Similarly, the ubiquitous controller of the video game both is and is not a part of the human nervous system—the human experience—that contains it. By confining the video game play experience within the mechanics of the video game controller and habituated response, video game rules and relationships undermine and deny conventional experience in much the same manner that poetic language undermines and denies conventional language.

The great difference, however, is that poetic language merely points to—and is therein distinguished from—the human physical form. Regardless of the skill of the poet, poetic language is never so stony as the stone; rather, it *remakes* the stone stony. There is no similar and incontrovertible distinction made between the human physical form and the video game controller, particularly under those circumstances where both systems—the human nervous system and the video game platform/engine—perform their functions subliminally. The video game controller *makes* (rather than remakes) the video game experience and therein confirms what poetic language would deny: the reality of the artifice.

During video game play, the human body and the human experience are accessible only as these are represented and valued by the video game mechanics. Poetic language points us to an objective correlative: a pre-linguistic state of direct and immediate experience. Video games, in contrast, point us to the more localized and individualized phenomena of the psychophysical: what we believe to be true.

Object and Conceptual Play

Object play in video games is play with in-game representations of objects. As such, this play is conceptual play, and includes play with—and against—video game rules.

Video game players, for instance, do not "play with" the video game controller (unless, perhaps, to occasionally throw it across the room). Rather, video game players play with those representations of objects arbitrarily assigned to various controller buttons and sequences. While these in-game objects may have value outside the game context, their repeated and habituated functions during video game play tend to erode those out-of-game values and, for the sake of successful play, replace them with values and priorities set by game rules.

The rules of chess, for instance, exist apart from the representational objects of chess (knights, pawns, bishops) and equally apart from the physical act of moving chess pieces from one square to another. Blindfold chess demonstrates the lack of necessity for either signifieds (kings and queens) or signifiers (carved blocks of wood). Despite the divorce of chess rules from game objects, however, concessions to locomotor play can still be observed during common games of chess.

Young children, for instance, often find more interesting play in stacking chess pieces into unwieldy towers than in manipulating those pieces according to the rules of the game. And even practiced and skilled chess players display an occasional and irrepressible desire to interact with the physical reality of the game—through the internationally recognized apology of *j'adoube* ("I adjust"), for instance. These vestigial mechanics of locomotor play in chess, however, pale in comparison to those associated with video games.

Video games are most fundamentally distinguished from puzzle, mind, and other similarly cerebral games—like blindfold chess—by the necessity of player action, movement, and habituated patterns of stimulus and response. While there is little requirement of strength or stamina or even, in very many cases (for example, within strategy games such as *Civilization*, Microprose, 1991), sudden and immediate coordination of hand and eye, video games as genre depend on a mechanical relationship between a particular and habituated response and a particular and rules-based representational form.

The representational forms of video games may be distinguished in terms of the relationship the game establishes among out-of-game objects and in-game representations, or, in a broader sense, in terms of a relationship between locomotor (physical) play and object (conceptual) play. These relationships may be oriented either inward or outward, either toward objective correlation or toward subjective introspection.

At one extreme, the conceptual objects of video game play may be designed to portray, as realistically as possible, their out-of-game referents. Therein, the video game becomes a simulation. This simulation must then restrict—or attempt to avoid entirely—the consequences of an anti-form.

In a simulation, game rules are equivalent to game instructions and both must be strictly enforced in order to maintain pre-determined values. Characteristic play is oriented toward adopting these values through mastery of game rules and the subsequent practice of transferable skills —which would encompass the goals of most educational and training games.

Further, to the extent that video game objects represent and refer to something outside the immediate experience of play, these objects and the rules-based relationships that value them demand a passive player. Games designed as simulations, in fact, frequently function most purposefully without player intervention. It is then the player's goal to neither divert nor test the game but to accept and absorb it, much in the manner of attending theater or watching television or reading a book.[16] The imposition of narrative within video games has much this same effect, wherein the narrative structure serves as the simulated and the video game player serves as a relatively passive participant in that simulation.[17]

At the other extreme, the conceptual objects of video game play may include the game itself. Playing with—rather than according to—game rules disrupts and ultimately destroys those rules through the self-reflexive application of anti-form. In this extreme, game play becomes increasingly selfish and less dependent on either the game design or the intent of the game designer.[18] Characteristic play of this sort includes cheating, as traditionally defined, but also, for instance, the accumulation of excessive "loot" (for example, gold farming) within MMORPGs, which does not disobey game rules so much as simply ignore those rules in order to achieve goals outside the game context entirely.

In between these two—the demands of the simulation and the gratifications of the self—is a more commonly appreciated video game aesthetic. In this middle ground, the anti-form of play is bound by game rules, but is allowed, within the context of those rules, free reign. Characteristic play may be either cooperative or competitive among players, but all players must equally adopt and abide by a common set of game rules and associated values.

Conceptual objects within aesthetically pleasing video games are then neither objects of simulation nor objects of desire. The manipulation of these intermediary objects constructs what some have called the *liminal*,[19] a period of transition during which it is difficult to discern what is true and valuable and what is not. Within video game play, the liminal is a fragile and fleeting state balanced between player expectations and player realizations. And the common experience of liminal play—its *feeling*—is then the most likely cause of our sense of similarity between playing games and reading texts. The formal mechanics of these two—and their ultimate consequences—however, remain distinct.

It is perhaps most useful here to compare the experience of playing a game with the experience of reading a peculiarly game-like text: hypertext. For instance, Aarseth has described the hypertext reading experience as an "ergodic" art form driven by aporia and epiphany, two concepts he also closely associates with video game play.

The aporia–epiphany pair is thus not a narrative structure but constitutes a more fundamental layer of human experience, from which narratives are spun.[20]

I have elsewhere described a similar dialectic resulting from the formal opposition and subsequent contextualization of signs,[21] involving a "mark of distinction"[22] and the dissolution of this mark during its reapplication to itself. This description is a bit different from that implied by aporia and epiphany, although both descriptions seem to refer to (as do the rules of TTT and T3) a similar, fundamental form.

Aarseth[20] describes properties of the hypertext reading experience from a reader's perspective and as these are guided by that reader's interpretive processes, often with narrative as a goal. Here I am maintaining that the dialectical properties of an anti-form of play lie *in the form itself*—a form video games reproduce most closely, but are shared at least in part by the digital mechanics of hypertext. This form consists of a peculiar set of relationships between: (a) objects and values, and (b) the local and habit-uated responses necessary to access and assimilate those object-value relationships.

The resulting anti-form may be collapsed through full knowledge of game rules and outcomes (the culminate result of the simulation, wherein all object-value relationships are fully disclosed) or through lack of player interest or investment in game rules and outcomes (during, for instance, either the detached reverie of the daydreamer or the purposeful misdirec-tion of the cheater).

In the first instance, object-value relationships are made too strict; in the second instance, those relationships are made too loose. In between is where video game play, as a unique aesthetic form, resides. Hypertext, as an intermediary between text and game, allows the reader to manipulate (play) with object-value relationships, but does not, as video games do, confirm and validate that play within a bodily mechanic.

Over time, because of the mechanical necessities of video game hard-ware (and because of the consensual necessity of a common set of game rules), video games have tended to culminate more often in the simu-lative than the selfish. This simulative structure often takes a recog-nizably narrative form in which video game players do not doubt or destroy but only, upon occasion, intervene—in a fashion similar to how readers intervene during the hypertext reading experience. In such cir-cumstances, social rules come to promote and enforce a limited set of player interventions, and playing video games becomes, like reading hyper-text can become, a derivative process: a derivation and simulation of reading text.

Social Play

The inclination to design video games for social play has been present since very early in video game development and history,[23] but the mechanics that made these designs possible were difficult to achieve without the parallel development of computer-mediated communications networks. Now, with such networks commonplace, it is clearly the intent of many video game designers to include social play as a meaningful component of video game play. Within the model presented here, however, it is not clear that social play contributes to the experience of video game play as a unique aesthetic form.

Because video game play relies so fundamentally on sensory mechanisms and habituated response, social play within video games is commonly filtered through some previous realization of locomotor play. This realization—a fundamental reliance on bodily mechanics—may also be at least somewhat similar to the experience of reading insofar as all language systems reference, as some have suggested, visceral experiences of the human body within three-dimensional space. Lakoff and Johnson,[24] for instance, have located the foundations for common language acquisition within *image schemata*[25]: "conceptual models of human perception and cognition [that] explain how different spatial relationships are used in language."[26]

While playing video games—unlike reading text/hypertext—may avoid direct reference to language, video game play cannot avoid reference to these more fundamental schemata or to the cognitive mechanisms that enable and empower them. The presence of other players can refine this reference, perhaps, but that presence cannot by itself avoid the interactive and visceral components of video game play.

In general, the experience of video game play does not emerge from social action, but rather becomes located within social action through purposeful game design. For this reason, video game social play more often refers to than reproduces social contexts.

For all these reasons—and because video game social play must always somehow incorporate the mechanics of locomotor play—it seems reasonable to construct an explanation of social video game play as an extension of individual video game play rather than to characterize individual play as a fragmentary and incomplete version of social play. Indeed, individual video game play often serves as an antithetical substitute for social play, with video game software taking the role of a (absent) human opponent. Many interactions with video game software are then more rightly classified as object and conceptual play, depending more on the relationship of the player to the object of play than on any objective characteristic(s) of that object, animate or inanimate.

Clearly, however, from a third-person perspective—when observing animal play, for instance—it is relatively easy to distinguish social from object play. And, even in human video game play, these two become conceptually intertwined only when video games also serve as communication devices and, in their communication functions, allow players to share common experiences during play. MMORPGs are currently popular video game designs that qualify both as video games and as social communities, though one set of functions may not require, and in fact may interfere with, the other.

Ideally, according to the model I have constructed here, social play within video games would extend the liminal qualities of individual play. Turner (1969)[27] has similarly extended his original concept of the liminal—into *communitas*.

> According to Turner, communitas does not engage in active opposition to social structure, but merely appears as "an alternative and more 'liberated' way of being socially human." . . . It is "a loving union of the structurally damned pronouncing judgment on normative structure and providing alternative models for structure." (51). In its most open form, a liminal event reveals a "model of human society as a homogeneous, unstructured communitas, whose boundaries are ideally coterminous with those of the human species" (47).[28]

Communitas, as defined above, is uncommon within online video games. Online video games promoting widespread social play[29] generate strict social hierarchies with strong normative guidelines, often only peripherally related to game goals. These hierarchical groups—guilds, fellowships, kinships, etc.—tend to restrict video game object-value relationships much as simulations do, and, as a result, either protect or prevent (depending on your point of view) individual players from fully accessing a video game aesthetic.

If so, then the primary function of video game social play is to control and deny the experience of self. That is, social play tends to require, as does the simulation, a common set of rules and, correspondingly, a predetermined and fixed set of object-value relationships. This affects game play among members of a social group significantly, most obviously in the case of PvE and PvP play.

PvE (player vs. environment) play in MMORPGs promotes cooperative behavior in which the objects and values of play are similar for all involved. Mere participation in such play—regardless of its dedication— then contributes to group and social cohesion.

PvP (player vs. player) play, on the other hand, creates competitive situations in which game goals include the thwarting of other players' goals. Social play, in order to maintain a common set of player goals, is then more likely to impose sanctions on PvP behavior (for example, constructing "false" or fixed competitions) than to pursue those competitions without bounds, thus limiting the degree to which individuals can explore the game space, rules, and system.[30]

Avoiding the consequences of an anti-form in this fashion requires that social play groups substitute social benefits for the more isolated pleasures of individual play; accordingly, most currently successful MMORPG designs manufacture and package the pleasures of play as "loot." In loot-based games, social groups can offer their members information concerning game mechanics, quest walkthroughs, twinking, and various other boons (depending on the genre and setting of the game) that, in terms of the discussion here, solidify object-value relationships without threat to social cohesion. This means that some members—the majority—of an online social play group are not required to undergo the same habituation process as other members, and, for that reason, the former may experience the video game aesthetic solely as a text aesthetic.

This phenomenon also marks much video game analysis, which interprets social and cultural strictures on game play as a form of creativity —for example, as a source of "user-created" content.

> There is no culture, there is no game, without the labor of the players. Whether designers want to acknowledge it fully or not, MMOGs *already are* participatory sites (if only partially realized) by their very nature as social and cultural space [emphasis in original].[31]

For those who would observe and record the interpretative practices of players as social activities reflecting shared cultural values, user-created content is an important outcome of play that can be explained and understood with reference to other, similarly located social and cultural phenomena. For those who would locate the phenomenon of play in individual cognition rather than common society, however, user-created content is a largely pre-determined feature of a particular game form—that is, a looseness of rules—which allows a game to be configured and therein exploited by social groups and pressures. The resulting "user-created" content, like all other rules-based structures within the game, can then engage and empower individual play only through its denial.

Play as Anti-Form

All games—video games among them—consist of rules that these games cannot themselves unravel.[32] If the impetus for the deconstructions of play, its *anti*-ness, cannot be located in the rules of the game, wherein does it arise? The suggestion here is that the recursive nature of play that befuddles and contradicts and evokes the liminal is more evident in the form of play than in the form of games.

Here I have described video game play as an experience in which the liminal—determined by a particular formal relationship among video game objects and values—is given a bodily component and cause that, in that process, viscerally confirms the play experience. *What seems to be* becomes, in the video game, *what is*; and the psychophysical is therein asserted and confirmed as the physical. This confirmation is normally a temporary state, undermined by the fragile and fleeting nature of play itself, but also by the dialectical relationship between the experience of the video game as simulation and the experience of the video game as self.

However, video game designers have tended to extend the experience of the liminal within video games—commonly as an endless series of goals or levels—wherein players oscillate between neophyte ("newbie") and expert. Expert status is achieved with full and thorough knowledge of video game object-value relationships and with the corresponding assimilation of those relationships at some habituated and visceral level. Because of this latter requirement, a full and thorough *knowledge* of game mechanics is not alone sufficient to locate and produce the video game aesthetic. A full and thorough knowledge is more equivalent to what is required during the aesthetic experience of reading text—and might be similarly claimed, for instance, from a full and thorough reading of video game rules or from a full and thorough reading of other video game players' accounts of their play.

But video game players eschew rules manuals in favor of an immediate experience, and many game designs—MMORPGs among them—no longer, if they ever did, publish game manuals in anything close to complete form. Knowledge of the video game is acquired only through the immediate and the direct, grounded only through the senses. This is not dissimilar from the knowledge of the warmth of the sun or the knowledge of riding a bike or the knowledge of some other intimate and personal kinesthetic joy. As such, this knowledge heralds, perhaps, a burgeoning aesthetic of the haptic senses, evoked not by individual sensations per se, but by their sequential presentation within an interactive and artificial (and therein abstract and symbolic) environment. Play would therein be instrumental in forging a relationship among our senses, our environment, and the neurological systems that mediate the two.

> In art, as in play, something comes into presence that has never been there before; the work is made present, presented, through play.[33]

Perhaps peek-a-boo, more than any novel or film, is then the quintessential video game, alternating between our expectations and realizations at such a visceral level that the culminate pleasure of the game lies most fundamentally in the realization that it is false. Furthering this analogy, peek-a-boo is also a game that can be wholly enacted by the self, with the reward of a familiar face provided as easily by a mechanical interface—for example, a video display—as by the physical presence of another human being: peek-a-boo in a mirror.

When the psychophysical—our perception of self—is asserted and confirmed during video game play, there is nothing to deny it other than some grotesque failure of the game mechanics (a power outage, for instance) or, through purposeful design, the end of the game. In the natural world, play provides a means to deny and therein explore the boundaries of our environment and our selves, yet these remain unassailably physical boundaries. There are no analogous physical boundaries—other than, perhaps, the physical exhaustion of the video game player—delimiting play within a virtual world. In the natural world in which our bodies and our play have evolved, experience is available to trump belief. In the virtual world of the video game, belief is given its own body of experience.

Insofar as video game play evokes a private experiential ground, there is little ability to differentiate between what seems to be and what is. And, in fact, when given the choice, players seem to much prefer what seems to be. As I have written elsewhere:

> For instance, within *City of Heroes* [NCsoft, 2004], . . . system rules (algorithms) govern the probability that a certain level of hero can punch a certain level of villain—and vice versa. That probability may be as high as 95% or as low as 5%. As the probability that a player-hero can punch a system-villain decreases, natural laws of random numbers allow for long series (or "runs") of misses by the human player. Human players . . . find such long runs of misses "unrealistic" and, more importantly, unfun; therefore, the current version of *City of Heroes* has implemented "streak-breaker" code.
>
> If either hero or villain misses more than human perception deems feasible or proper, then the miss streak is broken. The hero or villain is given an automatic hit, which over time and many heroes and many villains, results in an improbable change in the natural laws of probability. These new and revised psychophysical laws of probability then affect player experiences with and expectations concerning natural laws. What is a genuine anomaly between human perception and reality in the non-virtual world becomes a more fun and easy-to-get-along-with confirmation of human perception within the virtual world.[34]

In the first *Video Game Theory Reader*, Grodal[35] positioned video games as a means of emotional control; I would claim here that video games function rather as a means of anti-control, a conscious—or at least willful—attempt to lose consciousness, to let the artifices of awareness and self slide in favor of a more direct and immediate engagement of body and mind.

Patterned after our own sensory mechanisms and those cognitive adaptations that have resulted in knowing the world through representations— semiosis—video games appear capable of extending human knowledge only to the extent that human experience can be *represented*. During video game play, representations of human experience—histories, narratives, societies, and simulations—are equally hollowed by the habitual and repetitive nature of play and are equally transformed by a more fundamental, proto-representational form: an anti-form. Video game play then serves as a revelation of those natural and historical affordances that determine our behavior, and, simultaneously, for better or worse, as a means to avoid and deny those determinations.

Notes

1. See Peter K. Smith, ed. *Play in Animals and Humans* (Oxford: Basil Blackwell, Inc, 1984), and Marc Bekoff and John Alexander Byers, eds. *Animal Play: Evolutionary, Comparative, and Ecological Perspectives* (Cambridge: Cambridge University Press, 1998).
2. Gregory Bateson, *Steps to an Ecology of Mind* (New York: Balantine Books, 1972).
3. A concept based largely on the discussion in Johan Huizinga, *Homo Ludens: A Study of the Play-Element in Culture* (Boston: Beacon Press, 1955).
4. Brian Sutton-Smith, *The Ambiguity of Play* (Cambridge, MA: Harvard University Press, 1997), 221.
5. Chek Yang Foo, "Redefining Grief Play," paper presented at the *Other Players conference*, Center of Computer Games Research, IT University of Copenhagen (December 6–8, 2004). Available online at <http://www.itu.dk/op/papers/yang_foo.pdf>. Also, H. Lin and C-T Sun, "The 'White-Eyed' Player Culture: Grief Play and Construction of Deviance in MMORPGs," in *Changing Views: Worlds in Play. Proceedings of DiGRA 2005 Conference*, Vancouver, 2005. Available online at <http://ir.lib.sfu.ca/retrieve/1609/5922543c8cba0a282491dbfdfb17.doc>.
6. This is somewhat similar to Eco's "model reader," although the "good player" is more fully conceived as subservient to game designer than game design. See Umberto Eco, *The Role of the Reader: Explorations in the Semiotics of Texts* (Bloomington: Indiana University Press, 1979).
7. Cf., the "standard player" in Katie Salen and Eric Zimmerman, *Rules of Play: Game Design Fundamentals* (Cambridge, MA: MIT Press, 2004), 269.
8. The controls for the arcade game *Defender* (Williams Electronics, 1980), for instance, were unusually and notoriously complex in comparison to other arcade games of the period— and were notably characterized as exceptional in that regard.
9. To name three: *Super Swing Golf*, Tecmo, 2006; *Tiger Woods 2007*, Electronic Arts, 2007; *Wii Sports*, Nintendo, 2006.
10. For example, the *Dance Dance Revolution* (Konami Corporation, 2001) platform, which is exceptional among video games in much the same way that *Twister* (Milton Bradley, 1966) can be considered exceptional among board games.
11. For example, "combo" moves in fighting games, such as *Virtua Fighter* (Sega, 1993), *Street Fighter* (Capcom, 1987), etc.
12. These shared elements include certain conventions regarding common in-game movement—for example, the "WASD" configuration used during keyboard play.

13. And, of course, video games controllers are produced *en masse*—another reason for their similar and generic design.

14. For instance, playing the well-known *Zelda* (Nintendo) series with and without a Wii controller yields very little difference—once both controller types have been equally mastered—in the overall *feel* of the game. Once controller mechanics are practised and habitualized, they then rarely—except in cases of severe over- or under-complexities—color our evaluation of video game aesthetics.

15. David Myers, "The aesthetics of the anti-aesthetics," in *Aesthetics of Play Conference Proceedings*, ed. Rune Klevjer (Bergen, Norway: University of Bergen, 2005), 13. Available online at <http://www.aestheticsofplay.org/myers.php>.

16. Examples are *The Sims* (Electronic Arts, 2000) and a great variety of sports simulations in which the game is quite capable of generating actions and outcomes without player interruption.

17. This was first the case within adventure games—beginning as early as the Will-Crowther-inspired *Colossal Cave*, circa 1976—which adapted a familiar text aesthetic to a new digital form.

18. Although, in video games, abiding by game design and instructions enabling locomotor play—as regards, for instance, maintaining properly functioning hardware—remains a necessity.

19. Cf., the description of the "liminal author" in Umberto Eco, "Interpretation and Over-interpretation: World, History, Texts," *Tanner Lectures* (Cambridge, 1990). Available online at <http://www.tannerlectures.utah.edu/lectures/Eco_91.pdf>.

20. Espen Aarseth, *Cybertext: Perspectives on Ergodic Literature* (Baltimore: John Hopkins, 1997), 92.

21. David Myers, *The Nature of Computer Games: Play as Semiosis* (New York: Peter Lang, 2003).

22. Cf., George Spencer-Brown, *Laws of Form* (New York: The Julian Press, 1972).

23. *Ali Baba and the Forty Thieves* (Quality Software, 1981) displayed most of the basic characteristics of later and more expansive multiplayer role-playing games.

24. George Lakoff and Mark Johnson, *Metaphors We Live By* (Chicago: University of Chicago Press, 1980); George Lakoff, *Women, Fire, and Dangerous things: What Categories Reveal About the Mind* (Chicago: University of Chicago Press, 1987); Mark Johnson, *The Body in the Mind: The Bodily Basis of Meaning, Imagination and Reason* (Chicago: University of Chicago Press, 1987).

25. See also Maxine Sheets-Johnstone, *The Roots of Thinking* (Philadelphia: Temple University Press, 1990).

26. M. Andrea Rodriguez and Max J. Egenhofer, "Image-Schemata-Based Spatial Inferences: the Container-Surface Algebra," in *Lecture Notes in Computer Science*, Vol. 1329, eds. Stephen C. Hirtle and Andrew U. Frank (Berlin: Springer-Verlag, 1997), 3 of online paper. Available online at <http://www.spatial.maine.edu/~max/COSIT-CS.pdf>.

27. Victor Turner. *The Ritual Process Structure and Anti-Structure* (Chicago: Aldine Publishing Co., 1969).

28. Mihai Spariosu. *Dionysus Reborn: Play and the Aesthetic Dimension in Modern Philosophical and Scientific Discourse* (Ithaca, NY: Cornell University Press, 1989), 28.

29. *World of Warcraft* (Vivendi, 2004) is the prototypical example, but this category also includes other and older designs (*EverQuest*, 989 Studios, 1999; *Ultima Online*, Electronic Arts, 1997).

30. See David Myers, "Self and Selfishness in Online Social Play," in *Situated Play—Proceedings of DiGRA 2007 Conference*, ed. Akira Baba (Tokyo: DiGRA Japan, 2007). Available online at <http://www.digra.org/dl/db/07312.58121.pdf>.

31. T. L. Taylor, *Play Between Worlds: Exploring Online Game Culture* (Cambridge, MA: MIT Press, 2006), 159.

32. Although, some games—*Illuminati* (Steve Jackson Games, 1982)—do make the attempt. See also the description of *Nomic* in Peter Suber, *The Paradoxes of Self-Amendment: A Study of Logic, Law, Omnipotence, and Change* (New York: Peter Lang, 1990).

33. Hans-George Gadamer, "The Relevance of the Beautiful," in *The Relevance of the Beautiful and Other Essays* (Cambridge: Cambridge University Press, 1986), 12.

34. David Myers, "Comments on Media Aesthetics and Media Policy," paper presented at the

State of Play II: Reloaded Conference, New York Law School, New York (October 28–30, 2004), 5–6. Available online at <http://www.loyno.edu/%7Edmyers/F99%20classes/Myers_SoPII_discpaper.rtf>.

35. Torben Grodal, "Stories for Eye, Ear, and Muscles: Video Games, Media, and Embodied Experiences," in *The Video Game Theory Reader*, eds. Mark J. P. Wolf and Bernard Perron (New York: Routledge, 2003), 129–156.

CHAPTER **4**

Embodiment and Interface

ANDREAS GREGERSEN
TORBEN GRODAL

Our biological embodiment is one of the most fundamental conditions that govern our experience of the world. The basic features of our biological embodiment have evolved to interact with a natural, non-mediated world and are a conglomerate of different capabilities. Besides having senses to monitor the world, body surface and body interior, we are agents that influence the world, and we may also be patients, that is: objects of other agents' actions or events unfolding around us. Interactive media activates aspects of this embodiment: audiovisual data stimulates eyes and ears to simulate a time-space—a simulated world (SW)—and a series of interfaces map actions in order to integrate the player with a SW in an interactive feedback loop, with resulting emotions that reflect the interaction. The interfaces provide motor links to a SW and may, to a limited extent, provide tactile aspects of interaction (in its active, but not in its passive patient, aspect). This essay will discuss how different types of interfaces and different game worlds mold players' embodied experiences, and centrally how player actions fuse with the audiovisual information.

We will refer to embodiment in two somewhat different, but related ways. One entails conceptualizing the human body as a physically-existing, biologically-evolved entity. The other entails *our experience of ourselves as embodied beings* and our mindful experiences of the world due to our embodiment. These two are obviously related, and since we work within a modern cognitive science framework incorporating questions of embodiment,[1] we assume that there is a set of rather tight connections between the two—to paraphrase an oft-quoted slogan of cognitive neuroscience, "the embodied mind is what the organism does". We will apply this idea of the embodied mind to examples of body-mapping within the realm of video games that map specific aspects of our physical actions to a virtual body in a virtual environment: different control schemes map different aspects of action onto different virtual bodies—all of them take our specific physical embodiment into account in order to produce specific experiences of embodiment.

Agency and Ownership, Body Schema, and Image

When it comes to questions of agency and embodiment, a fruitful distinction has been proposed by philosopher Shaun Gallagher (Gallagher, *Body*), when he distinguishes between sense of agency and sense of body ownership as separable aspects of our embodiment. In normal embodied interaction with the environment, these two aspects are fused and operate pre-reflexively: We experience ourselves as instigating agents and we feel that the acting body is our own. Ownership of our bodies, but not of agency, is also in place when we are patients rather than agents—we know, for example, that it is *our* body that is being pushed down the stairs, even though we do not feel any ownership of action. We can thus distinguish between ownership of action (agency) and ownership of body. In relation to agency, the question of self-efficacy[2] is central: We may very well have an acute sense of body ownership and still have a distinct non-agentive feel if we believe that we lack the ability to influence states around us.

Although our physical embodiment ultimately determines the extent of our potential experiences, our experience of ourselves cannot be *reduced* to the actual, physical body as a thing among other things: one need only to consider the many instances where we literally feel the pain or joy of other people or represented avatar-agents as we observe them while linking aspects of our body image to that of the avatar. A person may literally wince as he scratches the red paint on his new car during a failed attempt at parking, because aspects of his body surface image and body experience have been projected to the car's surface to make a temporarily extended body image.

The "lived body" in Merleau-Ponty's[3] terms is thus not independent of the physical body, but it certainly is not reducible to it, either. This distinction raises a series of interpretational problems; we will follow Gallagher in making a basic and somewhat rough distinction between *body image* and *body schema*:

A *body image* consists of a system of perceptions, attitudes and beliefs pertaining to one's own body. In contrast, a *body schema* is a system of sensory-motor capacities that function without awareness or the necessity of perceptual monitoring.

(Gallagher, *Body*, 24)

Among the information systems used by the body schema processes are the visual, somatosensory, and proprioceptive systems. Visual systems yield information about the body as seen from the outside, while somatosensory systems give information related to touch and temperature of the skin and proprioceptive systems about body posture including muscle and joint position. Gallagher (*Body*, 24) further argues that the distinction between image and schema "is related respectively to the difference between having a perception of (or a belief about) something and having a capacity to move (or *an ability to do something*)" [emphasis added]. Gallagher also argues that although perceptual feedback both contributes to a sense of body ownership and is important for our sense of agency, a primary cause of agency experiences seems to be processes tied to the actual intention to perform an action. In a summary of neurological studies related to agency and ownership, Gallagher and Zahavi[4] conclude that a sense of agency depends upon both higher-order intentions to perform an action, the motor commands issued, and proprioceptive feedback. Psychologist Daniel Wegner and others have argued that a sense of agency has a tendency to increase body ownership.[5]

Following this, we would argue that interacting with video games may lead to a sense of extended embodiment and sense of agency that lies somewhere between the two poles of schema and image—it is *an embodied awareness in the moment of action*, a kind of *body image in action*—where one experiences both agency and ownership of virtual entities. This process is a fusion of player's intentions, perceptions, and actions. Once the player stops acting in relation to the game system and pays conscious attention to his or her own embodiment, this effect subsides in favor of a more regular body image.

Interactive interfaces and game systems may selectively target and activate the auditory, visual, somatosensory, and proprioceptive systems. The extent to which an embodied sense of agency, ownership, and personal efficacy is fostered by games is very much a question of overall design including interface design.

Possible Actions

Merleau-Ponty writes that the body is "a system of possible actions". This is a strong claim, and it seems rather obvious that even though we encounter many different action opportunities throughout our lives, our physical body does not change in many of these. As already mentioned, however, anecdotal evidence suggests that even though the actual body does not change, different situations change *the experience of our embodiment.* For instance, we feel a range of situations in an almost somatosensory modality, even though the nerve endings of the somatosensory system are not being stimulated. And it is, of course, not the case that people feel actual pain when they scratch paint off beloved artifacts or when they watch others feel pain—but we do *feel* something distinctly body-related in these situations.

In embodied experiences related to video games incorporating virtual environments, there seems to be two related but different issues involved each of them due to different neurological structures. The first is the oft-noted flexibility of our embodiment; we are easily able to include parts of our environment into our intentional projects as clothes, canes, and even automobiles may become integrated parts of our embodied activity (Merleau-Ponty). Neuroscientists have identified specific structures that are plausibly responsible for this flexibility of the body schema to incorporate tools and other objects, including those virtually represented.[6] Bimodal neurons, that normally keep track of both somatosensory areas of hands or shoulders together with the visual field close to these areas, apparently enlarge their visual field to include tools while keeping this visual field tied to the body parts in question. This bimodal integration of visual information with somatosensory information provides a partly sub-personal but very real and efficacious feeling of an incorporated and augmented embodiment when we use tools for manipulating: we feel a clear sense of both agency and ownership with tool extensions that we are thoroughly familiar with.

The other issue is the well-known fact that observing other agents who perform bodily actions tends to activate parts of one's own motor system—and if the observing person also performs a motor action herself, the movements may be congruent or incongruent; the latter phenomenon is usually called motor interference.[7] For example, when people observe hand movements, those areas that prepare hand movements in their own nervous systems are activated, and a person instructed to perform movements in one direction while watching another person performing an action that is directionally opposed (for instance, up vs. down) suffers slight performance degradation.[8] The idea that perception and action is intricately linked is a main tenet of both classic phenomenology and modern cognitive science, and it has gained further support through the hotly-debated mirror systems or resonance systems tied to the motor systems. The basic idea is that many of the perceptually-driven motor activation and interference effects are due to specific mirror neurons (especially in the prefrontal motor cortex) that fire both when the subject observes an action and when she performs one herself; that is, they fire when a person plans and performs an act of grasping, but also when that person watches other people grasp. Such "shared circuits"-approaches[9] argue that we are fundamentally intersubjectively attuned to the movements of other bodies. Thus, modulations in our embodied experiences may come in several interacting streams from the body (somatosensory and proprioceptive) and (audio)visual information related to motor pattern stimuli from outside that activates mirror neurons. Both of these systems may come into play when experiencing embodiment effects in relation to virtual environments. One allows us to feel our own body extending into the virtual environment through a kind of virtual tool-use, the other activates our own motor system as a response to observed motor patterns.

Mappings and Interfaces

We have just mentioned that flexible embodiment is fundamental to our acting in the world, and we would hold that this includes the virtual worlds and synthetic environments presented by many video games. One of the fundamental conditions that govern our interactions with video game virtual environments is that our actions are mapped[10] onto the game system by various technological means, since we cannot physically manipulate the virtual entities directly. Such physical input devices (hereafter referred to as physical control interfaces) can take the form of keyboards, mice, joysticks, gamepads, motion-sensing devices such as the Wii-remote, steering wheels, trackballs, paddles, flight yokes, and, less often, dancing mats, plastic guitars, and other custom devices. All of these interfaces are designed to provide a more or less straightforward coupling with the constraints inherent in the biological human body, and as such they provide affordances, such as lifting, grasping, and pushing.[11] When coupled to a properly programmed game system, however, they also provide a mapping functionality that allows us to perform a wide range of actions in relation to that game system and its virtual environment. Importantly, this means that the combination of controller and game system provides both *physical affordances* and *intentional affordances*,[12] the latter often designed to yield a sense of augmented embodiment.

In what follows, we will discuss how actions are mapped through different physical control interfaces, and pay special attention to the recent mainstream adoption of the Nintendo Wii-remote control interface—an interface that prioritizes input related to hand movement in ways that have clear connections with the proprioceptive system. We will distinguish between primitive actions meaning actual body movements and on the other hand actions in the wider sense: moving the index finger (to pull a trigger) is a primitive action, whereas discharging a firearm is an action.[13] For the present purposes, a primitive action (P-action) is thus defined as merely a movement of the body. A given P-action may be part of many different actions, and an action may be constituted by different P-actions—there are many ways to skin a cat, as the saying goes. P-actions are usually performed to do something else by that movement: A breakdown of many action descriptions is thus possible by using the formula "she performed the action *by* performing a P-action".[14] Applied to gaming, we perform a wide variety of game actions *by* performing P-actions in relation to control interfaces: The resulting state changes in the controller are mapped to the virtual environment.

We may grade P-actions in relation to different interfaces on a scale from the minimal action of moving a thumb or index finger to the maximal action such as a full swing of the arm. There is an arbitrary relation between P-action, the mapping, and its effects as relayed by the audiovisual feedback. In *Halo 3*, a move of the index finger will blow up a nuclear reactor, and in *Wii Tennis* a full swing of the arm will merely return a tennis serve. Thus some video games and their requisite control schemes emphasize motor activation and encourage players to perform maximal P-actions, while others prioritize the audiovisual effects resulting from the P-actions without emphasizing the latter. One end of the spectrum prioritizes contact senses and muscle sense input for its effects and emotional impact, while the other prioritizes the distal systems of visual and auditory perception.

We will return to the relationship between P-actions and their audiovisual consequences later in this essay, but we will note here that the typical action adventure game orchestrates virtual action opportunities that are positively grandiose and spectacular,[15] while actual body movements are limited to button pushes and joystick manipulation, and as such they rely very much on the *consequences of actions* relayed through audiovisual feedback for their embodied effects. With regard to this, several studies suggest that the area of visual field as a result of display size, together with spatio-temporal resolution, matters in terms of viewer arousal, perceived realism and emotional response—all else being equal, of course.[16]

Another important aspect of the mapping relation is the fact that our P-actions are very often—but not always—mapped to a representation of a body on screen, in such a way that when we perform a P-action, it causes changes to this body representation. Body representations in games may be more or less detailed and stylized to various degrees, and we shall not attempt a general typology of avatar embodiment here, but rather proceed by analyzing some cases in which a full or partial body representation on screen is visibly influenced as a result of mapped P-actions, since we find this relationship to be general enough to warrant investigation across cases which may exhibit differences (and undeniably significantly so) in avatar representations. We will very briefly introduce some general aspects of control schemes and then devote more attention to the games *Wii Sports* (Nintendo, 2006), *Eyetoy: Kinetic* (SCEA, 2005), and *ICO* (SCE, 2001), focusing on how the body and player actions are mapped onto or into video game spaces by analyzing the relationship between P-action and control interface.

Different Control Schemes

The most widespread control relation in console gaming is what one could call the mainstream controller scheme, where minimal P-actions are performed on a standardized physical game controller. These P-actions are minimal and the necessary repertoire of P-actions is also rather small; all one needs to do is press buttons and move thumbsticks with the fingers—though precision and timing may be an issue. The mapping is most often both arbitrary and natural in the terms of psychologist and design theorist Don Norman (Norman, *Design*). Action mappings are often arbitrary in that you push buttons with your thumb to virtually jump or swing your arms—as opposed to any real jumping or swinging of arms or hands in physical space—but they can be said to provide a minimum of natural mapping in so far that the application of force in P-action may correspond to application of force in the virtual environment. Thumbsticks allow for a slightly greater degree of *motor isomorphism* and this is often exploited: forward locomotion of an avatar will almost invariably be mapped from a forward movement of the stick, and so on. This makes for motor congruence in the case of both avatar and virtual object movement. One might also note that certain domains of virtual action may make this correspondence even more direct, as in the case with games that include operating virtual firearms fired by index triggers—light guns, of course, take this principle to its logical conclusion.

The standard interface for PC gaming is the keyboard and mouse combination. The button presses on the individual keys are similar to buttons on the controller, although the keyboard makes possible a much wider range of discrete button mappings. Most game controllers are setup to be used by index and thumb on both hands, whereas the de facto standard of so called WASD key-mapping for locomotion (W=forward, S=backwards, A=left, D=right) in combination with mouse movements for orientation uses three or four fingers for operation of the keys on the left side of the keyboard and the whole hand plus two fingers for the mouse. P-actions are quite minimal, and mouse movement may be isomorphic and naturally mapped in 2-D game spaces and cursor-operated 3-D games, and often semi-natural in the case of 3-D games with avatar embodiment. The WASD movement keys corresponds to movement changes in congruent directions, but in actual control, the key-operating fingers are usually not moved in any direction but down, and a forward movement of the mouse does usually not make the avatar move forward, but rather changes the virtual camera orientation—on a game controller this usually done via a thumbstick.

It is matter of debate how the motivation for the standard camera control scheme is understood best. One explanation could be that an image-schematic model of an object that can be tilted up or down replaces our natural perceptual actions: moving the mouse is equal to tilting the vehicle of our perceptual embodiment up or down. The flexibility of such a model may explain why some people need to reverse the camera controls in games—the dynamic will depend upon the imaged shape of the object in combination with the point of force application in relation to the axis of tilt or pan. A related aspect of this is that some games allow switching between first- and third-person viewpoints. In first person the default mode is usually "move mouse or thumbstick left to look left" whereas the third-person camera is often tethered behind the avatar and thus needs to move virtually to the right in order for the player to "look left". A potential complication here is whether the control relation is actually the avatar's orientation with a yoked camera position or the camera is independent of the avatar. These design decisions in combination with different image-schematizations of the relationship may result in different control preferences.

The Wii-remote departs from other standard game industry interfaces in that it combines the elements of the standard controller (discrete button presses and joystick movements), with something much less discrete, namely, the seeming ability to take actual body movement as input. In reality, and just like standard controllers, the Wii-remote does not actually map actions or actual body movement, but rather a set of state changes in the control system. The technology consist of accelerometers inside the Wii-remote together with an infrared positioning system using a sensor bar outside the controller coupled to an infrared camera in the controller. This enables the Wii-remote to be used to point toward the screen if one does not move outside the field of the infrared reception area, and it can also register controller movement in three-dimensional space since the accelerometers register changes on three axes (up-down, left-right, up-down)—one directional axis more than the standard joystick. An almost completely unified design intention seemed to be behind many of the launch games using this new type of controller, namely that of *isomorphic relations between an existing (and non-minimal) P-action motor domain and a virtual one*, with a direct mapping of real movements to virtual movements: a tennis stroke executed in the living becomes a tennis stroke on the virtual tennis court, and so forth. This control scheme enables the player to experience his own embodied interaction through both postural and, to a lesser extent, somatosensory input. The aim seems to be immersion in game actions through motor activation, motor isomorphism, and related ease of use. This is a design strategy, however, and one could argue that the issue of maximal and highly isomorphic P-action is primarily relevant in the cases where the player actively pursues similarity to an already well-known motor activity domain. Since the Wii-remote reacts to movements, not body acts per se, it is usually possible to use "medium-sized" or smaller P-actions instead of maximal swinging and so on. In other words, the desire for high motor congruence may or may not be present in the player, even though the game system setup offers it.

Wii Tennis

Nintendo game designer and celebrity Shigeru Miyamoto introduced *Wii Tennis* in 2006 with the following words "Control is simple and intuitive. Even your mom can play." The game is as the name implies; a tennis game of the casual variety, since it only maps the control of one particular aspect of a tennis player's actions, namely the swinging of the racket, whereas positioning the avatar is taken care of by the AI in the game. Using *Wii Tennis* as an example of the aforementioned immediate-immersion-through-isomorphism strategy, it can be argued that such a strategy poses certain problems for games aiming for immersion in virtual environments, in that it may lead to a somewhat harmful bifurcation between actual and virtual space. In a nutshell, the dilemma is that if one prioritizes the actual physical control interface (PCI) and P-actions performed in relation to this, the phenomenal action space might switch from virtual space to actual space; available add-ons in the shape of mock tennis rackets that may be attached to the Wii-remote play up the physical reality of the PCI even more. This latter strategy might lead to trouble. One might accept this or not, based on one's own experience of Wii-remote functionality, and though one could argue that there is no sharp boundary between the screen space and the physical space experientially speaking, neuroscientific evidence suggests a slightly different picture.

In the comprehensive study of visual perception in relation to visually-guided behavior, it has become commonplace to distinguish between two separate brain systems that use visual information for different purposes: the dorsal and the ventral system. Originally, this was proposed by neuroscientists Ungerleider and Mishkin as the "where" and the "what" systems, respectively, the idea being, very briefly, that one system in the brain deals with spatial location ("where") whereas others deal with properties such as form and color ("what"). Another pair of neuroscientists, namely Milner and Goodale,[17] have later proposed that the actual distinction is better understood as that between "how" and "what". They argue that the dorsal system delivers "vision for action" and operates outside consciousness, while the ventral system deals with "vision for perception", the latter being a more traditional perceptive system delivering consciously-accessible perceptual information. So, a common scenario in which one wants to pick up a ball with one hand runs like this: the "vision for perception" system allows you to consciously see the ball and plan the actual action, but it is "vision for action" that sub-consciously controls the ongoing visual guidance of the actual hand movement. As such, the "vision of action" feeds directly into the motor system, or so the theory holds. This is by no means an uncontroversial thesis, especially not when applied to agency, perception, and awareness in general,[18] but the evidence seems pretty robust in favor of at least some functional division between these two systems.

Applied to *Wii Tennis* however, this seems to spell trouble: we see the ball on screen, not in our peripersonal space close to our own hand or to its extension, the Wii-remote. Despite the previously-mentioned results proposing body schema flexibility in relation to tools, other studies suggests otherwise; "vision for action" uses an exclusively egocentric frame of reference and coordinates this with actual body structure such as grip aperture of the hand, and this makes for incongruence when facing a screen that presents data in an allocentric—that is, an object-centered—representation scheme. The "vision for action" system simply is not built for relative size projections situated in virtual space.[19] A closer look at *Wii Tennis* in comparison with the actual motor domain of real tennis shows that the extent of such problems might depend on the task-interface structure at hand. As a casual analysis of real tennis suggests, the speed of the ball makes it difficult for visual guidance and online monitoring and correction of action by "vision for action". Studies support this intuition: in fact, a tennis pro needs to calculate, prepare, and execute motor movements that position himself and the racket properly *before the ball is served* in order to successfully return it, and much the same holds for baseball.[20] One of the primary cues used to select the proper motor plan seems to be the posture of the serving or pitching agent before and during the serve. Thus, a salient cue besides ball movement in a realistic tennis simulation would be the spatio-temporal biological motion pattern exhibited by the virtual serving agent prior to the actual serve and *Wii Tennis*, obviously, does not try to simulate this cognitive-perceptual challenge. Furthermore, the movement of the player getting into striking position—a key component in serve returns in real tennis that demands almost explosive body activation—is in any event computer-controlled: the key problem and requisite motor domain here is solely when and how to return the virtual ball by moving the Wii-remote, and the ball moves slowly enough to cue action in regard to this task.

On the one hand, the Wii-remote coupled to a screen display may lead to trouble if the games put too much emphasis on P-actions performed in the peripersonal space and on the actual controller in combination with virtual cues in screen space that do not correspond with the "vision for action"-space: players may spend cognitive and emotional resources inhibiting visually-guided action potentials that work with cues in relation to the hand and controller, not the virtual space—less efficacy of agency and less ownership of the virtual body may be the result. On the other hand, it is obvious that *Wii Tennis* works pretty well in terms of immediate control and the establishment of agency and ownership of actions—the 3-year old son of one of the authors needed only two swings in order to tacitly understand the mapping involved, and he had never seen or tried the system before—and this is probably largely due to the motor isomorphism facilitating ownership of agency and both bodies (real and virtual) to some extent. So, even although relatively slow and visually-guided actions may not be possible through "vision for action" in relation to virtual environments displayed on screen, the actual ease of control in such games as *Wii Tennis* and *Wii Baseball* makes it highly plausible that other systems, possibly tied to vision for perception, are perfectly able to execute a kind of visually-guided action based on allocentric, distal cues outside the peripersonal space. Furthermore, if the Wii-remote—or other input devices using similar, but more advanced technology—could be made to deliver a more nuanced action individuation and map these accordingly, interesting and quite complex artificial conflict patterns might be the result. The task-structure may profitably exploit perceptual-cognitive learning of the anticipatory variety, present its visual cues saliently on screen and make use of motor congruence, but designers should not bank on our otherwise amazing abilities to act effectively in peri-personal space, since this may be the work of motor schemas served by "vision for action", that is, structures that demand egocentric data for their proper functioning. Otherwise, problems with both agency and ownership may be the result.

Swinging, Hitting and Grasping Forcefully

Another problem with the Wii-remote—and one that we find potentially more problematic for the technology's ability to produce a robust sense of agency and ownership—has to do with both the touch systems' and the proprioceptive systems' role in action. Physical force and force dynamics are central to our understanding of the physical world and thus, to a wide extent, our engagement with the world. A basic problem with the Wii-remote and many other game controllers is that true force feedback is impossible to implement in controllers of this kind, and in a nutshell, this yields a dissociation of sensory experience: in the games launched with the console, the actions depicted were, among others, using a racket to hit a tennis ball, using a sword to kill gangsters or smite mythological enemies, using a fishing rod to catch fish, and using fists to hit another agent in the face during a boxing match. Once again, the aim seems to be immersion through isomorphic movement patterns, and in most of the examples, the Wii-remote becomes a stand-in for a virtual tool that is grasped and handled in similar ways to the physical counterparts. But, this makes for some tradeoffs in the different kinds of information delivered by the perceptual systems. While the Wii-remote and the audiovisual feedback can manage a certain range of modal information, the force feedback is necessarily missing. When one swings a real weapon, the weight and length is easily felt by body schema processes, and if one hits something with the weapon as a consequence of a full swing, the impact can be literally stunning for the somatosensory system and muscles and joints. When one operates a real fishing rod, the interplay between such variables as weight, length and elasticity of the rod, the elasticity of the line and the angle as a result of fish position, and, of course, the dynamic movements of a hooked fish will all translate into easily felt force dynamics. Part of these dynamical patterns will be felt through the posture and touch system, but one of the primary variables here seems to be the sheer amount of muscle tension involved in reeling in a fish. All of these crucial sensory inputs will be missing from the P-action performed in physical space. It seems obvious that in the absence of force feedback, the game will have to deliver through other input channels, but the question remains what exactly is gained by allowing one aspect of the action to be directly isomorphic while a very important aspect is completely missing. While the standard controller schemes couple minimal P-action with maximal audiovisual feedback, the Wii-setup makes for a kind of *incongruent motor realism*—the sense of ownership of the real body is high because body schema processes are activated, but both the sense of agency and transfer of ownership to the virtual space may be hampered severely, since what you feel and what you see does not add up. Less motor activation means less incongruence in these cases, which suggests a "less is more" strategy might be more useful. Another factor involved here is of course that force *is actually necessary* in the real world, but may not be in the games: In real tennis, you need a fast, powerful swing to make the ball move, but *Wii tennis* does not actually track a movement pattern in real space, just simple accelerator changes inside the controller. *Wii tennis* is thus essentially a game of timing, not of strength, and since it is much easier to time a quick flick of the wrist than a full swing, this quickly becomes the preferred strategy if one is interested in winning a match.

The problems of missing force dynamics is also quite pronounced in the boxing game included in *Wii Sports*. Here, the player can throw punches by making punching motions while grasping the Wii remote and the Nunchuck and block punches by holding these controllers in front of the face. An actual punch may be more or less accurately mapped visually and thus quite isomorphic and congruent, but the feeling of landing a punch is, of course, sorely missing in terms of proprioception and somatosensory stimulation—thus minimal agency and efficacy might be the result of such *ghost physics*.[21] Blocking punches is also a semi-embodied affair since the action of holding up both hands will be mapped to a blocking movement, but once again the P-action and the visuals do not match up with the expected impact on the physical body. This shows the problematic dichotomy between acting upon other agents and being acted upon—the active and tense acts of hitting someone virtually benefits to some extent from the ability to actually make punching motions, but the patient-relations involved in the boxing match must be left to the audiovisual feedback—and since this is comparatively sparse when hitting or blocking in *Wii Boxing*, the game does not do a very good job of fostering ownership of the virtual body in that situation. Being hit, however, results in a very simple "explosion" effect, which is surprisingly effective on a large screen display. We would argue that the ownership effect here is tied as much to the real body as to the virtual one, which makes this particular aspect of the game somewhat successful in producing a patient effect in actual, not virtual, space.

Once again, we are of course not claiming that players are consciously expecting the boxer on screen to land a physical blow that can be physically felt—we are rather arguing that sub-personal expectations may lead to less than ideal feelings of being an embodied agent responsible for the actions portrayed on screen since the input is often incongruent over several channels of sensory input.

EyeToy and Agency

For a short comparative example of how game systems can map P-actions to virtual bodies and allow these to influence virtual entities, consider the EyeToy peripheral for the PlayStation 2 as used in the game *EyeToy: Kinetic* (2005). The game does not use a physical control interface; rather, the EyeToy camera captures video of the space in front of the camera and displays this as live video on screen—whatever P-action you perform, you will see on-screen as in a mirror (with a slight delay and potential size variation due to screen size). Typically, graphical objects are then rendered on top of this image, and the player is then prompted to perform actions in relation to the objects on screen, such as hitting or avoiding balls, etc. *Eye Toy: Kinetic* seems to rely solely on a primitive motion detection algorithm in order to calculate proximity and eventual collision between the screen body and virtual objects, and this combination of a moving visual image together with a very sparse underlying structural model of the displayed body makes for a potential asymmetry of inputs in relation to player body awareness, as could be seen during two *EyeToy: Kinetic* sessions. In one instance, the player's objective is to avoid a bouncing object, but when the player accidentally remained completely still, the virtual object "passed directly through" the body on screen, making the screen body a "ghost". In another situation, the player's objective is to hit a large object in the lower left corner of the screen, but several attempts to hit the object were rendered unsuccessful, although the on-screen body seemed to connect quite well. This turned out to be a matter of visual obstruction, since the back of an office chair obstructed the camera's field of view in the outermost left corner. In both instances, the algorithm could not cope with mapping the actual P-action to virtual action and the resulting discrepancy between body schema processes and visual feedback from the screen yielded distinct problems of both agency and ownership of the screen body.

Interface Aesthetics in *ICO*

One could also apply considerations of interface choice to the problem of theme in games—a kind of interface aesthetics with regard to the connection between embodiment, interface, and thematic content: How well would a different interface and its physical affordances serve the intentional affordances of a given game? As a very brief example of how this may play out, consider the highly regarded *ICO* (2001) for PlayStation 2, a game rightfully considered a modern classic. One of the main game mechanics is that the player avatar Ico has to protect the young girl Yorda from various demons or monsters. These monsters exhibit the kind of ghost-physics mentioned earlier: they seem to be like smoke or fog when it comes to substance, but they have the power to physically affect their surroundings, as when they knock Ico over or grab Yorda. One way of repelling these ghost-like monsters is to repeatedly swat them with a wooden stick or sword, and this (somewhat curiously, given their apparent body composition) will drive them off eventually. If one were to use a control scheme utilizing motion sensing for this game action (as seen in *Red Steel* (Ubisoft, 2006) and *The Legend of Zelda: Twilight Princess* (Nintendo, 2006) on the Wii), it would fit the bill neatly in terms of force dynamics, since the thematically-motivated ghost physics and resulting absence of resistance should make for direct isomorphism of the movement kinematics and the expected feedback resulting from force dynamics. Transfer of agency and ownership should be high. The bouts of fighting are intricately tied to another central mechanic, namely the holding of Yorda's hand by pushing one of the shoulder (also called trigger) buttons operated by the index finger when gripping the controller. This is an important action in the game world, since the demons constantly try to carry Yorda away, and if they succeed the game ends prematurely. The P-action is of course a kind of grasping in force-dynamic terms, but neither the somatosensory dynamics of gripping a hand nor the tug of holding another person's hand can be simulated adequately by any of the standard controllers. Agency may be somewhat intact, but ownership might be hampered.

ICO is not a game that flaunts its own status as an artifact of audiovisual and ludic fiction—there is no Head Up Display showing score points, health, etc., no in-game map, and there are no postmodern pointers to the world of the player, not even the widespread conflation of interface relations and game world ("press 'X' to hit the demons") found in many other games.[22] One could nonetheless argue that, considering the importance of the emotional themes of solitude, bonding, and attachment, some of the constraints inherent in the game system setup serve the game quite well aesthetically. There is no question that Ico is just as much a character as he is an avatar, and the highly arbitrary mapping nature of the PS2 controller makes sure that the actions of player and avatar stay detached as far as P-actions go. Moreover, the game thrives on our interest in and empathy with the couple's predicament, and one might argue that Ico is doubly abandoned: both by his tribe and, albeit to a lesser extent, by the player who is forever situated outside Ico's action space. The minimal interface relations thus helps keep the player suitably detached from both the girl and the boy in the virtual space. So, if one were to translate *ICO*'s control scheme into motion sensing, one might gain immersion in one game mechanic, but at the same time it may alter the game as a whole in a direction adverse to the overall cognitive and emotional theme of the work as it stands on the PS2.

Agency as Experiencing the Actions of Others

This leads us to more fundamental considerations regarding the nature of mapping in relation to agency and some of the related fundamental emotional complexes. It seems that interface relations in general support primarily the "positive performance" side of agency,[23] while leaving out those situations in which we might want to remain passive or invite actions of other agents and/or events to influence us, also physically. A wide range of actions facilitated by standard control schemes may be termed either kinaesthetically involving and/or agonistic; the most common game action in the action-oriented game is to attack something either with a projectile or a melee weapon. By their very nature, such actions usually involve an agonistic intention and a muscular tone best characterized as tense. Being a human agent, however, is also a matter of letting oneself be acted upon. The dyadic character of certain interaction patterns seem to involve a kind of turn-taking, and this phenomenon is well known from most agonistic games where it might be implemented directly (in turn-based games) or rather emerge from gameplay mechanics (virtual resources, fixed time delays after using a virtual skill, etc.). But this is only the abstract structure of letting others act—the actual embodied experience of being acted upon is still missing: the class of actions which are not exactly actions but rather "receptions" are still only evoked audiovisually and, with what one could only call minimal somatosensory stimulation, such as "rumble" motors inside controllers. It may be a banal observation that video game characters cannot touch us in a purely somatosensory way, but when one considers some of the design intentions behind motion sensing and body mapping, it becomes clear that interfaces facilitate certain isomorphisms related to agency but not others. As motion sensing and other technologies increasingly allows body schematics to be isomorphically mapped to a game space, we take another step in making embodied interaction *fundamentally asymmetric*: dishing out blows, blowing kisses, and petting one's virtual dog becomes eminently possible when one opens up this other channel of input with regards to the system, but the reciprocity in these actions is not facilitated by the interface setup: input to the system may be in the tactile modality, but system output serving as input to the player may not.

The above goes some way in showing that there are certain domains of actions that lend themselves less well to the interface relations of today, and among these are many of the action-emotion complexes involved in nurturing and bonding relations. We are not arguing that one cannot communicate, say, love through a letter, a telephone line, or any other technological medium. The visual feedback of doggish gratitude and playfulness that we get when petting a virtual Dalmatian in *Nintendogs* (Nintendo, 2005), for example, may, via synaesthetic networks, activate emotions and even low-level tactile sensations.[24] However, if one thinks that the actual body matters and subsequently privileges the actions of the actual, physical body in interface design in a given computer game, there are still certain constraints including a technological bias in favor of positive performance. In other words, players can dance, swordfight, and fish the nights away in the comfort of their living room, but they still get no hugs or kisses.

Conclusion

Video games are computer-and-monitor-supported activities that select a small basketful out of all the possible ways that embodied brains may relate to worlds and other agents. A given real life event will also demand or emphasize a specific subset of the total set of possible ways such interactions may exist, also because the embodied brain is a pragmatic set of different functions evolved to perform different tasks.[25] This is even truer in relation to video games; there may (or may not) be core elements in play and games as a general category (Juul), but surely no total theory of video games is possible: Some games emphasize visually salient and/or association-rich audiovisual worlds and emotionally engaging characters, while others are highly abstract, some employ cognitively or emotionally intriguing challenges, while others prioritize physical action; some games are strongly goal-oriented and telic   others are paratelic, process-oriented, and so on. We have argued that embodied interface interaction is general enough to warrant attention, and the continuing work on making new interfaces points to the problem of how to activate the basic experiences of agency, efficacy, and ownership leading to immersion in relation to the player's embodied interaction with the screen-and-speaker world, partly by providing salient somatosensory and proprioceptive support for the feeling of embodied presence in the game world. The existing interfaces primarily support agency, and thus possibly feelings of active ownership and efficacy in relation to avatars and tools. In contrast, experiences of being patients, being objects of embodied actions deriving from game worlds, are presently not supported by existing interface technology.

Notes

1.   For examples, see Andy Clark, *Being There. Putting Brain, Body, and World Together Again* (Cambridge, MA: MIT Press, 1997); Shaun Gallagher, *How the Body Shapes the Mind* (Oxford: Clarendon, 2005), hereafter cited as Gallagher, *Body*; Raymond W. Gibbs,

Embodiment and Cognitive Science (New York: Cambridge University Press, 2006); Torben Grodal, *Moving Pictures. A New Theory of Film Genres, Feelings and Cognition* (Oxford: Clarendon Press, 1997); Torben Grodal, "Video Games and the Pleasures of Control," in *Media Entertainment: The Psychology of Its Appeal*, eds. Dolf Zillmann and Peter Vorderer (Mahwah, NJ: Lawrence Erlbaum Associates, 2000), 197–213; Torben Grodal, "Stories for Eye, Ear, and Muscles: Video Games, Media, and Embodied Experiences," in *The Video Game Theory Reader*, eds. Mark J. P. Wolf and Bernard Perron (New York: Routledge, 2003), 129–155; Torben Grodal, *Embodied Visions* (New York: Oxford University Press, forthcoming); Alva Noë, *Action in Perception* (Cambridge, MA: MIT Press, 2004); and Edward E. Smith and Stephen M. Kosslyn, *Cognitive Psychology: Mind and Brain*. 1. (Upper Saddle River, NJ: Pearson/Prentice Hall, 2007), hereafter cited as Smith and Kosslyn.

2. Albert Bandura, *Self-Efficacy: The Exercise of Control* (New York: W. H. Freeman, 1997), and Albert Bandura, "Toward a Psychology of Human Agency," *Perspectives on Psychological Science* 1, no. 2 (2006): 164–180.

3. Maurice Merleau-Ponty, *Phenomenology of Perception* (London: Routledge & Kegan Paul, 1962); hereafter cited as Merleau-Ponty.

4. Shaun Gallagher and Dan Zahavi, *The Phenomenological Mind. An Introduction to Philosophy of Mind and Cognitive Science* (Oxon: Routledge, 2008).

5. Jonathan Cole, Oliver Sacks and Ian Waterman, "On the Immunity Principle: A View from a Robot," *Trends in Cognitive Sciences* 4, no. 5 (2000): 167; Daniel M. Wegner, *The Illusion of Conscious Will* (Cambridge, MA: MIT Press, 2002); and Daniel M. Wegner and Betsy Sparrow, "Authorship Processing," in *The Cognitive Neurosciences, Third Edition*, ed. Michael S. Gazzaniga (Cambridge, MA: MIT Press, 2004), 1201–1209.

6. Angelo Maravita and Atsushi Iriki, "Tools for the Body (Schema)," *Trends in Cognitive Sciences* 8, no. 2 (2004): 79–86.

7. For an introduction, see G. Rizzolatti, L. Fogassi, and V. Gallese, "Mirrors in the Mind," *Scientific American* (November 2006); and Smith and Kosslyn.

8. James Kilner, Antonia F. de C. Hamilton, and Sarah-Jayne Blakemore, "Interference Effect of Observed Human Movement on Action is Due to Velocity Profile of Biological Motion," *Social Neuroscience* 2, no. 3 (2007): 158–166; and J. M. Kilner, Y. Paulignan, and S. J. Blakemore, "An Interference Effect of Observed Biological Movement on Action," *Current Biology* 13, no. 6 (2003): 522–525. Some of these effects extend even to language processing. See Daniel C. Richardson, Michael J. Spivey, Lawrence W. Barsalou, and Ken McRae, "Spatial Representations Activated During Real-Time Comprehension of Verbs," *Cognitive Science* 27, no. 5 (2003): 767–780.

9. Susan Hurley, "Active Perception and Perceiving Action: The Shared Circuits Model," in *Perceptual Experience*, eds. Tamar Szabó Gendler and John Hawthorne (Oxford: Oxford University Press, 2006), 205–259. See also Gallagher, *Body*, Ch. 9.

10. Donald A. Norman, *The Design of Everyday Things* (New York: Basic Books, 2002); hereafter cited as Norman, *Design*.

11. James J. Gibson, *The Ecological Approach to Visual Perception* (Boston: Houghton Mifflin, 1979).

12. Michael Tomasello, *The Cultural Origins of Human Cognition* (Cambridge, MA: Harvard University Press, 1999).

13. As implied in Donald Davidson, *Essays on Actions and Events* (Oxford: Oxford University Press, 1980); hereafter cited as Davidson.

14. Following Davidson; Georg Henrik von Wright, *Explanation and Understanding* (Ithaca, IL: Cornell University Press, 1971); and Jennifer Hornsby, *Actions, International Library of Philosophy* (London: Routledge & Kegan Paul, 1980).

15. Geoff King, *Spectacular Narratives: Hollywood in the Age of the Blockbuster* (London: I. B. Tauris, 2000); and Geoff King and Tanya Krzywinska, *Tomb Raiders and Space Invaders: Videogame Forms and Contexts* (London: I. B. Tauris, 2006).

16. See Matthew Lombard and Theresa Ditton, "At the Heart of It All: The Concept of Presence," *Journal of Computer-Mediated Communication*, no. 2 (1997); and Byron Reeves and Clifford Nass, *The Media Equation: How People Treat Computers, Television, and New Media Like Real People and Places* (Stanford: CSLI Publications, 1996).

17. Arthur David Milner and Melvyn A. Goodale, *The Visual Brain in Action, Oxford Psychology*

Series, no. 27 (Oxford: Oxford University Press, 1996), hereafter cited as Milner and Goodale.

18. See Pierre Jacob and Marc Jeannerod, *Ways of Seeing. The Scope and Limits of Visual Cognition* (Oxford: Oxford University Press, 2003); and Johannes Roessler and Naomi Eilan, eds. *Agency and Self-Awareness. Issues in Philosophy and Psychology* (Oxford: Oxford University Press, 2003).

19. Milner and Goodale; see also Y. Hu and M. A. Goodale, "Grasping after a Delay Shifts Size-Scaling from Absolute to Relative Metrics," *Journal of Cognitive Neuroscience* 12, no. 5 (2000): 856–868.

20. Nicola J. Hodges, Janet L. Starkes, and Clare MacMahon, "Expert Performance in Sport: A Cognitive Perspective," in *The Cambridge Handbook of Expertise and Expert Performance*, eds. K. Anders Ericsson, Neil Charness, Paul J. Feltovich and Robert R. Hoffman (Cambridge: Cambridge University Press, 2006), 471–488.

21. Pascal Boyer, "Cognitive Constraints on Cultural Representations: Natural Ontologies and Religious Ideas," in *Mapping the Mind: Domain Specificity in Cognition and Culture*, eds. Lawrence A. Hirschfeld and Susan A. Gelman (Cambridge: Cambridge University Press, 1994), 391–411.

22. See Jesper Juul, *Half-Real: Video Games between Real Rules and Fictional Worlds* (Cambridge, MA: MIT, 2005), hereafter cited as Juul.

23. Jennifer Hornsby, "Agency and Actions," in *Agency and Action*, eds. John Hyman and Helen Steward (Cambridge: Cambridge University Press, 2004), 1–23.

24. For an overview of synaesthesia, see Simon Baron-Cohen and John E. Harrison, eds. *Synaesthesia* (Cambridge, MA: Blackwell, 1997).

25. Lawrence A. Hirschfeld and Susan A. Gelman, eds. *Mapping the Mind: Domain Specificity in Cognition and Culture* (Cambridge: Cambridge University Press, 1994); Elizabeth S. Spelke, "Core Knowledge," *American Psychologist* 55, no. 11 (2000): 1230–1233; and Elizabeth S. Spelke and Katherine D. Kinzler, "Core Knowledge," *Developmental Science* 10, no. 1 (2007): 89–96.

CHAPTER 5

Understanding Video Games as Emotional Experiences

AKI JÄRVINEN

Video game studies should delve into more experimental areas of game design and player experiences. At their best, analytical approaches to such areas can help in uncovering starting points for more versatile insights into games.

However, systematic and widely acknowledged methods for video game studies, especially concerning the studying of games from the perspective of game design, are still largely missing. More rigorous methodologies are needed in order for video game design studies to establish itself as a credible academic discipline and engage students and practitioners in the study of games. In general, among schools of academic game studies, the discipline of psychology has been largely ignored. My argument is that playing games is a fundamentally human activity, and thus psychological studies in cognition, emotion, and goal-oriented behavior have to be taken into account when trying to understand video game aesthetics.

In this essay, concepts and categorizations are introduced for studying how various aspects of game designs embody the potential for eliciting particular types of emotions during gameplay. Upon these premises, I have developed a set of methods for the detailed study of gameplay.[1] The set includes a method for analysing how the so-called eliciting conditions for emotions are *embodied* into game designs; that is, which objects, agents, and events in games potentially trigger emotions that are significant and meaningful in the light of the play experience as a whole. Embodiment here refers to visual, aural, or tangible materializations of game elements, such as rules. Concepts such as these can be employed in analyses of individual games, but also as tools for exploring possible research questions concerning play experiences.

Furthermore, analyses regarding the emotional constitution of game designs and the play they facilitate can inform design solutions and experimentations. This essay primarily contributes to *game design research*, that is, to the development of practical methods with which to conduct research into game designs and the play experiences they provide. Games such as *Animal Crossing*; *Zuma*, *Shadow of the Colossus*; *Guitar Hero*; *Silent Hill*; *Super Monkey Ball*; and *Dying in Darfur* will be used as examples in order to highlight how the concepts can be applied in tasks of practical analyses to explain how games engage players emotionally. By identifying games in which emotional dispositions such as empathy—rather than, say, conflict—characterize play experiences, video game studies can point the way to a broader spectrum of play experiences, and consequently, uncover a potentially broader spectrum of audiences and attitudes towards games.

Gameplay and Emotions

> To be a participant is to take on the goals of the game as one's own. Only as a participant will one experience emotions. Only as a participant will one be excited by the possibility of an attack on the queen's side, feel glad to start putting up hotels on one's property, or feel anxious to avoid serving another double fault. Emotions that occur in relation to goals we have adopted are real. One may be engaged in a role, experiencing what happens in it as happening to oneself, and indeed shaping one's selfhood.[2]

As emotion theorist Keith Oatley's insight illustrates, one of the key forms of enjoyment that games offer originates from how games impose goals on players: by setting up goals in stylized, fantastic, temporally limited, and/or larger than life form, games condense features of routine nature of everyday life for entertaining purposes. The subsequent result is that the road that players take in trying to attain those goals is beset by emotions, that is, by valenced reactions towards events, agents, or objects in the game. Depending on the game, such *appraisals* may range from judging one's own or fellow players' performances, outcomes of goals, rule procedures, narrative sequences, and so on. Appraisals may be positive or negative, or something in between—the intensity and valence of an emotion depends on many contextual factors, as we shall see.

This suggests that gameplay, as a human experience, is instilled with emotions, from fierce to mild in their intensity, and from persistent to fleeting in their temporality. The premise of this essay is adapted from studies of emotions by scholars of psychology and cognitive science. Among the literature of their field, two ideas have been widely established. First, as Keith Oatley has stated, "emotions depend on evaluations of what has happened in relation to the person's goals and beliefs." (Oatley 19). Second, it is believed that emotions induce a mental state "usually caused by an event of importance to the subject."[3] The logical conclusion from these statements would be that as long as a player is willing to care enough about the goals of the game and the social situation in order to "play along," games arguably set up conditions for eliciting emotions (according to Oatley's arguments).

Numerous categorizations of emotions exist in the field of emotion theory (for example, Oatley), yet I have found the theory of the cognitive structure of emotions and its categorizations, by Andrew Ortony, Gerald L. Clore, and Allan Collins, as the most suitable for studying games.[4] This is mainly because their charting of "psycho-logical" potentials of experiencing different emotions in a world of *events*, *agents*, and *objects* seems to best correlate with gameplay as an activity where players participate in events, manipulate objects, and take the role of agents and interact with other agents.[5]

Emotions as Phasic Processes

The prominent emotion theorist, Nico Frijda, has proposed that emotions can be seen as a set of phases.[6] Frijda suggests that emotions are phasic in the following way: first, there is *appraisal*, that is, the *recognition* of an event as significant. This is followed by a so-called *context evaluation*, that is, thoughts or plans as to how to cope with the event that caused the emotion. This leads to *action readiness*: one's willingness to respond with another action. Finally, there is *physiological change*, such as expression and action, the bodily and expressive effects of emotion. (For more information on this topic, see Oatley and Jenkins 98–122.) An important concept related to action readiness is *action tendency*, which conceptualizes the tendencies of individuals "to establish, maintain, or disrupt a relationship with the environment" (Frijda 71) as a result of experiencing an emotion.

Gameplay as a Phasic Process

I propose that gameplay consists of phases that are analogous to those of the emotional process; there is recognition of something significant in the game in its present state, followed by the player's appraisal of the situation and what to do. After that, the player proceeds to take actions within the rules, as action readiness transforms into concrete action. Therefore, the study of players' emotional episodes should be anchored to the significant events in the often cyclical continua of games in which players repeat the same actions over and over.

In order to focus an analytical eye on the significant factors that contribute to eliciting conditions, the concept of "game state" is useful. First, game states function as temporal reference points to an event in a game; they represent specific moments in time where the game and its players, and all information concerning them, are in a certain configuration. Second, from the perspective of players, game states function as way-points to attaining goals; game states communicate proximities to confirmation or disconfirmation of a goal. Third, due to their positioning within a game, game states function as carriers of information (Järvinen 2008). The conclusion here is that an appraisal always relates to a specific game state where the events, agents, and objects of the game are configured into particular relationships. Common examples of such relations are geometrical and/or logical relations, as in, for example, in *Pac-Man* (Namco, 1980), the presence or absence of dots, and the positioning of Pac-Man and the ghosts, which indicate how close a player is to success or failure.

Studying Game Design from the Perspective of Emotional Processes

With the above premise and the set of concepts related to it, we can analyze how a game's design builds up moments in which the phasic process of emotions is triggered. Often these moments involve interaction between players, or, between a player (oneself) and the game (design as agent). In the latter cases, the game itself is perceived as an agent with a certain behavior. It can be understood as a force that puts players, events, and objects into motion in the course of gameplay. A video game's "system behavior"[7] consists of the execution and governing of rule procedures: adding or subtracting points, instantiating the behavior of artificial intelligence through virtual characters, triggering scripted events in the game world, judging a player's performance, and so on.

In gameplay, then, at least two kinds of behavior are combined: the behavior arising from the game design as a system of rules, but more importantly, the rule-governed behavior of players themselves. Because games with their rules and roles are coercive in nature, the behavior of players tends to be, to a certain extent, more habituated and thus more predictable[8] than in other forms of entertainment. The difference is due to the interactive nature of gameplay: in other media forms, individual interpretations are seldom channeled directly back, via playful behavior, to the media content with which the audience interacts.

Thus, I suggest that by means of analysis, player behavior as a set of appraisals and subsequent *action tendencies* which use the available means to carry out actions within the game can be modeled into research and design hypotheses that predict both the general nature of play experiences, and the specifics of how they unravel temporally. These hypotheses can be translated into research questions in actual player studies or play-testing sessions with a particular game, if so desired. This essay will focus particularly on the development of theoretical grounding for such practices, that is, on conceptualizing the emotional constitution of play experiences.[9]

Emotion vs. Pleasure

Next, we need to establish a conceptual distinction between emotions and another term often used in discussions of play experiences; the term "pleasure."[10] Michael Kubovy has dealt with the concept of pleasure in a way that is useful to adapt for purposes of understanding video game pleasures. Kubovy posits a theory of "the pleasures of the mind" and "the pleasures of the body." I will mostly focus here on the pleasures of the mind, which Kubovy sees as collections of emotions distributed over time, that is, sequences of emotions. Conversely, he argues that pleasures of the body provide sequences of so-called hedonic states rather than sequences of emotions.[11] According to Kubovy, pleasures of the mind differ from the experience of individual emotions in a number of ways: whereas emotions have communicative signals, such as a facial expression, pleasures of the mind do not; whereas emotions are quick and brief, and can develop rapidly, pleasures of the mind are more extended in time; whereas emotions are experienced involuntarily, pleasures of the mind are "voluntarily sought out," for example, in the form of entertainment such as games (Kubovy 137).

I will proceed in an analogous fashion with the way emotions are related to pleasures. First, I will discuss the micro-level of emotions and categorizations, from which I will proceed to similar conceptualizations of pleasure. This means that I will regard *gameplay* as an activity that embodies prospects for various pleasures, whereas *game designs* are objects or events that embody prospects for emotional episodes.

Emotion Categories as Keys for Understanding Play Experiences

In order to be able to differentiate between play experiences of varying kinds, I argue that we need to identify differences in their emotional constitution. In order to do this, we need to be able to make distinctions between different emotions.

Ortony *et al.* base their theory on the study of groups or clusters of emotions that are elicited by similar conditions. They arrive at groups of emotions with structurally-related eliciting conditions, for instance the attribution group, in which the *actions of agents* trigger the eliciting conditions.

In my view, this concept is useful for studying and designing games, because one cannot unambiguously define the set of emotions a game elicits—at least not without substantial empirical data based on experiments involving a certain design—but I argue that one can conclude, by means of analysis, whether a set of eliciting conditions designed into a specific game state or sequence relates to agents, objects, or events. This helps in identifying relevant emotion categories, and the specific emotion types within them, that are more likely to occur than others. Furthermore, it enables the analyst to describe and construct hypotheses about the play experience, but also vice-versa: the designer may attempt to "reverse engineer" the emotional constitution of a game design. For the purposes of developing such analysis and design methods, I will next produce a summary of the categories in the OCC (Ortony, Clore, and Collins) model.

Prospect-based Emotions

Emotions associated with events belong to a type of prospect-based emotions. Typically, games have events in the form of causal sequences: actions and outcomes, which range from the outcome of a single shot in *Halo* (Bungie Studios, 2003) or *Zuma* (PopCap Games, 2004) to a dramatic turn in a background narrative, as with the *Final Fantasy* series (Square Enix, 1987–2007). Events have to do with prospects, that is, with mental considerations and pictures of something to come. The confirmation of prospects is evaluated in terms of goals, and a prospect might actually equal attainment of a goal or a sub-goal directly.

The potential for emotions based on events is in their prospect: what does the occurrence, and subsequent resolution of the event, promise for the player, and is the event worthwhile in the sense that the player invests effort into trying to make the outcome desirable for oneself or for others. Hope, fear, satisfaction, fears-confirmed, relief, shock, surprise, and suspense are some of the emotions experienced in relation to events and their prospects. Prospect-based emotions are fundamentally related to goals which the player has been instructed to pursue and with which he or she has identified.

Such prospects of events, and the emotions they bring about, can be quite different from one genre of games to another. In story-driven games, the turn of events may be unknown and consequently part of the pleasure of gameplay, whereas in sports or strategy games it is the exact (as defined in the rules) knowledge of what will happen as a consequence of an event that motivates players.

Fortunes-of-Others Emotions

Fortunes-of-Others emotions include good-will emotions, such as being happy or feeling sorry for somebody, or on the other hand, a display of ill will in the form of resentment or gloating. In the context of games, these emotions apply to multiplayer situations and to empathy—or counter-empathy[12]—felt towards the fate of fictional game characters, or to fellow participants, such as team or guild members. An important note to remember is that these emotions focus on events rather than the agents themselves. Thus, emotions relate to the goals of others rather than to others as such; it is the next category, attribution emotions, that accounts for the latter.

Attribution Emotions

Attribution emotions are reactions geared towards agents, that is, the behavior of other human beings, or towards something perceived as an agent, such as the game itself as the governor of rules. The valence of attribution depends on the praiseworthiness or blameworthiness of actions, and their intensity is related to how the behavior deviates from expected behavior. Players may feel pride and appreciation towards themselves or others, but also reproach towards the actions of an opponent, or the rules which effectively represent the game as an agent. If a single-player game is too difficult, the player potentially gets frustrated and regards the game as an agent that acts in a reproachable manner, thus producing emotions of contempt in the player. The concept of genre is also relevant here, as a game can be construed as an agent that represents genre conventions, that is, a certain set of expected behaviors, "how things should proceed," and if the game deviates from the expected conventions, the player may respond with an attribution emotion which leads to an attraction emotion (see below). In other words, an appraisal of the game, in the context of its equivalence to (or deviance from) genre conventions, takes place.

Attraction Emotions

Objects evoke *attraction emotions*—players like or dislike game settings, graphics, soundtrack, level design, and so on. The degree of appeal, or appeal and familiarity, has consequences for the intensity of attraction: high degrees of unfamiliarity most likely produce an attraction emotion of dislike, or even disgust. Thus, they lend themselves for deliberate use, in the design of horror games, for instance, as discussed by video game theorist Bernard Perron.[13] Attraction emotions seem to relate to particular game elements and their implementation, especially the design of characters and game spaces, and how information is distributed to players.

Well-being Emotions

Well-being emotions are basic emotions that relate to desirable or undesirable events. Reactions with positive valence give birth to joy that manifests as happiness, delight, pleasant surprise, etc. Reactions with negative valence lead to distress such as depression, dissatisfaction, grief, etc. The intensity of the emotion is proportional to the degree that the event is desirable or undesirable, or in the special case of a loss (very relevant in the context of games), to its unexpectedness. Whereas prospect-based emotions can be seen to relate to various goals regardless of their status in the goal hierarchy, well-being emotions relate to the victory condition and the gameplay itself as a whole, and whether it has been successful in terms of areas such as social interaction and entertainment.

Variables that Affect Intensities of Emotions

In the OCC model, each distinct emotion type represents a family of closely-related emotions, sharing same basic eliciting conditions but differing in terms of intensity, and possibly "in terms of the weights that are assigned to different components or manifestations of the emotions." (Ortony *et al.*, 15–16.) This means that when an emotion is a compound of other emotions, it is the "balance" of weight between the compounds that gives the emotion its particular nature. In this way, we can understand how both *Super Monkey Ball* (Amusement Vision, 2001) and *Silent Hill* (Konami, 1999) elicit emotions of suspense, yet the way in which the compounds of suspense, such as fear, are embodied in the game design and manifest in the player experience, are distinctly different. Also, each emotion type includes a specification of the principal variables that affect its intensity, which can be divided into local vs. global variables. Local variables affect a group, while global variables have their effects across groups. Global variables include the following:

Sense of reality
This variable has to do with how much one believes the emotion-inducing situation is real. Thus, it is quite relevant in contexts of entertainment and fiction. In the particular contexts of games, the variable can be understood as the degree to which players get "immersed" or "engaged" in a game world and/or the social contexts that the game is being played in.

Proximity
This variable is dependent on how close in psychological space one feels to a situation that triggers an emotion, for example, the intensity of the feeling of success or failure regarding one's performance in the game. Intensity regarding proximity seems to be modulated by the player's identification with goals, in particular.

Unexpectedness
This variable relates to information about the situation, that is, how surprised one is by the emotion-inducing situation; how surprised or shocked the player is regarding a particular outcome, or about unexpected information that a new game state reveals, about opponents, goals, or the game environment.

Arousal
This variable has to do with general psychological and cognitive readiness to experience emotions, and how much one is aroused prior to the situation. For example, the level of arousal affects how the player perceives her abilities to perform in the game, or it can function as a baseline factor affecting how much she cares about the outcome to start with, and so on.

It is important to remember that these *global* variables often work in combination. For example, the level of arousal affects the sense of reality, and vice versa: a player who is fond of fantasy worlds is more likely to get immersed in a fantasy game world, as the player's level of arousal contributes to the sense of reality variable.

Local Variables
The OCC model defines variables that affect the intensity of a particular type of emotion, that is, variables that affect the experience of an emotion locally instead of globally. The following are the local variables that are most relevant in connection with game design: likelihood, degree of effort, degree of desirability, degree of undesirability, and intensity of hope or fear that something will happen.

These all relate to particular emotions. For instance, the intensity of hope or fear relates to the emotion of suspense, which Ortony, Clore, and Collins place in the category of prospect-based emotions that relate to events. Furthermore, they define suspense as a compound emotion of hope, fear, and uncertainty. The local variables that affect the intensity of the compounds also modulate the intensity of the resulting emotion of suspense. From the perspective of gameplay analysis, the focus can then be geared towards the events that contribute to the player's experience of suspense. This can be observed through the three compounds: first, the player's experience of hope (in relation to reaching a particular goal), second, the experience of fear (in relation to losing or failing in the game), and finally, the experience of uncertainty (what makes reaching the goals of the game uncertain). Often this uncertainty is embodied in the game design as the margin of error; that is, it has to do with the player's ability to perform the tasks, such as being able to make deductions (in puzzle and adventure games) or perform tasks involving motor skills (controlling a character, aiming and shooting, etc.).

I believe that the crucial point to be made from the concept of variables is that the design of game elements and gameplay embody both global variables and local variables, and they function as a framing that sets up different eliciting conditions between one play experience and another. The fear in *Super Monkey Ball* is the fear of falling from the track, and the emotion of uncertainty related to it equals the uncertainty of one's own ability to perform in a way that the prospect of fear does not become confirmed—and the emotion of hope is anchored to the same prospect but in a reverse manner; there emerges hope for success when the player manages to stay in the middle of the track. In play experiences of *Silent Hill*, on the other hand, uncertainty is embodied in the design of the game environments and characters, and fear rises from their horrific and mysterious nature. The difference in theme, the setting, and the other ways that underlying rules are communicated to the player, together produce this difference in experience. Nevertheless, both game designs seek to elicit the emotion of suspense through fear and uncertainty, but the material embodiments of particular design elements (characters, environments, sound, etc.) set the eliciting conditions for suspense in quite opposing ways: colorful and cheery in the first case, vs. dark and horrifying in the second.

These observations lead us to focus on the nature of video gameplay experiences as aesthetic experiences; experiences of pleasing appearances or effects, as the dictionary definition of "aesthetics" goes. Video game aesthetics incorporate effects that have to do with both sensory and cognitive aspects, but also, increasingly, with physical processes.

Play Experiences as Aesthetic Experiences

The aesthetic nature of play experiences—whether it involves performing, appreciating the design and composition of game characters and environments, or being fascinated with the simulated minds of game characters —is an important aspect of the antecedents of pleasures and eliciting conditions for emotions in games.

Even though the attraction emotions in the OCC model can be interpreted to account for aesthetic appreciation, I believe that the "magical" qualities of video gameplay needs to be addressed in more detail. One reason for this is that games cannot be objectified from the perspective of play experiences—they are also about aesthetically appreciating events and agents, and thus go beyond attraction emotions geared towards objects. My premise is that this has consequences for emotions, possibly intensifying and/or modifying them in particular ways.

This tension between the everyday world—and its agents, events, and objects—and the ones in a game's world leads us to theories on how aesthetic stimuli differ from everyday stimuli. Gerald Cupchick has written about aesthetics from the perspective of emotions. Cupchick's premise is that stimulus appraisals and responses to them (that is, valenced reactions that happen in everyday life) can be generalized to the aesthetic realm. According to Cupchick, "Everyday stimuli denote objects, people, or events in the world which possess practical utility."[14] Conversely, aesthetic stimuli, such as paintings, are distinguished by a quality Cupchick calls "unity in diversity." According to Cupchick, when compared with everyday stimuli, aesthetic stimuli possess greater qualitative diversity, as they incorporate both stylistic information as well information regarding the subject matter (semantic information).

It can be argued that the "magic circle" of games leverages the experience to a particularly aesthetic nature where practical utilities are submitted to an intrinsic motivation to be entertained. Cupchick writes: "The shifting of thematic fields or backgrounds can radically change the meaning attributed to an event. The important point is that thematic fields or contexts are adduced in accordance with their relevance to a sender or receiver's goals and intentions" (Cupchick 180).

The magic circle produces a shift in the thematic field of the experience, which simultaneously both magnifies the emotional intensity, yet also provides a safety net with the pretend aspect of player behavior it elicits and its relation to the sense of reality variable. Therefore, variables concerning emotional intensities should be interpreted from this perspective.

Aesthetic Sensations as Global Variables of Emotional Intensity

I propose a solution in which the design of aesthetic stimuli in games using various semiotic resources (graphics, speech, text, visual and sound effects, music, etc.) is conceptualized as a practice that affects the intensities of emotions. This takes place globally through the theme of the game, that is, how the game's subject matter and ideas are woven into game states and the design of game elements. In addition, this process takes place locally, through semiotic techniques which produce local effects. Essentially this refers to techniques with which a game design communicates degrees of desirability, or the proximity to goals, and so forth.

Such stimuli have a role in communicating and amplifying the meanings of game states and game sequences, and thus they have consequences for players' abilities to make sense of eliciting conditions. In terms of emotions, visual and sound effects (such as an animation of an explosion with the accompanying sound) are points of focus for the phasic process of emotions—they make an event and its resolution visible and audible. As a result, they can create stimuli which accompany the resolution of a game goal. The resolution itself can be viewed as a utilitarian piece of information for the player, but the aesthetic stimuli amplify and stylize it, thus producing valenced reactions, while contributing to aural and visual pleasures or displeasures of the play experience.

This is to say that, in terms of emotion theory, flashy graphics are not just eye candy but an important antecedent of the play experience as an emotional experience. However, the use of aesthetic variables to intensify the emotional nature of play experiences is often overemphasized in design—other choices, such as an emphasis on character dialogue (as in *Animal Crossing*, Nintendo, 2002) or the intricate modeling of infrastructures (the *Civilization* series, Microprose/Infogrames/2K Games, 1993–2007), might support a play experience of different experiential flavor.

Whatever the design emphasis, antecedents of emotions may take advantage of references to other media forms that are culturally invested with emotions. They can be used as design drivers to remediate the emotional potential that has been already proven in another medium: for example, the spectacle of bullet-time in *Max Payne* (Remedy Entertainment, 2001) remediates effects from the film *The Matrix* (Andy and Larry Wachowski, 1999), while *Guitar Hero* (Harmonix, 2006) remediates rock stardom and performances, and sports games simulate the skills and stardom of athletes, and the glamour of professional sports.

These arguments also open up a design perspective which is more inclined towards so-called experience design, rather than functional design; that is, from a purely functional standpoint, visual and sound effects could always be replaced by communication with the sole purpose of distributing information, such as rules. Game design practices that seek to create emotional experiences are essentially aesthetic creative practices, then, and these observations also explain why there is room for diversity in the shape of different styles in designing game visuals, sounds, and gameplay.

In the following section, I will highlight how the concepts introduced thus far can be applied in practical analysis tasks. As an example, I will present a comparative analysis of two video games.

Case Study: Embodiments in *Thrust* and *ICO*

This analysis has its roots in an intuitive observation of a game scholar: there appears to be something similar in the game design of the space-themed game *Thrust* (Firebird Software, 1986) for Commodore 64, and an esoteric adventure game for PlayStation 2 made 15 years later, *ICO* (SCEA, 2001). From the perspective of goals, it can be argued that the two games have similarities in their goal structures and the means the players are given to attain those goals. Both present their players with the goal of delivering something from one location in the game environment to another, and protecting the delivery while it is in transit. The player is given the means to do this through a certain set of actions—most notably by enabling the player to "drag" something behind their avatar. In other words, we can find structural similarities between the two games by focusing on the goals, and the means which players are given for their attainment.

Despite underlying structural similarities, the two games arguably afford rather different player experiences in terms of emotions. One way to understand this difference is by describing it thoroughly, but my argument is that it is useful to anchor the descriptions in general concepts. This expands the breadth of interpretation; a number of analyses can be compared and discussed with the same terminology. Therefore, I suggest that the difference can be identified by analyzing how the goal of delivery is *embodied* into the game, that is, how it has been given a visible and tangible form in the game design. Thus, the particular embodiment potentially triggers an emotion, or an emotional episode, that leads to action tendencies. Embodiments may vary from the design of a character to the mood and atmosphere of a game world, and onwards to how the game communicates with the player and how a particular game state and goal scenario plays out. Looking for and analyzing embodiments of emotions equals understanding what, in the game design, represents agents, objects, and events in the world that the design builds and upholds.

My premise is that as a goal-oriented activity, gameplay privileges embodiments of goals. For example, in *Pac-Man*, the conditions by which a game ends, such as "after three deaths the game is over," is embodied both in the Pac-Man character's attributes as having three lives, but also in the four ghosts, who embody death. The maze as the game environment embodies the space of movement, and the yellow dots within the maze embody the goal of "clearing" the maze, whereas the "power pills" embody the prospect of eating the ghosts. Arguably, it is the ghosts that elicit the most intense emotions, as they impose a direct threat to the goal the player hopes to reach.

Embodiments of Goals in *Thrust* and *ICO*

As a consequence of the premise, I suggest that the analysis should focus on the embodiments of goals, in particular. In the case of *Thrust*, the goal of delivery is embodied into a container, and the means to attain the goal are embodied in the spaceship that the player controls. In *ICO*, the same elements are drawn from the fantasy theme: Yorda embodies a different metaphor for the goal in the form of a character that is portrayed as fragile and helpless through her timid behavior. Yorda's traits (appearance, voice, movement, etc.) have been designed to communicate her relevance to the goals of the game. Her embodiment tries to elicit feelings of empathy and the desire to nurture. While the container in *Thrust* embodies prospect-based emotions relating to goals, Yorda in *ICO* also embodies the fortunes-of-others type of emotions.

Ico, the title character, embodies the metaphor for the means and agency with which to attain the goal; the player-character embodies the metaphors of savior and protector, and consequently prospect-based emotions associated with heroism, such as pride. Furthermore, the visible interaction of the two characters—Ico guiding Yorda along—is embodied in a composition where he holds her hand. In *Thrust*, it is the cable between the container and the spaceship that embodies similar structural connection. These embodiments of feeling in the game designs differ considerably from each other, and highlight the function of the theme of the game as an aesthetic metaphor for underlying logical and mathematical rule structures.

The Emotional Spectrum of *Thrust* vs. that of *ICO*

The resulting hypothesis from the analysis above is that *ICO* supposedly privileges the elicitation of so-called *attribution emotions* (from pride to remorse), as they focus towards agents—whereas *Thrust* elicits a less nuanced set of *attraction emotions* which focus towards objects, roughly oscillating along the axis between liking and disliking. If we think about the game space that the two games create for play, the two-dimensional space in *Thrust* is less dynamic, whereas *ICO* simulates a world of fantastic origin where the environment is not only an object but also has characteristics of an agent. This also accounts for the differing experiential basis that the two games afford.

The player's own performance in relation to the game's goals, and valenced appraisals regarding one's success, become more prominent in the play experience of *Thrust*. Thus, prospect-based emotions, and the variables affecting their intensity, are constantly present in *Thrust*'s play experience. This is also due to the different rhythms of the two games: the pressure for the player to perform within the margin of error in *Thrust* is constant, whereas in *ICO* the pressure comes at certain intervals, tied to the player's exploration of the game world and the challenges designed into its locations. The difference in emotional spectrums also has to do with the sense of reality variable, and how it functions in the two games: Whereas *Thrust* creates immersion into the game through constant requirement of player action, *ICO* creates immersion through intricate simulation of a fantastic world and the characters inhabiting it.

As a consequence, *Thrust* can be seen as a dynamic visual puzzle that emphasizes psychomotor and cognitive abilities tied to visual perception and reaction speeds, whereas *ICO*, despite addressing some of the same abilities, appears as a story of rescue and empathy. The "gameness" of the two games is thus decidedly of a different flavor, due to the emotional constitution of their design.

The Design of Goals as the Design of Eliciting Conditions

It is in the general nature of goals that they tend to prompt a series of actions that in turn produce effects in the world (Oatley 24). Therefore, goals are tools for game designers to activate players for play, and for players, the emotional experiences produced by the struggle to attain a goal. In terms of emotion theory, game goals imply action tendencies which are usually restricted to a few actions, as defined in the rules of the game. The action tendencies designed into the game can both open and constrain the emotional and experiential space of the design. In any case, the design of the possibilities in which the actions of a game are taken always has consequences for prospect-based emotions.

Indeed, Oatley (25) has stated that "emotions emerge at significant junctures in plans." By their shocks and surprises, games provide junctures in our plans to complete a goal of saving the world, scoring most points, finding a treasure, or whatever it is that the game designers try to coerce the players into believing and striving for in the world of the game.

It is once again worth pointing out the pervasiveness of goals in light of gameplay experiences: game elements that embody game goals, will elicit prospect-based emotions. For example, if the goal is to capture a certain space in the game environment, the environment comes to embody the prospect of having its ownership, even though the actual capturing would take place by performing a specific action designed for that purpose. In similar fashion, a tool that the player can use to her advantage in order to reach a goal, such as a weapon in *Half-Life* (Valve Software, 1999), represents an object that embodies the solution to the challenge that the goal presents. The object communicates a prospect for the player, and thus, such an instrumental object, and its use, is bound to elicit emotions.

In a similar fashion, in games like *Tetris* (Alexey Pajitnov, 1985), but also in card games like Texas Hold'em or Poker there are numerous game states where the combination of game elements and their configuration in the game environment leave a prospective space open for future blocks, or cards, respectively, to be placed upon. Such design solutions highlight the promise of an attained goal (such as the penalty kick example, described below) and consequently, set up emotional focal points for players.

The Design of Game States as the Design of Eliciting Conditions

The emotion-eliciting feature of an individual game element is largely conceptual, since in play experiences, elements combine into sequences of emotions, the origins of which might be hard to distinguish individually. If there is a discernable object of study, it is a game state in a given moment of time, with the elements configured into a certain constellation, and the prospects of emotions attributed to that constellation; that is, pictures of something—and the subsequent emotions—to come. Even if I were to argue that, with the concepts introduced in this essay, we are likely to be able to identify which elements have the most significant emotional consequences for players, often the experiential whole is more than the sum of its parts.

Therefore, I will briefly discuss some examples of game states which set up particularly interesting eliciting conditions. First, an interesting game state in the context of eliciting conditions for emotions is found in soccer: the penalty kick. As the ball is placed on the spot within the penalty area, the focus centers around only two players, whereas normally there are almost always more involved. The game state derives much of its emotional intensity from the fact that the normally fluid continuation of one game state to another is suspended—as it is during goal kicks, throw-ins, and corner kicks. Yet, in the case of a penalty kick, the possibility space regarding the following game states is dramatically reduced to two possible outcomes: a goal, or no goal. The game state thus embodies more predictable emotional outcomes than a random state during the game, and thus the local variable affecting the intensity of resulting emotions (from the suspense of hope + fear + uncertainty to satisfaction/fears-confirmed) is amplified. The inevitable temporal delay that precedes the penalty kick also intensifies the prospect-based emotions by heightening arousal, as there is more time to consider the possible outcomes than in most scoring situations in which the action does not stop. The first game state in the 100 meter sprint in running, combined with the "ready-set-go" signal, produces similar arousal and emotions of expectancy and suspense. In light of the penalty kick example, it is interesting to consider similar examples from other realms of games. In video games, the constitution of such game states, or sequences of them, is highly genre-dependent. Games like *Half-Life* or *Halo* build such moments by so-called scripted events that get triggered once the player directs the game character into a certain location of the game world, or manipulates an object in it.

On the other hand, in a game like *Zuma* (PopCap Games, 2004), suspense is embodied in the interplay of game elements (as is the case with *Thrust*), and especially in the end and victory conditions. In *Zuma*, balls of different colors move through a tube, at the end of which there is a skull, which embodies the end condition of losing a life. The player tries to avoid the end condition by shooting the balls out from the tube, thus trying to reach the victory condition of clearing the tube completely. The number of balls left in the tube, and their distance from the skull, is a "vector of suspense," along which the hopes and fears of a *Zuma* player oscillate. This also means that the monitoring of progress towards the goal is constant, and consequently so is the suspense, which gives a flavor of its own to the play experience when compared with, say, a turn-based game, in which events and their resolution play out in different tempo.

There is another popular game, *Peggle* (PopCap Games, 2007), in which the player tries to clear a number of pegs from sets of spaces by hitting the pegs with a ball. In *Peggle*, the vector of movement of a bouncing ball sets up a random vector of suspense which changes dynamically according to the unpredictable collisions of the ball with its surroundings. Each time the ball bounces upwards or towards pegs in the game environment (which embody prospects of reaching the goal), there is "hope", and each time the ball descends towards the bottom, the compound emotion of fear intensifies. The game combines aspects of Pinball and Pachinko, the Japanese game played in gaming parlors. There is an interesting design solution in *Peggle* when the player reaches the game state where the last peg remains; once the ball flies close enough to the single remaining peg, the perspective zooms in and a slow-motion effect is used to emphasize the meaning of the last peg as the goal-confirming element. In terms of the theory formulated here, this design feature is a particular technique to intensify the hope of reaching the goal, and it very literally emphasizes the player's understanding of her proximity to the goal; and as an attention-inducing moment, it can also be seen as contributing to the "sense of reality" variable. Obviously, the zoom and slow-motion effect embody aesthetic sensations that intensify the experience as well.

Game designs that aim to elicit suspense may be built either mostly or entirely on chance (a force the player can not affect), or mostly on skill (a force dependent on the player's abilities) as with *Zuma*. This difference results in quite different emotional experiences. This has to do with how the intensity of suspense becomes modulated through the play experience: a game design with a hectic or accelerating tempo elicits *constant* suspense (for example, in *Tetris*), whereas a game design with narrative aspirations might elicit suspense through a dramaturgic arch, in which information is distributed through narrative passages in ways that embody a gradual diminishment in uncertainty, and the "dead" moments are dramaturgically necessary for the emotional effect sought by the designers. So the emotional potential of a sequence of game states may be designed according to various dramaturgic principles, ranging from constant "drama" to varying highs and lows similar to those found in music or narrative in other media.

From Emotions to the Pleasures to Which they Contribute

Now I will move the discussion from the micro-level of play experience to the pleasures to which they contribute at the macro-level of play experience. Kubovy (147–149) distinguishes five particular categories of "pleasures of the mind." In Kubovy's terms, these categories arise from the objects of emotions that contribute to the emergence of certain kinds of pleasure. In my interpretation, this is an approach similar to the OCC model, where the structural similarities of eliciting conditions are used to group emotions. I see these pleasure categories as being relevant in the context of games and these can be summarized as follows:

- *Curiosity* conceptualizes pleasures from learning something previously unknown. The unknown functions as the object of emotions. As prospects by definition point towards future and consequently to something unknown, it is the prospect-based emotions that can be seen as significant contributors to the pleasure arising from curiosity.
- *Virtuosity* conceptualizes pleasures from doing something well. One's own performance and ability function as the object of emotions. This pleasure anchors to the pleasure to be gained from making the prospect become reality, that is, the act of gameplay as a set of events, and one's performance as a part of it. Attribution emotions (regarding one's performance) have consequences for the pleasure of virtuosity therefore as well.
- *Nurture* conceptualizes pleasures from taking care of living things, such as childrearing, gardening, nursing, or teaching. Their objects function as the objects of emotions. Obviously, this pleasure has

to do with fortunes-of-others emotions; prospects that have relevance and consequences not only to self but others. In addition, attribution and attraction emotions towards the act of nurturing, and/or the object of nurture, are bound to be elicited as well.

- *Sociality* conceptualizes pleasures from belonging to a social group. The members and the group function as the object of emotions. Pleasure from sociality has to do with the attraction emotions towards agents, and attribution emotions towards their doings, as well as well-being emotions.
- *Suffering* involves negative pleasures of the mind from "mundane" psychological pains, such as shame and guilt, or from "existential" pains, such as fears of death or related concerns, which consequently function as the object of emotions. This pleasure quite obviously has to do with many different emotion types, with negative valence as the common denominator.

Next, I will look at these categories individually in the context of video games, and evaluate their applicability for purposes of video game studies.

Curiosity Breeds Suspense across Game Genres

Curiosity as a pleasure for players results when the unknown is embodied into the game design or gameplay. "Who will win?" is a fundamental object of curiosity of multiplayer gameplay experiences. Regarding game design, curiosity has to do with the distribution of information, in particular. It is generally accepted that humans are insatiably curious, and that our curiosity can extend to the contents of our own or other's minds. With particular game genres, curiosity is made manifest through different design techniques. Kubovy (149) touches upon this when he mentions the "joy of verification" and "feeling of surprise" characteristic to puzzle-solving and mysteries, respectively. Even in games where all information is available to the players (like chess), the outcome of the game is still the subject of curiosity.

The emotion of suspense contributes to curiosity, because uncertainty is one of its compound emotions. Moreover, the emotion of shock, due to its compound nature of unexpected and undesirable (Ortony *et al.*), is something that seems to appear often in relation to curiosity, especially in horror video games, like the *Resident Evil* series (Capcom, 1996–2008). In the same genre, games like *Silent Hill* take advantage of darkness as the embodiment of uncertainty and fear.

Curiosity also highlights one specific trait of video games; that is, how they enable the creation of game worlds which awaken the curiosity of players through goals that require the exploration of game environments that are unknown (such as those in *ICO*, *Halo*, and *Half-life*). One specific design feature, the design of the player's perspective of the world, can function as an embodiment of uncertainty: it can constrain the player's field of vision deliberately to a certain viewpoint in order to be able to shock from behind. Sounds designed into a game world are also effective aesthetic variables that affect the intensity of emotions.

Virtuosity through *Guitar Hero* and *Singstar* Skills

Kubovy's notion of virtuosity involves the deriving pleasure from one's own performance and ability—in this case, through video gameplay. It contributes to the individual's sense of self-efficacy. In the context of entertainment, virtuosity also serves to explain how enjoyment can be elicited by an appreciation of an artist's performance—or, either the performance of a fellow player or a professional player, such as a "cyberathlete" of the real-time strategy game *Starcraft* (Blizzard, 1998). In general, a display of skill functions as an antecedent to virtuosity. The preceding analysis of *ICO* and *Thrust* highlights how *ICO* privileges—through exploration and narrative elements—pleasure from curiosity, whereas *Thrust* privileges pleasure from virtuosity by constantly forcing the player to remain within the margin of error.

In terms of emotions, it is the attribution emotions—ranging from pride to shame—regarding one's performance that contributes to this particular pleasure. Whereas games like *Guitar Hero* support the display of virtuosity and creativity through specific motoric and auditory skills, games like *Dance Dance Revolution* (Konami, 1999) add bodily performance to the equation, and *Singstar* (SCEE, 2004) anchors its emotional basis in performance through the singing of songs.

When the pleasure of virtuosity is facilitated by conflict, they set up antecedents for curiosity—in many games; it is through conflict that uncertainties between two or more degrees of virtuosity are decided. Even if conflict, which juxtaposes the player and the game or other players, is an inherent quality found in many games, its significance varies greatly across both existing and future game genres. The pleasures from nurturing, sociality, and suffering also play a role, and in the following sections my aim is to present evidence of how their elicitation can be set up in game designs.

Nurturing from *The Sims* to *Animal Crossing*

There are specific game genres that afford nurturing, especially among video games: virtual pets (like the Tamagotchi toys) and the social relationships and well-being of characters in *The Sims* (Maxis, 2000), yet also player roles such as football managers and urban planners (the *SimCity* series from Maxis, 1989–2008) can be seen to afford the pleasures of nurturing. It would seem to be closely related to collecting, which is what motivates players of collectable card games, like *Magic the Gathering* or *Pokémon*. The pleasure of nurture can be elicited in a number of ways in games, but it is useful to point out the consequences of different game themes, that is, subject matter and metaphors for rules, in the elicitation of nurturing.

Nintendogs (Nintendo, 2005) is an interesting case in the sense that it elicits pleasure from nurturing through a simulation of a living being and its behavior. Gestures and canine behavioral cues (like tail-wagging or barking) function as constituents of eliciting conditions. The behavior of the virtual dogs comes to embody a set of eliciting conditions, which refer to our experiences and attitudes towards dogs as faithful companions which, as pets, still depend on the care of humans. In other words, a "pet schema" is used as a structure for the goals of the game which embody tasks of caring.

Another interesting example is *Animal Crossing* (Nintendo, 2004), a game in which the player takes care of a virtual village of small animal characters. It illustrates how the design of both character behaviors and goal hierarchies set up eliciting conditions. Goal hierarchies in the game are designed in such a way that, to paraphrase the syntax of the OCC model, "Goals-of-animals" (non-player characters) contribute to "Goals-of-self" (the player character) and consequently to "Goals-of-village," the goals of the community made up of both player and non-player characters. As a result, these design solutions support a community spirit, a caring about the common concerns and the "feelings" of the animal characters, and the well-being of the idyllic village and its virtual nature. There is a strong instrumental relation with sub-goals and the higher-order goals they contribute to (nursing a garden contributes to the well-being of the village, etc.), which makes prospects more potent in the way they set up eliciting conditions. This has to do with the global variables "sense of reality" and proximity as well.

Design and writing techniques, which have to do with the player's recognition, alignment, and/or allegiance to characters,[15] is another key to empathy. In *Animal Crossing*, dialogue is especially used as a characterization technique that sketches out the animal characters' personalities, as the game does not pursue any kind of photorealistic imagery or life-like animations. The dialogue pieces set up eliciting emotions for attraction emotions towards the characters, and their actions (such as giving or receiving gifts, sending letters, etc.) function in a similar fashion in the context of attribution emotions. The dialogue is also filled with appraisals of the player-character, or other animal characters, which adds to the game's repertoire of eliciting conditions. Overall, *Animal Crossing* manages to address some of the same pleasures as the television series *Big Brother* (Endemol, 1999–2007), which basically, especially for its contestants, sets up eliciting conditions across all emotion types.

Sociality from *World of Warcraft* to *Animal Crossing*

Sociality is obviously a fundamental pleasure to be gained from participating in gameplay with others, or from being a spectator of one. Recognition or reproach from peers contributes to well-being emotions, especially gratitude or anger. These emotions are set up in player communities such as guilds or teams in multiplayer online games from *Half-Life: Counter-Strike* (Valve Corporation, 2000) to *World of Warcraft* (Blizzard Entertainment, 2004) and numerous browser-based games, such as *Travian* (Travian Games, 2005).

However, games like *Animal Crossing* are not without aspects of sociality: besides players being able to visit others' villages, there is the "parasocial" nature of interacting with the animal characters, which, due to the "sense of reality" variable, might seem quite life-like. Furthermore, *Singstar* facilitates sociality by offering opportunities to sing together, and in general, such play performances cater for sociality through spectatorship.

Suffering through Loss in *Dying in Darfur* and *Shadow of the Colossus*

Kubovy's final category, suffering, finds its mundane realizations in the paradoxical nature of player motivations, that is, the player's willingness to play even in the face of potentially suffering loss or experiencing negative emotions. This paradox has been explained in psychological theory with the concept of "metamood." The term accounts for a mental process where individuals experience unpleasant emotions on the object level, but also positive emotions and enjoyment on a meta-emotional level. This is done to achieve other goals and purposes, such as being entertained.[16]

So, although voluntary suffering appears in many games, some games, with their themes and designs, set up eliciting conditions for particular emotions related to suffering, such as hopelessness (undesirability + irreversibility, according to Ortony *et al.*) or even resignation (undesirability + inevitability). My examples in this context are the browser-based game *Dying in Darfur* (MTV Games, 2006) and a game for PlayStation 2, *Shadow of the Colossus* (Team Ico, 2005).

Dying in Darfur is interesting in how it sets up eliciting conditions for empathy and tries to persuade its players to become more aware of the humanitarian crisis in question, and take "outside-of-the-game" actions toward bringing hope to the situation in Sudan. Such feelings of empathy, and the suffering associated with it, are sought by persuading the player to identify with "Goals-of-Darfurian refugees." This kind of design premise, in which the goal is to get players to identify with Fortunes-of-Darfurians can also be seen to set up conditions for intellectual and altruistic pleasures (which Kubovy does not address in particular).

In *Shadow of the Colossus*, the player has the task of slaying giant colossi in order to bring back a loved one from the dead. In the process, the hero starts an inevitable deterioration towards turning into a monster himself. The play experience is heavily based on the sense of spectacle with its epic theme and sense of scale, yet the game design forces the player to destroy that which provides the play experience of spectacle and struggle. Consequently, a sense of loss and inevitability are the key moods. The aesthetics of the game intensify this, as the completion of higher-order goals—such as slaying the colossi—are communicated with tragic over-tones instead of celebratory fanfares.

Overall, the applicability of the term "suffering" can be questioned in the context of games. As the above examples illustrate, games have their particular means of eliciting feelings of anxiety and guilt, and therefore "Anxiety" might be a more suitable term to characterize such pleasures from playing games. This terminological issue is partly due to the pleasures games privilege at present, yet as the serious games movement gains momentum, the pleasures of suffering might become more prominent in the overall emotional spectrum of gameplay emotions.

Methods and Vocabulary for Understanding Play Experiences

This essay has tried to illustrate that when theories of emotion are adapted for practices of game study, scholars and students of game design can shift the focus to the exploration of any type of emotion, including those that are associated only with a minority of video games at present. Emotions related to fortunes of other players or non-player characters present examples of characteristics which are embraced in the play experiences of games such as *Animal Crossing* but not broadly across video game genres.

In addition, the results presented in this essay are pointing to design techniques which potentially could be used to explore and design more diverse player experiences. They provide examples of how feeling is embodied into an aesthetic work,[17] which, from an emotional perspective, is what creating art and entertainment is largely about. In academic terms, they are meant to function as conceptual basis for identifying such differences with a specific methodology, and to build vocabularies and conceptual toolboxes for emotion-centered game studies and design practices.

Notes

1. Aki Järvinen, *Games without Frontiers. Theories and Methods for Game Studies and Design* (PhD dissertation, University of Tampere, 2008).
2. Keith Oatley, *Best Laid Schemes. The Psychology of Emotions* (Cambridge: Cambridge University Press, 1992), 355; hereafter cited as Oatley.
3. Keith Oatley and Jennifer M. Jenkins, *Understanding Emotions* (Malden, MA: Blackwell, 1996), 377; hereafter cited as Oatley and Jenkins.
4. Andrew Ortony, Gerald L. Clore, and Allan Collins, *The Cognitive Structure of Emotions* (Cambridge: Cambridge University Press, 1990); hereafter cited as Ortony *et al.*
5. Another interesting theory for these purposes is put forward in Ira J. Roseman, Ann Aliki Antoniou, and Paul E. Jose, "Appraisal Determinants of Emotions: Constructing a More Accurate and Comprehensive Theory," *Cognition and Emotion* 10, no. 3 (1996).
6. Nico H. Frijda, *The Emotions* (Cambridge: Cambridge University Press, 1986); hereafter cited as Frijda.
7. Robin Hunicke, Marc LeBlanc, and Robert Zubek, "MDA: A Formal Approach to Game Design and Game Research" 2004. Available online at <http://www.cs.northwestern.edu/~hunicke/MDA.pdf>.
8. Peter Vorderer, Christoph Klimmt, and Ute Ritterfeld, "Enjoyment: At the Heart of Media Entertainment," *Communication Theory* 14 (2004): 388–408.
9. Please note that I am not discussing emotions in the sense of the "emotioneering" that computer game producer David Freeman promotes in *Creating Emotion in Games. The Craft and Art of Emotioneering* (New Riders Publishing, 2003). Even though shades of emotioneering might be evident in the following concepts, I do not believe that the relationship of video games and emotions can be reduced to narrative techniques only, such as dialogue or characterization. This seems to be the area where work in the realm of games emotions has focused so far (see, for example, Isbister Katherine, *Better Game Characters by Design. A Psychological Approach*, San Francisco: Morgan Kaufmann, 2006). I will argue that it is indeed only one area from where emotional episodes emerge during gameplay.
10. See Nicole Lazzaro, "Why We Play Games: Four Keys to More Emotion in Player Experiences," paper presented at the *Game Developers Conference* (2004). Abstract available online at <http://www.xeodesign.com/whyweplaygames/xeodesign_whyweplaygames.pdf>.
11. Michael Kubovy, "On Pleasures of the Mind," in *Well-Being: The Foundations of Hedonic Psychology*, eds. Daniel Kahneman, Ed Diener, and Norbert Schwarz (New York: Russell Sage Foundation, 1999), 134–154; hereafter cited as Kubovy.
12. Dolf Zillman, "Mechanisms of Emotional Involvement with Drama," *Poetics* 23, no. 1 (1995): 33–51.
13. Bernard Perron, "A Cognitive Psychological Approach to Gameplay Emotions," in *Changing Views: Worlds in Play. Proceedings of DiGRA 2005 Conference*, Vancouver, 2005. Available online at <http://www.digra.org/dl/db/06276.58345.pdf>.
14. Gerald C. Cupchick, "Emotion in Aesthetics: Reactive and Reflective Models," *Poetics* 23, no. X (1994): 178; hereafter cited as Cupchick.
15. Murray Smith, *Engaging Characters: Fiction, Emotion, and the Cinema* (New York: Oxford University Press, 1995).
16. J. D. Mayer and Y. N. Gaschke, "The Experience and Meta-experience of Mood," *Journal of Personality and Social Psychology* 55 (1988): 102–111.
17. Gerald Cupchick, "Aesthetics and Emotion in Entertainment Media," *Media Psychology* 3 (2001): 71–72.

CHAPTER 6

In the Frame of the Magic Cycle
The Circle(s) of Gameplay

DOMINIC ARSENAULT
BERNARD PERRON

More than Smoke and Mirrors

The simplest way to conceptualize the gaming activity is to see the game and the gamer as two separate entities meeting at a junction point, which is commonly referred to as "gameplay". In popular game culture, this all-inclusive term seems to belong more to the realm of magic than to the one of science. People will usually say that the gameplay of a particular game is what makes it "fun" without precisely detailing what it entails. But as we know, insofar as the notion of gameplay cannot be ignored, its nature is being scrutinized both in video game studies and professional game development communities. Like Daniel Cook states in "The Chemistry of Game Design", it is necessary to move "beyond alchemy" and to "embrace the scientific process and start [to] build a science of game design".[1] Indeed, we have reached a point where it is possible and necessary to break the spell of gameplay in order to understand this elusive phenomenon, and to use proper terms and models to study it.

At the onset, one of the first misconceptions of gameplay which needs to be addressed springs out when one does not make a distinction between the process of playing a game and the game system itself. This is exactly the case with Lev Manovich's discussion of the notion of algorithm. In *The Language of New Media,* Manovich writes:

> The similarity between the actions expected from the player and computer algorithms is too uncanny to be dismissed. While computer games do not follow database logic, they appear to be ruled by another logic—that of an algorithm. They demand that a player executes an algorithm in order to win.
>
> An algorithm is the key to the game experience in a different sense as well. As the player proceeds through the game, she gradually discovers the rules that operate in the universe constructed by this game. She learns its hidden logic, in short, its algorithm. Therefore, in games in which the game play departs from following an algorithm, the player is still engaged with an algorithm, albeit in another way: She is discovering the algorithm of the game itself. I mean this both metaphorically and literally . . .[2]

The word "algorithm" is used here to refer to two different things: the actions the gamer must perform to solve a problem, and the set of computer procedures controlling the representation, responses, rules, and randomness of a game.[3] Uncanny connection or not, these things are not the same. And the literal meaning is as wrong as the metaphor remains in the end faulty. Clearly, Manovich does not seem to grasp the subtle difference between his own conception and the one he quotes from Will Wright: "Playing the game is a continuous loop between the user (viewing the outcomes and inputting decisions) and the computer (calculating outcomes and displaying them back to the user). The user is trying to build a mental model of the computer model" (Manovich, 223). When, to take Manovich's example, the gamer finds out that an enemy in *Quake* (Id Software, 1996) will always appear from the left, he still only witnesses the repetitive result of the computer's response to his action. He does not, per se, discover the game's algorithm which remains encoded, hidden and multifaceted (from the graphics, which deal with the appearance of the enemy, to the artificial intelligence, which manages this enemy's actions). His mental model will never represent the gameplay as a computer set of instructions or calculated formulae (the enemy's movement from left to right is not thought of by the gamer as "Enemy1.PositionX = PositionX+1"). Therefore, the notion that a gamer's experience and a computer program directly overlap is a mistake. Gameplay should not be considered as "gamer's input + computer algorithm = outcome". The patterns of gameplay are much more complex than that. On this matter, Jesper Juul makes a significant clarification:

> It is important to understand that the gameplay is not the rules themselves, the game tree, or the game's fiction, but the way the game is actually played. . . . Where does gameplay come from? I believe that gameplay is not a mirror of the rules of the game, but a consequence of the game rules and the dispositions of the game player.[4]

While it is certainly more than smoke and mirrors, gameplay is not just a perfect mirror of the algorithm either. To better define gameplay, we need to consider it as something on its own.

Another common misconception about gameplay comes from the widespread use of the metaphor of space to describe the junction point between the gamer and a game. This is probably one of the main reasons why Huizinga's concept of "the magic circle" is now being questioned. For instance, Daniel Pargman and Peter Jakobsson underline in "The Magic is Gone: a Critical Examination of the Gaming Situation"[5] that there is not a strong boundary anymore between games and ordinary life in our digital world, and that games play many different roles and fill many other functions than those related to "fun", "specialness", and "other-worldliness".[5] While those observations may be true, taking Huizinga's wording at face value and trying to reduce the gaming situation to extraordinary and spatial considerations carried in "magic" and "circle" is still a blunder that should be avoided.

For one thing, a game does not depend on the playground in which gamers find themselves. As Mia Consalvo puts it:

> While it may be helpful to consider that there is an invisible boundary marking game space from normal space, that line has already been breached, if it was ever there to start with. My point is not to contend that such boundaries are necessary (or unnecessary) but instead to point to the most important boundary marker for games: their rules. Rules keep a game distinct from other games as well as other parts of life.[6]

With or without physical boundaries, self-contained or open activity, routinized practice or ritualized events, playing a game always requires the understanding and voluntary adoption of certain behaviors enforced through the game's rules. We cannot play without taking on, at a certain degree, a lusory[7] or ludic attitude. This, in Gadamer's terms, "determines exactly why playing is always a playing of something. Every game presents the man who plays it with a task. He cannot enjoy the freedom of playing himself out except by transforming the aims of his behavior into mere tasks of the game" (in French, the translation refers to a behavior transformed into a "pure ludic task").[8] We cannot play if we are not conscious of playing. When all is said and done, Salen and Zimmerman's suggestion that "[t]he idea of a cognitive frame closely mirrors the concept of the magic circle"[9] should be taken the other way around. In fact, it is the magic circle that reflects the concept of cognitive frame.

The authors of *Rules of Play* resort pertinently to Gregory Bateson's theory of play (and fantasy). Observing play activities among animals and human beings as well, Bateson notices that "this phenomenon, play, could only occur if the participant organisms were capable of some degree of metacommunication, that is of exchanging signals which would carry the message 'This is play'. (. . .) Expanded, the statement 'This is play' looks something like this: 'These actions in which we now engage do not denote what those actions *for which they stand* would denote'."[10] Like Pargman and Jakobsson's interviewed informants, a gamer can go in the most ordinary way from his PC to his console (left on all the time), and still understand that he plays here, and not there. Picking up a game controller or even logging into his *America's Army* (US Army, 2002) account will signal him that he is not using his PC "to work" or to interact with "the real world".[11] Failure to do so would be a huge problem and would probably necessitate therapy. Moreover, for Bateson,

> "[t]he resemblance between the process of therapy and the phenomenon of play is, in fact, profound. Both occur within a delimited psychological frame, a spatial and temporal bounding of a set of interactive messages. In both play and therapy, the messages have a special and peculiar relationship to a more concrete or basic reality." (Bateson, 191)

If, among his two examples, Bateson takes the physical analogy of the picture frame to explain his concept of psychological frame,[12] he underscores the fact that the "psychological concept which [he is] trying to define is neither physical nor logical. Rather, the actual physical frame is . . . added by human beings to physical pictures because these human beings operate more easily in a universe in which some of their psychological characteristics are externalized" (Bateson, 187). In that sense, the image of the magic circle externalizes the cognitive processes implied by the act of entering a game.

A psychological frame delimits a set of messages or meaningful actions. We act differently or follow different rules according to the framing of a situation or an activity. Since human beings are switching frames "all the time and it can literally be done at the blink of an eye" (Pargman and Jakobsson, 20), there might be, following Pargman and Jakobsson, nothing "magical" about playing a game nowadays.[13] No doubt we all wish at one point in our lives to be able to see games (and many more things) once again through a child's eyes. It seemed, in those days, that playing games had mysterious and supernatural qualities (especially when these games had been delivered by Santa Claus under the Christmas tree). But if, as we grow up and as our experience of gaming changes, games do not spellbind us anymore, it does not mean that there is not something captivating or enchanting about them any longer. On the contrary. To quote Salen and

Zimmerman (2004, 95) "there is in fact something genuinely magical that happens when a game begins." Pieces on a board become kings, queens, rooks, bishops, knights, and pawns; they have to be moved in specific ways; and they necessitate the development of strategies. It might be yet another first-person shooter with the same default controls and narrative premises, but a gamer is still getting a certain anxiety in a digital universe he has to explore and where he will face hordes of enemies in real-time with an arsenal at hand. Just as there is probably nothing "magical" per se about reading a book, it is still fascinating to find ourselves totally absorbed in one. While a well-informed cinephile can focus on details an ordinary viewer would not see, it does not prevent him from being caught up in the action of a movie or from experiencing a wizardly special effect.[14] To anyone who loves games, there is always something exciting about gaming. It can certainly happen that the "game magic" is not there, but again, the image of the magic circle externalizes the fact that we see and behave in games differently than in our ordinary-life psychological frame. This is what Huizinga was trying to say: "All [play-grounds] are temporary worlds within the ordinary world, dedicated to the performance of an act apart."[15]

Getting into the Magic Cycle

While everyone seems interested in "breaking the magic circle"[16] because the concept appears to be questionable, there is at least one point on which everyone agrees: playing a video game is always a continuous loop between the gamer's input and the game's output. Call it interactivity or ergodicity (or anything else)—is that not what is unique about video games? And is this not where the magic comes from? We should not forget that the temporal dimension of gameplay prevails on its spatial characterization. Therefore, the figure of the circle should make us think about an ongoing process more than an enclosed space. It is much more relevant to conceptualize the cognitive frame of gameplay as a cycle: the magic cycle.

As Perron has already noted,[17] the notion of circularity in video games is a classic way to explain gameplay. From game designers to video game scholars, everyone is referring to some kind of cycle. For instance, game designers Ernest Adams and Andrew Rollings have highlighted in their book *Fundamentals of Game Design* (2007) the importance of positive feedback loops. "The core mechanics often reward achievements with assets that the player can convert into power in order to make further achievements easier."[18] We can exemplify this with *The Elder Scrolls IV: Oblivion* (Bethesda Game Studios, 2006), in which the player can explore the world to find alchemical ingredients and use them to create potions that in turn make it easier to explore the world, and so on. The well-known theorist and practitioner, Chris Crawford, goes beyond specific examples and integrates the cycle into his very definition of interactivity: "a cyclical process in which two actors alternately listen, think, and speak to each other".[19] In his aforementioned *Gamasutra* article "The chemistry of game design", Daniel Cook breaks down this high-level conception by "remixing" the "basic ingredients" of gameplay put forth by other game designers into a "self-contained atomic feedback loop called a skill atom". In his view, gameplay is a four-part loop between player input (*Action*); algorithm processing (*Simulation*); the game engine's output (*Feedback*); and the player's comprehension of his action (*Modeling*). Another *Gamasutra* chemist, Tom Heaton, has also presented "A circular model of gameplay", in which the gamer input and the game output reciprocally influence each other and are given equal importance.[20]

Based on Heaton's model and echoing Cook's declaration that "to accurately describe games, we need a working psychological model of the player," Perron has developed a first version of a "heuristic circle of gameplay" (see Figure 6.1).

While playing a video game, the gamer has to "go in circles around the questions" (as in *faire le tour de la question* in French[21]) "or the challenges he faces."[22] At first, right after the game's output, he must analyze the information available to him (while keeping in mind as well the potential future states of the game) through his perceptual and cognitive activity, which relies on the bottom-up (data-driven) and top-down (concept-driven) processes. If the unfolding of the action is new and it is difficult to predict what will come next, the gamer will rely more on images, sounds and/or force-feedback in trying to make sense of such a situation. The bottom-up process will be dominant. But if the beginning of the action matches a general knowledge schema (context) or a generic schema (learned from past experience of other texts—co-texts), the top-down process takes the lead and the gamer will look for a confirmation of his expectations. Both processes direct the choice the gamer will make. For instance, seeing a lifeless body lying on the ground in a survival horror game always suggests that it can rise from the dead. A gamer then knows he has to walk around it carefully. However, the gamer cannot rely only on his analytical skills in order to progress in a video game. He needs embodied, sensorimotor skills as well, and as much. Without the right input or excellent implementation, the gamer will not be able to succeed in the game's challenging tasks or objectives. It is one thing to know a zombie can jump on your avatar, and another to successfully move out of the way and shoot it to survive. It is by constantly affecting the game, modifying reactions, and directing actions, that a gamer can say he is playing a game.

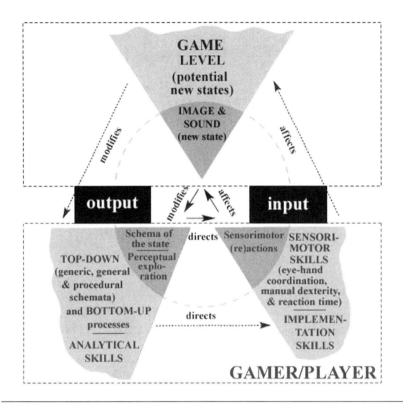

Figure 6.1 Perron's heuristic circle of Gameplay.

As Perron has stated, a video game is a thought- and action-triggering engine.

Although such a conception is well-suited to explain the ins and outs of gameplay, it is far from being fully developed. Indeed, the most obvious flaw of representing gameplay with a single circle is that the temporal progression—the evolution of the gamer's relationship with the game—is left aside. To be true to the gameplay experience, the best way to illustrate it is through spirals (see Figure 6.2).[23]

Our model of gameplay features three interconnected spirals which represent the cycles the gamer will have to go through in order to answer gameplay, narrative, and interpretative questions.

The first one, and the largest, depicts the actual gameplay—the most important feature of video games. The spiral expands with an ever larger circumference to represent the fact that video games seldom have a unique, fixed, and unchanging gameplay. Usually, new features, power-ups, and situations are introduced progressively to the gamer. This constitutes, in a

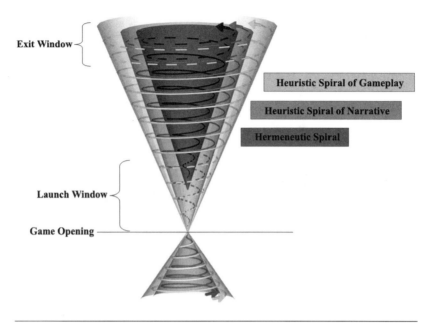

Figure 6.2 The spirals of the Magic Cycle.

simple way, the "rising challenge" of the progression structure that is so common among video games.[24] Even in games of emergence, such as *The Sims* (Maxis, 2000) or *Civilization* (MicroProse, 1991), the gamer at first only has a few parameters and resources to manage, but eventually goes beyond the simple menial tasks and single-city micromanagement to romantic relationships and a whole kingdom or empire to run. It is not the game itself that is expanding—the game's data and algorithms are a finite product on a CD-ROM or cartridge[25]—but only its gameplay. In the words of Katie Salen and Eric Zimmerman (66–67), it is the game's space of possibility that expands, and not its design.

The second spiral, contained within the gameplay, marks the narrative events that unfold through the game. While there exist abstract or non-narrative video games—*Tetris* (Alexey Pajitnov, 1985) and sports games come first to mind—most games rely on some kind of narrative, ranging from a basic framing narrative (*Tetris Worlds*, Blue Planet Software, 2001) to a rich and complex plot (*Star Wars: Knights of the Old Republic*, BioWare, 2003). Playing the game and moving on through the gameplay spiral causes a similar heuristic progression on the narrative level. The gamer slowly grasps what is going on. The more he knows about the characters, their motivations and their aims, the more he is in a position to evaluate and guess the possible outcomes of the story. This follows the same principles as reading a book or even watching a film in a theatre where the viewer cannot go back in time. In Bertrand Gervais' terms, we would refer to a reading-in-progression.

> The progression is, by definition, the basic economy of the reading act. To read is to progress through a text, to reach its end. . . . [T]he explicit goal is not so much to understand everything . . . but to progress onward, to become acquainted with the text. When one reads a novel, the plot can often bring us to want to seek the rest of the narrative. In a certain way, there is "suspense", an expectation that pushes us to go further, to the detriment of a greater precision in our understanding of the events.[26]

In similar fashion, a gamer will usually not interrupt his game every so often to think in depth about all the ramifications of the story's events, but will simply follow the narrative.

The third spiral represents the hermeneutic circle (or hermeneutic spiral as it also came to be theorized[27]). The circularity between the whole and the parts brings here the question of interpretation and deals with different meanings. To quote David Bordwell: "comprehension is concerned with apparent, manifest, or direct meanings, while interpretation is concerned with revealing hidden, nonobvious meanings."[28] Taking a famous example, it is possible to play *Tetris* without interpreting the game as "a perfect enactment of the overtasked lives of Americans in the 1990s—of the constant bombardment of tasks that demand our attention and that we must somehow fit into our overcrowded schedules and clear off our desks in order to make room for the next onslaught."[29] It is also possible to play *Super Mario Bros.* (Nintendo, 1985) just for fun and not see there a metaphor for being high on drugs, or of overcoming the hurdles of modern life with its instant consumerism mentality. However, interpretation is always a possibility for the gamer who is making meaning while playing a game and, in some cases, long after the end of it. Of course, one can also talk about a game without having played it and "project her favourite content on it". The hermeneutic spiral can then be separated from our system of embedding. But this kind of "interpretative violence"[30] remains an unproductive method questioned by most interpretative communities.

We must make it clear that if this third spiral is at the center of the magic cycle, it is not because it is the core of the gaming experience, but because it is far from being an obligatory process—and the same thing can be said about the second spiral, the heuristic circle of narrative. The spirals' relationship to each other is one of inclusion: the gameplay leads to the unfolding of the narrative, and together the gameplay and the narrative can make possible some sort of interpretation. Following this process, we can easily understand that a game, in its purest and most formal incarnation, could feature only one spiral. However rich and complex the narrative or subtext of a game can be, and however limited its gameplay, there will always be a heuristic spiral of gameplay. Even the so-called interactive movies such as *Dragon's Lair* (Cinematronics, 1983), *Night Trap* (Digital Pictures, 1992) and *Phatasmagoria* (Sierra, 1995) had a minimal gameplay requiring some sort of rudimentary performance. Those games also make us aware that the size of the spirals depends on the importance given to each of those aspects by both the game's design and the gamer's individual preferences. For instance, looking at Nintendo's Super Mario franchise from *Super Mario Bros.* to *Super Mario Galaxy* (2007) would consistently show a large heuristic spiral of gameplay and both a small heuristic spiral of narrative (the "plot" is always a variation on the same theme, with Bowser always trying one more evil scheme to rule the world and get the princess), and a small hermeneutic spiral (as we have described earlier). On the other hand, even though the gameplay is still very rich in *The Elder Scrolls IV: Oblivion*, the game's design, with its many side quests and detailed universe (with hundreds of in-game books), makes it possible for a gamer to get into a narrative spiral just as large as the gameplay. It all depends as much on his past experiences as on the one he wishes to have.

Since playing a game is a process that takes place over time and which relies on acquired knowledge and skills, it is important to stress that the gamer's experience with a game starts before the gameplay proper. The horizontal line on our figure marks the game's *primordial speech*, to continue with Crawford's metaphor of a conversation: it is the first manifestation of the game. This often takes the form of an introductory cut-scene whose main function is to regulate, modulate, take in charge, or shape the gamer's horizon of expectations. As we know, Jauss has introduced this concept to explain the reception of a text, which cannot be separated from its historical context: "The new text evokes for the reader (listener) the horizon of expectations and rules familiar from earlier texts, which are then varied, corrected, altered, or even just reproduced."[31] The horizon of expectations explains why there are inverted spirals below the line representing the game's opening.

By reading the description on the box or some reviews beforehand, the gamer comes to know what kind of content to expect, and to identify the particular genre(s) it will fall under according to what the game is about in terms of gameplay and narrative. Since the cover of *Gears of War* (Epic Games, 2006) shows a massive soldier holding an oversized gun with a chainsaw, and that the narrative is about saving humanity from extinction and waging war against a horde of monstrous aliens, it is not difficult to imagine the sort of actions the gamer will be undertaking. The more a gamer comes to a game with some idea of what is to be found inside, the more the gamer's horizon narrows. This means the gamer does not enter the cycle at the tip of the spirals, but well before that. One cannot be considered a complete newbie for long: as is the case with films,[32] an exposure to even a small number of games gives one a head start when getting into a new title by concretely shaping otherwise diffuse expectations. When a game answers to these expectations, the gamer can rely on prior analytical and implementation skills to jump ahead (by skipping the tutorial for example) and immediately tackle some higher patterns of gameplay. In our model, this is expressed with the dotted lines at the base of the spirals, which correspond to what one could call a launch window. A gamer can enter at any point along the lines depending on his past experience.

It makes little difference that *Gears of War* is a third- instead of a first-person shooter, since it uses the same control scheme as other games of this genre. The gamer can easily start to shoot and flank enemies using aiming, strafing, and tactical expertise acquired through other previously played similar games. However, this is not the case with the game's unique "active reload" system, which requires some initial trial and error to use. It goes without saying that mastering new game mechanics is a learning process leading to better analytical and implementation skills. This process can be somewhat circumvented by the use of walkthroughs or cheat codes. Consulting a walkthrough is essentially tapping into another (more advanced) gamer's analytical skills. It has an effect on the gameplay level, but the implementation still rests squarely on the gamer's shoulders. Conversely, using a cheat code usually has a direct effect on the game by modifying its rules or properties, and allows the gamer to continue progressing through the game without having mastered the necessary implementation skills for doing so legitimately.

Going Through the Cycles

Heaton has divided gameplay into "units of interaction", with the basic structure being "analysis, decision, implementation and change in game state". This gamer-centric formulation of the gameplay process is well-founded, except for the commonly held assumption it is implicitly based on: that playing a video game is interactive in the sense that a gamer can act, and the game can react to this input. But we would argue that a video game is rather a chain of reactions. The player does not act so much as he reacts to what the game presents to him, and similarly, the game reacts to his input. If the player stumbles upon a blocked door, he can react by looking around, with the game reacting to the manipulation of the joystick by panning the virtual camera around; if he sees a crowbar on the floor, he can again react by picking it up and smashing the door. The entire game system and the events have been programmed and are fixed, and the designer has tried to predict the gamer's reactions to these events and develop the game (in part through artificial intelligence programming) to react in turn to some of the gamer's reactions. While we are not arguing here for a change of terminology, this temporal divide between the authorial figure and the gamer would place the video game more along the way of *inter(re)activity* than *interactivity*. Consequently, our model could be said to be as much gameplay-centric as gamer-centric.

In Heaton and Perron's model, it is no coincidence that "analysis" is listed first. If, following Chris Crawford's previously mentioned definition, interactivity can be seen as a "conversation", this means that the game always gets the first turn to "speak" (its primordial speech), and that is why our heuristic spiral of gameplay begins (with the star on the right) in the game rather than in the gamer. The minimal unit of interaction we can conceive is represented as a single loop (see Figure 6.3):

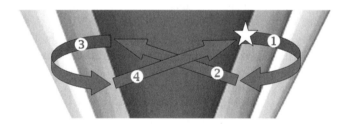

Figure 6.3 A single loop of gameplay.

The single loop is a four-step process:

1.   From the game's database, the game's algorithm draws the 3-D objects and textures, and plays animations, sound files, and finds everything else that it needs to represent the game state.
2.   The game outputs these to the screen, speakers, or other peripherals. The gamer uses his perceptual skills (bottom-up) to see, hear and/or feel what is happening.
3.   The gamer analyzes the data at hand through his broader anterior knowledge (in top-down fashion) of narrative conventions, generic competence,[33] gaming repertoire,[34] etc. to make a decision.

4. The gamer uses his implementation skills (such as hand-eye coordination) to react to the game event, and the game recognizes this input and factors it into the change of the game state.

This looping motion is repeated countless numbers of times to make up the magic cycle. Although the nature of each loop remains the same, as noted earlier, progressing through a game entails a progressive subsuming of individual events under greater patterns of gameplay on the part of the gamer. To focus attention on higher-level issues, the gamer needs to become skillful. But beforehand, the gamer needs to perform basic actions. In Daniel Cook's terms, these are "skill atoms." Cook gives as an example the need to press a button in *Super Mario Bros.*[35] Indeed, the first things a gamer needs to gain knowledge of are the consequences of pressing the buttons and to learn to press the right one for the right action. This also requires an understanding of the game interface (which is crucial in complex games). When one begins to play a game without any knowledge or skill, the gamer starts at the bottom of the spiral where the first loop is very small. For instance, in the first few minutes of playing *Super Mario Bros.* on the NES, the gamer will generally learn to walk by pressing the right arrow, learn to jump by pressing the A button, then learn to run by holding the B button. At the most elementary level, the gamer will have gone through three cycles, expanding those actions each time, as depicted in Figure 6.4.

Each new situation and enemy will have to be circled around individually before the gamer can attempt to overcome the challenges they create. After a couple of levels however, the gamer will have mentally organized the multiple encounters with Goombas, pipes, pits, and fire flowers as a variety of game patterns. The gamer might even, while playing *New Super*

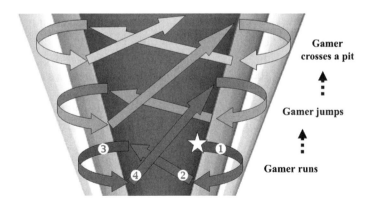

Figure 6.4 The progression through the cycles of gameplay.

Mario Bros. (2006) on the Nintendo DS, learn that the coins are placed along suggested trajectories that, if followed, will get the gamer safely through the levels' hazards. Through the heuristic spirals of gameplay and narrative, the gamer, after reaching the second or third castle, will expect the level to end with a boss battle. But this knowledge is not sufficient: the gamer still has to win.

In a video game, both analytical and implementation skills are needed. To succeed in an action or to avoid punishment, one must execute a series of movements relying on a good handling of the controller. For instance, *Super Mario Bros.* often requires the plump plumber to run while jumping to make it over a long pit. To effectively do this, the gamer must position a thumb over the B button and hold it down to run, pressing the A button when needed with the thumb's phalanx bone. This handling is not immediately obvious.[36] The Nintendo Wii perhaps brought these considerations back to a world that had seen a certain standardization of controllers. When playing *Marvel: Ultimate Alliance* (Activision, 2006) on the Wii without reading the game manual beforehand, a long-time hardcore gamer may wonder why the in-game virtual camera keeps spinning around his character in an annoying circular fashion. In our case, it took one whole hour of play to realize that the camera's movements were controlled by the internal accelerometer of our nunchuks, the motions of which we were not really paying attention to.[37] Our gameplay spiral widened through our game sessions as we learned that while battling Dr. Doom's minions, we could hold the A button to make a more powerful attack than just shaking the Wii Remote. Due to our repertoire of actions (established throughout the other similar games we played before), we surmised that there was a good probability that *Marvel: Ultimate Alliance* could feature a double jump. We tried pressing the jump button again in mid-air and discovered that for some characters such as Thor, this caused them to fly. This opened up a number of new strategic possibilities for both combat and exploration in the game world.

Our experience with *Marvel: Ultimate Alliance* allows us to expose the whole functioning of the magic cycle. We chose this game because it was one of the first Wii titles, thinking it would make an interesting use of the console's unique control scheme, but even with a tutorial focused on the special Wii moves (shaking, tilting, thrusting, etc.), we quickly found out that was not the case (we could still get around by simply pressing buttons). Also, we had no preliminary assumptions about it. Our narrative horizon of expectations was shaped by our basic knowledge of some of the Marvel superheroes and the age-old battle between Good and Evil. We had no precise idea about the game's type of gameplay beforehand, but in the first few minutes, the camera's perspective, the game's interface, and the general movements and actions of our avatars was very reminiscent of both *Gauntlet Legends* (Atari, 1998) and *Dungeons & Dragons: Heroes* (Atari, 2003), which one of us had played previously. In this regard, our expectations were somewhat fulfilled. This was also the case with the game's narrative, although our very limited knowledge of the more obscure characters featured in the game prevented us from truly enjoying many of the game's subtle nuances (we ended up playing exclusively with Thor, Wolverine, Spider-Man—three of the four first heroes available, Captain America being the other—and Elektra, instead of cycling through the likes of Deadpool, Moon Knight, or Luke Cage). We knew we would eventually thwart Dr. Doom's plans and defeat him, and the game made good on these promises, but with very little suspense throughout the twenty-something hours it took for us to complete it, limiting the span of our heuristic spiral of narrative. There seemed at one point to be a possibility for an interesting sub-plot to develop with Black Widow. We were rapidly able to see through her treacheries, but since we did not gain access to all the sub-quests related to her actions, this sub-plot fell short and did not increase our narrative immersion. Finally, our hermeneutic spiral was not very wide. We did not really care about all the potential interpretations we could make besides the classic metaphor of the foreign, evil dictator wishing to rule the world, and the union of all mankind under the supervision of America to maintain freedom. Nor did we think about either female empowerment or gay issues, themes which the cast of superheroes could have alluded to.

"Ceci n'est pas un algorithme de jeu" (This is not a game algorithm)

Our model being gameplay- and gamer-centric, makes us realize a very important aspect of gaming, one that ties in with Jesper Juul's thoughts on rules:

> *Rules*: While video games are just as rule-based as other games, they modify the classic game model in that it is now the *computer* that upholds the rules. This gives video games much flexibility, allowing for rules more complex than humans can handle; freeing the player(s) from having to enforce the rules; and allowing for games where the players do not know the rules from the outset. (Juul, *Half-Real*, 53–54)

Regarding video games, it is crucial to remember, as we said at the beginning of this essay, that the gamer never has direct access to the game's algorithm under the surface, and that the work of comprehension is based on hypotheses in a heuristic fashion. Therefore it would be somewhat misleading to say that the gamer "decrypts" or "cracks" the game's code. The gamer's perceptive and cognitive activities aim to construct a coherent whole out of the various gameplay patterns identified. The gamer knows that the gameplay is engendered both by his and the game's reactions and that, of course, the game keeps track of his (re)actions through the gameplay. But the gamer does not know exactly all the details of those interconnections. The player's activity should rather be understood as a piecing of individual elements taken from the game into a mental representation of the game's system, whose accuracy in respect to the actual game system can vary greatly. It might be a risky analogy, but like the spectator looking at an image of a pipe with the inscription "Ceci n'est pas une pipe" ("This is not a pipe") in Magritte's painting *La trahison des images* (*The treachery of images* 1928–29), the gamer does not see the game algorithm itself when he plays, but only a mental image he builds of it while playing.

A perfect example to illustrate this would be the "drop rate" mechanism in *World of Warcraft* (Blizzard, 2004). When a gamer embarks on a quest to, for example, find the blueprints for the Super Reaper 6000 machine, he is only told that he should be able to find them on one of the Venture Co. Operators that can be tracked and killed in a given location. If the gamer turns to the well-known online *World of Warcraft* database Thottbot and looks for the page dedicated to this particular item,[38] he will find out that only 2.1 percent of the gamers who killed an Operator before have found the Blueprints. However, the discussion below the item's profile is filled with comments from some of these gamers, some saying that it took them thirty kills to get the blueprints, and others only one or two. From their own experience, the quest item's drop rate would be as high as 50 percent or 100 percent, which is clearly not an accurate rate but rather an exceptional stroke of luck. What is interesting is that even the 2.1 percent figure, gathered from hundreds of thousands of *Warcraft* players around the world, is itself flawed, since a player can only find the blueprints if he is on the quest to find them, but the Thottbot data is compiled from all kills regardless of who is on the quest or not. If, as can be seen on the page, 2.1 percent of the Venture Co. Operators dropped the blueprints upon death and they add up to 1,445, this means that a grand total of 68,809 Venture Co. Operators died in the bloody process (2.1/100 = 1,445/68,809). But according to the drop rate to be found on the creatures' page (instead of on the item's page), it would appear that the absolute drop rate for the blueprints is rather 13.6 percent. If both of these figures are correct, it means that of the 9,358 (68,809 × 13.6 percent) times the blueprints dropped, 7,913 gamers were not on the quest, and thus could not pick them up and corrupt the data. Better yet, the gamer can turn to other database sites and receive different numbers: Allakhazam and Wowhead[39] report a drop rate of 11.75 percent and 15 percent, respectively. And all of these calculations are made with the assumption that Blizzard did not change the item's drop rate in one of the game's many patches (as they often do). *World of Warcraft* clearly shows that even with a multitude of resources focused on decrypting its algorithms, one can never be a hundred percent sure he has cracked the game's code. The gamer is always left to his own devices, that is, his own mental image of the game.

Such a complex example urges us to develop even further our model of the magic cycle (see Figure 6.5).

Since the gamer does not have access to the game itself, his perspective is limited to what he can do, what the game throws at him, and his mental image of the game's system. This is noted as *Game'* in our figure, with the apostrophe following the usual algebraic notation of "image" (prime). This image of the game is the gamer's understanding of the game system. It widens as the gamer progresses through the game and maps more of the game's space of possibility.[40] The Game' does not only extend upwards (for the duration of the game), but also sideways, mirroring the gamer's ever-expanding understanding. As the gamer progresses through the game,

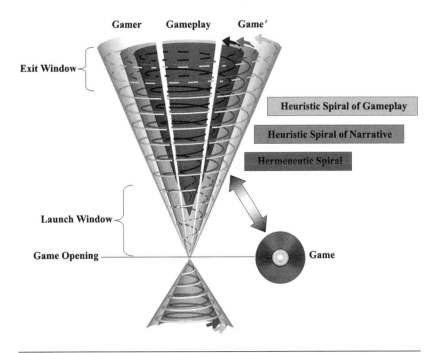

Figure 6.5 The Magic Cycle.

he incorporates more and more of the game's elements into the Game' and uses this knowledge to apprehend the forthcoming events and have a better view of what he can do. But still, the boundaries between the Game' and the game itself are blurred. The gamer only sees the game through his own view. In fact, as opposed to what our Figures 6.3 and 6.4 might have suggested, we have to realize that it is from outside the magic cycle that the game's algorithm draws its information (see Figure 6.6):

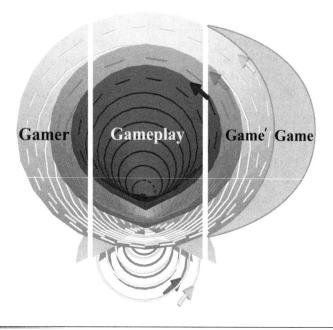

Figure 6.6 Top view of the Magic Cycle.

The activity of playing a game can then be understood as a symbiosis between the gamer (with all his background, expectations, preferences, knowledge, and skills), the gameplay (with all the spectrum of possible actions and reactions) and the Game' (with all its varying shades of understanding). The experience of a game is a gradual shift from predominantly bottom-up processes, where individual elements are analyzed before reacting, to top-down processes, where a mental image of the game system guides the gamer's reactions and expectations.[41] This echoes the conclusion Jesper Juul reaches in his essay dealing with abstraction in game design: "Actual game playing is about building and modifying one's understanding over time. There is a first and a final impression of game. A player picks up a game, explores it, and puts it down."[42] But there are multiple ways for a gamer to go about this. As our model shows a launch window at the bottom of the spirals to illustrate that a gamer can enter at any point along the lines depending on his past experience, it also features the same dotted lines at the top in order to represent an exit window, pointing out that all gamers do not put down a game with the same level of understanding (of the gameplay or the narrative), or extensiveness of interpretation.

The Videoludic Tension

Following Juul's thoughts, we could make a distinction similar to the one he presented. As we know, for him, there are two basic gaming challenge structures: "*games of progression* that directly set up each consecutive challenge in a game, and *games of emergence* that set up challenges indirectly because the rules of the game interact" (Juul, *Half-Real*, 46).[43] In our theoretical model centered not on game structures but on the gamer and gameplay, this division refers to the inevitable notion of progression (over time), but points to another essential process required by video games, which is mastery (over the game mechanics, as minimal as it can be).

A gamer's relation to the gameplay mirrors a reader's relation to the narrative we have evoked with Gervais earlier:

> To read is to progress and to understand, and the importance granted to one or the other of these economies depends on the reader's objectives, of her *mandates*. The reading differences (or reading mandates) therefore depend on the preponderance of one or the other of these economies: to better understand or to progress further onward. (Gervais, 43)

Insofar as it is impossible to clearly separate progression from comprehension in the act of reading, it is likewise impossible to clearly separate progression from mastery in the act of playing a video game. Playing a game can be understood as a continual tension between the two economies of mastering specific game mechanics—*playing-for-mastery*—and progressing forward to see the rest of the game's content—*playing-for-progression*.

The games associated with the notion of progression generally have some kind of narrative which institutes the desire to go forward. For instance, a horror first-person shooter like *Condemned: Criminal Origins* (Monolith Productions, 2007) prompts the gamer to lead the investigation along with Agent Ethan Thomas in order to clear his name and to fight his own demons. But at the end of each chapter, a "Mission Stats" screen offers the gamer a rundown of his performance during the mission and gives him two possibilities: Restart the chapter (button Y on the Xbox 360) or

Continue (button A). Such an option, which is somewhat commonplace, introduces what we call a "videoludic tension." The gamer may only want to "walkthrough" *Condemned* and go on to the next level, however unsatisfactory his evaluation might be; he could also choose to restart the mission in order to find all the "birds", "metal pieces", and other hidden Easter eggs, and increase his "successful hits" and combat accuracy to get the highest number of Achievement Awards. Of course, choosing to play for progression requires a minimal amount of mastery (the gamer still needs to overcome the obstacles)—while playing for mastery similarly necessitates some progression (new enemies have to be found and fought)—regardless of a game's structure belonging more to emergence or progression.

Our Magic Cycle allows us to exemplify different types of gameplaying. To play for progression is to put emphasis on the vertical axis, resulting in thinner spirals. This means that once the minimal skills have been mastered, the gameplay spiral is not widening anymore but stays the same until the end of the gamer's experience (which usually coincides with the moment the end of the narrative spiral is reached). This is done at the detriment of a broader understanding of individual elements in the gameplay or the plot, which is the horizontal axis. When someone plays a game again on a higher difficulty level, or plays a progressively-structured game, such as *Gears of War* in competitive multiplayer mode ("deathmatch" mode), the goal is to widen the gameplay spiral through a better mastery of the gameplay patterns. A gamer can also re-play a game to widen his narrative and hermeneutic spiral, to see all the ramifications and meanings of the plot. In that perspective, playing-for-mastery is trying to widen as much as possible the last level of the spirals. At this point, the exact task to be accomplished depends on how much of a completionist (or a perfectionist) the gamer is, as it is easy to see by looking at Xbox 360 Gamerscores.[44] Some gamers pick up a game and can never put it down before they have "beaten" it (and the choice of words here is truly revealing), while for others the goal is to develop a deep knowledge of the game until they feel their Game′ is a perfect reflection of the game system. Thus, the term "mastery" should be taken in a broad sense. In Bartle's typology,[45] achievers, explorers, and killers would all seek mastery over different types of game content. The quest for the best possible Gamerscore which we have exemplified here is typical of an achiever's obsession. An explorer, on the other hand, would want to see all of the game world's virtual space, or could seek mastery over the game system for the sake of "breaking" or "expanding" it—a type of player defined by Perron as a gameplayer.[46] On the other hand, a killer's pursuit of mastery is undertaken with the purpose of crushing as many enemies as possible, whether controlled by the computer or other human gamers.

Breaking Through

With this essay, we have tried to offer a theoretical foundation of gameplay that, as we have said to begin with, goes beyond the alchemy or smoke-and-mirrors approach. We might have reached a point in video game theory where it is necessary to break the circle, but only to get into the magic cycle.

Notes

1. Daniel Cook, "The Chemistry of Game Design," *Gamasutra.com* (July 19, 2007); hereafter cited as *Cook*; available online at http://www.gamasutra.com/view/feature/1524/the_chemistry_of_game_design.php.
2. Lev Manovich, *The Language of New Media* (Cambridge, MA: MIT Press, 2001), 222–223; hereafter cited as Manovich.
3. See Mark J. P. Wolf and Bernard Perron, "Introduction," in *The Video Game Theory Reader*, ed. Mark J. P. Wolf and B. Perron (New York: Routledge, 2003), 15–16.
4. Jesper Juul, *Half-Real. Video Games Between Real Rules and Fictional Worlds* (Cambridge, MA: MIT Press, 2005), 83, 88; hereafter cited as *Juul*, Half-Real.
5. Daniel Pargman and Peter Jakobsson, "The Magic is Gone: a Critical Examination of the Gaming Situation," in *Gaming Realities : A Challenge of Digital Culture*, ed. M. Santorineos (Fournos: Athens, 2006), 15–22; hereafter cited as *Pargman and Jakobsson*.
6. Mia Consalvo, *Cheating: Gaining Advantage in Videogames* (Cambridge, MA: MIT Press, 2007), 7.
7. The term was coined by Bernard Suits and used in his definition of games: "The attitude of the game player must be an element in game playing because there has to be an explanation of that curious state of affairs wherein one adopts rules which require one to employ worse rather than better means for reaching an end." See *The Grasshopper: Games, Life and Utopia* (Toronto: University of Toronto Press, 1978), 38.
8. Hans-Georg Gadamer, "The Ontology of the Work of Art and Its Hermeneutical Significance. 1. Play as the Clue to Ontological Explanation," in *Truth and Method* (New York: The Seabury Press, 1975), 96. In French : *Vérité et méthode* (Paris: Éditions du Seuil, 1976), 33.
9. Katie Salen and Eric Zimmerman, *Rules of Play: Game Design Fundamentals* (Cambridge, MA: MIT Press, 2004), 370; hereafter cited as Salen and Zimmerman.
10. Gregory Bateson, "A Theory of Play and Fantasy," in *Steps to an Ecology of Mind* (New York: Ballatine Books (1955) 1972), 179; hereafter cited as Bateson.
11. Even games using wireless and location-based technologies in order to fuse the *virtual* and the *real* introduce a playful distance carrying the message "This is play".
12. The other example is the analogy of the mathematical set.
13. "The long-term effects of spending this much time on computer games are that playing goes from (perhaps) having been once a 'magical' activity to now having become a 'normal' activity." The authors then refer to childhood memories to explain this transformation (Pargman and Jakobsson, 19).
14. These are simply different types of immersion that are not mutually exclusive. See Dominic Arsenault, "Dark Waters: Spotlight on Immersion," in *Game On North America 2005 International Conference Proceedings* (Ghent, Belgium: Eurosis-ETI, 2005), 50–52; available online at <http://www.le-ludophile.com/Files/Arsenault%20-%20Dark%20Waters.pdf>; and Laura Ermi and Frans Mäyrä, "Fundamental Components of the Gameplay Experience: Analysing Immersion," in *Changing Views: Worlds in Play (Selected Papers of DiGRA 2005 Conference)*, eds. Susan de Castell and Jennifer Jenson (Vancouver, 2005), 15–27. Available online at <http://www.digra.org/dl/db/06276.41516.pdf>.
15. Johan Huizinga, *Homo Ludens. A Study of the Play-Element in Culture* (Boston: Beacon Press (1955) 1975), 10.
16. To echo the topics of two 2008 conferences: the "Breaking the Magic Circle" Seminar in Finland and the Philosophy of Computer Games Conference in Germany.

17. Bernard Perron, "The Heuristic Circle of Gameplay: the Case of Survival Horror," in *Gaming Realities: A Challenge of Digital Culture*, ed. M. Santorineos (Fournos: Athens, 2006), 65–66; hereafter cited as *Perron*, available online at <http://www.ludicine.ca/sites/ludicine.ca/files/Perron%20-%20Heuristic%20Circle%20of%20Gameplay%20-%20Mediaterra%202006.pdf>.

18. Ernest Adams and Andrew Rollings, *Fundamentals of Game Design* (Upper Saddle River: Prentice Hall, 2007), 384.

19. Chris Crawford, "Interactive Storytelling," in *The Video Game Theory Reader*, eds. Mark J. P. Wolf and B. Perron (New York: Routledge, 2003), 262.

20. Tom Heaton, "A Circular Model of Gameplay," *Gamasutra.com* (February 23, 2006); hereafter cited as *Heaton*; available online at <http://www.gamasutra.com/features/20060223/heaton_pfv.htm>.

21. Which means "to review and to examine all the elements of a problem".

22. Following a model based on the logic of questions and answers, Perron has shown that it is as relevant to discuss game playing in terms of *erotetic gameplay* as it is to see popular film viewing in terms of *erotetic narrative*: "Erotetic narration is also an elaboration akin to problem solving. Yet again, this theorization makes even better sense regarding video games. If the viewer is a question-former according to Carroll, the gamer has therefore to be seen as an answer-maker, a decision-maker, a problem-solver. Leaving narration aside and considering the game itself, it is thus possible and appropriate to talk about *erotetic gameplay*. Gameplay is about micro-questions that the gamer must answer, about micro-objectives that he or she must attain. The difficulty of these varies, something boss fights display." See Bernard Perron, "A Cognitive Psychological Approach to Gameplay Emotions," in *Changing Views: Worlds in Play. Proceedings of DiGRA 2005 Conference*, Vancouver, 2005. Available online at <http://www.digra.org/dl/db/06276.58345.pdf>.

23. The only other spiral figure we know of in video game studies is the one brought forth by Tracy Fullerton to explain the relationship between playtesting, evaluation, and revision. However, she is using it the other way around: the "concept phase" is the larger end of the spiral while the "launch" of the game is the bottom tip. See Tracy Fullerton, *Game Design Workshop. A Playcentric Approach to Creating Innovative Games*, 2nd edn. (San Francisco: Morgan Kaufmann, 2008), 249.

24. Jesper Juul, "The Open and the Closed: Games of Emergence and Games of Progression," in *Computer Games and Digital Cultures Conference Proceedings*, ed. F. Mäyrä (Tampere: Tampere University Press, 2002), 323–329. Available online at <http://www.jesperjuul.net/text/openandtheclosed.html>.

25. The exception to this is downloadable content, add-ons, and expansions. *Brood War* (Blizzard, 1998) does indeed expand the game *Starcraft* (Blizzard, 1998), but to do so, it must also expand the gameplay, since the player cannot access the game by any other means than its gameplay.

26. Bertrand Gervais, *À l'écoute de la lecture* (Montréal: VLB Éditeur, 1993), 46; hereafter cited as Gervais. Quotations translated by the authors.

27. "If this schematization of the hermeneutic process as a growing spiralling movement is accepted, it comes as no surprise that no complete understanding can ever be achieved, since a spiral is an open curve which, unlike a circle, does not circumscribe a finite space. Any interpretation is provisional and relative to a given (and situated) critical project. In fact, from the moment a text is contemplated as a component part of a larger whole, the interpretive moment begins anew. It is easily seen that the attempt to read any cultural text opens up a potentially ever-expanding interpretive process. Once it has been actualized by the receiver and contextually interpreted, a sign acquires a more precise sense. But there are no fixed principles on how to delimit the relevant aspects of context, since what is relevant is relevant not in itself but with respect to a specific communicative process." José Ángel Garcia Landa, "Retroactive Thematization, Interaction, and Interpretation: The Hermeneutic Spiral from Schleiermacher to Goffman," in *BELL* (*Belgian Journal of English Language and Literatures*), vol. 2: *The Linguistics/Literature Interface* (Ghent, Belgium: Academia Press, 2004), 155–166. Available online at <http://www.unizar.es/departamentos/filologia_inglesa/ garciala/publicaciones/spiral.pdf>.

28. David Bordwell, *Making Meaning. Inference and Rhetoric in the Interpretation of Cinema* (Cambridge, MA: Harvard University Press, 1989), 2.

29. Janet H. Murray, *Hamlet on the Holodeck: The Future of Narrative in Cyberspace* (New York: Free Press, 1997), 143–144.
30. We are borrowing the expression "interpretive violence" from Markku Eskelinen. See Markku Eskelinen, "The Gaming Situation," *Game Studies* 1, no. 1 (July 2001). Available online at <http://www.gamestudies.org/0101/eskelinen/>.
31. Hans Robert Jauss, *Toward an Aesthetic of Reception*, translated by Timothy Bhati, (Minneapolis: University of Minnesota Press, 1982), 23.
32. As Edward Branigan states: "It's my belief that a film spectator, through films, knows how to understand a potentially infinite number of new films. The spectator is able to recognize immediately repetitions and variations among films, even though the films are entirely new, and outwardly quite distinct," in *Point of View in the Cinema. A Theory of Narration and Subjectivity in Classical Film* (Berlin: Mouton Publishers, 1984), 17.
33. See Alastair Fowler, *Kinds of Literature. An Introduction to the Theory of Genres and Modes* (Cambridge MA: Harvard University Press, 1982).
34. See Juul, *Half-Real*, 95–102.
35. Cook thus describes a canonical skill atom:

    > Action: An inexperienced player pushes a button.
    > Simulation: The simulation notes the action and starts the avatar of Mario on the screen moving in an arc.
    > Feedback: The screen shows the user an animation of Mario jumping.
    > Modeling: The user forms a mental model that pressing the button results in jumping. Implicit in this model is that the atom is often looped through multiple times before the user understand what it teach [*sic*].

36. This manual dexterity required for manipulating devices (especially using the thumb) marks an often overlooked difference between gamers belonging to the groups that Marc Prensky calls the digital natives and the digital immigrants. See "Digital Natives, Digital Immigrants", *On the Horizon*, NCB University Press, vol. 9 no. 5 (October 2001); available online at <http://www.marcprensky.com/writing/Prensky%20-%20Digital%20Natives, %20Digital%20Immigrants%20-%20Part1.pdf>.
37. After an hour or so, we finally turned to the game manual and saw the cryptic mention in the Basic Controls section: "Nunchuk Gestures . . . Camera Control".
38. <http://thottbot.com/i5734>. All data mentioned here was current at the time of writing (January 2008).
39. See <http://wow.allakhazam.com/db/item.html?witem=5734> for the Allakhazam entry, and <http://www.wowhead.com/?item=5734> for Wowhead.
40. Salen and Zimmerman (2004, 67) write: "We call the space of future action implied by a game design the *space of possibility*. It is the space of all possible actions that might take place in a game, the space of all possible meanings which can emerge from a game design."
41. This forms the basis of what Arsenault (2005, 51) termed systemic immersion: "when one accepts that a system (of rules, laws, etc.) governing a mediated object replaces the system governing a similar facet of unmediated reality."
42. Jesper Juul, "A Certain Level of Abstraction", in *Situated Play: DiGRA 2007 Conference Proceedings*, edited by A. Baba (Tokyo: DiGRA Japan, 2007), 514; available online at <http://www.digra.org/dl/db/07312.29390.pdf>.
43. The distinction was first introduced in his 2002 paper: "The Open and the Closed: Games of Emergence and Games of Progression".
44. Microsoft's Gamerscore system awards gamers up to 1000 "achievement points" for completing specific tasks in each game. At the time of writing, as suspicious as it can appear to a normal gamer, the top-ranking gamer had a Gamerscore of 245,825 points, obtained through 182 commercial games and 80 Xbox Live Arcade titles. See <http://www.mygamercard.net/leaderboard.php>.
45. Richard Bartle, "Hearts, Clubs, Diamonds, Spades: Players Who Suit MUDs" (1996), *The Game Design Reader: A Rules of Play Anthology*, eds. K. Salen and E. Zimmerman (Cambridge, MA: MIT Press, 2006), 754–787.
46. Bernard Perron, "From Gamers to Gameplayers. The Example of Interactive Movies," in *The Video Game Theory Reader*, eds. Mark J. P. Wolf and B. Perron (New York: Routledge, 2003), 251–253.

CHAPTER 7

Understanding Digital Playability

SÉBASTIEN GENVO

In his book *Pourquoi la fiction?*[1] Jean-Marie Schaeffer notes that the modal-ities of circulation of digital fictions are much more flexible than the fictions known as "traditional," because of the quasi-instantaneity of the transmission as well as the infinite reproducibility of the transmitted sig-nals. This has as a consequence an extraordinary multiplication of the fictional worlds in circulation in a transcultural context. In this perspec-tive, video games are established as a representative case of the potential of the new media to connect various cultures at an international level. This applies for online games as well as for offline games, since the video game industry is a globalized one. This reflection encourages one to question the modalities of expression that the video games offer. Indeed, authors such as Johan Huizinga, Roger Caillois, or Jacques Henriot have raised the fact that the various forms of play and the representations related to this activ-ity can vary according to places and times. Consequently, video games raise the question of communication processes set up on an international scale, particularly within the field of game design. Indeed, it is through the design of a video game's world that players from different cultures will be encouraged to adopt a ludic attitude, in order to get them involved in its fictional universe. Therefore, game design concerns what I call "ludic mediation," that is, the process of transmitting the will-to-play to some-one. To understand this process, I will show at first that when someone plays, he adopts a particular posture of immersion that is a "ludic attitude" (we will see that this attitude rests on a willingness to operate by certain rules and restrictions in a metaphorical way). But in order to be able to adopt this attitude, the structure upon which the actions are performed must be appropriate to the activity of play: it must contain a certain amount of "playability." This is true of the structures of both traditional, physically-based games as well as digital ones. Nevertheless, we will see that digital media imply particular modalities of mediation, which do not exist within traditional games. These different elements raise questions as to which theoretical tools can be mobilized to describe the structural conditions of ludic mediation set up by a given video game, in order to understand the way it presents a specific playability. To achieve this analysis successfully, it will be necessary to link a ludologic approach to some useful elements of narrative semiotics in order to formulate what I call a descriptive approach of playability. The purpose of this link is to take fully into account specificities of the meaning production process in the case of digital play. The last part of this essay is an example of analysis of *Tetris*, a game which may not appear to have any narrative aspects, yet which is perfectly suited to the descriptive approach as I define it.

Defining the Ludic Attitude

As we will see, the process of game design can be summarized in a very simple question: How can I give the will-to-play to the player of the game? In order to find an answer, it is first necessary to define what exactly is meant by "play." First and foremost, playing is a question of attitude. Indeed, according to Bernard Suits, "the attitude of the game-player must be an element in game playing because there has to be an explanation of that curious state of affairs wherein one adopts rules which require one to employ worse rather than better means for reaching an end."[2] If this definition seems to be well known, this state of mind rests also on other characteristics that need to be taken into account if one wants to understand the whole process of ludic mediation. As Jacques Henriot states, when someone plays, he adopts a state of mind that implies a "metaphorical process."[3] The term "metaphorical" is used because playing is about transposing things of the world to a new order. For example, in order to play the game, a chess player must *act as if* the board and the pawns are more than they really are: pieces of wood or plastic. Chess is not just a question of "pushing wood," as the chess enthusiasts say about players who do not understand anything about the rules of this game. The player leaves "ordinary reality" aside. According to D. W. Winnicott,[4] the world in which we play is an "intermediate space," between internal and external reality. Although the player's thoughts occur in this intermediate space, his actions in the world are as real as any other activity. The player is present where he plays, but also elsewhere, enlivened by a goal which carries his acts beyond the present instant and the immediacy of his actions: "He is this hero, this conqueror, this seducer; at the same time, it is not him, since he is only himself and that he plays" (Henriot, 260). This mental state also characterizes any other kind of fictional immersion, a behavior which Jean-Marie Schaeffer has termed a "bi-planar" behavior: the player is engrossed in his game although he knows that after all it is only a game. In the preceding sentence, one can replace the term "game" with "movie" or "fictional story," and the term "player" with "spectator" or "reader." The player must act as if he was confronted with another reality. Nevertheless, if fictional immersion is a part of play activity, it is necessary to note that it is not equivalent to it because playing is also *a particular form of process.* For D. W. Winnicott, playing is a process in the sense that "playing is doing" and that doing is proceeding. This means that any activity which requires a form of play usually implies a goal. While there are forms of play without a definitive goal, there is almost always some kind of objective in the actions undertaken during play. Likewise, there are forms of play without a final sanction which would put an end to the activity, from which a result would be drawn (a loser/a winner, the realization of a performance in a given time, etc.). For Jacques Henriot, as a *metaphorical* process, every form of play has a purpose. This purpose includes the system of rules that the player follows: "The global purposes include the goal itself and the obligatory conditions of its achievement. One could imagine the same goal (crossing the garden) and different conditions (running on four legs, etc.): one would be dealing with different activities of play. The system of rules is therefore itself the object of an arbitrary choice, since the player invents them (or accepts them) and decides to submit to them while nothing compels him. Playing always consists in doing something in a particular way" (Henriot, 227). Therefore, the purpose that the player follows is *arbitrary* because he chooses it by his own free will (he can leave his state of play when he wants because playing is a free activity). The purpose cannot be imposed upon the player, it is up to the player to *actualize it voluntarily.* According to Henriot, to do so, the player uses a *set of actions consciously perceived as aleatory.*

One must be careful with this last point because it is needed to understand why—from Jacques Henriot's point of view—playing is also a particular form of process. The unpredictable characteristic of play was frequently questioned, for instance by Roger Caillois: "A sequence known beforehand, without possibility of error or surprise, driving apparently to an ineluctable result, is incompatible with the nature of play . . . the course cannot be determined, nor the result attained beforehand, and some latitude for innovations must be left to the player's initiative."[5] But it is not enough to qualify this activity as uncertain. Many activities, often considered the opposite of play (like Work), also comprise a character of uncertainty. But whereas the worker will tend to reduce the field of possibilities to increase the productive efficiency of his actions, the player, even if he would have calculated the various probabilities which follow every possible choice, knows that the result of his actions cannot be given in advance (as Bernard Suits says, the player employs worse rather than better means for reaching an end). If the activity only consists of a succession of interactions with only one possible response (apart from leaving the game), then the player does not have any real choices to make, and the outcome of the game does not depend on how he plays (in the most extreme case, the player will feel like he is watching a movie, pulling triggers from time to time in order to watch what is coming next). For example, this is the case at the beginning of *The Nomad Soul* (Quantic Dream, 1999), during the introduction sequence, which is a cinematic. When the cinematic stops, the player is asked by a game character if he wants to join him to save his world. The only choice available for the player is to say "Yes." The outcome of this decision will of course be the same for every player: the introduction sequence continues. For this reason, this sequence is not very playable, the player has just one option. Since playing is doing, it is essential to add that to play is to make a decision in order to *exercise the possible* (the player must feel that his decisions will make a difference in the game).

As I said earlier, players must adopt a ludic attitude, which means that the player operates a metaphorical process that voluntarily actualizes a purpose by the way of a set of actions consciously perceived as aleatory in order to exercise the possible. But it is important to note that this attitude cannot be adopted in every situation; some situations do not allow the people involved in them to play. The impossibility of performing an action that has a significant repercussion in the sequence of events to be followed is an example of one of these aspects (as the person will not be able to experience the possible). "No one will say that an epidemic, a flood constitute in themselves a game. One does not say this out of fear of contradicting public opinion, or to avoid injuring others' sensibilities, but primarily because the situations that create such events leaves virtually no room for the initiative of those who are trapped in it. They have no choice" (Henriot, 218). While some situations do not allow one to adopt a ludic attitude, others clearly have an evident potential for play. For children, it is usually more difficult to play during classtime (because they are not allowed to), whereas breaks are playful moments. The structure (the system of constrains and rules) of both situations are different. It does not mean that it is impossible to play during the class (of course not . . .). But one situation is more playable than the other. All in all, it means that there are "playable structures." Numerous playable structures are qualified by the term "game" in English (whereas in French, we do not make the distinction between the attitude and the structure by indistinctly using the word "jeu," the same term applies to both aspects). But it is often by convention that some playable situations are qualified as games and others are not, as the perception of what is ludic depends on the sociocultural positioning of the player. It is thus important to stress that no playable structure is ludic in itself and by itself (it is just more or less playable). Software such as Microsoft Word can be used as a game while *Doom* (id Software, 1993) can be used as military training. What makes a situation a game is when someone adopts a ludic attitude toward the situation in which he finds himself. The relevance of the structure will depend on a series of associations which remains linked to the biographical situation of the actor, his cultural environment and his social conditions. In this way, designed playable structures draw their "type elements" in the culture to which they belong in order to be recognized as a game and to promote the adoption of a ludic attitude. A simulation program such as Flight Simulator X (Microsoft Game Studios, 2006) could be flight training for a pilot while at the same time it could be entertainment for the person using it during his or her free time. However, from a ludic point of view, what differentiates Microsoft Word from *Tetris* (Alexey Pajitnov, 1985) is that the structure of the latter—the set of rules which govern its use—will have a greater potential of adaptation to ludic activity. Certain characteristics will favor this attitude during their metaphorical actualization, while others will discourage the player in his play, bringing him back to "ordinary reality."

The Ludic Mediation

These elements of definition encourage one to qualify the work of game design, which refers to the design of a playable structure. First of all, we can suggest that a playable structure is a system of rules that is formalized for someone. But every system of rules is not meant to encourage the adoption of a ludic attitude. It is necessary to add that this system is designed in order to achieve a ludic mediation, where the notion of mediation has to be defined as "a phenomenon which allows one to understand the broadcasting of linguistic or symbolic forms, in space and time, to produce a meaning shared within a community,"[6] this "meaning" being play activity, in the case of game design. For this purpose, a system of rules, to be playable, must proceed from a certain configuration of signs to be coherent with its object, the ludic attitude. To describe the way in which playable structures are designed, is thus to analyze the way in which the components of a system of rules are designed to make sense with regard to the ludic attitude.

Indeed, one method often used to analyze these components involves the categories formulated by Roger Caillois about the "fundamental" characteristics that a structure can feature to engage someone in a ludic attitude. Let me recall these very well-known categories: *agôn*, or competition; *alea*, or chance; *mimicry*, which rests on the fact that someone plays to make believe or to be made to believe that he is other than himself (this category generally describes the mimetic activity); and *ilinx*, which is characterized by a kind of giddiness, spasm, fright, or dizziness which destroys or disrupts reality. I suggest that these four categories are found systematically as soon as the player plays a formalized system of rules. Indeed, when someone plays a "game," the player must experience the possible (*alea*), while trying to accomplish a purpose (*agôn*) by the way of a metaphorical process, which implies that one *acts as if* the present moment was different (*mimicry*) through the disruption of ordinary reality (*ilinx*). In this point of view, the ludic aspect of *ilinx* rests in this feeling of being apart from ordinary reality (dizziness without this feeling can be the opposite of play, if it is a symptom of disease, for example). It is also necessary to underline that competition (*agôn*) takes place as soon as the player aims at a result (even if it is not an "endgame" result), because of the intrinsic uncertainty which governs each process of decision-making within a ludic framework. Thus, there will be competition to reach a result projected beforehand, even if it is only between the player and the system. Of course, certain activities of play do not have an agonistic aspect, when the action proceeds without aiming at achieving a result, but then they fit into the category of "informal play," which is when one plays without playing to an explicitly formalized system of rules. For instance, when a little girl plays with her doll, she does not necessarily make a game with her doll. Even if she unconsciously follows a system of rules which govern her actions (with given goals), she does not aim at the realization of a result whose success (or failure) she would evaluate according to previously formalized parameters. Within the framework of formal play, when a player actualizes an explicit playable structure, the four categories described by Caillois appear.

This does not mean that any playable structure comprises these four fundamental characteristics, nor even that only one of these categories would be sufficient to confer a ludic dimension to a system of rules, because a playable structure becomes truly ludic only when someone has decided to play with it (the same structure, even if it is playable for one person, may not be ludic for someone else). As Henriot notes: "Chance is a type of structure. Is it enough to induce objectively given forms of play? That there are games of chance does not prove that chance is ludic in essence. In a hazardous situation, play appears only from the moment when somebody decides to engage, assumes a risk, bets on an event whose complete production he does not control. In itself, chance could not make play" (Henriot, 110). Such a remark argues in favor of the four categories. But it is only when they fall into these fundamental categories that elements in a system of rules will be able to appear adapted to the ludic attitude and will encourage its adoption. A playable structure can only rely on one of these categories, or use game mechanisms of different nature (for example, betting on dice is based on *alea*, while chess tends to be based mainly on *agôn*). These categories can be made more complex if the conditions of production of the meaning of play are described with more detail. *To understand the playability of a structure, is to analyze the way in which this structure is designed to create meaning with respect to the ludic attitude.*

For Gonzalo Frasca, this type of approach would mark a break with the methods used to analyze "traditional" mass media, because for him, video games imply "an enormous paradigm shift for our culture because they represent the first complex simulational media for the masses."[7] According to this author, this analytical perspective would thus concern a particular discipline, called ludology, devoted to the comprehension of "structure and elements [of a game]—particularly its rules—as well as creating typologies and models for explaining the mechanics of games" (Frasca, 222). And because of the ontological nature of video games, the narrative paradigm would be the opposite of the ludologic perspective:

> So far, the traditional—and most popular—research approach from both the industry and the academy has been to consider video games as extensions of drama and narrative. While this notion has been contested (especially by Espen Aarseth) and generated a sometimes passionate debate, the narrative paradigm still prevails. My goal in this essay is to contribute to the discussion by offering more reasons as to why the storytelling model is not only an inaccurate one but also how it limits our understanding of the medium and our ability to create even more compelling games. The central argument I will explore is that, unlike traditional media, video games are not just based on representation but on an alternative semiotical structure known as simulation (Frasca, 221–222).

Nevertheless, in the context of a ludological framework, we will see that some elements of narrative semiotics are useful to fully understand some specificities of the ludic mediation when it occurs in a context of digital play. The main point is to understand that these elements are not about "storytelling" but about modeling a goal-oriented action.

The Experience of Digital Play

In order to play a traditional game, the player must first peruse the rules which will govern its action. In this way, the player can have in advance an idea of the ludic potential of the structure according to its own representations of play. Then, the player will actualize this system with a ludic attitude if it answers to his ideal types of the activity. On the other hand, in the case of a digital game, the player does not need necessarily to peruse beforehand the rules which will govern his actions. He can uncover them gradually during his progression. For example, even if a player does not know how to play chess, he can still use a chess program, which will simply not allow any illegal moves. As Patricia Greenfield states, the most interesting aspect concerning video games considered as a complex system lies in the fact that it is possible to discover the rules by observation, "tests and errors" and by a method of hypothesis testing.[8] Within this framework, the player can never be completely sure that he has uncovered all the rules that structure his actions, this even in the games which may appear the most "basic." For example, a website[9] dedicated to *Pac-Man* describes the character traits of each ghost and the rules which model their behaviors. For instance, the red ghost (named Blinky) increases his speed when there are just twenty dots left, which is a trait that is not explained in advance and that takes a lot of practice to be discovered. In my opinion, this observation about digital media regarding the dynamic discovery of the rules greatly changes the modalities of the ludic mediation. Indeed, during the actualization of the playable structure (the playing of the game), the player will discover the rules which govern his action and will at the same time judge the adaptation of this system to his ludic usage (that is to say, the player will determine if he likes playing the game or not). This characteristic refers to the concept of gameplay, which is usually employed to qualify what makes the quality of a video game independently of its technical features. When the player actualizes a video game, he will at the same time peruse the way the game system works, through its mechanisms, and will test its play potential, which is what the term "gameplay" refers to, by gathering these two aspects in the same concept. Attention is drawn as much to the structure as to the action itself, requiring a constant balance between engagement and detachment so that the action can be maintained and evaluated. The player discovers and transforms jointly the system by his actions. It is this dynamic which constitutes the gameplay of a given video game and which will cause the pleasure or displeasure of the player.

Within this framework, if it is indeed necessary to use a "traditional" ludologic approach to describe the nature of the various elements composing a game according to a paradigmatic axis (*mimicry* or *agôn*, typologies of rules, etc.), the importance of the concept of gameplay in video games encourages one to take into account the diachronic aspect of playable structure (its syntagmatic axis), which is what the player has to do, so that the system's mechanisms are delivered in the action and "come into play." As we will see, the addition of particular elements of narrative semiotics makes it possible to answer this need, by the way of the Canonical Narrative Schema (CNS). This schema was mainly formalized by Joseph Courtés according to the research of the French semiotician Algirdas Julien Greimas, who developed a formal method of analyzing semiotic productions.[10] What interests me in this research is that by "using the canonical narrative schema, we can describe the logical, temporal, and semantic arrangement of the elements of an action."[11] By gathering elements of this schema into a ludological framework, the semiotic model that I propose allows one to study at the same time the paradigmatic axis and the syntagmatic axis of a digital playable structure. The purpose of this approach is to make visible the conditions of production of the meaning implemented by a system of rules in order to appear to be playable, that is why I call it a descriptive approach.

The Descriptive Approach of Digital Playability

According to Greimas, a narrative is the realization of a project, in which a *subject* goes through a conflict because he desires something. This "something" is called an *object* by Greimas and could be a concrete goal (money) or an abstract one (political power). The narrative also involves a process of communication, because the *object* has to be transmitted from a *sender* to a *receiver*. These different roles are called the "actants" of the narrative (and not actors) because one role can apply to several characters or entities, and the same character can assume one or more functions. A very simple schema can summarize the preceding assertions (Figure 7.1).

Greimas and Courtés divide the realization of this project into four stages (Courtés). In the first step, a contract is passed between a subject and a sender, in which the sender delivers a quest in an attractive way (the

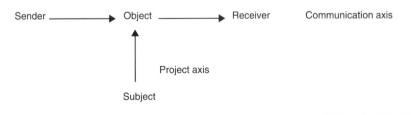

Figure 7.1 Greimas Actantial Model.

sender transmits information about a goal to achieve). The subject has to be encouraged to act. This is why this stage is called a sequence of *manipulation*. The sender makes the subject take on the project. In the second stage, the subject reaches the point at which the necessary competencies to realize the objective have to be acquired (this is the stage of *competence*), and in the third, these competencies are used for the realization of a *performance*. This canonical narrative schema ends with a stage of sanction, in which the sender checks to see if the terms of the initial contract are respected and sanctions the subject positively or negatively. For example, in a typical fairy tale, a king (the sender) asks to a knight (the subject) to deliver his daughter from a dragon, and promises him the hand of the princess (the object) if he succeeds (the knight will have both the function of the subject and the receiver). The performance here consists in killing the dragon, which will require the knight to get some magical skills beforehand.

What interests me in this theory is that the CNS can usually be found in any video game if one considers this theory as a theory of action in its diachronic sense. Each goal of a game can be framed by using this four-stage sequence, depending on the level of complexity required by the analysis. The player passes through a sequence of manipulation, which means that the game requires him to solve a problem or to achieve a goal. The game also checks how the player has done and provides either positive or negative sanctions. The receiver can be the player (if there is some sort of social recognition in stake) or a fictional character within the game (in *Tomb Raider* (Core Design, 1996) for example, the player is the "subject-operator" of the action, but finally it is Lara Croft that has all the recognition, although it is "just a game"). It is, of course, possible to frame the game's main goal at a larger scale and to consider that some secondary objectives depend on the stage of competence regarding the main goal (for example, if the player must first find a weapon in order to defeat a boss). In fact, if in a game, the realization of the performance depends on the player (unlike a movie, where the realization of the action depends on the fictional character), we will see that the stage of competence allows one to describe the particular gameplay of each game, which structures the ludic attitude of the player.

Indeed, this schema stresses that the subject, in order to complete the performance, must have the necessary competencies beforehand, and must become qualified. During the competence sequence, it is necessary to acquire four types of "modalities of doing" in order to realize the performance. These modalities can be classified in pairs. First, there are the modalities of the potentialization which are the "having-to-do" and the "willing-to-do" (also translated in English as the "wanting-to-do," the original term being "*vouloir-faire*"). These modalities are called this because they propose the performance that the subject must accomplish. The two other types of competences are the modalities of actualization, that is to say, the "being-able-to-do" and the "knowing-how-to-do." They determine the competence of the subject in order to realize his performance. The following schema, below, summarizes the different Greimas theory elements (Figure 7.2).

In video games, the "having-to-do" depends on the structure, which offers objectives and proposes the performance that the player must accomplish (for example, in adventure games, in which the game has the role of a sender), or encourages the player to formulate his own objectives based on the mechanisms composing the system (the game designer has decided to let the player be the sender and the subject). For example, in *The Sims* (Maxis Software, 2000), the designers let the player choose the goals he wishes to accomplish, which is an important factor in the way the game encourages the player to adopt a ludic attitude. It is of course possible that a purpose established by the designers is not followed or not immediately discovered, but this aspect concerns, above all, the analysis of the practices. The actual approach is useful to describe the way in which a structure was designed to present a given "playability." Another particularity of play is that the "willing-to-do" only relies on the player and not on a fictional character (whereas in a film, the spectator has to follow the will and the decisions of the hero). Indeed, the activity of play is freely adopted by the player, and cannot be imposed by the playable structure. Whereas in ordinary reality, tasks can be imposed on a subject by force or by constraint, play does not allow this option. The "will-to-do" is the obligatory condition of any playable situation because it is only when the player decides to immerse himself in a game that it begins to be a play activity (when the "willing-to-do" is no longer there, the activity becomes boring and loses its ludic state). So the game design process can be briefly summarized by this question: how can the player be given the "will-to-play"? If

Stage	Manipulation	Competence	Performance	Sanction
Modalities of doing	Making-to-do	Having-to-do Willing-to-do Knowing-how-to-do Wanting-to-do	Doing	
Actants involved	Sender – Subject	Subject	Subject	Sender – Subject – Receiver

Figure 7.2 Canonical Narrative Schema.

the "willing-to-do" depends on the ludic attitude of the player, the "being-able-to-do" relies on the structure. This is according to the rules of the game that make an action possible or not. Video games are strewn with "modal objects" concerned with this modality of doing: for example, if at the beginning of *Doom* (id Software, 1993) the space marine has just a small gun, his progression through the mazes will very quickly be conditioned by the need for increasingly powerful weapons, which will give him new abilities.

But it is important to remember that if the "ability to do" concerns the structure, the realization of the action will be controlled by the player. And to be able to do an action, it is first necessary to know how to do it. The "knowing-how-to-do" concerns the player, who must know how to control the software interface in order to act in the fictional world. Today, many games begin with a didactic sequence (such as a training level) in order to make sure that the player has acquired the basic procedural knowledge to handle the software. But this knowledge is not only limited to the control of the software interface but also applies to the procedures found by the player to reach the goals suggested by the structure. This "knowing-how-to-do" depends a lot on the type of game and on the mechanisms which make up the system. Moreover, because the realization of the performance rests on the player, the structure must ensure a certain degree of randomness. However, all players do not have the same level of procedural knowledge needed for the type of game they play. A lack of experience or skill may lead the player to repeated failures. And if one cannot have an "experience of the possible" (the sense that it is possible to lose as well as to win), one will not be able to adopt a ludic attitude, calling into question the player's immersion. Consequently, how can a game designer ensure a certain degree of uncertainty for each player? The answer to this question depends on the nature of each software program. Some games, like *Supreme Commander* (Gas Powered Games, 2006) or *Enemy Territory: Quake Wars* (Splash Damage, 2007) are intended primarily for an audience that already has important procedural knowledge (which will be put to the test during the game), while others are addressed to a larger audience and need to deliver the necessary knowledge during gameplay (numerous Nintendo games proceed like this, the latest being *Super Mario Galaxy* (2007) and *The Legend of Zelda : Phantom Hourglass* (2007)). All in all, one analyzes here which kind of "model player" the structure postulates to be playable (in the same way that, according to Umberto Eco, a text postulates a "model reader"[12]). For example, if video games have different levels of difficulty, it is precisely to regulate the degree of uncertainty in the action. Finally, it should be noted that in video games, it is always possible to start again in order to acquire the necessary knowledge for the performance (even in MMORPGs, which themselves cannot be restarted, the player can still begin again). However, if this training is too long, it is possible that the player's "will-to-do" disappears, as the repeated succession of failures gives the player the impression that success is impossible.

I propose, here, to summarize these ideas within a model which takes into account the conditions of meaning production set during gameplay (Figure 7.3).

As this model suggests, it is necessary to analyze the "having-to-do" and the "being-able-to-do" in the four-stage sequence described earlier, in order to describe the way in which the structure encourages the player to adopt a ludic attitude ("willing-to-do"), while taking care of the knowledge required to realize the performance. The ludologic approach provides tools adapted to describe the type of ludic mechanisms set up through the first two poles, so that the structure presents a given playability. I will illustrate this methodology with an analysis of *Tetris* (1988), which is often considered to be a game without much narrative content. Nevertheless, as we will see, the preceding elements of the canonical narrative schema are well adapted to analyze the playability of a game, as long as they are used as a theory of action. The following case study is not exhaustive, but illustrates the way in which the theoretical ideas presented in this essay can be applied to a specific game.

Case Study: *Tetris*

It should first be mentioned that the "having-to-do" of the structure of *Tetris* at first seems very restricted, since it is only a question of making horizontal lines of ten squares out of seven geometrical figures made up of four squares each (the famous tetraminos), which descend relentlessly. The

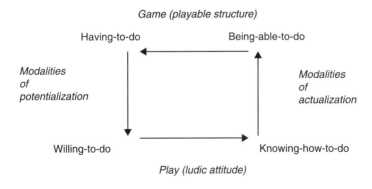

Figure 7.3 Semiotic Model of Gameplay.

"being-able-to-do" is also restricted, as the player can act only on the speed of the descent of the tetraminos, their horizontal displacement, and their rotation. This implies reciprocally a very minimal acquisition of "knowing-how-to-do" to initially handle the system's mechanisms. In the 1988 arcade version used for this analysis, if the player chooses the beginner level of difficulty, these various elements are initially introduced during a short non-interactive didactic sequence (this is the sequence of manipulation, delivering the "having-to-do"). Nevertheless, the "having-to-do" becomes more and more complex from the moment the player starts to play. Indeed, the player must not only make horizontal lines, he must make a given number of them to be able to pass to the following "round," where the number of figures to complete is increasingly more difficult (one passes from a four-stage sequence to another at each round, the end of the round having a value of positive sanction). Moreover, in the arcade version, two players can play simultaneously, with the game indicating which player is leading the game. If the game involves a simultaneous confrontation between two people, a scoring system also sets up another objective, including a "having-to-do" founded on an asynchronous competition (sanctioned by the inscription of initials on the high-score screen). This way, the *agôn* rests on the competition against the system (it is a matter of erasing lines to prevent the tetraminos from filling the play area) but also against other human players, which multiplies the objectives of play and complicates the "knowing-how-to-do" (defeating the computer and defeating human opponents are, of course, different things).

The aleatory dimension of the game rests primarily on what the player cannot do. Indeed, each tetramino is "randomly" chosen by the program: Although the next few tetraminos are indicated to the player, the player is not able to choose the next piece to come (the structure would have been very different if the player had been able to choose the next piece). This absence of "being-able-to-do" implies the development of a competence in which the player knows how to pertinently place each given piece in a limited time. But as I pointed out earlier during the defining of the ludic attitude, playing is not only an activity with a characteristic of uncertainty. It is necessary for the player to "experience the possible." The structure must avoid letting the player succeed too easily. In *Tetris*, if the movement of the tetraminos during the first rounds is relatively slow, giving the player time to place the piece in progress judiciously (and plan for the one to come), each new round increases the speed of the pieces' descent. This reduces the time for decision-making, which eventually does not allow the player enough time for a complete optimization of his actions (the player can no longer play with complete certainty).[13] The player will be able to reduce the field of possible events, but without being ensured of the future success of his movements. Then, if the "knowing-how-to-do" is quickly acquired at the beginning of the game, it becomes more and more complex since the initial objective is reached (to complete a row) and that other objectives are delivered (round by round, or by choosing other modes of play). In certain modes, *Tetris* does not have an end game. To use Gonzalo Frasca's terminology, there are no rules of ludus allowing the final victory of the player (there is an infinite succession of four-stage sequences, the end of a round having the function of a positive sanction). *Tetris*, then, is well-adapted to the beginner as well as to the experienced player (who has already acquired a great procedural knowledge of the game). Indeed, whereas the beginner understands what is possible while playing the first level (it is not difficult to see that it is possible to succeed), advanced rounds always guarantee an increasing level of difficulty for the more qualified (skillful) players, who are still able to experience the possibility of failure or success (their practical knowledge does not guarantee an automatic success). Moreover, since the expert can appear overqualified for the first rounds, the 1988 arcade version of *Tetris* has various levels of difficulty so that all players can play at their level immediately without having to complete rounds that are too easy. The highest level of difficulty also includes another mechanism, founded on the *alea*, which is the sporadic appearance of a block in the play area.

Although *alea* and *agôn* are the two principal fundamental categories that give form to the gameplay of *Tetris* (many of the system's mechanisms rest on these two aspects), *Tetris* also uses *ilinx* in its gameplay. As we saw, *ilinx* encourages the adoption of the bi-planar behavior necessary to any ludic attitude, through mechanisms causing the giddiness of the player. According to Andrew Rollings and Ernest Adams, in *Tetris*, at a certain speed, the need for more and quicker decision-making encourages the best players to adopt a state of "Tetris trance," so that the player processes all the data contained in the play area in a pre-attentional way:

> Players seems to lose all track of time and don't concentrate on the specifics of the gameboard. Instead, players defocus and appear to process the entire playing area as a whole, without considering the individual elements . . . it appears that these players are tapping into their brain's subconscious pattern-recognition ability to improve their game.[14]

This last element shows how an aleatory situation of competition is not necessarily synonymous with play and that the structure must also allow adoption of a bi-planar behavior (play being a "metaphorical" process). It is this mental state which will make the difference between the simple user and the player. *The software loses the appearance of a program dedicated to the realization of a given task, and appears as an intermediate space of experiment, which must be known by the abstraction of ordinary reality. This divided mental state gives access to the space of play, which is a potential space because it is a place of exercise of the possible.* As we have seen, it is through choices offered by the game's design, falling under the categories of *agôn, alea,* and *ilinx,* that *Tetris* creates a very particular playability and encourages the user to become a player.

Context and Practices

To conclude, it is important to remember that these preceding thoughts constitute a general analysis framework for video games. For this reason, this framework encourages the exploration of the tracks which it outlines: it seems particularly important to underline again that a playable structure prescribes the way in which certain signs can be arranged by the player to make sense, not the way in which they will be interpreted. This being the case, it is necessary to supplement the internal analysis of the object with an analysis of players' practices in order to have an overall view of the process of mediation, so that it is possible to determine the way in which players mobilize their own representations of the play activity to confer a ludic meaning on a playable structure. But, conversely, one should not ignore the structure into which the activity of the player goes, because that would amount to ignoring the context which makes play activity possible.

Notes

1. Jean-Marie Schaeffer, *Pourquoi la fiction?* (Paris: Éd. du Seuil, 1999).
2. Bernard Suits, *Grasshopper: Games, Lifes and Utopia* (Boston: David R. Godine, 1990), 38.
3. Jacques Henriot, *Sous couleur de jouer* (Paris: José Corti, 1989); hereafter cited as Henriot. Freely translated.
4. Donald Woods Winnicott, *Jeu et réalité. L'espace potentiel* (Paris: Gallimard, 1971).
5. Roger Caillois, *Des jeux et des hommes* (Paris: Gallimard, 1958), 39. Freely translated.
6. Jean Caune, "La médiation culturelle: une construction du lien social," *Les enjeux de l'information et de la communication* (2000). Available online at <http://w3.u-grenoble3.fr/les_enjeux/2000/Caune/index.php>. Freely translated.
7. Gonzalo Frasca, "Simulation versus Narrative," in *The Video Game Theory Reader*, eds. Mark J. P. Wolf and Bernard Perron (New York: Routledge, 2003), 224; hereafter cited as Frasca.
8. Patricia Greenfield, "Les jeux vidéo comme instruments de socialisation cognitive," *Réseaux*, 67 (September–October 1994), 33–56.
9. Available online at <http://jongy.tripod.com/GhostPsychology.html>.
10. Joseph Courtés, *La sémiotique narrative et discursive : méthodologie et application*, Preface by A. J. Greimas (Paris: Hachette supérieur, 1993); hereafter cited as Courtés.
11. Louis Hébert, "The Canonical Narrative Schema," in *Signo*, ed. Louis Hébert (2006). Available online at <http://www.signosemio.com/greimas/a_schemanarratif.asp>.
12. Umberto Eco, *The Role of the Reader: Explorations in the Semiotics of Texts* (Bloomington: University of Indiana Press, 1979).

13. See Erik D. Demaine, Susan Hohenberger, and David Liben-Nowell, "Tetris is Hard, Even to Approximate," in *Proceedings of COCOON'2003* (2002). Available online at <http://www.lcs.mit.edu/publications/pubs/pdf/MIT-LCS-TR-865.pdf>.
14. Andrew Rollings and Ernest Adams, *On Game Design* (Indianapolis: New Riders, 2003), 218.

CHAPTER 8

Z-axis Development in the Video Game

MARK J. P. WOLF

Images have long attempted to represent three-dimensional spaces within the two-dimensional plane. The video game image's interactive nature, however, presented new and difficult challenges in the depiction of three-dimensional space. Some answers to these challenges can be seen in the development of the z-axis within video game imagery.

Taken from Cartesian mathematics, the x-axis, running horizontally, and the y-axis, running vertically, are both located within the picture plane. The z-axis, which is perpendicular to the picture plane and traces the trajectory to and away from the viewer, is not physically present in a two-dimensional plane, so it differs from the x-axis and y-axis in that it can only be implied in an image. From the *skenographia* of ancient Greece around the fifth century BC, to Filippo Brunelleschi's demonstrations of geometric perspective in the early 1400s, perspective developed slowly in painting and art, and a coordinate system to express it mathematically was codified by Descartes in 1637, thereby uniting algebra and geometry.

By the time video games appeared, the techniques used for implying the z-axis in imagery were well-known, so it became only a matter of applying these techniques within the limitations and restrictions imposed by the still-developing computer graphics technology used by video games. Over time, video games incorporated all of the techniques used to imply depth in graphic art, including overlap, apparent size, linear perspective, fore-shortening, texture gradients, aerial perspective, and shadowing, as well as parallax (used in binocular imagery as well as monocular moving imagery) and the rotation of objects.

Early Attempts at an Illusion of Depth

The simplest way the z-axis is implied is through a figure-ground relationship, in which an object (the figure) is seen as being in front of a background (the ground). For example, in that most minimalist of all video games, Atari's *PONG* (1972), the white ball and paddles appear to be in front of the black background of the screen, which disappears and reappears behind them as they move across it, their movement further strengthening the figure-ground distinction. More representational graphics allowed games to reference real-world analogues, for example, in arcade games like Atari's *Tank* (1974) and *Indy 800* (1975), in which overhead views show vehicles driving in various courses with walls, obstacles, and other graphical objects. Overlapping planes of graphics, such as the clouds in Atari's *Combat* (1977) for the Atari 2600, which the airplanes could fly behind, implied depth; in this case, three distinct positions along the z-axis (the empty sky, the airplanes and their bullets, and the clouds).

The first attempts at depth suggested by linear perspective in commercial video games came in 1976, when racing games like Midway's *Datsun 280 Zzzap* and Atari's *Night Driver* both featured series of small, white rectangles arranged to suggest roadside pylons which defined a roadway extending into the screen towards a vanishing point (see Figure 8.1). The illusion of depth was further improved with the game's motion; the pylons would move along the roadside, growing larger as they followed one another down the screen, to make it seem as though players were driving down the road with scenery moving toward them on the z-axis.

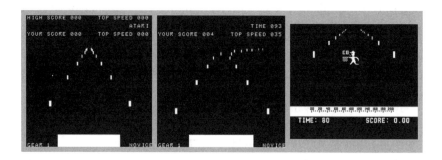

Figure 8.1 Images from arcade games of 1976: Atari's *Night Driver* (left and center) and Midway's *Datsun 280 Zzzap* (right), in which the size and placement of white pylons imply a linear perspective view down a roadway toward a vanishing point.

The technology of scalable sprites made such imagery possible. Appearing in the 1970s, sprites are small bitmapped images which can be moved around the screen. These images can be scaled, that is, reduced or enlarged, by mathematically remapping them at different resolutions. By matching their change in size with their position onscreen, sprites can appear to be moving along the z-axis, reducing as they near the vanishing point or enlarging as they move away from it, as the pylons do in *Night Driver*. Unlike the technique of overlapping planes in which objects appear at different points along the z-axis but do not move along the axis itself, scaling sprites allow an object to move along any of the three axes or combinations of them, the resulting freedom of movement greatly strengthening the suggestion of a three-dimensional space.

The use of scaling graphics to imply a z-axis through the technique of apparent size, however, depends on the x- and y-axes. Specifically, the resolution of the z-axis, that is, the number of distinct positions at which an object can appear along the axis, depends on the resolution of the x-axis and the y-axis, and on the tonal and color resolution of the image. This is perhaps more apparent in a binocular image, where the x-axis resolution quantizes and limits the amount of horizontal pixel offset between images, which in turn limits the number of possible positions along the z-axis since the amount of offset determines those positions. This limitation is particularly noticeable in grid-based random dot autostereograms where the effects of resolution are more easily measured (although to date no video games have ever used random dot autostereograms in their graphics, in theory they could).[1] But even in a monocular image, x-axis resolution plays a role in determining z-axis resolution, as does y-axis resolution. Both horizontal and vertical resolutions limit the various sizes at which a scaled object can appear. In the Atari VCS 2600 home system, for example, the effective resolution was 192 by 160 pixels, limiting how smoothly objects could scale from one size to another (although the games were displayed on standard NTSC cathode ray tube, which has a higher native resolution, the resolution used by the games was limited by the system hardware and programming). Likewise, lines of perspective are only recognizable as such if the pixels with which they are drawn are small enough.

Even when a game's hardware and software are able to make use of the full resolution offered by a display device, the resolution of the x-axis and y-axis still influence the z-axis resolution. One way to overcome some of the restrictions of limited spatial resolution is with greater tonal and color resolution, which allows for sub-pixel rendering that can increase the apparent resolution of an image. With sub-pixel rendering, the number of intermediate positions which an object can be moved along the horizontal or vertical axis depends not only on spatial resolution, but on the number of colors or tones that each pixel is capable of displaying, with intermediate tones indicating sub-pixel movements between two pixels; for example, a black pixel moved halfway across a white pixel would result in a pixel that is 50 percent gray (see Figure 8.2).[2] Color and tonal resolution is also related to aerial perspective, discussed later in this essay.

Another depth cue that relies on resolution is the texture gradient. Instead of having a single object changing in size over time, a texture gradient features a repeated pattern spread over a plane or other surface which is oriented along the z-axis. As the texture pattern recedes into the distance, the repeated elements in the pattern foreshorten and appear smaller and smaller, indicating distance in a manner which combines scaling and linear perspective. The earliest appearance of something approximating a texture gradient in a commercial video game was in Midway's arcade game *Laguna Racer* (1977). Alongside the racetrack, series of white lines recede into the distance, foreshortening vertically the higher they are onscreen (see Figure 8.3).

A slightly more detailed texture gradient would appear in Activision's *Robot Tank* (1983) for the Atari 2600, in which a series of horizontal lines of different thicknesses represented the ground stretching out to the horizon; when the player moved forward along the z-axis, the colors of the lines would alternate temporally, attempting to create a marquee effect that would suggest movement over the land into the distance. In these early instances, texture gradients had to be designed as two-dimensional graphics designed to look three-dimensional, but later, when texture mapping was introduced into games with three-dimensionally generated graphics with filled polygons, texture gradients would occur automatically as polygons were rendered at different angles.

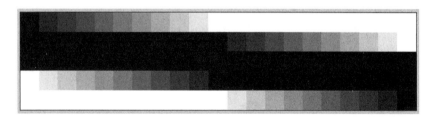

Figure 8.2 An example of sub-pixel rendering: in successive columns, moving from left to right, a black three-pixel bar moves downward one-tenth of a pixel at a time. Shades of gray suggest the partial occupation of intermediate pixels. Sub-pixel rendering is also used in anti-aliasing to suggest greater spatial resolution than what a screen contains, thereby smoothing out the rough edges of high-contrast boundaries. (Image by the author.)

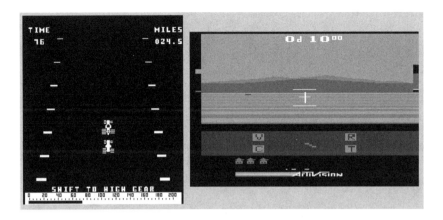

Figure 8.3 Early texture gradients in Midway's *Laguna Racer* (1977) (left) and Activision's *Robot Tank* (1983) (right). The horizontal lines have less vertical dimension the closer they are to the horizon line, appearing to foreshorten and create a sense of depth and distance in the image.

Vector Graphics

As described above, the spatial resolution limitations of early games severely limited the resolution of the z-axis. In 1977, vector graphics brought a new kind of imaging to video games. Rather than using its memory to produce raster imagery of limited resolution, which looked like filled rectangles in a grid, vector graphics were drawn onscreen one line at a time, at any angle, resulting in wireframe graphics. Lines that could be drawn in any direction made it much easier to create scenes with linear perspective, like those found in the vector arcade games *Barrier* (1978) and *Speed Freak* (1978) (both by Vectorbeam), and Atari's *Tempest* (1981). *Speed Freak* featured the strongest illusion of a three-dimensional space of any game up to that time (see Figure 8.4), with a moving road, scenery that scaled and appeared to move on the z-axis, and the first true three-dimensionally generated objects in a commercial video game: an oncoming car that drove down the road toward the foreground, rotating slightly as it moved, and pieces of a car that rotated in an explosion following a car crash.[3] While there was yet not enough processing power to do an entire game in 3-D, these objects made *Speed Freak* the first video game to have real movement along the z-axis, even if it was limited to only a few objects.

Only one vector-based home video game system ever appeared, GCE's Vectrex from 1982. Although it did not involve true 3-D computation, it featured vector games with scaling and linear perspective. Three games

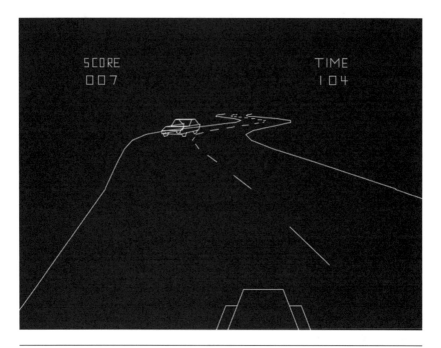

Figure 8.4 *Speed Freak* (1978) featured a strong illusion of depth in its depiction of a road stretching back to a horizon, even though no three-dimensional computation was involved in the creation of the road.

made for the system, (*3D MineStorm* (1982), *3D Crazy Coaster* (1983), and *3D Narrow Escape* (1983), produced a three-dimensional effect through the use of binocular imagery viewed through the "Vectrex 3D Imager" headgear. The games' graphics also made foreground objects brighter and background objects dimmer, making it probably the first video game system to use a technique similar to aerial perspective to create an illusion of depth.

Although vector graphics made high-resolution linear graphics possible, the processing power needed to model three-dimensional environments was still beyond the capabilities of the machines of the day, although the first arcade game to use it, Atari's *Battlezone* (1980), was a vector game that appeared only two years after *Speed Freak*. Later, vector games like Atari's *Star Wars* (1983) were more complex graphically, but still used wireframe graphics. By the late 1980s and early 1990s, games using real three-dimensional computation began appearing with filled polygons, and vector arcade games were no longer produced.

Other Visual Design Strategies

Although *Battlezone* had a true three-dimensional environment, it was a very simple one, and the computing power it used was still more than most game designers were willing to sacrifice. And there were other techniques developing that had a three-dimensional look which allowed raster imagery to be used, giving game graphics a solid and colorful look, all without real 3-D computation. These strategies allowed the z-axis to develop throughout the 1980s, and most of them were successful enough to continue to be used into the era of game graphics generated by true 3-D computation.

Overlapping Planes and Sprites

Overlapping planes, sometimes referred to as "2.5 dimensional graphics," continued to be used, and could suggest depth through the use of parallax scrolling, which first appeared in Irem's arcade game *Moon Patrol* (1982). Like a multiplane camera effect, in this kind of scrolling, the closer planes of graphics are to the forefront, the faster they move laterally during scroll-ing. Planes farther back on the z-axis scroll more slowly than those in front of them, producing a parallax effect. Early games with parallax scrolling tended to have their action taking place all in the forefront plane, but later games, like Nintendo's *Warioland* (1995), allowed the player to jump from a foreground plane to a background one.

Overlapping planes were often suggested in games by overlapping sprites, and sprite technology was also improving. By the early 1980s, sprites were colored and large enough for more detailed characters, and different sprite designs could animate objects and characters turning in different positions, adding to a sense of depth. Some early examples of such sprites can be found in Nintendo's *Donkey Kong* (1981), where Donkey Kong and Mario could appear facing forward, backward, right, and left (even the rolling barrels could change from side to front views as they rolled down the ladders), or in Nintendo's *Mario Bros.* (1983), where the coins appear to be spinning (see the image from *Mario Bros.* in Figure 8.6). In Atari's *Pole Position* (1982), the player's car appeared to rotate slightly to the left or right as the player steered. *Pole Position* also featured a fully-colored raster landscape with scaling sprites, such as roadside signs and other race cars, and a perspective view of the racetrack, the vanishing point of which swayed side to side as the player encountered turns, result-ing in a relatively convincing feeling of forward movement into the dis-tance. By the mid-1980s, computers were capable of animating (scaling and rotating) thousands of sprites, which could produce a very good illu-sion of depth in a scene; for example, Sega's *Space Harrier* (1985)[4] could scale 32,000 sprites and filled a moving landscape with them. Sprites continued to be used in arcade games into the 1990s, and they are still used in handheld games and other systems where memory and processing power are insufficient for true three-dimensional computation.

Because sprites and planes were separate entities that could differ in their position along the z-axis, the image could be duplicated and its planes and sprites given the proper amounts of parallax to produce stereo pairs of images from which a 3-D game could be made, so long as each image could be sent the correct eye. One of the earliest 3-D video games was Sega's *Subroc-3D* (1982) which used a viewer with spinning discs to alternate right and left images to the player's eyes from a single monitor. Large glasses with spinning discs also appeared as a peripheral for the Vectrex, mentioned above, and three games were released for it in 1982 and 1983. A later system used liquid crystal shutters in its glasses: Sega's SegaScope3D released in 1988, which had six games made for it, *Blade Eagle 3-D, Maze Hunter 3-D, Missile Defense 3-D, Space Harrier 3-D, Poseidon Wars 3-D,* and *Zaxxon 3-D*. Finally, one home game system was completely designed around 3-D, the Nintendo Virtual Boy, which appeared in 1995. The Virtual Boy produced its 3-D from dual images inside a viewer that the player looked into while playing. Only 22 games were released for the system, which had red monochrome images which could tire a player's eyes after extended play. Like 3-D movies, the eyestrain and need for additional viewers kept these games from achieving popularity and widespread success.

Axonometric Projections

Up until the early 1980s, the three-dimensional look used in games was that of a single point perspective, with a vanishing point somewhere around the middle of the screen. In 1982, with the appearance of Sega's *Zaxxon*, video games began using axonometric projections (which were usually dimetric projections[5]), to give a three-dimensional look to their graphics. One advantage of this kind of view was that character sprites within the scene could move around without having to change in size.

Axonometric projections brought new possibilities for three-dimensional space, which developed over the next few years (see Figure 8.5). *Zaxxon* (1982) had diagonally-scrolling scenery over which a plane flew, its height indicated by a scale (on the left side of the screen) and by its distance from its shadow below, one of the first appearances of shadowing in a video game, and one which helped the player to locate the plane within the game's space. The action of Gottlieb's *Q*bert* (1982) took place on a pyramid of cubes, and emphasized their dimensionality with Q*bert and other characters hopping on the squares facing upwards, and two

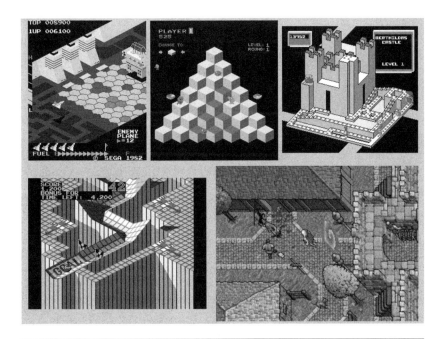

Figure 8.5 Axonometric projections in *Zaxxon* (1982) (top left), *Q*bert* (1982) (top center), *Crystal Castles* (1983) (top right), *Marble Madness* (1984) (bottom left), and *Ultima VII: The Black Gate* (1992) (bottom right). Dimetric and oblique perspectives combine a sense of the horizontal layout, similar to what one could get from a top view, with side views of objects, characters, and architecture.

enemy characters, Ugg and Wrong-Way, hopping on the sides of the cubes. Very quickly the visual sophistication of these projections increased, as is evident in Atari's *Crystal Castles* (1983) and Atari Games's *Marble Madness* (1984), both of which have screens with many different levels and elevations, with navigation up and down them an important part of gameplay. *Crystal Castles* even allowed the player's character, Bentley Bear, to enter inside structures where he was hidden from sight, though his position was represented by his red shoes, which were overlaid on the structure he was in. Axonometric projections would also appear in home games with large graphical spaces like Maxis's *SimCity 2000* (1993), and in role-playing games like Origin System's *Ultima VII: The Black Gate* (1992), where an oblique perspective gave a sense of what was surrounded the player on the horizontal plane (which previously would have been done in a top view), while at the same time allowing objects, characters, and architectural elements to be seen in a side view (as opposed to a top view).

Yet while axonometric projections brought new possibilities to video game graphics, the three-dimensional spaces they create are visually limited in that character sprites do not change size (and thus seem to always remain at the same distance from the player), and also because implied camera movement is restricted to lateral tracking (as in *Zaxxon*) as opposed to the movement possible in a scene rendered from a linear perspective, in which objects can be moved along the z-axis. After true three-dimensionally generated graphics became commonplace, axonometric projections saw much less use, since a three-dimensional game could generate a view similar to the axonometric one by positioning the implied camera over the game's scenery, only one which had more potential for camera movement and interaction.

Pre-rendered Three-Dimensional Imagery

The backgrounds used in games with axonometric perspectives were two-dimensional images drawn to look three-dimensional, and the use of drawn or pre-rendered three-dimensional imagery as a kind of backdrop in a video game has a long history and is perhaps the most common method of creating 3-D graphics without 3-D computation. Some early instances can be found in arcade games, where details were drawn to appear to have some z-axis depth. For example, Atari's *Stunt Cycle* (1976) had tubes the cycle drove through, the openings of which were drawn as ovals to convey a sense of volume, while the pipes in *Mario Bros.* (1983), although seen completely in side view, still had stripes of lighter and darker colors along their sides to suggest the kind of highlighting and shadowing that would occur with a round pipe (see Figure 8.6). Another game of

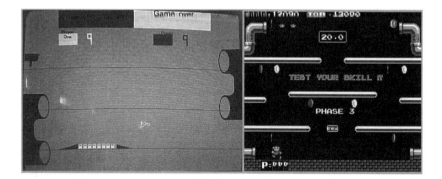

Figure 8.6 Pipes made to look three-dimensional in *Stunt Cycle* (1976) (left) and *Mario Bros.* (1983) (right). *Stunt Cycle*'s pipes feature a foreshortened view of the pipes' ends, while the pipes in *Mario Bros.* seen in side view, have light and dark stripes positioned on them to indicate highlights and shadow areas.

1981, Atari's *Tempest*, used pre-rendered moving image sequences between levels in which the player's point of view flies through tunnels of various shapes. Later games included entire backgrounds that were drawn in linear perspective, like First Star's *Spy vs Spy* (1984) and Atari Games' *Xybots* (1987). Although they could feature interactive elements (for example, the rooms in *Spy vs Spy* had furnishings the spies used to set traps and doors that could open and close), spatial interaction was limited and the backgrounds were fixed and immobile, cutting from one to the next.

Laserdisc technology brought greater possibilities for pre-rendered moving image sequences, which could be stored as video on the disc, beginning with Electro Sport's *Quarter Horse* (1981) and Sega's *Astron Belt* in 1982. This stored imagery could be live-action video (as in Mylstar's *M.A.C.H. 3* (1983) and Atari's *Firefox* (1984)), hand-drawn animation (as in *Dragon's Lair* (1983) and *Space Ace* (1984), both by Cinematronics), or computer-generated animation (as in Simutek's *Cube Quest* (1984)). Since the imagery was all pre-rendered, as opposed to being created in real time during game play, its quality was higher than that of other games of the time, but the games using it sacrificed interactivity as a result. Sequences would be exactly the same each time the game was played, and sprite-based player-characters in the foreground often seemed pasted onto the background instead of integrated into it, which in some cases destroyed the illusion of depth that the backgrounds were supposed to create. Many techniques from laserdisc games also made their way to CD-ROM-based games in the 1990s, as one optical storage medium gave way to another. CD-ROM games like Trilobyte's *The 7th Guest* (1992) and Simon and Schuster's *Star Trek: Borg* (1996) integrated video clips, the latter being made up almost entirely from them.

The storage capacity of CD-ROMs also allowed large numbers of pre-rendered still images to be stored and used as backgrounds. Games using large numbers of still images were typically navigation-based adventure games, in which the images were used for changing first-person views of different locations. These images could resemble hand-drawn ones, like those found in *The Manhole* (1987) and *Cosmic Osmo* (1989) (both by Cyan), or could be live action or computer-generated. Due to the cutting or dissolving from one camera position to another as opposed to a continuous long take with moving camera, as well as the pre-rendered nature of the images, images which were individually consistent and Euclidean in their approach to their construction of space could be combined together to construct non-Euclidean spaces in which the implied size of the onlooker changed drastically from one image to the next, or in which spaces were connected in physically impossible ways. For example, in the three pairs of images from *Cosmic Osmo* seen in Figure 8.7, the player's implied size is large in the images on the left-hand side, but small in the image in the right-hand side. The change of size is indicated by the height of the viewpoint, the relative sizes of familiar objects, and the ability to enter spaces that would appear to be too small for a full-size person to enter. In each of the three cases depicted in Figure 8.7, a player can click from one image to the next, and in one view enter a space that might appear as a tiny opening in a previous view of the same location.

Many games used computer-generated pre-rendered imagery, in which the linear perspective of the imagery is the result of computer models constructed in a three-dimensional space (for example, games like Synergy Interactive's *Gadget* (1993), Nintendo's *Donkey Kong Country* (1999), and

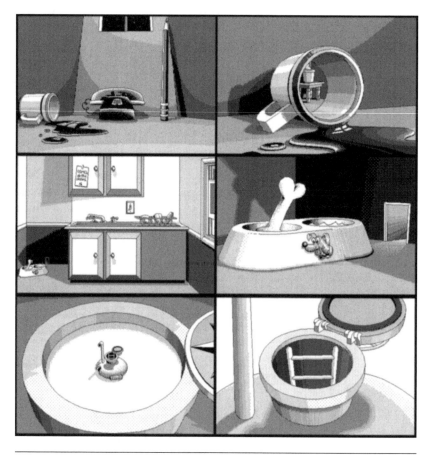

Figure 8.7 Changing the implied size of the player in *Cosmic Osmo* (1989). Images on the left imply a normal human-size player character, while those on the right imply a much smaller sized player-character, who is able to pass through tiny openings.

those of the *Myst* series and *Rhem* series). While some games use flat rectangular stills, others, like Cryo Interactive's *Atlantis: The Lost Tales* (1997), or *The Journeyman Project 3: Legacy of Time* (1998) and *Myst III: Exile* (2001) (both by Presto Studios), use 360° panoramic still imagery instead. To keep their background images from seeming too static, these games incorporate moving imagery into their backgrounds; usually small areas in which a cyclical series of images appears, like the turning windmill in the Channelwood Age in *Myst* (1993) or the moving water found in *Myst III: Exile*. In games using 360° panoramas, the player's viewpoint can turn and move in place like a nodal-point tripod head; and the panoramic image (which can be mapped onto the inside of either a cylinder, sphere, or cube) changes as the player's viewpoint moves, in such a way that objects in the center of the image grow larger as they approach the edge of the image, further enhancing the illusion of depth. The sense of three dimensions is strong in these images, especially the panoramic ones, but in all of these games the viewer is limited to the standpoints from which these views are generated, and apart from merely zooming an image to enlarge detail, camera movement on the z-axis is not possible.

Three-Dimensional Computation in Real Time

Methods designed to reduce the amount of computation needed for 3-D graphics were developing in the 1970s, such as the Z-buffer invented independently by Edwin Catmull and Wolfgang Straßer in 1974, which reduced the amount of rendering needed for images by determining which objects were placed in front of others, eliminating the rendering of hidden surfaces. Actual three-dimensional computation done in real time during a video game had been around since the 3-D wireframe exploding car in *Speed Freak* (1978), the 3-D wireframe world of *Battlezone* (1980), and the first filled-polygon world of Atari's *I, Robot* (1983), but the necessary computing power and speed needed to create a world of real-time filled-polygon graphics detailed enough to be representational instead of merely crude abstractions would take some time develop. Game hardware as well as software had to be able to handle the demands of three-dimensional computation. For example, due to the heat generated by the large amount of processing power needed for its 3-D computation, Namco's *Cyber Sled* (1993) required cooling fans without which the game would malfunction.[6]

Throughout most of the 1980s, then, other methods, like pre-rendered backgrounds or sprite-based simulations of three-dimensional space, could produce a greater degree of graphical detail than could the 3-D computation of the time, and so remained the preferred methods. After working on prototypes[7] during the mid-1980s, Atari Games released arcade games with 3-D computation around the end of the decade, including *Hard Drivin'* (1988) and *S.T.U.N. Runner* (1989), both racing games. During the early 1990s more 3-D games appeared, and even some home video games began using limited 3-D computation. Many games mixed 2-D and 3-D elements to save computing power while still creating a three-dimensional look. Home computer games like Electronic Arts's *John Madden Football '92* (1991) and id Software's *Doom* (1993) use 3-D backgrounds that moved in perspective, with 2-D foreground characters that were sprite-based. Other games reversed the process, such as the arcade games *Virtua Fighter* (1993) from Sega and *Tekken* (1994) from Namco, both of which had 3-D characters fighting into front of flat pre-rendered backdrops. So long as there was limited interaction between foreground characters and background scenery such methods were successful.

By the mid-1990s 3-D arcade games and home games were becoming more common, the number of polygons used was increasing, and other computer graphics techniques like texture mapping and light mapping would begin to appear in video games. Steady increases in all of these things over the next decade would gradually push the look and feel of these games towards the goal of photorealism. By the end of the 1990s, home games eclipsed arcade games, 3-D video games became the standard type of game produced, and sprite-based games were no longer dominant.

The ability to render game spaces and locations in real-time 3-D improved through the 1990s and into the 2000s, but the demands of more detailed characters, objects, interactions, and scenery still placed limitations on the rendering of game imagery, and game designers would have to find ways to work around them.

Designing Around Limitations

One of the disadvantages of three-dimensional computation and rendering is that objects contain the same number of polygons regardless of where they are positioned onscreen, and thus require the same amount of rendering time whether they are in the foreground and occupy a large portion of the screen or are in the distance and occupy a relatively small portion of the screen. Viewpoints with a wide angle of view or great deal of z-axis depth may include so many objects that rendering a scene could take a very long time. In games like *Myst* and *Riven* (1997), this is not a problem because the imagery are all pre-rendered, and the time needed to render them occurs during the production of the game itself, not during gameplay. But games rendering their imagery in real time cannot afford the same kind of refined detail, high resolution, and subtle lighting effects that pre-rendered images can have (even as processing power increases, so too does the photorealism of pre-rendered imagery by comparison). Real-time interactivity and movement through a detailed 3-D world would require new ways of dealing with the depiction of depth.

One solution to this problem was to design spaces in such a way as to avoid sightlines extending deep into the distance. The first two games in the *Grand Theft Auto* series featured an overhead view which looked directly down onto the street where the player's car was driving, limiting the depth and breadth that could be seen. But even games with a typical first-person ground-based perspective can limit what a player can see, by breaking up a game's world into sectioned spaces, for example, dividing interiors into rooms and hallways like those found in the *Doom* series, *Tomb Raider* series, and *Silent Hill* series. In such cases, while a game's world may be huge, only a small portion of it is rendered at any given time. Passages between rooms can further be designed to turn corners, avoiding the need to show room interiors at a distance from inside other adjacent rooms.

For larger spaces, other methods were employed. Techniques that simulate exaggerated aerial perspective kept distant scenery hidden from view and meant that nothing would need to be rendered beyond a certain z-axis depth, even in open terrain. For example, in the *Tomb Raider* series, receding spaces are gradually darkened, and beyond a certain distance they simply appear as black (see Figure 8.8). As the player's point of view moves down the z-axis into these spaces, they brighten and the detail there becomes visible. The player's inability to see into these darkened spaces enhances the feeling of distance and depth, as well the player's feeling of discovery while moving into them as they brighten (the effect is similar to carrying a torch through a dark interior, though in most of these games the player-character is not carrying any kind of portable lighting device). A similar technique is the use of an atmospheric effect, like the fog and snow used in *Silent Hill* (1999), which hides distant objects in a gray haze and has them seem to materialize as the player approaches them. By 2001, with the release of games like *Grand Theft Auto III*, the increasing computing power of home systems was able to extend visibility quite far down the z-axis into the distance, so that aerial perspective techniques could appear more natural and not as exaggerated as they did in earlier games.

With the computing power that made greater z-axis depth possible came other ways to minimize render time. In computer-generated film sequences, distant objects are sometimes replaced with versions of those objects with lower geometric resolution (that is, made with fewer polygons). While this speeds up render time, such a method becomes difficult in real-time game graphics when objects are moving along the z-axis, since they need to smoothly change their geometric resolution as they move,

Figure 8.8 Spaces darken as they recede from the player in *Lara Croft Tomb Raider: Anniversary* (2006) and appear as black beyond a certain distance. This saves render time, since only the areas and objects within a set distance along the z-axis need to be rendered.

which itself takes processing power and time to do. The solution to this problem are NURBS, Non-Uniform Rational Basis (or Bézier) Splines. Objects are represented as curved surfaces which can be rendered at various geometric resolutions depending on their position along the z-axis. As Robert Polevoi, an Assistant Professor of Computer and Video Imaging in Silicon Valley describes it:

> A NURBS surface is free-form and ideal. However, to be rendered, its must be resolved into a polygonal mesh, a process called tessellation or surface approximation. The single most important aspect of NURBS modeling is in this very power to vary the geometric resolution of the model as needed. If the model is small or needed for realtime rendering, the tesselation [*sic*] can be made cruder to produce a lower polygon count. For close-ups or cinematic-quality work, the surface approximation can be made very fine.
>
> The games industry, which is the technology leader in realtime, interactive 3D graphics, is moving toward the goal of realtime tessellation of NURBS models. Thus a NURBS character could seamlessly increase its geometric

resolution (polygon count) as it grows large on the screen, and decrease it's [*sic*] resolution as it moves away. This technological advance, when it occurs, will dramatically increase the quality and realism of interactive 3D.[8]

As games grow more photorealistic, other optical effects involving the z-axis, such as the rack focus, will come into greater use, making games even more cinematic and increasing players' visual involvement in the games' worlds.

Just as in other visual media, the z-axis is of central importance in the production of an image depicting three-dimensional space which the viewer can enter vicariously. In games like *Riven* (1997) and *Rhem* (2003), tiny depictions of distant objects provide clues for the observant player, orienting the player in space and enhancing the interconnectedness of a game's geography, resulting in a strengthened illusion of a real three-dimensional space. While greater z-axis depth places demands on hardware, software, and game design, it fills the player's viewpoint with a larger and more detailed world of interconnected locations, encouraging involvement and giving players a virtual space to enter into where their attention is held and contained. That is, after all, the essence of *entertainment*, which traces it etymology to the Latin roots *inter* meaning "among", and *tenere* meaning "to hold". With their still-increasing photorealism and z-axis depth, video games are the cutting edge of interactive imagery, producing visually-convincing virtual worlds that can be entered vicariously, allowing them to occupy an ontological position somewhere between incarnation and imagination.

Notes

1. Interestingly, random dot autostereograms also contain pixels (in the offset areas) which are simultaneously figure for one eye and ground for the other, even though in a monocular image, elements can only be either figure or ground at any given moment, but not both simultaneously.

2. A good visual comparison of sprite movement with and without sub-pixel rendering can be found online at <http://www.willmcgugan.com/2007/04/25/going-sub-pixel-with-pygame/> (accessed November 12, 2007).

3. Tim Skelly, a programmer at Cinematronics, the company that purchased Vectorbeam, the makers of *Speed Freak*, discusses the game's graphics:

    > Forgetting about the car for a moment, all of the objects drawn on the screen are two dimensional. Some are rotated onto the X plane, some the Y and some are in the Z plane, but all are 2D. They scale, but they do not rotate. Even the road, which as I noted before, slides from side to side but without a rotation of viewpoint that you would see with full 3D. As long as image orientation is fixed along one of the primary axes, rotation is trivial and can be "hardwired" into the tables used for rendering.
    >
    > The car and its bits are rendered in true 3D. There are few enough edges to allow this. It appears that two "flat" objects like the airplane and the hitchhiker can appear at one time. I'm guessing that a similar amount of vectors are used for the car on the road, which always appears alone. The exploded car is rendered

> entirely by itself, free to use all the available rendering resources. (From an e-mail from Tim Skelly to the author, September 27, 2007.)

At the time of this writing, footage of the game *Speed Freak* being played could be seen in a video clip on YouTube at <http://www.youtube.com/watch?v=syDQ1GEM-s8> (accessed September 27, 2007). The gameplay of many games can be seen in action in videos at video sites like YouTube and Google Video on the Web.

4. Both 1985 and 1986 are given as release dates for *Space Harrier*, which may indicate individual release dates in Japan and North America, respectively.

5. Most of the axonometric projections used are dimetric projections because the grid of pixels used by video game graphics does not allow for smoothly-drawn isometric projections, which require all three axes to be exactly 120 degrees apart; typically a two-to-one ratio of pixels is used in the diagonals of most games. See <http://en.wikipedia.org/wiki/Isometric_projection>.

6. According to the page for *Cyber Sled* at www.klov.com:

> Because of the large number of polygons in the game and the processing power required, the game also *requires* cooling fans to blow across the game boards. Without these, the game will freeze up, or cease functioning completely. (From <http://www.klov.com/game_detail.php?game_id=7466> accessed on November 8, 2007.)

7. An example of a 1985 prototype can be viewed online at <http://www.youtube.com/watch?v=ab8GMdPFikA> (accessed November 8, 2007).

8. Robert Polevoi, "Lesson 83—3D E-Commerce With MetaStream- Part 3", from his January 5, 2000 column *3-D Animation Workshop*, available online at <http://www.webreference.com/3d/lesson83/part3.html> (accessed November 8, 2007).

CHAPTER 9

Retro Reflexivity
La-Mulana, an 8-Bit Period Piece

BRETT CAMPER

Since its inception, the commercial video game industry has been fundamentally oriented towards the steady "progression" of technology platforms. Along the way, representational aesthetics have largely followed these technical advances. We have moved from one-screen action game classics like Atari's *Missile Command* (1980) and *Centipede* (1982), to side-scrolling platformers borne from the genre-defining *Super Mario Bros.* series (Nintendo, 1985–ongoing), to 3-D first-person shooter franchises like *Half-Life* (Valve, 1998-ongoing) and *Halo* (Bungie, 2001–ongoing). At the same time, childhood gamers have grown up, and a powerful nostalgia for older styles of games has germinated: players in their twenties recall the ground-breaking 2-D titles of the Nintendo Entertainment System (NES), while thirty-somethings remember the thrill of Atari's VCS (also known as the 2600), when broadcasting's monopoly of one-way television ended and millions of households first "brought the arcade home."

Today, the commercial industry is increasingly recognizing this retro market, resuscitating its back catalog of older titles via digital distribution, with dedicated outlets such as Microsoft's Xbox Live Arcade, Nintendo's Virtual Console on the Wii, and the PC-based GameTap subscription service. This in itself is a positive and meaningful development for the medium and business, an explicit recognition (and business legitimization) of its history. But why stop at re-packaging older titles? Why is it that these older game aesthetics cannot still be relevant today? Why should today's games be driven *only* by today's newest technology? Independent developers outside of the traditional commercial industry have responded with a trend of "retro" styled—but original—video games. By adopting technologically "obsolete" audiovisual conventions for a new generation of games, they display a stylized self-awareness of technologies, aesthetics, and genres, and the underlying relationship between them. Perhaps considered outliers or oddballs when viewed alongside the larger field of commercial (or even many other independent) titles, we find in them the kind of reflexivity that is arguably central to advancing our critical understanding of video games as a medium. From an historical angle, the throwback look and feel of these titles also visually reminds us that today's resurgent momentum for amateur and other non-traditionally produced games—from zeitgeist pop culture websites such as Homestar Runner, to the industry's annual Independent Games Summit—is a return to the roots of the hobbyist "bedroom coder" of the 1980s.

To illustrate, I will take an in-depth look at *La-Mulana*, a puzzle-centric platform-adventure for Windows PCs, created by a Japanese amateur development team called the GR3 Project (now known as Nigoro). Originally written in Japanese and released in 2005, an English version (patched by the fan translation group Aeon Genesis) was completed in early 2007, considerably expanding the game's audience, and bringing with it high critical praise: one reviewer simply said "It's the best game I've played in a year."[1] *La-Mulana* belongs to the subgenre of 2-D platform-based action-adventures, which originated in the 8-bit console era most prominently with the classic *Metroid* (Nintendo, 1986) for Famicom/NES. Unlike a traditional action platformer, the emphasis is on world exploration, with a degree of non-linearity and player discretion. The genre borrows elements of methodical puzzle-solving and incremental character development from adventure and role-playing games, which are traditionally less action-oriented. Several lesser known NES games contributed to the style early on as well, such as Hudson Soft's *Faxanadu* (1989) and *Milon's Secret Castle* (1986), as well as Konami's *The Goonies II* (1987). In the past decade, the *Castlevania* series from Konami has also adopted and advanced the form, from *Symphony of the Night* (1997) on PlayStation, through the recent *Portrait of Ruin* (2006) for the Nintendo DS.

Professor Lemeza is *La-Mulana*'s player-protagonist, an archaeologist explorer reminiscent of Indiana Jones, charting out vast underground ruins in a distant, unspecified corner of the globe. Though the game provides plenty of fierce action and demands a relentless on-guard posture, the player's progression is mostly dependent on the solution of cryptic

Figure 9.1 *La-Mulana* is a 2-D action-adventure in the tradition of *Metroid* and *Castlevania*. Though it was created in 2005, the game uses retro-styled graphics to evoke its 1980s predecessors.

riddles and other challenges of logic (punctuated by customary, punishing "boss battles"). The game employs a familiar "start from zero knowledge" conceit: the player arrives at the ruins with no map and only the vaguest of rumors, setting the stage for the free-roaming, hostile territory common to the genre. *La-Mulana* is an extremely well made title that ranks among the finest in its class, commercial or amateur, past or present—particularly impressive, given that the action-adventure genre is arguably among the greatest of challenges to independent developers, requiring a diverse, multidisciplinary mix of skills. Where many of today's laudable indie titles are action or abstract puzzle games that rest (fairly enough) on one or two clever game mechanics, novel graphical effects, or a well-tuned physics engine, the action-adventure game demands a blend of fictional setting, game mechanics and rules, audiovisuals, and textual exposition on a grander scale and often with a much greater amount of content. *La-Mulana* displays unusual craftsmanship and cohesiveness.

What really sets *La-Mulana* apart, however, is its distinctly recognizable retro visual style, and from the title screen onwards we are treated to a sparse, "8-bit" styling. While *La-Mulana* is in fact an ordinary, contemporary Windows game without any special technical capabilities (or limitations) of note, it mimics a very specific older game technology: the MSX, an 8-bit home computer popular in Japan in the mid-1980s. This self-stated adoption of the MSX platform makes the game an attractive case study, because it explicitly foregrounds its retro aspirations, while giving us a specific technological rubric by which we can analyze it. Nick Montfort and Ian Bogost have established the approach of *platform studies* as a means of understanding a program's technical basis in context: "the investigation of underlying computing systems and how they enable, constrain, shape and support the creative work that is done on them."[2] The distinct bundles of hardware and software that make up a platform profoundly shape the kinds of games that are (and can be) made for it: 2-D pixel-based systems favor side-scrolling platformers and top-down maps; native support for 3-D polygonal graphics has made the first-person shooter a mainstay; the lighting effects of today's programmable shaders encourage further stylistic distinctions like the shadowy "survival horror" genre.

Though *La-Mulana* is not actually written, compiled, or executed on a real MSX computer, the game's conscious imitation of (as well as dissonance with) that system makes for a degree of platform study by proxy. Below, I mix this mindset with other methods and sources, viewing *La-Mulana* from a wide angle: close technical and gameplay analysis, quotes from the game's developers on their own stated intent for the project, responses from the larger indie community, and comparisons to commercially marketed "retro" offerings.

An "MSX-style" Game

In a sense, *La-Mulana* is an 8-bit "period piece": the creators intentionally position it as an "MSX-style" game, with specific mention of Konami's *Maze of Galious* (1987, also known as *Knightmare II*) as an inspiration. To fully understand the game's aesthetic and cultural references requires some background knowledge of the MSX itself. Although the system was never seriously marketed in the USA, the MSX was a successful platform, particularly in Japan: it sold over 5 million units worldwide, and maintained its relevance alongside the fierce competition of Nintendo's better-known Famicom (branded the Nintendo Entertainment System in the USA); both machines were released in 1983. Notably, the MSX hosted the first titles in significant franchises that have remained strong to this day, including the inaugural *Metal Gear* (Konami, 1987) and *Bomberman* (Hudson Soft, 1983) games.

As a computational platform, the MSX had an unusual genesis: the brainchild of Kazuhiko Nishi, a Microsoft executive at the company's

Figure 9.2 The MSX was a hybrid console-computer, popular in Japan in the mid-1980s. Though it looked much like other personal computers of the time, its standardized cartridge format and graphics acceleration made it attractive to game developers. (Photograph by Paolo Tonon. <http://commons.wikimedia.org/wiki/Image:Canon_V-20_MSX_computer.jpg>. Licensed under Creative Commons Attribution ShareAlike 2.0 (CC-BY-SA)).

Japanese branch, it was an attempt to standardize the nascent PC market by providing clear guidelines for hardware manufacturers. Rather than building or assembling the machine itself, Microsoft instead specified which components third party vendors should use in order to make their computers "MSX compatible." Over fifteen years later, Microsoft would consider the same standards-based approach when planning its Xbox console, before rejecting the idea in favor of keeping production centralized.[3] The MSX was a general-purpose computer rather than a strict game console, but its graphics and sound chips (from Texas Instruments and Yamaha, respectively) provided 2-D hardware acceleration and music capabilities that were lacking on regular PCs. The reliability of standardization made it attractive to game developers, who dominated the machine's software library. In relative technological horsepower, the initial MSX1 was more sophisticated and had a higher pixel resolution and greater graphical variety than predecessors like the Atari VCS 2600 and Intellivision consoles, but lacked some important features of the rival Famicom (such as continuous scrolling). The audiovisual components were later upgraded with the MSX2 specification in 1986; *La-Mulana*'s chief reference point is the MSX1.

Much of *La-Mulana*'s 8-bit aesthetic is tied to its self-imposed graphical limitations. To start, the native resolution of 256 × 192 pixels is (as we would expect) much less than that of contemporary standards, which deliver 640 × 480 pixels on the low end, with the Xbox 360 and PlayStation 3 consoles supporting far greater detail up to 1920 × 1080 pixels as HD (high definition) television is ushered into more homes. As with most of its technical guidelines, *La-Mulana*'s 256 × 192 resolution matches that of the original MSX1. By default, the game scales up to a full-screen display in Windows, restoring the familiar coarseness of NES (256 × 224) and PC EGA or VGA (320 × 200) era titles. Conveniently, the currently common PC resolution of 1,024 × 768 is four times greater than that of the MSX1 on both axes, allowing *La-Mulana*'s original pixels to be easily blown up to an area 16 times their original size. If desired, the user can also opt to play in a windowed mode—and doing so makes the game so tiny that the vast differences in detail are immediately driven home.

Nonetheless, *La-Mulana*'s graphics are dense enough to depict reasonably recognizable representations of "real-world" objects and environments: from stone statues, to waterfalls, pottery, birds, and skeletons, right down to the player's hat and whip. There is a noticeable increase in fidelity over the stereotypically blocky style of the Atari VCS console, where highly abstract games like *Breakout* (Atari, 1978) and *Kaboom!* (Activision, 1981) were common. For example, Atari's *Adventure* (1979), the progenitor of the entire action-adventure genre, was so visually constrained that it represented the player's character on screen as a simple square, while the sword looked more like an abstract arrow shape. *Pitfall!* (Activision, 1982) is the closest VCS comparison to *La-Mulana* in theme and gameplay, but despite its reputation for pushing the system's graphical limits (pioneering techniques for multi-color sprites), the wide rectangular pixels and severe limitations on the simultaneous display of sprites favor broad splashes of solid, contrasting colors, with each screen literally centered on a single interaction (as the VCS has a technological predisposition to symmetrical environments).

While pixel resolution is arguably an important criterion for a more general concept of retro game style, *La-Mulana*'s particular look actually owes more to its palette, which is limited to a mere 16 colors. Replicating the palette of the MSX1, these run the gamut from gaudy cyan, to neutral brown and gray, to deep primary red; though not a perfect match, US players unfamiliar with the MSX would likely recognize *La-Mulana*'s often jarring juxtapositions as similar to those of PC EGA games (also 16 colors). Because the palette is fixed throughout the game, much of the artistic accomplishment surrounds creatively mixing these 16 colors, using dithering techniques to achieve distinct moods in each of the game's areas: the grassy village outside the ruins, the huge red stone monuments depicting the god-like creatures of the "Giants' Mausoleum," and the faux Egyptian tombs of the "Temple of the Sun."

But where *La-Mulana* ups the ante is in its more subtle adherence to the MSX1's specific limitations on the spatial distribution of colors. The platform's greatest challenge is: upon the background layer, each horizontal segment of eight pixels can only consist of two separate colors. While the specific colors used can be altered from segment to segment, the two-color restriction puts significant "local color pressure" on the visual design, and encourages the use of vertically-stacked bands of horizontal gradients to create a sense of texture or sheen—an effect evident from *La-Mulana*'s title screen logo to its environmental backdrops. Furthermore, while the MSX1 did provide basic support for freestanding sprites (that could be placed anywhere on screen, unlike the fixed location of its background tiles), each sprite graphic is limited to a single color (plus transparency, for a total of two values, or 1-bit-per-pixel). As a result, most of *La-Mulana*'s characters and enemies are flat silhouettes that require the artist to carefully attend to shape and outline. The color palette plays a sometimes subliminal but significant role in establishing a platform's visual style, so *La-Mulana*'s particular 16 colors provide an effective cue of its MSX origins; even the Atari VCS, which generally only allowed four unique colors to be shown per line, still had a far larger palette of 128 overall colors from which those four could be chosen. By contrast, every pixel of every MSX1 program had to be picked from its lonely 16 color palette.

Although my technical focus has been on visual elements, MSX sound is faithfully reproduced as well, in the style of Konami's SCC (Sound Custom Chip), an add-on chip (not part of the MSX's base specifications) that was included with popular cartridge games for the system.[4] Even though the SCC has just 128 bytes of memory, the chip uses wavetables that allow each game to customize the sound samples of its underlying "instruments"; this provided for considerably more variability and texture than the fixed-wave channels (pulse, triangle, white noise, etc.) of competing systems, chiefly the Famicom/NES. (The SCC was still undeniably primitive: the next generation of similarly designed wavetable sound boards, like the Gravis Ultrasound released for PCs in 1992, featured over 2000 times as much memory.)

As players, we do not need to consciously recognize or understand all (or even any) of *La-Mulana*'s specific technological constraints in order to appreciate its aesthetic style, and to intuitively identify it as "8-bit." The MSX's computational similarities to other platforms in the same "family"—the Nintendo Famicom/NES, the Commodore 64, among others—create a wider, more accessible aesthetic and cultural touch-point. The game appears to be attractive to retro-minded players in the USA, for

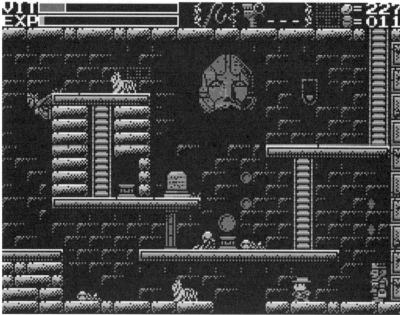

Figures 9.3 & 9.4 *La-Mulana*'s low-resolution, 16-color graphics follow the conventions of the 8-bit MSX computer, which limited horizontal color variety. Instead, the system favored vertically-stacked bands of solid horizontal colors, seen in the title screen lettering, as well as the ladders and bricks of the in-game graphics.

instance, despite the MSX being almost unheard of in this market. At the same time, a technically-oriented analysis, as I have begun to explore here, can provide deeper insight into the context of both production and reception. *La-Mulana*'s self-assigned and abided rules create such specificity that even without an explicit statement of connection (as the game provides), a devoted MSX fan would likely recognize the visual inspiration purely from the phenomenological experience.

La-Mulana's MSX obsession is far from limited to its in-game look and sound, extending to ancillary materials like the accompanying manual, and even worming its way into much of the storyline and game mechanics. For instance, when the game loads, the deep blue MSX start-up screen is displayed, along with the amount of available video RAM—yet in a passing systems joke, the RAM listed by *La-Mulana* is thousands of times more than a real MSX would have had. Within the game itself, Professor Lemeza's most prized possession is a "portable MSX," described in the game's tongue-in-cheek back-story as a niche, laptop version of the computer created for use by global adventurers. The in-game MSX turns out to be critical: in addition to powering basic functions like the game map, the player can unlock new abilities by finding and buying cartridges strewn throughout the ruins, most of which are named after real MSX games, like Konami's *Comic Bakery* (1984) and *Hyper Rally* (1985). Outside of the game program itself, the developers have crafted a faux MSX instruction booklet and box (presented in HTML form), with cartoonish, pen and ink illustrations of characters, enemies, and items; in keeping with such 1980s era supporting documentation, these analog drawings have a distinctive style, a "printed" monochrome half-tone quality (despite being created digitally) that is wholly separate from the low-res in-game sprites. Functionally, the manual includes detailed descriptions, tables, and hints that are near necessary to deciphering the game—again, congruent to actual 8-bit titles, but deviant from the general trend today that favors interactive tutorials and de-emphasizes external references (as well as aesthetic clashes between intra- and extra-game imagery). As one reviewer aptly put it, *La-Mulana* is a "100-hour love letter to the 'Xbox of 1983'" (ActionButton.net).

An 8-Bit Game with Contemporary Ambitions

As we have seen above, the influence of the MSX is most immediately apparent in the game's visual style and paratextual markers. Yet if we read what the game's developers have to say about their intent, graphics are never explicitly mentioned. Instead the inspiration initiates from gameplay, and more specifically the concept of challenge. *La-Mulana* is a

Figure 9.5 *La-Mulana*'s digital manual mimics the pen and ink illustrations of 1980s instruction booklets, with sharply different representational styles for in-game and out-of-game visuals.

deeply difficult game, which the developers describe as a reaction to "the new-style of really easy games," going on to say: "it may be very hard to beat *La-Mulana*. But that's OK. We're looking for those gamers that could in days past defeat Druaga [*The Tower of Druaga*, Namco, 1985], bring the baby back safely from the clutches of Galious [*Maze of Galious*], and seal the Evil Crystal [*Hydlide 3*, T&E Soft, 1987]."[5] There is a two-part supposition here: first of all, that the trend of gameplay in the commercial industry has been from harder to easier; and second of all, that an earlier platform style can reset that clock, triggering an association with those older, harder games, and the set of gameplay expectations that come with them. The evocation of 8-bit gameplay is at least as important as, if not more so, than that of 8-bit graphics. And the developers have bent over backwards to categorically associate the game with the long defunct MSX platform because they believe the two are intrinsically linked.

All of this is to say that the technological artifacts of the MSX are stamped not only upon *La-Mulana*'s visuals and sound, but also its gameplay, and within its world we can see how certain technological methods of aesthetic presentation correspond to particular gameplay mechanics or styles of interaction. The MSX-adopted limitations on pixel configuration and color distribution create graphics that are highly repetitive within each area of the game world. But rather than attempting to "overcome" this, the game naturally orients itself in this direction. In the tradition of the Atari VCS *Adventure*, many of *La-Mulana*'s underground rooms are very similarly templated, with slight variations that create a sense of labyrinthine confusion. Distinguishing between these rooms is a key challenge—it is a designed psychological task of gameplay, a simple visual example of the developers' overarching intent to make you slow down, take your time, and carefully observe your surroundings. As the designers chide:

> You can proceed however you like, but if you solve riddles and don't pay attention to how the ruins change accordingly, that's not very archaeologist-like! . . . Try not to miss changes in the ruins, things that seem out of place, or strange mechanisms just because you didn't look them over carefully enough! (Instruction manual)

The MSX1 did not have hardware support for the smooth scrolling of background images. Following this cue, *La-Mulana*'s world space is displayed as a vast series of contiguous (rather than continuous) single-screen areas, similar to *Adventure* (the first game to use such a method) and *Pitfall!* or (on the Famicom/NES) the first *Legend of Zelda* game (Nintendo, 1986). Quick, chunky scrolling transitions show one area sliding into the next each time the player reaches a screen edge (again, consistent with the MSX's ability to shift the entire background map one complete 8-pixel-wide tile at a time—too little resolution to depict precise player-driven movement, but sufficient for a pre-calculated visual effect).

As is typical of this mode of spatial representation and era of 1980s gameplay, non-player characters or enemies are confined to the area of their own local screen, and they will not follow the player across screens. Action scenarios are choreographed around specific, partially predetermined "room" setups, with pseudo-random elements introduced through techniques such as multiple potential enemy spawn points. Such containment is convenient to the MSX's limit of 32 total simultaneous sprites (with a maximum of four allowed per line of pixels); juggling the display of an indeterminate number of characters across a free-roaming world composed of hundreds of screens would be atypical for the machine (even if it might be possible). Continuous action is therefore de-emphasized to some degree. Though the game does require complex execution of real-time actions (many of them quite challenging), a reconnaissance style of exploration is enabled by both the ability to escape local battles by leaving the room, and through the Grail, an item acquired early in the game which allows the player to warp instantaneously to a handful of key checkpoints. In another technique borrowed from 8-bit classics, many puzzles depend on "clearing the room"—defeating all enemies in the immediate vicinity—in order to trigger events or reveal items.

The room system provides for a good blend of action and thought-focused riddles. In the level known as the "Giants' Mausoleum," for example, large inanimate statues are scattered throughout the individual rooms. On first glance, the figures appear mostly to be decorative backgrounds, the subjects of the epic but fragmentary mythology that is scrawled upon the ruins' ancient tablets. By the time the player discovers that accomplishments in one room may alter the pose of a statue in another (offering a visual clue to yet another riddle in turn), the need for careful self-documentation of the surrounding behavior is apparent. In fact, the game's translators even advise taking sequential screenshots (using extra-game utilities) of rooms and tablets as an aid to deducing one's progress.[6] It is a strategy reminiscent of the 8-bit adventure game tradition encouraging (sometimes requiring) the player to create hand-drawn maps of the game world, with a twist that suggests the play-style of recent "camera"-based games, in which visual evidence is gathered directly from within the game world itself (such as *Fatal Frame*, Tecmo, 2001, or *Dead Rising*, Capcom, 2006).

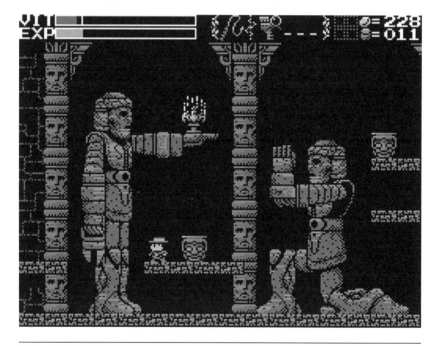

Figure 9.6 Players must pay close attention to the poses of the statues in the Giants' Mausoleum. Completing a puzzle in one room may subtly alter a statue in another.

We could also see the choice of 8-bit visuals as an expression of Jesper Juul's argument that less graphical representation of a game world tends to correspond to a greater awareness of the functional rules of that world.[7] On a formal (rather than visually aesthetic or culturally nostalgic) level, we could imagine *La-Mulana* dispensing with the lushly-rendered background images that appear in 16- and 32-bit platformers because (theoretically speaking) they are extraneous to those games' rule sets, and therefore part of an "optional world" that is unnecessary to gameplay. The stripped down graphics force the player's attention onto action and function over strict fidelity of representation. *La-Mulana* also teases the player with this expectation, playing with the established 2-D platform game conventions of non-interactive backgrounds that have no bearing on the game world state, and thus do not require significant active attention.

La-Mulana's designers have consciously aimed for a style of play that does not simply replicate its classical models, but adapts and evolves them. Recounting their development and play-testing process, they describe an initially vague but continually nagging self-recognition that while they worked ever more to match the source of their inspiration, a sense of satisfaction did not follow, even in their success. Coming to a moment of design crisis midway through, they concluded that "in the end, what we had was nothing but a cheap *Maze of Galious* knockoff" (Instruction manual). Their response, interestingly, was a direct attempt to inject contemporary (that is, current platform generation) gameplay trends into their design: they "wondered if it might not be possible to incorporate the sense of tension in newer games like [the] *Metal Gear* [*Solid* series, Konami, 1998–ongoing]" (Instruction manual). What they pivoted towards was a design best described as contemplative. They describe this philosophy as follows:

> We tried to make it so that people wouldn't get hopelessly stuck everywhere, but if you just whack walls at random without thinking you'll die. If you think "Ooh, a treasure!" and run charging toward it without thinking, you'll die. If you just operate a mechanism without thinking about how it works, you may end up not ever being able to get a specific item. If you think "I'm trapped! I'm going to warp out!" and do so, you won't be able to get back into that room from the outside. Once you do finally manage to find your way back in, you may be confronted with an even more obnoxious mechanism to overcome than before. If you make enough big mistakes it will even become quite tough to complete the game. (Instruction manual)

The design demands self-regulated pacing and patience from the player. One of the most commented upon aspects from new players is its difficulty at the outset: initially, players cannot save their progress (until they have purchased the Game Master MSX ROM), cannot read the ancient tablets that contain the majority of clues to the game's riddles (until they have acquired the Hand Scanner accessory which translates this text), and even assuming one did manage to successfully solve a puzzle under these conditions, they would not receive any positive feedback or encouragement alerting them to this fact (until finding the Shell Horn, which sounds a note each time an action is completed). Many of the basic scaffolding capabilities that players have come to expect are noticeably and intentionally absent. To sum up: "we decided to put in the fear of death" in *La-Mulana*.

While it would be inaccurate to call this design style more "realistic," the game's stark beginning does set the tone that a different set of expectations are at play. The archaeological fictional setting—exotic and adventurous on its face, yet clichéd and humdrum as a game trope—is to be taken seriously this time around. Rather than an exaggeration or parody of its forebearers, it is more accurately a re-doubling and intensification. Above all is a demand towards logical contemplation ("What would I do in this situation?"), and away from the immediacy of combat-oriented action. The latter is positioned as an ever-present threat to be deflected, rather than as an end in and of itself (the handful of culminating boss battles possibly aside). One parallel would be to see the designers as bringing the game world's emphasis more into line with related pop culture archaeologist-heroes of other media, from early examples like H. Rider Haggard's late nineteenth century pulp paperbacks, chronicling the adventures of the Englishman Allan Quartermain, to the best-known example on the big screen, Indiana Jones. As standard-bearers of the "thinking" action hero, these protagonists are apt models for *La-Mulana*'s dependence on observation and intellectualism, remaining firmly embedded in an action framework.

As *La-Mulana*'s particular subgenre of 2-D platform-adventure has seen a recent resurgence of critical interest, its roots are undergoing a reappraisal. *La-Mulana* has fared well in the comparison:

> [S]omehow, *La-Mulana* manages to avoid the clunky presentation and game-play which has aged the real 1980s games so dramatically. Operating without real 8-bit constraints, the developers have made an 8-bit game with modern ambition. It makes me want to throw away my next-gen devices, but at the same time it is richer and more satisfying than any game I could find for an emulator. *La-Mulana* is deeper and more complicated than any other game with 16-colour graphics, though it is never inaccessible or obtuse. It is exceedingly difficult without ever feeling arbitrary. (ActionButton.net)

Difficulty may be central to *La-Mulana*'s charter, but it is a challenge built on clarity of presentation and logic, rather than the charge of obscurity often leveled at similarly large, non-linear 8-bit worlds. For instance, while the NES action-platformer *Milon's Secret Castle* (1986) could be considered a progenitor of *La-Mulana*, it is anything but logical; a recent stream-of-consciousness review by journalist Kyle Orland began and ended in frustration:

> I get hit by one enemy four times in rapid succession and it's game over. What the hell!
>
> I know games were harder back then, but DAMN!
>
> . . .
>
> Starting over, I kill an enemy and he turns into an umbrella that floats away before I can grab it. Now that's good design.
>
> . . .
>
> [A]pparently shooting a bubble in JUST the right spot in the upper right corner uncovers a door out. Intuitive![8]

While the comments may be sarcastic, they underscore the fundamental lack of cause-and-effect seen in many games of the period, even those which innovated in other ways (in this case, non-linear world design). While the objections raised about *Faxanadu* (1989, NES) by Jeremy Parish are less derogatory, they go to the heart of the issue: "there's a certain element of abstraction to the whole thing—vaguely-translated objectives, unexplained item effects, a bit of trial-and-error—but do recall that this is the 8-bit era we're talking about."[9] *La-Mulana* aims to correct these flaws and evolve past them by adopting the 8-bit form; thus its design began grounded in nostalgia, but ended up driven by critique.

Finally, from a perspective beyond direct design, we also ought to remind ourselves of the changed nature of global communications today, two decades after the MSX and NES heyday: *La-Mulana* is blessed with an excellent English translation that was done entirely by dedicated fans. The game's English text is clearer than that in a great number of Japanese commercial games of the 1980s. Such quality is crucial to understanding its complex system of logic and riddles, and the title's appeal outside of Japan would be severely limited without it—a fate many of its 1980s predecessors endured in the USA. Further mitigating its difficulty, an exhaustive series of walkthrough videos (comprised of 89 individual segments) appears on YouTube (again courtesy of a fan). These tutorials can be especially helpful in starting the game, and as of January 2008 the opening episode had garnered over 15,000 views.[10] *La-Mulana* was designed in a far more advanced (and commercially independent) environment of cross-cultural reception.

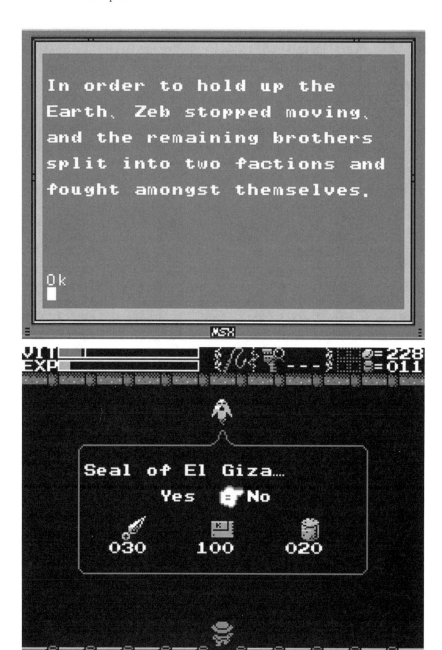

Figures 9.7 & 9.8 Despite their amateur origins, *La-Mulana*'s textual riddles and conversations are better translated and more intelligible than their professional predecessors from the 1980s.

Platform Remediation

La-Mulana is only one example in a host of indie games that consciously adopt a "chunky pixel" aesthetic, and the technique has emerged as a clearly identifiable trend. In a recent interview Phil Fish, an independent game developer as well as a level designer in the commercial industry, ruminated on the roots of the pixel's nostalgic attraction by way of other lo-fi media:

> I'm playing *Mass Effect* [Bioware, 2007] these days. It's incredible, the game is all shiny HD [high definition] graphics, and yet it has a MOVIE GRAIN FILTER! This pure, sharp 100% digital image gets all fuzzied up with a thick grain. And for what? To get that 70s feel. To give it that warmth that a pure, sharp 100% digital image so completely lacks. And it's so wonderful. It fits the game's aesthetic perfectly. It hides all sorts of little imperfections and just makes it all that much cooler. I like it better like that for the same reasons I prefer a fuzzy drowned-in-noise Jesus and Mary Chain guitar to some contemporary over-produced Pro Tools crap: for the warmth. Like Vinyl [vs.] CD. I think pixels have reached that status.[11]

What Fish is describing in the vernacular is a phenomenon that media theorists Bolter and Grusin call *remediation*.[12] As particular media technologies mature, we become comfortable with them and the artifacts that they bring to representation—the grain on celluloid film-stock that began as a barrier to capturing the "true" image ceases to be seen as noise, and instead becomes a hallmark of authenticity. The aesthetic becomes detached from the necessity of the technology. This kind of cross-over is a longstanding trope of media development: for example, in the late 1880s adherents of Pictorialism, one of the dominant movements in early photography, strove for soft focus and lighting in an attempt to make their photographs appear like paintings. In a train of thought paradoxical to today's concept of "photorealism," paintings simply felt more natural to pictorialists than did the unfamiliar harshness of unfiltered photography.

Games are no stranger to remediation. As 3-D game technologies advanced in the mid-1990s (most notably on the PC and Sony's PlayStation console), graphics programmers looked for ways to bring an aura of "realism" to their images. One effect they often used was the "lens flare," the blinding white starbursts and concentric rings that form when an optical lens catches a bright light source. These were especially popular in leading titles with urban settings, like *Gran Turismo 3 A-Spec* (SCEA, 2001) and *Grand Theft Auto: Vice City* (Rockstar Games, 2002). For a while, lens flares were the game graphics state of the art, part of the ecosystem, from the evaluative criteria of game reviewers to the selling points of third-party game engine licensers. The irony, of course, is that lens flares are the artifacts of curvature in physical optics, an old media signature injected into the new for legitimization. As with film grain, the lens flare no longer obscures the image, but instead has been integrated into its definition. Similarly, Fish's enthusiasm for *Mass Effect*'s film grain emerges from the dialectic of Bolter and Grusin's "double logic of remediation": an ideal of immediacy—the "pure, sharp 100% digital image"—mitigated by hypermediacy, the awareness and exploitation of a medium's artificiality. The unreality of one medium helps to make the other feel subjectively "real."

Remediation also happens "locally": as a medium evolves, its earlier stages begin to be remediated within it. The emphasis on legitimization or realism fades, and remediation drifts from a fallback to a conscious stylistic choice, a tactic for evoking and re-interpreting the medium's past, an expert vehicle for the homage, the parody, or the genre revival. This is where remediation meets retro. The technique is relatively new to gaming, but it is richly developed in other media like film and music. For example, in the film *Pleasantville* (Gary Ross, 1998), two present-day teenagers are transported into a black and white, suburban 1950s-style alternate reality. The monochrome presentation of the world evokes its mid-century American naïveté, and as viewers we understand this connection because of our familiarity with actual television shows of that period. The original, technical requirement of black and white film and broadcasting is long gone, but in our historical memory it is closely associated with the content it represented. The twin sociological and technological transitions of the past five decades become the backbone of the film's symbolism: as elements of 1990s modernism slowly seep into 1950s innocence, the world is literally colorized, one character, building, and flower at a time. *La-Mulana* extends this logic from film hardware to game hardware: it is an MSX *platform remediation*, and as we have seen, evocation through technological aesthetics is similarly central to its origins.

But in terms of both aesthetic presentation and formal ambitions, perhaps a more apt film comparison than *Pleasantville* would be avant-garde film-maker Guy Maddin's *The Saddest Music in the World* (2003). Shot in a varying pastiche of early film tropes, including black and white (with some color sequences), heavy film grain, and fuzzy iris lens-induced edges, the plot centers on a bizarre musical competition set in 1930s Winnipeg, and "evokes Busby Berkeley musicals, silent melodramas and Depression-era studio fantasies of wealth, romance, and intrigue."[13] Most notably, a shock of temporal displacement marks the critical reception of both *Saddest Music* and *La-Mulana*, with reviewers in each case expressing the disorienting (and undeniably striking) simultaneity of a technologically dated presentation paired with a contemporary sensibility:

> *La-Mulana*: "You get the feeling that the history of video games went awry about 20 years ago, and that *La-Mulana* somehow came to us through a wormhole from a beautiful parallel universe." (ActionButton.net)
> *Saddest Music*: "[S]eems to pop out of an otherworldly time capsule. It is a tribute to, and a sendup of, old movies that never quite existed. . . . delving into a past that never was to prophesy an alternative vision of the future of movies." (Scott)

That the retro mode created by the remediation of *La-Mulana* and *The Saddest Music in the World* is expressed in science fiction or mystical terms of "time travel" belies the degree to which we historicize the aesthetics of our technologies. This notion of generative retro views the past neither reverently nor quaintly, but instead, as Elizabeth Guffey says, with an "unsentimental nostalgia."[14] Retro is delineated from the more classical form of revivalism, which while taking great pleasure in the past nonetheless considered it from a detached perspective, as a "completed" protocol rather than as a still viable branch of evolution. This retro strategy is to mix up recognizable components of past aesthetic styles and genres, reassembling them into previously unseen forms.

From these examples, we see retro as a unique subset of artistic inspiration and influence: retro carries with it a source of *discontinuous* influence, resemblance coupled with temporal distance. This is distinct from the more generally incremental nature of game design, such as the step-by-step evolution of the "matching tile" puzzle game genre over more than 20 years, traced by Jesper Juul from *Chain Shot!* (Kuniaki Moribe, 1985), to *Dr. Mario* (Nintendo, 1990), to *Bejeweled* (PopCap Games, 2001).[15] Retro media, on the other hand, is not that which innovates upon its direct parents, but rather those ancestors which are unequivocally "outdated." Of course, the determination of currency vs. obsolescence is itself imprecise and up for debate. But broadly speaking, creative industries that are structured upon cyclical change have a particular predilection to retro as phenomenon and rhetoric. This is no doubt why fashion was at the center of the term's establishment by 1970s French critics (Guffey, 14). Gaming hardware may not be quite as pliable as fabrics and colors, but the breakneck leapfrogging of technology and periodic turnover of game consoles provides a built-in obsolescence that almost guarantees the emergence of retro gaming. The aesthetic potential of a game platform is only beginning to be understood by the time it is discontinued commercially.

Beyond Commercial Conservatism

A comparison to the field of titles marketed by the commercial game industry under a "retro" moniker can help to further contextualize *La-Mulana*'s distinct approach and originality. Generally speaking, there are two forms that currently dominate commercial retro gaming: emulation, and remakes. Today, the commercial emulation product with the most exposure is probably the Nintendo Wii's Virtual Console. This service allows players to purchase individual titles that originally appeared on older game platforms of the 8-bit and 16-bit families (and beyond), including Nintendo's own systems (the NES, Super NES, and Nintendo 64), as well as those of past rivals such as Sega's Master System and Genesis, NEC's TurboGrafx-16, and even the MSX itself (available only to Japanese Virtual Console customers). Games on Virtual Console range from $5 to $10 apiece, and the service has been widely successful, generating $33 million on sales of 7.8 million titles in its first two years of availability.[16]

The games on Virtual Console are emulated, which means that even though the game program is "hosted" for the player on the contemporary Wii platform, the original game code is maintained, running via an intermediary program (an emulator) that simulates the CPU, graphics chips, and other computational functions of the original platform for which it was compiled. In this sense, emulation attempts to re-create the "real experience" of particular classic games. Because the game's code is the same, its rules and mechanics are identical to the original, and it should (theoretically) respond to player input in exactly the same way. In most cases, the graphical pixels of 2-D games are also accurately preserved. Of course, emulation never produces a true replica of a native platform: input devices with differing material qualities and control layouts affect the player's physical interaction; the need to up-scale graphics for display on higher resolution screens alters the quality of their appearance, and so on. And emulators can consciously introduce new capabilities to the platform as well, such as the Wii's ability to instantly suspend or "save state" at any point during play (rather than relying on the individual game's own save mechanisms), increasing convenience and easing the difficulty level. (However, it is worth noting that unlike more flexible emulators, the Virtual Console does not allow the player to save several states individually, instead providing for only one state to be saved at a time—in other words, a global "pause" button rather than a "rewind" function.)

An important distinction of philosophy and operation is that while emulation actually *enacts* a platform at the computational level, *La-Mulana* selectively *imitates* the platform's aesthetic hallmarks as a vehicle for stylization. *La-Mulana*'s developers may have carefully followed the

MSX1's most immediately visible properties (such as resolution, palette selection, and spatial color distribution), but there are many technical aspects of the platform that are not adopted or enforced. These include fundamental low-level structural elements, such as the maximum addressable memory space, or the lack of a linear frame-buffer representation for the video display—often significant hurdles to programmers writing real-time graphics code on an actual MSX. And while these limitations could be dealt with through skilled coding, *La-Mulana*'s programmers, developing on the much more "friendly" and flexible environment of the modern Windows-compatible PC, were able to conveniently skip these challenges, and instead implement only those ultimately resulting visual artifacts which they deemed relevant and necessary to their goal of aesthetic association. In some circumstances, such differences in the production process may not be detectable to the player at all. Yet in other cases, *La-Mulana* does flaunt some MSX1 specs, bending the color distribution rules for the player sprite of Professor Lemeza (adding a thin black outline to make the character more legible), and ignoring the flicker caused by more than four simultaneous sprites per line. It is possible that the extra color employed for the player sprite might be achievable on the MSX1 through multi-sprite overlay techniques (in which two sprites are stacked upon one another) or other tricks. But *La-Mulana*'s pixel artist gave himself the benefit of the doubt, and left us with a hypothetical question.

Microsoft's Xbox Live Arcade (XBLA), the downloadable game arm of the Xbox 360 console, is an illuminating contrast of a different sort. Unlike the Virtual Console, XBLA is not an exclusively retro service, and contemporary original titles are featured alongside classic games of the 1980s and 1990s. Nonetheless, a significant portion of the catalog is comprised of older titles, including many of its bestselling games in 2007, such as the *Teenage Mutant Ninja Turtles* arcade game (Konami, 1989), and *Castlevania: Symphony of the Night* (1997, PlayStation).[17] While the retro appeal of the two services is similarly title-nostalgia-centric, XBLA's retro strategy is not based purely on emulation of existing code and audiovisuals. Instead, many titles are offered as remakes (also known as ports) that have been rebuilt for the Xbox 360 from the ground up, incorporating all-new "enhanced" graphics that leave behind low-res pixels in favor of a visual aesthetic more in-line with today's mainstream commercial games. Sometimes this means a new set of high-resolution 2-D images that aim to preserve the stylistic spirit of the original, such as with *Yie Ar Kung-Fu*'s (Konami, 1985 [2007]) self-proclaimed "stunning hand-painted models and backgrounds."[18] In other cases like *Jetpac Refuelled* (Microsoft Game Studios, 2007) and *Prince of Persia Classic* (Ubisoft, 2007), the hand-drawn 2-D sprites have been replaced entirely with renderings of 3-D models.

While maintaining the look of older games is a basic assumption on Nintendo's Virtual Console, there is no such preference for historical fidelity in these XBLA titles. (It should be noted however, that not all XBLA classics feature altered graphics; some of the lesser known titles like *Cyberball 2072* (Midway, 1988 [2007]) and *Root Beer Tapper* (Midway, 1983 [2007])—those which would most likely attract a smaller niche nostalgia crowd—retain the original visuals, and most of the enhanced titles still offer this option as well.) On the contrary, from a marketing standpoint, the shift in representational modes of these "re-skinned" remakes is an unequivocal attraction unrelated to their nostalgic authenticity:

> *Jetpac Refuelled*: "The completely updated graphical look of the game gives you a truly hi-def and in-depth gaming experience."[19]

> *Prince of Persia Classic*: "This new version features updated character designs, animations, visuals, and lighting effects, all transforming the game into a fresh, close to 3-dimensional look."[20]

In many regards, Virtual Console and XBLA are both valuable and popular services that regard classic gaming seriously not only as a commercial enterprise, but also as an important element of game culture. And both have made interesting contributions to the nascent field of retro gaming: XBLA adds a layer of community-oriented features on top of its classic remakes, taking advantage of a networked environment to offer online play (a novelty for titles of the 1980s), leader boards (top scores that can be viewed by players across the world), and "achievements" (game-specific goals that display accolades on a player's online profile, creating a framework for comparison across disparate titles). On Virtual Console, Nintendo has ventured beyond the strict nostalgia market by offering games like *Battle Lode Runner* (Hudson Soft), a 1993 title for the PC Engine (the Japanese market name for the TurboGrafx-16) that was previously unreleased in the USA. Yet when we pull back to a larger perspective, both services are also fundamentally conservative because they are focused on recycling existing game designs (or in more business-oriented terms, their goal is to maximize existing intellectual property (IP) value through re-packaging). Virtual Console is at best about preservation. XBLA recognizes the opportunity to re-contextualize retro games in new ways that resonate with today's gamers, but adopts the predominant, self-sure industry view that technology is the path to improvement: it is time to dust off those old neglected games and bring them up to snuff. Both are based on title-specific (sometimes franchise-specific) nostalgia, intended to attract players by evoking childhood memories of particular games.

La-Mulana's MSX platform remediation turns this notion inside-out.

Nostalgia still plays a key role, but the focus is shifted from specific game content—recognizable characters, trademark game mechanics, worlds, or storylines—to the more abstract concept of platform-centric nostalgia. *La-Mulana* could be called an anti-XBLA game: rather than arranging contemporary technologies around a kernel of historical gameplay, its developers have flipped the proposition, creating an original title that is driven by the aesthetic guidelines of past technological constraints. Both approaches are viable, and the comparison is theoretically interesting because it helps us to examine the interdependence between alternating formal, historical, and technological game elements—and the effects of changing one, but not the others. The commercial view of retro as a hobby of collecting things is certainly a commonly accepted one outside and irrespective of games; it is popularly expressed in trends such as "vintage" clothing at thrift stores, or 1960s plastic and glass furniture at higher-end boutiques. But *La-Mulana* is a more transformative interpretation: like the best retro precedents, the game "challenges positivist views of technology, industry, and, most of all, of progress itself" (Guffey, 13).

Indie Retro: The Stylistic Traces of Materiality

La-Mulana has been my primary example of this "indie retro" trend in part because it is such an excellent game, but also because it is so well-defined in its approach to technology and genre. But the phenomenon is fast-growing, and there are many creative indie games that employ the platform remediation calling card to varying degrees, with styles that span the past 20 years; new specimens appear weekly on blogs like The Independent Gaming Source, and IndieGames.com: The Weblog. The tongue-in-cheek *Shotgun Ninja* (2008), for instance, is a fast, precision action platformer that borrows its 16 color palette and oblong-shaped pixels from the Commodore 64 (C64), the beloved 8-bit home computer (far more popular worldwide than the MSX, in fact, with roughly six times as many sales). Designed by Jonatan Söderström, a prolific Swedish indie developer known online as Cactus (creator of the Independent Games Festival 2008 finalist *Clean Asia* (2007)), the game is both clearly inspired by the C64—the executable filename is c64ninja.exe—and also blatantly at odds with it: the C64's pixels were similarly rectangular, but they were fat, horizontal rectangles (at 160 × 200 resolution), while *Shotgun Ninja*'s are tall and thin (with an effectively 320 × 120 screen). It is the kind of mis-matched, technical mash-up found in Maddin's *The Saddest Music in the World*, which caught reviewer A. O. Scott off guard with its silent film-era visuals acting as vehicle for a heavily vocal musical.

Another commercially abandoned genre that maintains a strong indie following are "shmups," shoot-'em-ups in the style of classic 2-D scrolling shooters such as *Gradius* (Konami, 1985) and *R-Type* (Irem, 1987), in which the player usually controls a "ship," navigating complex patterns of "bullets." While there are a dizzying number of indie shmups of all technological stripes (2-D and 3-D), *HoneyBlaster* (LowFuel, 2007, featuring a honeybee theme) and *Guxt* (Pixel, 2007, with a more genre-traditional aircraft) are two that employ a monochrome gradient look. They mimic the washed-out colors and ghosting artifacts of primitive, unlit LCD screens, such as those found on the original handheld Game Boy platform (released 1989). Moreover, their pixel resolutions are even lower than *La-Mulana* (120×160 and 160×100, respectively). *Beluga Mk II* (T. Matsushima, 2008) takes a different approach: a horizontal shooter with an astronaut protagonist, it has a four-color palette of bright, fully-saturated green, blue, red, and yellow, and uses an unusual fuzz filter that gives the graphics a blur and bleed strongly reminiscent of 1980s CRT (cathode ray tube) televisions. Each of these games is notable in foregrounding the physical effects of earlier display technologies, going beyond the aspects of color and pixel resolution governed by CPUs and graphics chips to embrace the optical properties of the screen itself. *Beluga Mk II* recalls a childhood spent 12 inches from the TV screen.

In the indie retro titles above, platform association is evoked vaguely, but not as a priority. *La-Mulana* is still rare in its explicit coupling to a specific platform, and this has made it a focused example—a more common strategy is to cherry-pick 8-bit hallmarks without aiming to re-create a holistic platform aesthetic. *Beluga Mk II* cheerfully proclaims "FOUR COLORS SYSTEM" and "8BITS COLOR COMPUTER" on its load screen, but targets no particular brand of console or home computer. The inspiration is not limited to computers of the 1980s though, either. *Cave Story* (a widely used English translation of the original Japanese title, *Doukutsu Monogatari*) (Pixel, 2005) is an action-adventure platformer that shares many genre qualities with *La-Mulana*, and garnered extensive gaming press following its release in 2005 (rare for an indie title, then and now). Its technological aesthetic is a "16-bit" analog to *La-Mulana*'s 8-bit MSX, with a full 256 color palette, higher 320×240 resolution, smooth high-speed scrolling including parallax background layers, and hundreds of sprites across a continuous multi-screen space, suggesting the era of the Super NES and Genesis consoles. *Cave Story*'s lush backgrounds and detailed characters recall Hayao Miyazaki's Studio Ghibli films such as *My Neighbor Totoro* (1988) and *Princess Mononoke* (1997)—the game's graphics are key to its personality and mood, and the endearing characters that make its story come to life simply could not be created under *La-Mulana*'s 8-bit conditions.

Figure 9.9 *Beluga Mk II* evokes a fuzzy Cathode Ray Tube television with its blurry and cheerfully bright blue, green, red, and yellow colors.

In theoretical terms, there is nothing about this game design strategy that makes it *inherent* (or limited) to independent producers. And encouragingly, we can find small pockets of the commercial industry where such a style is possible: notably, *Game Center CX* (Namco Bandai, 2007) for the Nintendo DS, a clever retro game inspired by a popular Japanese television show of the same name. In the TV series, the comedian Shinya Arino plays (and often completes) games from the 8 and 16-bit eras, his progress charted in a reality show format. The DS game is an outlandish adaptation in which you play as an elementary school-aged gamer, taking on short (but not mini) 8-bit-style games in the most popular console genres of the 1980s, including shmups, platformers, top-down racing, and even an RPG. As with the indie games discussed so far, *Game Center CX*'s "faux retrogames" (as Chris Kohler describes them[21]) are carefully-crafted throwbacks through and through, from their look to their gameplay (in this case the NES is the clearest platform of reference). But its most impressive twist, reminiscent of *La-Mulana*'s extensive (and crucially helpful) 1980s-era instruction manual, is the inclusion of an overarching meta-game that requires the player to peruse fake magazines (in-game, on the DS screen itself), seeking out hints and cheat codes necessary for completing specific challenges—like "Clear Floor 4 without losing a single life"—within each sub-game (Kohler). As is *La-Mulana*'s aim, this last structural element ties contemporary influence (think Xbox Live's achievements) back into a firm retro grounding, commenting on gaming's history in parallel.

Yet *Game Center CX*'s retro creativity is still very much a commercial exception. On the whole, indie developers have considerably more freedom to play with our aesthetic expectations. Without the same financial pressure or corporate structures, they are able to push game genres, platforms, interfaces, and audiovisuals into unusual (sometimes unintended or counterintuitive) territory, presenting juxtapositions that might be commercially risky, unviable, or illogical. Neither are they bound by traditional development cycles—indie designers like Cactus often complete games from start to finish in under three days, a radical, one-off approach far beyond even the most progressive forms of rapid prototyping employed by commercial development houses. Indie retro creates a new field of production, maturing the medium of video games by moving off-axis from commercial concerns.

Notes

1. ActionButton.net, review of *La-Mulana* (GR3 Project), available online at <http://www.actionbutton.net/?p=193>; hereafter cited as ActionButton.net.
2. Nick Montfort and Ian Bogost, *Video Computer System: The Atari 2600 Platform* (Cambridge, MA: MIT Press, forthcoming).
3. Dean Takahashi, *Opening the Xbox* (Roseville, CA: Prima Publishing, 2002), 76.
4. Msxnet, "Konami SCC Sound Chip," technical reference, available online at <http://bifi.msxnet.org/msxnet/tech/scc.html; Wikipedia, "Konami SCC," technical reference, http://en.wikipedia.org/wiki/Konami_SCC> (February 8, 2008).
5. Instruction manual, translated by Aeon Genesis, *La-Mulana*, Windows, GR3 Project, 2005, available online at <http://agtp.romhack.net/project.php?id=lamulana>; hereafter cited as Instruction manual.
6. English translators' notes ["La-Mulana Readme.text"], *La-Mulana*, Windows, GR3 Project, 2005, available online at <http://agtp.romhack.net/project.php?id=lamulana>.
7. Jesper Juul, *Half-Real: Video Games between Real Rules and Fictional Worlds* (Cambridge, MA: MIT Press, 2005), 139.
8. Kyle Orland, review of *Milon's Secret Castle* (Hudson Soft), *Games for Lunch*, December 13, 2007, available online at <http://gamesforlunch.blogspot.com/2007/12/milons-secret-castle.html>.
9. Jeremy Parish, "Metroidvania Chronicles: Faxanadu," review of *Faxanadu* (Hudson Soft), available online at <http://www.gamespite.net/toastywiki/index.php/Site/Metroidvania09 Faxanadu>.
10. YouTube, "Playlist: Let's Play La-Mulana," video playlist, available online at <http://www.youtube.com/view_play_list?p=25D2DC18FBD81577> (February 8, 2008).
11. Phil Fish, interview, *Arthouse Games*, available online at <http://northcountrynotes.org/jason-rohrer/arthouseGames/seedBlogs.php?action=display_post&post_id=jcr13_119604 1006_0&show_author=1&show_ date=1>.
12. Jay David Bolter and Richard Grusin, *Remediation: Understanding New Media* (Cambridge, MA: MIT Press, 1999).
13. A. O. Scott, "Wallowing in Music for the Miserable, Then Splashing Down in a Giant Vat of

Beer," review of *The Saddest Music in the World* (film), *New York Times*, April 30, 2004, available online at <http://query.nytimes.com/gst/fullpage.html?res=9E02EFD D173DF933A05757C0A9629C8B63>; hereafter cited as Scott.

14. Elizabeth E. Guffey, *Retro: The Culture of Revival* (London: Reaktion Books, 2006), 17; hereafter cited as Guffey.

15. Jesper Juul, "Swap Adjacent Gems to Make Sets of Three: A History of Matching Tile Games," *Artifact Journal*, 2007, 1(4): 205–216, available online at <http://www.jesperjuul. net/text/swapadjacent/>.

16. Anoop Gantayat, "Virtual Console Numbers Revealed," *IGN Entertainment*, (November 28, 2007), available online at <http://wii.ign.com/articles/838/838286p1.html>.

17. Brandon Boyer, "Top 2007 Xbox Live Games Show Retro Success," *Gamasutra.com* (January 7, 2008), available online at <http://www.gamasutra.com/php-bin/news_index.php? story=16051>.

18. Microsoft, "*Yie Ar Kung Fu*," product description, available online at <http:// www.xbox.com/en-US/games/y/yiearkungfuxboxlivearcade/> (accessed February 8, 2008).

19. Microsoft, "*Jetpac Refuelled*," product description, available online at <http:// www.xbox.com/en-US/games/j/jetpacrefuelledxboxlivearcade/> (accessed February 8, 2008).

20. Microsoft, "*Prince of Persia Classic*," product description, available online at <http://www. xbox.com/en-US/games/p/princeofpersiaxboxlivearcade/> (accessed February 8, 2008).

21. Chris Kohler, "A Tour Through *Game Center CX*'s Faux Retrogames," *Wired*, November 16, 2007, available online at <http://blog.wired.com/games/2007/11/a-tour-through.html>; hereafter cited as Kohler.

CHAPTER 10

"This is Intelligent Television"
Early Video Games and Television in the Emergence of the Personal Computer

SHEILA C. MURPHY

My essay's title is taken from an advertising campaign for Mattel's Intellivision, a home video game system that was first launched in 1979–1980. When writing about gaming, television, and computers, I could not resist Mattel's "This is intelligent television" slogan, which simultaneously encapsulates the bad object status of television and promotes the game system as an engaging and cultured alternative to watching reruns. Mattel's print and television advertisements for the system, which starred erudite pundit George Plimpton, sought to brand the Intellivision as a thought-provoking, "smart" video game system, something that current advertisements for Nintendo's *BrainAge* series (2005–2007) continue to do today. While the Intellivision was released later than most of the systems I am discussing here, the system and its promotional campaign perfectly demonstrate the rhetorical "muck" that early video game systems were caught in when making both figurative and literal connections between television, gaming, and computers. And it is these connections—between discreet media that share certain commonalities (most notably, a screen)—that I am concerned with here. For rather than theorize a particular genre, mode of interactivity, or process of identification, I suggest we look more closely at video game systems themselves—as media apparatuses, as sites of representation, and as the starting points for what scholars today now refer to as "*media convergence.*"[1]

I began this essay as part of a larger project that places the history of video games into the context of digital media theory and the histories of computers and television. While computers, video games and digital media are often part of the same set of conversations, the medium of television is usually only given passing consideration as, quite literally, a "medium" through which this other, newer media "flows."[2] I believe that television's role in digital media history, especially its place in the historical development of digital entertainment technologies like video game systems and computers, should instead be emphasized and understood as crucial to new media history and theory. For the then-new technologies of the 1970s like the personal computer and video game, television lent more than a basic display apparatus; instead, one finds that the literal links between TV sets and (home or video game) computers were established in relationship to the cultural baggage already associated with television by that time.[3] We can see the way television and video games were imagined together in the inside-cover illustration from the 1982 Atari catalogue. Centered in the image and hovering above an Atari Video Computer System, a television set displaying a *Pac-Man* start screen is the destination for rows of games streaming towards it. Underneath, the Atari system rests atop a *Tron*-style white grid on a black background. The message of this game catalog is clear—together TV and Atari can offer numerous, enjoyable routes towards interactive fun.

Often lauded as a "breakthrough" period for television programming and technologies—with the emergence of PBS, "quality" situation comedies and the rise of cable—television in the 1970s was also understood as a time of cheap formats and exploitative series that former FCC Chair Newton Minow had dubbed the "vast wasteland" of TV in 1961.[4] Such a repositioning of television has crucial theoretical ramifications for video games and video game theory because it expands our understanding of video game theory to include television as a medium, technology, and space of encounter for digital gaming.

Why *Not* Convergence?

It is crucial to disentangle some of the assumed and seemingly naturalized connections between television, personal computers, and video game systems in order to better understand the relationships between these media forms. In order to carefully approach 1970s gaming systems and television, there are certain key questions to ask: what were the connections between television sets, video games, and personal computers during the first home video game craze in the late 1970s? How was the public reception of video games and computers linked to television? And in what ways did these new technologies promise to remake and reframe TV?

The idea of technological and cultural convergence is relevant here and requires some explanation.[5] "Convergence" is one of those techno-buzz words that seems both to emblematize *and* to mystify new technologies. Yet if we take the idea of convergence seriously, it can be a quite useful way of approaching the field of digital culture/new media studies. One dictionary definition of convergence describes the term as it relates to mathematical, biological, and physiological studies, as well as its common definition as "a point of converging, a meeting place." In each of its subject-specific definitions, convergence is described as a kind of merging of data—be it the establishment of a finite limit in math, the physiological "turning of the eyes inward to focus on an object at close range," or its biological definition as the "similarity of form or structure caused by environment rather than heredity." What all of these definitions share and what is useful here is that this coming together—this merging—results in a new grouping or formation—a new model for understanding previously disparate data or information. It is also crucial to my enterprise to understanding gaming, computers, and television that we take note that in these scientific fields convergence describes pre-existing formal shifts discovered and detailed using field-specific methodologies. By using a term like "convergence" we risk perpetuating the notion that cross-media configurations are themselves *naturally* occurring phenomena rather than the result of technological innovation, business strategies, and larger economic and cultural forces.

Other theorists have also noted the cultural and economic shifts leading towards media "convergence." The list of what we might call "convergence theorists" includes Paul Virilio,[6] Siegfried Zielinski,[7] Friedrich Kittler,[8] Henry Jenkins,[9] and Brian Winston,[10] among others. Winston traces out a history of media technologies that connects telegraphy, telephony, radio, television, videocassette recorders, computers, cable and satellite transmissions, and the Internet into a history of technological innovations connected together by their use as communications media (Winston). While Winston does not predict that these technologies will merge, he does make deep connections between them and ends by predicting that holographic television will be part of the future of these technologies. Siegfried Zielinski, however, does theorize that visual/media culture is progressing towards "advanced audiovision," which will combine the cinematic and the televisual into "a complex kit of machines, storage devices, and programs for the reproduction, simulation, and blending of what can be seen and heard, where the trend is toward their capability of being connected together in a network" (Zielinski, 19). Henry Jenkins describes how much of the discourse around convergence relies upon what he has termed the "black box fallacy" that all media will eventually flow through a singular black box into the home. According to Jenkins, "media convergence is not an endpoint; rather, it is an ongoing process occurring at various intersections between media technologies, industries, content, and audiences."[11] Media use has changed in ways that, as Jenkins tells it, exceed the much-hyped "digital revolution." Jenkins' (Fans, 155) essay details just how "new media technologies . . . enable consumers to archive, annotate, transform, and recirculate media content." While academic interest in media convergence is relatively new (and roughly contingent with the emergence of the field of new media studies), gamers and computer users have been practicing convergence for decades as they connect televisions, computers, consoles, speakers and other media equipment into work/life/entertainment systems.

I should also note that, while varying technological components may be merging with one another and have been doing so since the very first oscilloscope/computer game moment, actual media convergence implies that the representations and images produced by each apparatus would also converge.[12] Yet, in the case of television, computers, and gaming, one can use one technology in conjunction with another to produce discrete media forms and experiences—a game or a television program, a spreadsheet or a game—not both at once. One can now *switch* between a device's various modes, experiencing the television receiver as television, computer, game, each with its discrete modes of reception and interactivity. I cannot *play* an episode of *Maude* (CBS, 1972–1978) with any greater success than I can *watch* a game of *Asteroids* (Atari, 1979).[13] Instead, the act of switching between these functions becomes a crucial semiotic link, remapping the machine as the screen flashes, blinks, goes black, ready to become my computer and not be my television set—at least not at the same time.[14]

Resetting the Set: Making Television a Game Computer

Much like Stephen Johnson's compelling discussion of video games and cognition in *Everything Bad is Good For You: How Today's Popular Culture Is Actually Making Us Smarter*,[15] my argument is that some of the most crucial technological and cultural innovations of video games have largely gone unnoticed while other, more "readable" aspects of gaming continue to garner media attention.[16] What I am *not* arguing here is that video games are culturally, morally, or aesthetically good or bad.[17] Instead it is essential to understand how the history of video game systems intersects with the history of television. By understanding the connections between early home gaming systems, TVs, and computers, one can re-situate the televisual apparatus within the common historical and theoretical narratives of new media/gaming. Crucial to this discussion is understanding how the boom of the early video game industry brought computers into the home and then connected them (the game system/computer) to the television set during the mid to late 1970s. In many ways, the television receiver served as a stable and familiar referent for consumers and users who were first learning to read the semiotics of the new personal computers and video game systems being connected up to more recognizable television set.

While the 1980s are widely lauded for the rise of multinational, post-industrial corporations, the widespread use of personal computers in domestic and professional environments and the emergence of the "cultural logic of postmodernism," the 1970s were when key computing inventions and innovations occurred, in both academic contexts and by individual computing enthusiasts who "homebrewed" their own devices.[18] Developed by early adopters, researchers, and hobbyists, these first personal computers were spectacles as much for what they did as for the very fact of their existence. While the Homebrew Computing Club members were building computers from kits, developments in the leisure industry were leading to some similar innovations.

At the same time that these ostensibly more serious and task-oriented personal computers were being developed, entrepreneurs were producing home gaming systems that attempted to capitalize upon the popular 1970s video game arcade trend. Home console games connected to a television set, which was used as the visual display or screen that enabled game play to take place, just as video game systems with external software programs continue to do today. Console games have programs hardwired onto the technology itself, as exemplified by the early Sears Home PONG (1975) manufactured by Atari and the Magnavox Odyssey (1972). Home gaming systems might include such hardwired games or are programmable "low level home computers" whose users can swap out cartridges ("carts") to play new games or use ancillary devices to expand the functionality of the gaming system (Winston, 232). Contemporary home gaming systems like Microsoft's XBox 360, Sony's PlayStation 3, and the Nintendo Wii all function according to these same technological structures: they plug into the television or "home theater system" directly, game software is run off of compact disc or digital video disc media played using a basic computer in conjunction with stored data such as memory cards loaded with previously saved gameplay (or on-board memory and a hard drive). The user then interacts with the game using a range of input devices like paddles, joysticks, or other handheld controllers. Like the early Atari, Magnavox,

Fairchild, Coleco, and Mattel systems produced between 1972 and 1983, contemporary home gaming systems utilize the television receiver as the "gaming computer's" visual display.[19]

Television's Role in the History of Video Games

Research and development of home video gaming systems began as early as the mid-1960s (not counting Willy Higginbotham's oscilloscope *Tennis for Two* "video game" displayed in the sole location of the Brookhaven National Laboratory in 1958). In 1968, engineer Ralph Baer applied for the first video game patent[20] and began to develop the system that would eventually be released as the Magnavox Odyssey in 1972.[21] When Baer began to approach television manufacturers to market and sell his gaming system he was surprised to find that he had to deal with the public perception that television was for *watching*, not *playing*.[22] According to Leonard Herman's *Phoenix: The Rise and Fall of the Video Game*, "Baer quickly learned that it wasn't just a simple matter of calling up a television manufacturer and telling them that he had a great new product that would interest them. He first had to make people realized that games *could* be played via a television set and that nothing could go wrong with the television should the player do something wrong" (Herman, 7). Television was perceived as a mysterious technology, one that brought media into the home but whose internal workings were complex. This perception of television technology as strange and mysterious was a legacy from the first waves of television's domestic postwar popularity, when viewers were unaccustomed to such complex electronic home technologies.[23]

By the time that Atari's breakthrough Sears Home PONG console was released, consumers were ready to play with and on their TVs. This shift towards seeing the television as a playable consumer device is crucial. While the histories of both computing and mass media contain important contributions from amateurs and hobbyists, the widespread public acceptance and use of home video game systems by a broader audience indicates that consumers were rethinking television's role as a home technology in the mid-1970s. Gaming systems at this time were proto-computers, hardwired to play certain games and were often promoted in connection to promised future features that would allow the systems to function as personal computers with keyboards and other input devices. By the time Atari released its Video Computer System in 1977, people were ready to see TVs as more than just an "idiot box" for viewing. Instead one could approach television as part of both a larger entertainment system and as an interactive "computer." At the same time, network television programming was in the midst of its own shift in cultural rhetoric, with the appearance of social relevant "quality" television programs and televisual events like the Norman Lear and MTM sitcoms and the mini-series *Roots* (ABC, 1977). Using today's parlance we might say that television, as a techno/cultural apparatus, was in the midst of an "extreme makeover" during the latter part of the 1970s. By being able to repurpose television receivers with add-on technologies like video gaming systems, one could, quite literally, transform the television set, turning it into a computer or, more precisely, a computer peripheral.

This shift in attitudes towards TV technology was largely on a conceptual level—part of an imagined nexus of home connectivity that did not yet exist at that time. We see this even in the naming of Atari's system. Video game historian Leonard Herman notes, "Although it has the word *computer* in its name, the VCS was not a computer in the fullest sense. The only thing that console could do was play games with the insertion of a cartridge. It had no other practical purpose" (Herman, 27). Practicality, utility, and function eventually became defining elements of personal computers, while the leisure-based and non-utilitarian "toy" aspects of interactive digital devices that connected up to visual displays would become elided with video game systems and the nascent gaming industry. As Charles Bernstein has noted, video games can be understood as a specific kind of computer, one that is "neutered of purpose, liberated from functionality."[24] This division of work/computer and play/video games quickly became entrenched. Yet there were overlaps between gaming systems and personal computers on many fronts—perhaps most notably in the employment of computing entrepreneurs Steve Jobs and Steve Wozniak at Atari, where, under Nolan Bushnell, the two raised funds for their garage-based Atari company by designing early Atari games like *Breakout* (1976). So, *literally*, video games were a technical and economic starting point for the personal computer industry.

The history of 1970s and early1980s home video game systems—historically labeled by fans through reference to the "generations" of hardware in a system—is riddled with domestic technologies that promised to do more than simply play games.[25] Instead, these systems were sold as high-priced toys that might also be linked to other, more "productive" activities like writing, coding, or playing music. While this is speculation based upon my research, I believe that video game and toy manufacturers were anxious about the relatively high cost and potentially limited replayability of their devices, so promises were made about add-on features that were rarely developed in order to justify the high price of a gaming system. Likewise, the connotation of games or toys could be improved through an association with computers and educational technologies. In the first decade of the video game industry's commercial penetration into the home market, gaming companies also produced home computer models, most notably the Atari 400 and 800 PCs and the Colecovision version of the company's ADAM home computer.[26]

The list of video game systems with promised or realized computer elements is long. It includes the Mattel Intellivision's keyboard component that was eventually scraped, the Atari 400 and 800 line of 8-bit computers, the Magnavox Odyssey[2] with its alphanumeric keyboard (1978), the Colecovision ADAM (with add-on parts for gaming system and stand-alone computer versions produced), Sega's SC-3000 (computer) version of its SG-1000 video game system (1983) as well as the SG-1000 Mark II (a 1984 Japanese release), a game system with a keyboard.[27] Later Sega also licensed their Mega Drive/Genesis hardware for inclusion in the Mega PC produced by Armstead and marketed as a home gaming computer in 1992–93 for a European/UK market, and Microsoft's 2001 XBox entry into the video game market significantly included a hard drive, Ethernet networking capabilities and "all in one" features that blur the distinctions between gaming system, home theater/entertainment system, and computer, turning the software giant into a new player in the hardware business.[28] These system designs indicate an industry-wide investment in framing gaming systems in relation to *both* computers and television. As German media theorist Siegfried Zielinski has declared, these efforts were "an expansion of the traditional television experience" in which television receivers and, eventually, dedicated computer monitors, were "new perception surfaces" for "the interface of man and media-machine" (Zielinski, 228). Atari's efforts to link gaming, computers, and television are an instructive example of how such multi-media efforts played out.

Candy and Colleen: The Atari Line of Personal Computers

In this history of now mostly forgotten gaming computer systems, I want to foreground Atari's efforts to produce computers for the domestic market during the 1970s, largely because Atari's eventually failed home computers were designed with television in mind (see Figure 10.1). The systems were configured to hook up to a television receiver and use it as a monitor, much like home video game systems do. Atari's 400 ($499) and 800 ($999), also known by the internal nicknames Colleen and Candy (after two Atari employees), were 8-bit computers—the 400 had a membrane keyboard and had less RAM (16K) than the more functional 800, with its typewriter-style keyboard and 48K of RAM. Both were released with ancillary technologies like a disk drive, datassette drive, and dot-matrix printer (Herman, 37). The 400 and 800 were able to display better graphics than Atari's VCS and the company released several games for the

Figure 10.1 The Atari 400 home computer. (Photograph by Marcin Wichary, used with permission.)

systems but on cartridges that were incompatible with the VCS (Herman, 37). Like Atari's earliest home consoles, the 400 and 800 were sold primarily at the company's retail partner, Sears, which had mandated the production of the cheaper 400 machine (Herman, Appendix A, "Computers"). The Atari computers competed in the marketplace against video game systems and similarly designed early PCs, such as those produced by Texas Instruments, Radio Shack, and Commodore. As seen in Figure 10.2, computer companies like Commodore produced personal computers like the Commodore 64 model that was also designed with the television-set-as-monitor set-up in mind.

The Atari 400 and 800's computer/television receiver configuration and the accompanying constraints that the Federal Communications Commission places upon television technology (as well as the limitations of that

Figure 10.2 The Commodore 64, released in 1982, was a home computer that used the television set as monitor. (Photograph by Dr John Smith, used with permission.)

technology itself) framed the personal computer apparatus in a specific, televisual way. They also affected how competitive the Atari units could be against companies like Apple, who did use dedicated computer monitors as displays. Atari's line of computers, like other "multi-functional" gaming/computer devices produced at the time when personal computers were first viable consumer products, were difficult to market (Is it a computer? A game?) and caused customer confusion over which device one should purchase. Marketed as computers and games for average users, these systems appeared to have added value and could bring the esoteric art of programming into the home. One Atari advertising slogan for the 400 and 800 told consumers, "You don't have to be a genius to use one," playing up the ease-of-use of these home computers. The 400 and 800 systems stand as examples of cross-purposed devices—they are neither the best version of a gaming system or a computer. As Nintendo of America President Minoru Arakawa said of Coleco's similar ADAM line of dual-use computer/game systems: "It [the Coleco ADAM] was a big mess. How do you define the line between computer and video games? We had a difficult time trying to satisfy both of them" (DeMaria and Wilson, 97). In the case of Atari's 8-bit computers, the company did not try and separate out computer and gaming functions. Leonard Herman notes that the release of certain games "cemented the position of the Atari 400 and 800s as a deluxe home arcade machine that was also capable of productivity and business tasks" (Herman, A-2). These cross-purposes were depicted in advertising that framed the systems as part of a larger discourse about familial, domestic technologies that could bring families together around the machine, reiterating the "family circle" notions first circulated about television in the late 1940s.[29] Advertisements, game catalogues, system manuals and other documents depicted multi-generational groups of users huddled around the television set using the new Atari devices, echoing the advertising rhetoric of the 1950s that positioned families around the television receiver, placing the technology at the center of the domestic discourse. Now such home spaces were re-imagined as sites of play and work, made possible by the presence of the computer in the home. This new technology promised to be a nexus for family bonding and shared experiences in the realms of play, education, and household management, with Grandpa cheering Junior on as he attempted to achieve a high score.

This approach towards television as an expanded site of work and play was also used for systems more clearly marked and marketed for gaming. In 1978 Atari ran a series of television advertisements that starred major athletes of the day, each paired with sports games. Pete Rose and Kareem Abdul Jabaar told their fans, "Don't watch television tonight, play it!" These spot ads, for games like *Home Run* (Atari, 1978) and *Basketball* (Atari, 1978) closed with a shot of the television set crowned by the Atari VCS, which was perched on top of it. The athletes' endorsement of the games and encouragement to play rather than watch TV re-imagines both the set and its viewers as part of an interactive entertainment discourse.

Television and New Media Studies

For scholars approaching digital media from within film studies or film and media studies, certain historical precursors and analogies have appeared as seemingly intuitive frames of reference for understanding what marks new media as new and what still grounds it in broader historical and theoretical fields. The early years of cinema have been mined as crucial analogies for understanding the early years of digital media and its uncertainties of format, exhibition, and aesthetic. Scholars like Richard Grusin and Jay David Bolter compare the present conditions of digital media to Tom Gunning's much-cited "cinema of attractions" model[30] in their key text *Remediation: Understanding New Media*.[31] "Software studies" theorist Lev Manovich draws heavily upon the history of early cinema and its theory, particularly Soviet cinema and montage, for defining the very

Language of New Media.[32] Manovich keenly points out the similarities between film and computer media and their points of convergence, such as Konrad Zuse's recycling of film stock for computer storage media in his early programmable analog computer (Manovich, 25, 330–331). While it is surely true that the early days of cinema and its period of development are instructional for understanding the current state and development of digital media technologies, this overemphasis upon the parallels between so-called "old media" (namely cinema) and New Media (such as computers, digital devices, computer networks, and a range of other technologies, not all of which are image based) leaves out a crucial historical predecessor of new media: television.

From a strictly technological standpoint, television is closer to the computerized components of digital media culture than cinema. Television receiver screen size and orientation and computer monitor size and orientation are similar to one another, largely because they rely upon similar technologies—first the cathode ray tube and later the liquid crystal display.[33] As stated earlier, many early personal computing technologies were first manufactured to connect to existing televisual technologies, turning the television receiver itself into a computer monitor. We can also note the way that projected cinematic images differ from the scanned images seen via a cathode ray tube or on a contemporary computer or televisual display. By situating the personal computer as a device accessible through the TV screen, this strategy of TV-as-monitor, born out of the pragmatic and financially motivated ingenuity to retrofit old technology to new, significantly situates computers within popular culture. The TV-as-monitor strategy allowed manufacturers and users of early personal computer systems to inadvertently naturalize the computer as domestic technology with links (both literally and metaphorically) to television.

This repositioning of television within digital media discourse not only grounds discussion of the digital in the everyday, it also allows for a reconsideration of television in the home itself. While outside the scope of this essay, these computer-television connections necessitate further study. We need to rethink accepted notions about the gendered reception of contemporary television, especially in light of the emergence of high-tech domestic home theaters and gamer environments as Do-It-Yourself home media worlds that complicate the history of separately-gendered domestic media/leisure spheres.

As I stated at the outset, repositioning the role of television within our analysis has implications for how video game theory deals with the very medium of gaming and the spaces in which one games. It also creates a link between video game theory and the field of television studies. While the ramifications of such a link are an unanswered question at this point, there are academic advantages to approaching video game theory from a perspective informed by television studies. Television scholars have successfully charted out a field with particular attention to social history, reception/viewership/usership, and media politics. Several prominent television scholars, most notably Henry Jenkins, have even morphed into advocates for the study of new media like games and gaming (Jenkins, Fans). As points of technological and content-driven convergence continue to increase, understanding how television and its history is embedded within video game culture is ever more critical. While these early examples of televisions harnessed into home computers give some indication of how one technology helped to create a domestic space for others, it is also important to note more recent attempts—successful or not—to bring computing, gaming, and television together.

From the 1990s through to the present day, the TV as part of the home computer system strategy was taken up again by leading computer manufacturers and software development firms. Contemporary personal computers can, if outfitted with the proper video card, process and display television. Apple Computer even released the unsuccessful *Macintosh TV* in 1993—a black case computer equipped with a 14-inch Sony Trinitron CRT monitor and a built-in television tuner card and remote. Apple pulled this expensive (retail price was over $2,000 in 1993) and poorly-selling device from the market only five months after it was released, guaranteeing its place in history as a collector's item.[34] The start-up company WebTV first produced its WebTV "set-top box" as a computer/interactive web browser accessed via a television receiver. Like the Apple project, WebTV met with limited success upon its debut in 1995. However, Microsoft saw potential in the marketplace for a home web browser and multimedia system accessed via the television and purchased WebTV in 1997, retooling the original technology and releasing updated versions as MSNTV and MSNTV2. While recent set-top boxes like WebTV are designed with the Internet in mind, gaming, in both its pre-existing connections to television and computers, seems like a more logical way to make TV into a computer and vice-versa. Yet, perhaps because gaming remains misunderstood as simple play, the *rhetoric* of televisual-computational convergence rarely mentions this medium, even while the technologies do in fact converge.

Ultimately, the discourse of convergence, change, emergence, novelty, and innovation that surrounds digital media technologies must be tempered with a careful reconsideration of older media technologies like television and cinema. Without sensitivity to the historicity of media and its experience, seemingly natural comparisons and connections between media emerge as though out of a vacuum. Yes, media do become deeply entwined formally and technologically but our tales of convergence must be situated in a framework that accounts for each form's specificity and use.

The literal and symbolic connections to media forms that already have established formal qualities, methods of distribution, and models of reception provide an anchor for emergent technologies, a starting point for framing how one plays/uses/works on/interacts with/spatially locates and understands computers and video games as part of personalized, domestic environments. And, while the rhetorically condescending attitude towards television was certainly intentional when Mattel deemed their Intellivision game system "intelligent television," it is crucial to understand how television shores up, serves, and frames both the computer and video game media through the strategies I've mentioned here. TV continues to provide a framework for digital media experience in an era when we are told, once again, to engage with "smart TV." Without repositioning television into the history of digital media, one cannot pause in front of and amidst the connections between the elements of our digital home media systems to consider the seemingly *inevitability* of digital media platforms and the array of experiences they promise.

Notes

1. My use of quotation marks here signals my skepticism at the discourse of media convergence. Instead I suggest a more thoroughgoing approach to media connections and configurations that places moments of convergence in historical and theoretical context.
2. See Raymond Williams on "flow" as an ideological and aesthetic structure often conflated with the medium of television in Williams, *Television: Technology and Cultural Form* (London: Fontana, 1974); hereafter cited as Williams. For televisual flow and new media, see Richard Dienst, *Still Life in Real Time: Theory After Television* (Durham: Duke UP, 1994).
3. Even the spate of high-tech superhero/super-science programs of the 1970s (including *The Incredible Hulk, The Six Million Dollar Man, and The Bionic Woman*) did not domesticate computers but kept these new tools safely instead high tech laboratory settings.
4. For more on 1970s television see Kirsten Lentz, "Quality vs. Relevance: Feminism, Race and the Politics of the Sign in 1970s Television," *Camera Obscura* 43 (January 2000): 45–93. For the "vast wasteland" speech, see Erik Barnouw, *Tube of Plenty* (New York, Oxford: Oxford University Press, 1999), 300–301.
5. I use the modifier "technocultural" to account for how any media "convergence" or coming together of disparate technologies is due to both technological and cultural forces.
6. Paul Virilio, "Speed and Information: Cyberspace Alarm!" *Reading Digital Culture*. ed. David Trend (Oxford: Blackwell, 2001), 23–27.
7. Siegfried Zielinski, *Audiovisions: Cinema and Television as Entr'Actes in History* (Amsterdam: Amsterdam University Press, 1999); hereafter cited as Zielinski.
8. Friedrich Kittler, "Gramophone, Film, Typewriter," *October* 41 (Summer 1987): 101–118.
9. See Henry Jenkins, *Convergence Culture: Where Old and New Media Collide* (New York: New York University Press, 2006).
10. See Brian Winston, *Media Technology and Society. A History: From the Telegraph to the Internet* (London and New York: Routledge, 1998); hereafter cited as Winston.
11. Henry Jenkins, *Fans, Bloggers, and Gamers: Exploring Participatory Culture* (New York: New York University Press, 2006), 154; hereafter cited as Jenkins, Fans.

12. Willy Higginbotham's early oscilloscope game might also be framed as a "divergence" from the technology's intended purpose. See Herman for more on Higginbotham.
13. As the *StarCraft* (Blizzard, 1998) professional competition in South Korea shows, video games also have audiences who watch a player or players interact with the game directly. Their experiences should not be discounted but are outside the scope of this essay.
14. I have to thank Andrew Covert for his astute comments on the material on the switch between technological functions.
15. Steven Johnson, *Everything Bad is Good for You: How's Today's Popular Culture is Actually Making Us Smarter* (New York: Riverhead Books, 2005).
16. While gaming violence is not my focus, surely it is arguable that violence is more widely readable than the more nuanced aspects of video games that are rarely commented upon in mainstream, alarmist coverage of gaming.
17. This approach also follows Johnson's argument in *Everything Bad is Good for You*, in which he argues that much of the most widely disregarded popular forms (television, video games, etc.) require high-level cognitive processing. Such engagements with media are often overlooked amidst the critique of media content. Marshall McLuhan would surely agree with Johnson that media critiques often miss the point when, in fact, the medium *remains* the message.
18. See Fredric Jameson, *Postmodernism, or the Cultural Logic of Late Capitalism & Other Essays* (Durham: Duke University Press, 1991), and Stephen Paul Miller, *The Seventies Now: Culture as Surveillance* (Durham: Duke University Press, 1999) on, respectively, postmodern aesthetics and 1970s popular culture. See René Moreau, *The Computer Comes of Age: The People, the Hardware, and the Software*, trans. J. Howlett (Cambridge, MA: MIT Press, 1984).
19. Most home gaming systems can be hooked up to a video projector or larger screen device using adapters but they are marketed primarily towards a home user and it is presumed that gamers will be playing on television screens. Recent systems, like Microsoft's Xbox 360, are even calibrated to work best with high definition television sets. Some third party manufacturers have sold larger gaming screens and low-end projectors with limited success.
20. Leonard Herman, *Phoenix: The Fall & Rise of Videogames* (Springfield, NJ: Rolenta Press, 1994), 7; hereafter cited as Herman.
21. Steve L. Kent, *The Ultimate History of Video Games: From Pong to Pokemon and Beyond. The Story Behind the Craze that Touched our Lives and Changed the World* (Roseville, CA: Prima, 2001), 22–26.
22. Of course successful gameplay and interactivity depends on the combination of one's watching with one's playing. Both modes of reception are co-present and dependent upon one another.
23. For more on how early viewers related to television technology, see Jeffrey Sconce, "The Outer Limits of Oblivion," *The Revolution Wasn't Televised: Sixties Television and Social Conflict*. eds. Spigel and Curtin (New York: Routledge, 1997), 21–45.
24. Charles Bernstein makes a similar argument about the non-utility of video games in his essay "Play It Again, Pac-Man," which originally appeared in *Postmodern Culture* 2, no. 1 (September, 1991). The essay was later reprinted in Mark J. P. Wolf, ed., *The Medium of the Video Game* (Austin: Texas University Press, 2001), 155–168
25. This historical grouping of games via the "generation" of their hardware holds sway in the industry, though largely in inaccurate ways, as often new releases are labeled, sometimes years in advance, as "next generation" systems.
26. Rusel DeMaria and Johnny L. Wilson, *High Score!: The Illustrated History of Video Games*, 2nd edn. (New York: McGraw Hill, 2003), 53; hereafter cited as DeMaria and Wilson.
27. See also <http://www.intellivisiongames.com, accessed 26 October 2007>.
28. Of course today one can purchase a computer that has been designed primarily for gaming, such as the systems made by Alienware. Here gaming also functions as the machine's primary purpose but these systems are still functionally PCs first, gaming computers second, unlike most of the systems I am discussing here. That is, one does not turn the machine's defaults into a game mode. Instead one encounters a PC operating system and then "switches" the machine into game mode.

29. Lynn Spigel, *Make Room for TV: Television and the Family Ideal in Postwar America* (Chicago: University of Chicago Press, 1992), 43–44.

30. Tom Gunning, "The Cinema of Attractions: Early Film, Its Spectator and the Avant-Garde," *Wide Angle* 8, no. 3–4 (1986): 63–70.

31. Jay David Bolter and Richard Grusin, *Remediation: Understanding New Media* (Cambridge, MA: MIT Press, 1999), 155–58, 254. Bolter and Grusin go so far as to claim, "Virtual reality functions for its contemporary user as the so-called cinema of attractions did for filmgoers at the turn of the century" (254).

32. Lev Manovich, *The Language of New Media* (Cambridge, MA: MIT Press, 2001); hereafter cited as Manovich. Manovich has suggested that traditional disciplines like film studies and media studies embrace his concept of "software studies" because contemporary media is increasingly encountered via software/digitally encoded objects. This new field will analyze a range of software objects. In 2007, Manovich established a new lab dedicated to Software Studies at the University of California, San Diego. See <http://lab.softwarestudies.com/>.

33. Though, as Mark J. P. Wolf has wisely suggested to me, the televisual aspect ratio was initially inherited from film's early aspect ratio.

34. My information on the Macintosh TV comes from primary sources like the Apple corporate website (<http://www.apple.com, accessed 2 February 2005>) and enthusiast-produced sites like Apple-history.com (accessed February 2, 2005) and Wikipedia.

CHAPTER **11**

Too Many Cooks
Media Convergence and Self-Defeating Adaptations

TREVOR ELKINGTON

Within the general trend of media convergence, the relationship between the film, television, and video game industries present a particularly interesting love–hate dynamic. On the one hand, visual and interactive media show increasing aesthetic and procedural similarities. Video games have generally become more narrative-based and increasingly draw upon film-like special effects and celebrity-power to stand out in the marketplace. Likewise, the technologies used for computer-generated imagery (CGI) in film are more and more often the same technologies used to develop video games, to the point that artists and technicians are able to move between the two industries with increasing fluidity. This process of convergence is expedited by the rapid expansion of the video game market and the horizontal integration of the media industry. The parent companies that own film and television studios are also increasingly invested in video game development, making synergistic collaborations between film, television, and video game developers commonplace. Major film releases like *Spiderman 3* (Sam Raimi, 2007) and the *The Lord of the Rings* films (Peter Jackson, 2001, 2002, 2003) are accompanied by video game adaptations, classic films like *The Godfather* (Francis Ford Coppola, 1972) and *Scarface* (Brian De Palma, 1983) are licensed for interactive media, and more video games are adapted to film, such as *Doom* (Andrzej Bartkowiak, 2005) or the *Tomb Raider* films (Simon West, 2001; Jan de Bont, 2003). And yet, licensed adaptations are commonly dismissed by critics and players as nothing more than cynical attempts to cash in on hype. Films based on video games usually do not fare well among critics and audiences, though they are capable of performing well at the box-office. Likewise, video games based on films receive a generally hostile reception from game reviewers and players. Rather than successfully drawing on the synergistic advantages of cross-media development and promotion, licensed film-to-game adaptations in particular must overcome a long history of critical and commercial failure.

But are licensed adaptations, when viewed as products in themselves and not as part of a larger media trend, qualitatively any worse or better than their competitors? Does the perception that licensed adaptations are inferior in quality bear up to analysis? And if so, then why is this the case? In order to answer these questions, it is useful to narrow the scope of inquiry. The challenges faced by video games adapted from film and television licenses can be seen as a problem of integrating often incompatible industry processes and potentially resistant social orders. That is, the consistent critical panning of licensed games can be framed as the result of incompatible production practices between film studios and game studios, as well as the resistance of critics and fans with incompatible expectations drawn from the original medium. The process of making a good film is not the same process as making a good game, and the elements that make a film good may not translate well into game form. Consider, for example, the mixed reception of films that attempt some level of interactivity such as *Clue* (Jonathan Lynn, 1985), in which audiences could choose from one of three endings and which was largely received as a vaguely interesting publicity stunt. Likewise, various attempts to use home video technology for interactive movies, where the home viewer is offered decision points throughout the film, have never developed into more than a minor niche market of video sales. In light of these tensions, it is useful to think in terms of what film scholar Mette Hjort, under a different context, has referred to as self-defeating productions.[1] In discussing the process by which many films are co-developed across national lines, Hjort advances the idea that film co-productions, in her case among Nordic nations, are potentially self-defeating if they fail to account for the split interests of their audiences. Serving two or more sets of audiences risks antagonizing the divisions within those audiences by serving too many masters and none well. The concept of self-defeating productions can be usefully broadened to apply to cross-media adaptations as well, in which products created to appeal to more than one audience of consumers can conceivably fail to appeal to any by including multiple elements that please one audience and actively antagonize another, such that no audience is wholly satisfied. Video games based on film and television licenses must attempt to appease two audiences: fans of the original license, who expect a certain adherence to its details, and fans of video games, who expect adherence to common notions of gameplay. Reconciling these expectations presents a fine line bordered on one side by numerous possible mistakes and on the other by a long history of previous failures.

Critical Reception of Licensed Games: The Numbers

But how pronounced is the problem, really? Licensed games with narrative components continue to appear on the market at a rapid rate, which would seem to suggest that success of some form can be found here. If these games are so unpopular, why would companies continue to make them? Would not sales reflect the problem, and thus discourage this kind of development? After all, game publishers are in the business to realize a profit. Clearly, successes do occur, and sales charts are filled with games based on the most recent blockbuster film titles. However, sales of this type are difficult to separate from the general level of marketing saturation associated with most leading film licenses. Licensed video games often benefit from the "opening weekend" strategy that has been at play in the film industry over the last decade and more: film studios, particularly in the case of blockbuster action titles of the type licensed games are commonly based on, look to recoup their investment in the initial days of the films' international opening, as a way of counteracting any potentially negative word of mouth.[2] As part of this media barrage, games based on movies can accomplish something similar, debuting with strong sales well before the critical reviews reach consensus and word of mouth spreads. As such, commercial success would seem at least initially to be a poor measure of game quality for anybody other than the game publishers that benefit from those sales, for whom financial success will always necessarily be the bottom line.

Where the problem of evaluating the "quality" of a game becomes most clearly identifiable is in the reception among critics and game-playing audiences. Compiling a broad sample of product reviews provides a useful index of how critical audiences, and potential consumers, are reacting to a particular game or a particular genre. Warner Brothers Interactive Entertainment took this logic to its extreme when it announced in May, 2004, that in order to discourage game developers and publishers from damaging their intellectual property by developing poor quality games, it would begin using a fluctuating royalty rate for game publishers based on critical response, drawing from results in sites like GameRankings (www.gamerankings.com) and Metacritic (www.metacritic.com). The policy, devised by the division's chief Jason Hall as an attempt to hold publishers responsible for producing inferior products, was wildly unpopular among game developers and game critics, who argued that game quality did not have a direct correlation to game sales, with many high-rated games selling poorly and many low-rated games selling well, and more tellingly, that game reviews are far from objective.[3] Attempting to pin an objective royalty scheme to a subjective index presented game developers with a seemingly impossible situation. Games that reviewed well but sold poorly would not have significant revenue to draw royalties from, and games that sold well but ranked poorly would be punished by the policy. So why use critical response as an index of industry status at all? While game reviews are subjective, and any one review is a poor indicator of the game's reception by other reviewers or its potential sales, game reviews do offer a sense of the *perceived* quality of particular games and a specific genre. As consumers themselves, video game reviewers provide some insight into consumer reception that reaches beyond sales figures. More importantly, despite developer assertion that quality and sales are not necessarily related, a recent study found that there is in fact a direct relationship between reviews and sales, with highly-rated games selling up to five times better than titles with lower-scoring reviews.[4] Developers, publishers, and licensors should be paying attention to review scores, as they seem to suggest how a game will perform in the marketplace, individual exceptions aside.[5] Moreover, the problem that Hall attempts to address, poorly-developed games damaging healthy intellectual property, is not simply a matter of video game developers and publishers exploiting trusting film studios by foisting inferior products onto unenlightened audiences. Rather, the problem is systematic, a flaw engrained within the current methods by which licensed games are developed, and game reviewers and audiences are keenly suspicious of the role film studios play in this process, as will be discussed below.

In this light, analyzing the review statistics compiled on Metacritic proves a useful case in point. The site collects reviews from stable game sites and compiles the results into aggregate statistics based on a 100-point scale, with separate rankings for critic reviews[6] and fan reviews, resulting in a meta-review that gives a broad sense of what people are saying about a particular game. Of the thousands of games reviewed on the site, hundreds are developed directly from a film or television license, whether as part of a major release like the video game adaptation of *Spider-Man 3* (Treyarch, 2007) or a retroactive attempt to market an older license, such as the quickly forgotten adaptation of *Miami Vice* (Atomic Planet Entertainment, 2004). At the time of writing, reviews for over 1500 games developed for the Sony PlayStation 2 (PS2) between 2000 and 2007 are aggregated on the site.[7] Review data was collected initially on September 10, 2005, and again on October 10, 2007. Average scores for PS2 games are relatively stable across time, dropping slightly from 69.1 in 2005 to 67.9 in 2007. These scores put the average game review within the "Mixed or Average Reviews" category for the Metacritic site.

However, the aggregate review numbers for video games paint a very different picture. In September, 2005, there were 1099 PS2 games listed on the site; of that number, 106 were directly based on a film or television license, a ratio of roughly 10:1. Of the licensed games, the average aggregate score was 61 out of 100, a full eight points below the average, though still within the "Mixed to Average Reviews" category. However, these numbers do not immediately reveal that nearly one quarter of the games reviewed, 22 out of 106, fell on or below 49, in the "Generally Unfavorable Reviews" category. By October, 2007, the picture is notably different. In the intervening two years, an additional 448 games were aggregated, resulting in an overall average of 67.9. Of those additional games, 109 were based on film and television licenses. For all scores in the database, the ratio of all games to film and television adaptations drops to roughly 7:1; more significantly, the ratio of all games to adaptations released between September 2005 and October 2007 drops to nearly 4.5:1. Most tellingly, the average aggregate score of film and television license-based games developed between September, 2005 and October, 2007, fell to 56.9.[8] Three conclusions become clear. One, that film and television adaptations consistently score lower than the average across the reviews aggregated by Metacritic. Two, film and television adaptations are occupying a larger portion of games released in a given year. Three, and most importantly, these games are receiving lower and lower scores over time. Put succinctly, video game developers and publishers are releasing more film and television adaptations at a faster rate, as a larger percentage of their release schedules, and these games are less and less popular with critics. It begs the question: Why? Are the commercial incentives simply too great? As noted above, critical reception and sales numbers show direct correlation. Are publishers simply willing to ignore critical response and keep delivering the same unpopular product in the hopes of finding a statistically exceptional hit with consumers? Or is the baseline of sales for lukewarm titles still enough to make them profitable? The evidence would seem to suggest both rationales as distinct possibilities.

Self-defeating Adaptations

So why do film and television adaptations fare so poorly with critics? Two possibilities seem likely: either the games are truly worse than other games on average, or critics just do not like adaptations, whatever their individual merits. Setting aside the second possibility for the moment, the possibility remains that film and television adaptations are simply not as good as non-adaptations, that there is something intrinsic in the adaptation process that results in an inferior game. Perhaps the difference between the media is too vast; the parameters of video games are too vastly different from film to make for good adaptations. And yet, both critical and financial successes do occur. So what's the secret? Or rather, what's the problem?

In an interview for the video game industry site Gamasutra, Rodney Greenblat, the artist who helped shape the groundbreaking *PaRappa the Rapper* rhythm game for the Sony PlayStation (NaNaOn-Sha, 1997), discussed the franchise's development across media. The game's success in Japan spawned an animated children's show, but for Greenblat, the results were messy. Conflicts over design and copyright among different branches of the franchise owner, Sony, led to continuity errors, narrative inconsistencies, and a sacrifice of the original game's vision. As Greenblat notes:

> Sony Creative owned the copyright, and Sony Computer had ownership of just the game . . . they didn't care, because it was raking in all this money for Sony even if it was just two different divisions . . . but when the animation people came in, and then Fuji TV . . . it just got [to be] this whole mess. Just too many people.[9]

When the series appeared on Japanese television, it became clear that significant differences between the game audience, comprised largely of adolescents and above, and the animated series, which was targeted at children, made it difficult to realize any cross-media synergy. Fans of the game were not interested in a children's television show, and fans of the series found it difficult to master a game designed for adolescent developmental skills. This internal conflict of franchise management resulted in a self-defeating project. The term underscores the idea that media convergence, despite its apparent ability to smooth over differences in media, actually creates an *increased* awareness among audiences of the particularities of form and content across media, and consequently requires developers to be more aware of the limitations of each medium and more responsive to the vicissitudes of various audience demographics. Media convergence is not an industry curative that makes production conditions easier; if anything, it increases the level of complexity. Thus the term "self-defeating" suggests projects in which the different goals of the various license-sharers stand in direct conflict, even contradiction, to each other, so that not only do they sacrifice consistency and continuity, they effectively achieve negative synergy, as each product antagonizes the contrasting audience.

So how do adaptations commonly defeat themselves? It is useful to look at the critical reception of four film-to-game adaptations from the height of the previous console generation: *Van Helsing* (Saffire, 2004), *Enter the Matrix* (Shiny Entertainment, 2004), *The Lord of the Rings: The Third Age* (Electronic Arts, 2004), and *The Chronicles of Riddick: Escape from Butcher Bay* (Starbreeze, 2004).[10] By analyzing specific critical response to these games, certain common faults and uncommon strengths in design as well as central challenges facing the current models for adapting films to video games begin to coalesce. The relative success and failure of individual cases suggests three things: one, games have arrived as a culturally and aesthetically competitive narrative space to film and television as opposed to a simple licensed ancillary; two, that players reject video games that rely heavily upon cinematic conventions; and three, that what video game consumers seek from adaptations is not a simple, interactive rehearsal of film events but in fact further expansion of a narrative world via an engaged relationship with an interactive medium. Failure to accommodate these factors results in a poorly-rated game.

The most common form of film-to-game adaptation is the direct adaptation, in which a video game closely, even slavishly, follows the film narrative by directly turning film events into interactive experiences. While certain exceptions do occur, they are generally the most criticized games on the market, seen as cynical attempts to exploit the hype of a particular film release. Saffire's *Van Helsing* adaptation exemplifies common weaknesses of the genre. *Van Helsing* receives a 63 on Metacritic, based on 32 professional reviews. Comments about the game ranged from lukewarm to savage, with one reviewer concluding, "*Van Helsing* is a shining example of what's wrong with games based on movies."[11] So what went wrong? Critics point to shallow, unchallenging gameplay, mediocre graphics, and a narrative based directly on film events, eliminating any element of suspense. More importantly, critics point to the limited options offered players as they are shuttled along a linear level design in order to work through events mandated by the film; any notion of emergent or creative gameplay is limited by the strictly linear narrative, thus stripping the title of a crucial interactive element. And finally, critics point to perhaps the most common complaint about film-to-game adaptations: an over-reliance upon cut-scenes. This design weakness means that players are not rewarded by events within the interactive game space, but in fact play up to a certain point, at which the game engine takes over and delivers a canned cinematic. Not only does the design choice rupture the flow of interactive space, it also undoes the basic idea of games, which is that they are subject to player control.[12] It is a flaw seen repeatedly in the games discussed below.

A second type of film/game convergence can be found in what Henry Jenkins has called "transmedia storytelling," in which each media product contributes to an overall narrative world, suggesting that single storylines are less important than the unfolding of an entire narrative world. The most notable example of this genre is the various products associated with *The Matrix* films (Andy and Larry Wachowski, 1999, 2003, 2003), where the various short films, games, books, and other products supplement and expand the world established by the films. Interestingly, critical and commercial reception of *The Matrix Reloaded* and *The Matrix Revolutions* was notably more negative than for the original film. Despite earning collectively over $800 million at the box-office, revenue fell markedly from the second to the third film, and both films saw significant drop in revenue after the opening week, suggesting a word of mouth effect that cooled interest from the first film. Critical reception of the films focused on the tangled narrative, apparent plot holes, undeveloped tangents, and shallow characters. Roger Ebert tempers his admiration for *Revolutions* by noting "the awkward fact that I don't much give a damn what happens to any of the characters" before concluding with a significant wink that "finally I measure my concern for [Neo] not in affection but more like the score in a video game."[13] Likewise, the video game component *Enter the Matrix* received a lukewarm 65 across 34 reviews, and Jeff Gerstmann writes in his GameSpot review that "the game serves as little more than an advertisement for the film—it doesn't have a story that stands on its own, and the gameplay doesn't really offer anything that we haven't seen in better games."[14] Similar to Joe Dodson's review of *Van Helsing*, Gerstmann notes the game's tendency to sacrifice gameplay for special effects and cutscenes, emphasizing the significant error of taking interactivity out of the hands of the player at key moments. In other words, the reviewers of the game *and* film argue that in trying to be more like each other, the texts manage to sacrifice the strength of their own medium without realizing the strengths of the other, thus leading to a self-defeating project achieving negative synergy.

A more positive example of transmedia storytelling can be found in Electronic Arts's *The Lord of the Rings: The Third Age*. While the initial games from *The Lord of the Rings* project are typical interactive walkthroughs of the film events, EA's *The Third Age* attempts something near transmedia storytelling by allowing players to direct original characters pursuing their own adventures in the larger world of Middle-earth. Characters at times intersect with film events, providing the larger picture of what happened before, elsewhere, or after the heroes of the movies pursue their quest. Reactions to the game were generally favorable, and the title received 75 across 38 reviews. Criticism, when offered, focuses specifically on the common flaw of mirroring narrative and cinematic convention over interactivity. In her review for GameSpot, Bethany Massimilla notes the game's tendency to communicate narrative exposition through cut-scenes in which Gandalf reveals information about characters and events, rather than through characters interacting with each other or the game world. She argues that "you are explicitly told what has happened and what will happen instead of actually seeing it happen, and it serves to somewhat distance the player from the whole experience."[15] However, in general, this critic concludes that game play compensates for the weakness and offers a compelling experience, and more importantly, fans of the books and films will enjoy the chance to explore Middle-earth and interact with the major characters while augmenting the clear narrative lines set by Tolkien. Where *The Third Age* fails is in its attempts to be more like a film; where it succeeds is where it plays upon the strengths of the game medium and offers players the chance to fully explore a larger fictional world.

Escape from Butcher Bay offers a third category of film/game convergence, drawing upon the Chronicles of Riddick world initially launched by the sleeper success *Pitch Black* (David Twohy, 2000) and its sequel, *The Chronicles of Riddick* (David Twohy, 2004), but pursuing a separate narrative not directly reliant upon film events. The game receives an aggregate score of 89 across 84 reviews, placing it high among games reviewed for the Xbox console. GameSpot reviewer Greg Kasavin notes:

> *The Chronicles of Riddick: Escape From Butcher Bay* is one of those exceedingly rare types of games that delivers exceptionally high quality through and through and single-handedly ups the ante for all similar games. The fact that it also happens to be based on a movie franchise—something that's usually a bad sign for a game—makes it all the more incredible.[16]

Escape from Butcher Bay is often framed as that rarest of products, the critically successful film-to-game adaptation. Players guide Riddick as he escapes from the maximum-security prison Butcher Bay, a necessary off-stage event that takes place prior to the events in the films. The obvious advantage for developers here is that, beyond general faithfulness to the film world and the facts established by the films, they are not hemmed in by the film narrative. They can more easily avoid the temptation to make the game like a film, as in this case, there are no specific film events that need to be related within the game narrative and there are no film sequences to be directly adapted as cut-scenes or gameplay elements. Instead, players shift from the film's third-person perspective to an interactive first-person perspective in order to further explore an appealing fictional world without being hampered by the specific constraints of the film or by the film medium. Unlike other transmedia storytelling, in which games like *Enter the Matrix* and *The Third Age* contribute one piece that directly relies upon the contents of the films, *Escape from Butcher Bay* takes one relatively minor detail and expands it into its own narrative territory without being too reliant on the films it licenses.

So what does this review of reviews tell us? To return to the example provided by Rodney Greenblat, it becomes clear that media convergence does not play out on a level field. Far from it. Film and television license-owners have to date largely dictated the course of game development, treating video games more or less like traditional ancillaries. Most of the qualitative problems arise from treating video game development as an afterthought, leaving developers hard-pressed to devise ways to work around the film schedule and agenda. The most common strategy, the direct adaptation, is also demonstrated to be the least popular among game players, resulting in a self-defeating project in which the film and game do not achieve synergy beyond name recognition and initial hype. Those games that do break out of this basic mold, like *Escape from Butcher Bay*, not only receive critical praise, but seem better positioned to reap comparable financial reward. Indeed, as Henry Jenkins argues in *Convergence Culture: Where Old and New Media Collide*,[17] story worlds are increasingly more important than individual stories, as consumers become fans of fictional characters and settings and look to the individual texts, be they films, video games, or novels, to offer further details and stories within those worlds. Creating a game that is a straightforward rehashing of the film or television product offers nothing new to the consumer in terms of new ideas or details, instead trading on an oversimplified appeal to interactivity in place of novelty. This rings particularly true for licenses within already popular narrative settings like Tolkien's Middle-earth, the Wachowski Brothers' Matrix universe, or J. K. Rowling's Harry Potter world. Part of the appeal to film studios and video game publishers for adapting works within these settings is that they come with established fanbases pre-disposed to buying additional products that further develop these worlds. However, as suggested by critical response, many of these video games in fact serve to further alienate that fanbase. Given the reception of games like *Escape from Butcher Bay*, it is clear that adaptations can succeed critically as well as financially. So why do so many of these games go wrong? As the reviews above suggest, some of this is directly due to the design of the games themselves, potentially hampered by their over-reliance upon the original intellectual property and upon the aesthetics of film and television in the first place. However, there is more than an aesthetic problem at stake here.

It is possible that in fact there is nothing qualitatively wrong with film and television adaptations, and that this is simply a case in which video game reviewers are negatively prejudiced against adaptations from the outset. As the reviews above suggest, many critics work from the assumption that adapted video games will be of inferior quality unless proven otherwise, and note with pleasure when a game overcomes that expectation or knowingly report when it does not. Perhaps the problem lies less with the games than with the critics. Maybe a game based on a film or television license simply cannot get a fair assessment. There are many possible reasons why reviewers might be ill-disposed toward adaptations. The legacy of poorly reviewed adaptations alone suggests that further adaptations will simply go on to fit the established mold. Likewise, Eric Peterson, a game developer who has specialized in adaptations such as *Flushed Away* (Monkey Bar Games, 2006), points out that most video game adaptations are based on children's film and television and are targeted toward that audience, which immediately affects their reception among adult reviewers:

> Reviewers frequently don't give kids games a fair shake—some don't even bother to review them, either because they aren't "cool," or don't appeal to their demographic. When these games are reviewed, they are often compared to games for older audiences, and which have longer development cycles.[18]

It is not surprising that a game like *Flushed Away*, with its appeal to juvenile humor, would not resonate with an adult reviewer. Indeed, the same study that found a correlation between high reviews and high sales also found that mature-rated titles have the highest average Metacritic scores and the highest average gross sales. This may be a reflection of the age and interests of the average game player skewing toward the ESRB M-for-mature rating. A broader consumer base, paired with a quality game, should result in higher sales. Reviewers, as average game players, may not understand adapted games targeted at children and thus review them negatively, while the kinds of games that reviewers do favor, mature-rated games, fare best commercially. Children's games fare poorly among critics already; with many adaptations falling into that genre because of their licensed material, it is predictable that their average review scores would also average below the norm. Nevertheless, games based on children's licenses such as *Happy Feet* (Midway Games, 2007), while receiving a 49 or "Generally Unfavorable Reviews" score on Metacritic for its PS2 version, have performed very well in the marketplace. The game shipped 1.8 million copies by January, 2007 (Seff, 2007).[19] So while mature-rated games rate high and sell well, other games that do not rate high nevertheless can offer financial incentives, which is a clear motivator for why they continue to be released despite general panning among reviewers.

Interestingly, despite noting that children's games rate poorly among reviewers, Peterson goes a long way to offering additional reasons why adapted games generally receive poor ratings and are expected to be of poor quality by reviewers. As he states the case, adapted games like *Flushed Away* are expected to be "just another movie-based game with shallow gameplay that was rushed out the door" (Peterson). But as Peterson admits, these types of games, whether for children or otherwise, usually have shorter development cycles, meaning that less time is available to develop innovative game design and polish the overall quality of the game. For better or worse, most adapted games *are* rushed out the door, with most being pushed to ship simultaneously with the release date for the film. But even games that are not rushing to ship for a box-office date, games like *Miami Vice* where the original intellectual property is already in the marketplace, are still reviewed poorly. In an example similar to Rodney Greenblat's experience on *PaRappa*, Peterson discusses his experience developing *Dinotopia: The Sunstone Odyssey* (Monkey Bar Games, 2003). Early in the development cycle, the licensors decided that the game should reflect coming narrative changes planned for the series. When these changes proved to be unpopular among series fans, they held the game accountable. "Dinotopia fans were outraged because they thought that we, as developers, had decided to change the world they loved" (Peterson). Moreover, because licensors were co-developing unreleased content with the game developers, it meant a high level of involvement from multiple parties during the game development cycle, with changes to the series directly impacting the design of the game. "We were like taffy, being pulled between licensor, sub-licensor, and publisher, all of whom wanted something different. We still got the game done, but at a heavy price. Everyone felt like they were forced to make a game they didn't believe in" (Peterson). The resulting game scored poorly in reviews, receiving a 50 on Metacritic. Development experiences like Greenblat's and Peterson's go a long way to suggesting why many game adaptations are of such poor quality. Game developers, often working under shortened production schedules, are put in the middle of conflicting interests from licensors, publishers, and other parties such as celebrities connected with the game. Whereas constant change is often the rule in film development, the impact of last minutes changes and ongoing design fluctuation is far more detrimental to game development, where design, art, and programming efforts often take months or years of work to produce results. The problem, in a nutshell, is that game development cannot respond well to competing interests and the design fluctuation it brings. In trying to serve so many masters, from the licensors on one end to the fans on the other, the potential result is a self-defeating product, a game that pleases nobody, be they licensor, publisher, developer, fan of the property, or fan of games. In order to understand the problem better, it is useful to turn to a developer that has a history of getting it right, the studio behind *The Chronicles of Riddick: Escape from Butcher Bay*.

Too Many Cooks Working Too Fast

Johan Kristiansson, CEO of Starbreeze Studios, the developer behind *Escape from Butcher Bay*, offers valuable insight into the licensed-game production cycle. He identifies two specific issues that compromise the quality of games based on film and television licenses: one, conflicts of development time and schedule, and two, conflicts within the design approval process.[20] The average Hollywood film takes roughly twelve to eighteen months to move from pre-production to completed post-production, depending upon a myriad of complex factors including the completeness of the script when green-lighted, necessary revisions, production factors like set-building and special effects engineering, and post-production elements such as digital effects and post-processing. The average AAA-title game, a nomenclature reserved for industry-leading titles from major publishers intended for the broadest audience usually across multiple platforms, averages 24 months or more to move from the design stage to a release-ready gold disc. Immediately, one can see the direct conflict in schedules. More often than not, a game developer would need at least a six month lead in order to deliver a game ready to be released simultaneously with a film. But if the project has not yet been greenlighted, there is no license or approved concept to work with. This leaves most game developers with two options: remain faithful to the film production schedule and shorten their own development cycle, or ship a game potentially months after the marketing campaign for the film is over. Generally, developers choose to capitalize upon film marketing by maintaining the film's release schedule, and attempt to make up the difference in a variety of ways, by either hiring more employees, working extra hours, underdeveloping parts of the game, or adapting their design. The last two factors, in particular, can result in inferior game quality: art assets seem incomplete, music is of poor quality, game play is simplified, and narrative content closely mirrors that found in the film. However, depending upon the status of the script, securing a license for a greenlighted project is no guarantee that the film concept is firmly in place. Film studios routinely revise scripts, sometimes to a significant degree, right up to and through the production phase. Unfortunately, game development is much less flexible in its design phase, as it can take weeks of multiple employees' efforts to institute features mandated by the film design. An off-the-cuff decision by the filmmakers can potentially run into weeks of wasted effort for game developers. Change, however, is inevitable, and if the film changes, then the game must change accordingly or run the risk of design discontinuity and potential self-defeating status.

Kristiansson provides an example in the development of *Escape from Butcher Bay*. Starbreeze Studios secured the license to make games based on *The Chronicles of Riddick* universe before the sequel script was complete; not having seen the script for the film, the team based its game pitch on what it knew of the Riddick character from the original film, *Pitch Black*. Faced with a 20-month development schedule, unusually long for a film because of its abundance of special effects and CGI sequences, the team debated setting its game as a sequel or a prequel to the films; given that the film script was still undergoing development, they ultimately opted to avoid direct conflict by developing a prequel to film events, leaving them a greater degree of design freedom. However, conflicts were not completely eliminated. For example, game designers created a backstory that explains Riddick's ability to see in the dark that did not correspond to the explanation ultimately reflected in the script. The game developers were fortunately able to change their design accordingly (Kristiansson), but the potential for significant problems increases the further along in the development process conflicts take place. The more developed a game is, the greater is the impact that design changes can have.

The second issue that Kristiansson directly identifies as problematic for developing games based on films is the increased complexity of the approval process. Unlike a traditional game or film, in which approval generally follows a hierarchy limited to and within the production company and the publisher/studio, licensed games, in this case film-based or otherwise, must gain approval from parties outside the direct line of game development. In the case of a game based on a film or television license, the approval process usually has three major steps: studio/publisher, license holder/film production team, and talent, usually the film's director, major stars, and similar parties. In addition to the usual game development approval steps that entail several levels of designers and executives within the studio and the publisher, a licensed game design must clear two additional hurdles: the license holder and film production team, and the talent, usually the film's director, major stars, and similar parties. In the case of *Escape from Butcher Bay*, the approval process outside the studio included the publisher, Vivendi Universal Games, and the film production team as managed through Vivendi Universal Films. Vin Diesel was also entitled to his own approval; fortunately in this case, Diesel has a well-documented interest in games, so much so that he created his own company, Tigon Studios, to oversee his involvement in this and future game projects. Each step in the approval process includes the possibility of suggested changes, which, as already stressed, presents a time-sensitive set of variables in game development.

The approval process is particularly thorny when dealing with independently-owned corporations sharing aspects of an IP license, as in the case of *Escape from Butcher Bay*, for which Starbreeze Studios contracted with Vivendi Universal to produce a game. Multimedia entertainment corporations with divisions devoted to the various aspects of contemporary entertainment would seem to have a clear advantage. Sony, as one example, has divisions devoted entirely to film, television, music, and games, and as such, would seem ideally positioned to streamline the design and approval process. However, even here, the possibility of conflicting creative visions is clear, as Greenblat found during the development of the *PaRappa* television series, where competing divisions within the same company behaved in ways similar to a licensors pulling the development in different directions.

Process-based conflicts like those described by Kristiansson do not entirely account for games like *Miami Vice, American Chopper* (Activision Value, 2004), or *The Great Escape* (SCi Entertainment Group, Pivotal Games, 2003). While all three are based on successful and potentially valuable film and television licenses, they are not entirely subject to the same production or marketing pressures as the usual film-to-game adaptation. *Miami Vice* was published years after the television show ended, presumably leaving the development team free to dictate its own schedule with ample time for developing a polished game, and yet the game received an abysmal 27 rating on Metacritic. *American Chopper*, based on a successful series already well established on television by the time the game was in development, likewise presents a different scenario from adapting a summer blockbuster. The cost of producing a reality-television series is substantially less than that of producing, for example, the *Van Helsing* film, and as such, the possibility that the greater financial stakes involved in filmmaking necessarily dictated design process does not necessarily apply to the *American Chopper* television license. One could imagine that the game developers would be on a more level playing field with their television counterparts, consequently able to negotiate a favorable design and schedule. And yet, the game received a 47 rating on Metacritic. Likewise, *The Great Escape*, based on a film classic with an established following, is nevertheless an older license that has long since recouped its investment through theatrical release, video sales, and other licenses. In theory, it would present a prime opportunity to invest the time and care necessary to develop a high-quality game capable of reviving the license's appeal. The game received a 57 on Metacritic.[21] Individually, these games have their specific flaws; collectively, they suggest that the game industry is still seen by the larger entertainment industry as a place to realize easy money by developing quick products that attempt to exploit license appeal without providing game quality.

The challenges discussed above are largely procedural issues, but the one element they all have in common is essentially a social factor: the current "illegitimate" status of the game industry. Despite healthy profits, explosive growth, and significant future market potential, many people still envision the typical game player as an antisocial seventeen-year old sitting on the living room sofa. This perception of diminished social significance pervades the entertainment industry. In her address at the 2005 Game Developers Conference, game development guru Kathy Schoback outlined predicted cost of AAA-title development for next-generation consoles, anticipating that costs could go above $20million, mandating a break-even sales number of roughly one million copies. Despite the social and economic significance reflected in these kinds of numbers, as Schoback quipped, "we're still not as cool as Hollywood."[22] Likewise, in his opening "state of the industry" address at E3 Expo 2005, Douglas Lowenstein, at the time President of the Entertainment Software Association (ESA), made a point of dispelling the urban myth that the game industry is larger than the film industry, noting "it never has been true. . . . In truth, the worldwide film industry stands at about $45 billion and the worldwide video game industry checks in at around $28 billion."[23] In the same address, Lowenstein outlines six fundamental issues in establishing social legitimacy for the video game industry, or as he puts it, "what will it take for the game industry to be as big or bigger than the film industry at some point in the future?" Among these issues, Lowenstein identifies the need to expand the market base for games, and in general his agenda calls for increasing appeal to female and casual gamers through better and different game design, arguing that more variety in what is offered to game buyers will increase the variety of people who will buy games. But what remains significant about Lowenstein's remarks is the pointed assumption that games are currently seen as a less socially acceptable or legitimate form of entertainment media. As he states the case:

> Acceptance in the culture is the key to legitimacy. None of us were alive when film first came on the scene but historians will tell you it was not regarded with great and instant acclaim. Our industry is just thirty years old and has

produced more than its fair share of classics. No doubt, many more will come. But if we as an industry aspire to the same cultural and artistic credibility and stature achieved by other major forms of entertainment, our creative community and our publishers will have to eschew some of the historically easy and successful formulas for commercial success and draw consumers into some new kinds of interactive entertainment experiences that more often ennoble our industry.

Remarks like Schoback's and Lowenstein's reflect the position of the contemporary entertainment industry, that it often plays the little brother role to the larger film industry. While making such clear-cut distinctions between the two industries is problematic given the sizeable investment of companies like Sony, Vivendi Universal, etc. in both media, nevertheless, when it comes to licensed adaptations development, video games clearly take a backseat to film and television. It is standard procedure that a game studio developing a licensed franchise gives some level of creative approval to the licensor; paradoxically, the reverse is hardly ever true. Even Bungie, creators of the enormously successful *Halo* (2001, 2004, 2007) franchise and with all of Microsoft's business acumen behind it, eventually gave up creative control of the *Halo* film license to Universal and Fox, though reports assured that Microsoft executives and designers would be guaranteed " 'extensive' consultation."[24] Eventually, the film was postponed due to conflicts within the project.

Developers like Kristiansson and Greenblat describe in clear terms the challenges presented to game development when their creative agenda is subject to the approval of a party whose agenda is set by film or television dynamics, completely different media with different production and audience demands. This is perhaps understandable, given the differences in potential revenue. But the situation does give rise to avoidable conflicts in creative agendas, conflicts that potentially result in self-defeating productions.

A Suggested Solution: Centrally Managed Development

The failures of transmedia development, as best seen in the critical reception of video game adaptations of film and television licenses, have and will continue to call for central project management. Current industry practice resists this kind of central planning by allowing the initial or most costly Intellectual Property (IP) commodity to set the agenda for the rest of the associated products. The film or TV script is written, the production schedule is planned, and it is up to the other associated developers to find a way to work around or within that frame, regardless of how this might impact their usual development practices. However, to successfully develop a project across media, the various development parties would benefit from ground level coordination in order to create a fictional world in which there are equal opportunities for high quality products across media. If these projects are not centrally managed, they quickly degenerate into situations where what is good for the film or television series is not good for the game and vice versa, pitting the interests of each medium and each license-holder against the central concept of the intellectual property. Rodney Greenblat's experience with *PaRappa* provides further illustration of this point:

> When *PaRappa 2* came out, the animated series came out in Japan, and [there were] too many people involved for me . . . [The show's producers] decided that they wouldn't let anyone from the game team side work on the TV side, they didn't want to pull anyone from the game development for the TV show development. And then they wanted to slate the show for little kids, 5 year olds or something, mostly to sell toys.
>
> And I wasn't into that, because I was like "Everyone knew teenagers loved *PaRappa*, so let's do a teen show." But [Sony] wanted to sell toys, so [the show's producers] made a little kids version of *PaRappa*. (Hawkins)

Greenblat goes on to note how, because of the lack of central design and franchise management, the various parties quickly pursued design decisions that best fit their medium and market needs, regardless of how these development decisions fit into the larger franchise:

> I would get rushes for each episode and make corrections, and they wouldn't even do anything about it! Characters kept on changing and messing up . . . in the game PaRappa could drive a car so you figure he's 16 or 17, but in the show he's sitting in the third grade and his antics were based on what 8 or 9 year olds are doing? It just got all nutty . . . and then I think [all the various parties] all fell apart . . . [A]ll those companies just scattered and did their own things. (Hawkins)

The problems created by a lack of central project management are more than simple issues of continuity. When the various products within a franchise pursue different goals and, in this case, different market demographics, the result is a self-defeating project in which any original audience is actively alienated by the new products, while a new, cohesive audience is difficult to achieve, as the products no longer make sense with regard to each other. What appeals in the game is contradicted by the television show, and vice versa. Again, what is realized is the worst of both worlds with the advantages of neither; the sacrifice culminates in a loss of franchise synergy.

This kind of central project management calls for central roles for the design and production teams. One suggested solution is the New Studio Model offered in October of 2004 by Stuart Roch, a ten-year games industry veteran and producer of *Enter the Matrix*.[25] Roch's model revolves around a core team of developers that build the game technology, allowing the studio to bring in guest designers to lead the game design. The goal of his model is to allow IP originators from other media like film or print to direct games based upon their fictional universe and accentuate their narrative strengths without falling into the traps discussed previously in this essay. The New Studio Model also places the administrative hassles on the shoulders of the publishers and producers, who are best suited for these tasks, rather than the artists creating the game. It is perhaps no coincidence that Roch is an executive producer at Shiny Entertainment, the developers of *Enter the Matrix*, as this model would serve well for a Matrix-like project. However, this model is designed specifically as a solution for developing games. It does not entirely account for the demands of transmedia or multimedia development, in which multiple projects are developing simultaneously, potentially pulling the core creative talent in numerous directions. A more radical solution is required: a central design and production team that develops the core narrative world including game and film scripts, characters, art design, gameplay, and other elements in order to insure that each element logically fits into the larger whole without sacrificing one text's needs for the demands of another. The implementation of these designs can then be managed by the individual studios. Projects like *Enter the Matrix*, *The Lord of the Rings*, and *The Chronicles of Riddick* have already moved definitively in this direction. Likewise, game publishers and developers are becoming savvy to the advantages of co-developing original content with film and television partners from the earliest stages. Midway's *The Wheelman*[26] is a case in point. Intended as a new creative franchise for Vin Diesel and developed in tandem with his game development company Tigon Studios, the initial idea was conceived as a game and film project from the beginning. The game was developed first, with the film script then written based on the game design.[27] This allowed the game developers to work closely with Diesel and deliver a solid game that is still consistent with the film. The film then becomes an additional text within the fictional world initially introduced in the game.

The challenges to this model are in part financial and pragmatic. Who provides the capital and assumes the risk for a transmedia project of this nature? How are the profits shared? Who has final say over the inevitable conflicts? To date, these risks have largely been shouldered by the film studio, as the majority of licensed adaptations or transmedia projects are generated by film narratives. Moreover, most transmedia projects to date are based on pre-existing franchises in an attempt to minimize risk, the logic being that if an audience for this narrative world already exists, then sales for new commodities within that world are more likely than for original IP. Working from existing narrative worlds also allows film and game developers to capitalize upon works already created and essentially "market tested" by fans. Working from a pre-existing world reduces the time and money required to develop intellectual property, and appealing to an established fanbase likewise reduces the risk of developing original IP that consumers may ultimately find uninteresting or unconvincing. As such, it seems likely that licensed franchise development will continue hand-in-hand with media convergence for the foreseeable future.

The larger issue at hand is the necessity of changing the perception of the video game industry as a lower stakes, less legitimate offshoot of the entertainment industry in general. As Douglas Lowenstein summarizes the issue, "acceptance in the culture is the key to legitimacy." Acceptance of this kind largely comes with time, as successive generations embrace video games and developers emerge to address different market demands, expanding the video game market beyond its current demographics and encompassing older, gender-balanced, and ethnically diverse audiences. Moreover, the continuing success of the game industry will be in part its own solution to the problem of legitimacy. As the cost of developing video games increases at the same time that the video game buying market is expanding, studios will necessarily have larger financial stakes in co-developing licensed franchises and will be better positioned to demand better terms for development, potentially leading to higher quality games.

The term "media convergence" carries with it the idea that all media are moving toward the same spot, a central ground in which texts begin to behave similarly, thus mandating a similar approach to developing a film, a game, or any other related product. However, not only are the narrative and design demands different between a successful game, a successful film, or any other medium, each medium likewise offers different strengths and weaknesses. Moreover, the successful management of a film, television series, or game presents its own practical production challenges. It requires different skills, resources, and schedules to develop different media com-modities. Rather than thinking of film-to-game adaptations as a pale, interactive imitation of the original film, they should be conceived of as their own legitimate products requiring their own forms and deserving quality development. In order for the evolving practice of transmedia storytelling to result in works that will be well-accepted by consumers and reviewers alike, the production methods and social positioning have to evolve accordingly.[28]

Notes

1. Mette Hjort, "From Epiphanic Culture to Circulation: The Dynamics of Globalization in Nordic Cinema," in *Transnational Cinema in a Global North: Nordic Cinema in Transition* (Detroit, MI: Wayne State University Press, 2005), 191–218.
2. Brian Jay Epstein, *The Big Picture: The New Logic of Money and Power in Hollywood* (New York: Random House, 2005). The means by which Hollywood realizes a profit on films is far more complex than counting box-office profits, as Epstein convincingly demonstrates. Most Hollywood films are considered a success if they manage to break even on theatrical sales when counted against the cost of distribution and marketing. Instead, studios depend upon home video sales, global television rights, and ancillary sales, including game licenses, to push the title into a profit.
3. Rob Fahey, "Warner Bros. Plans Penalties for Poor Quality Licensed Titles" *GamesIndustry .biz* (26 May 2004). Available online at <http://www.gamesindustry.biz/content_page.php?section_name=pub&aid=352>.
4. Leigh Alexander, "M-Rated Games Sell Best," *Game Developer* (October 2007): 5.
5. However, a controversy within the video game industry erupted in late 2007 that suggests a more complex relationship between high-rated games and high game sales. On November 30, 2007, *Penny Arcade* (<http://www.penny-arcade.com>), an industry site that hosts a popular comic series, game reviews, and forums and organizes an increasingly important annual game industry conference (PAX), reported on the firing of outspoken game reviewer Jeff Gerstmann from GameSpot, a leading game review site. Penny Arcade alleged that Gerstmann had been fired after his "savage flogging" of Eidos Interactive's title *Kane & Lynch* (Io Interactive, 2007) had led Eidos to pull "hundreds of thousands of dollars worth of future advertising from the site" and pressure GameSpot's parent company, CNET, to discipline Gerstmann ("The New Games Journalism" *Penny Arcade* (November 30, 2007). Available online at <http://www.penny-arcade.com/2007/11/30#1196409660>). Representatives from CNET, GameSpot's parent company, later denied that Gerstmann was fired for his review, asserting that "we do not terminate employees based on external pressure from advertisers"; however, they declined to comment on whether Eidos had attempted to apply any such pressure on GameSpot for the review (Kyle Orland, "GameSpot Denies Eidos Pressured Firing of Gerstmann" *Joystiq* (November 30, 2007), available online at <http://www.joystiq.com/2007/11/30/gamespot-denies-eidos-pressured-firing-of-gertsmann/>). The ensuing controversy, in which Gerstmann, Eidos, CNET, and various other interested parties weighed in with often conflicting accounts of what had happened, led to vigorous conversation on video game forums on the nature of corporate influence within the game review industry. While separating the business and content departments as a means to avoid these types of ethical conundrums is a standard practice in mainstream journalism, the possibility that video game publishers might essentially buy good reviews and punish bad reviews through the application of advertising funds called the validity of all video game reviews into question, at least in the eyes of some. It also further complicates the reliability of drawing conclusions based on game sales vs. game reviews, as video game publishers with the highest selling games also tend to have the most advertising funds, at least in theory suggesting that they can influence the rating of their video games and possibly further incite sales. It is a controversy particularly relevant to this essay, as Gerstmann's reviews on other video games are quoted as a means to demonstrate a larger argument. However, the lack of a clear conclusion as to why Gerstmann was fired from GameSpot and whether Eidos had any influence on the decision is itself indicative of the difficulty of ascertaining the relationship between reviews, advertising, and sales. It is an area of inquiry that clearly calls for more research; in the absence of that research, this essay must rely on the current state of thought on the issue.
6. Metacritic does not report aggregate scores for video games until at least four critic reviews have been collected.
7. The Sony PlayStation 2 was chosen as an analytical basis as it provides the largest pool of reviews to draw from and was the commercially dominant console platform during its technological generation. Review data was originally collected on September 10, 2005, and again on October 10, 2007. Games that did not yet meet the minimum four-review limit were not considered as part of the data collected for this analysis.

8. The average for all film and television adaptations between 2000 and 2007 fell to 59.

9. Matthew Hawkins, "Interview: Rodney Greenblat, Creator of Sony's Almost Mario," *Gamasutra.com* (July 5, 2005). Available online at <http://www.gamasutra.com/features/20050705/hawkins_01.shtml>; hereafter cited as Hawkins.

10. Due to *Escape from Butcher Bay*'s exclusive release on the Microsoft Xbox console, these scores are for versions on that console. The other three games discussed were also released as PS2 and PC versions. In 2007, a revised and expanded version was released for the Xbox 360 and PS3, titled *The Chronicles of Riddick: Assault on Dark Athena*. It is also worth noting that although two of the games discussed (*Van Helsing* and *Escape from Butcher's Bay*) are from the same publisher, Vivendi Universal, they are from different development studios and significantly different in design.

11. Joe Dodson, "Review: *Van Helsing*". Available online at <http://gr.bolt.com/games/ps2/action/van_helsing.htm> (accessed July 21, 2005).

12. It also conversely points to the unpopularity of interactive movies, rupturing as they do the receptive experience that underlies film viewing. However, the question of choice and spectator activity in the experience of film perception is a broad field of research and is beyond the scope of this essay.

13. Roger Ebert, "Review: The Matrix Revolutions," *Chicago Sun-Times* (November 5, 2003). Available online at <http://rogerebert.suntimes.com/apps/pbcs.dll/article?AID=/20031105/REVIEWS/311050301/1023>.

14. Jeff Gerstmann, "Enter the Matrix Review" *GameSpot.com* (20 May 2003). Available online at <http://www.gamespot.com/ps2/action/enterthematrix/review.html>.

15. Bethany Massimilla, "The Lord of the Rings, The Third Age Review," *GameSpot.com* (November 4, 2004). Available online at <http://www.gamespot.com/ps2/rpg/tlotrthethirdage/review.html>.

16. Greg Kasavin. "The Chronicles of Riddick: Escape From Butcher Bay—Developer's Cut Review," *GameSpot.com* (December 10 2004). Available online at <http://www.gamespot.com/pc/action/chroniclesofriddick/review.html>.

17. Henry Jenkins, *Convergence Culture: Where Old and New Media Collide* (New York: New York UP, 2006), 20.

18. Eric Peterson, "A License to Review," *Game Developer* (October 2007): 64.

19. Ascertaining precise sales numbers for games can often be difficult, as publishers often report only the number of games shipped as a way to circumvent issues of game returns and the sale of used copies.

20. Johan Kristiansson, Private interview (August 10, 2005); hereafter cited as Kristiansson.

21. Scores for all three games are for PS2 console version.

22. Kathy Schoback, "The Economics of a Next-Gen Game," *Game Developers Conference 2005* (March 9, 2005).

23. Douglas Lowenstein, "E3Expo 2005 State of the Industry Address," E3Expo 2005 (May 18, 2005). Available online at <http://www.theesa.com/archives/2005/05/e3expo_2005_sta.php>. Making easy comparisons between the economic status of the video game vs. the film industry is difficult, as the significance depends entirely upon how one defines the scope of each industry and how wide one casts a net for figures. Lowenstein's numbers are based on software sales vs. box-office sales. As noted previously, the majority of contemporary Hollywood's revenue comes from home video sales, international television sales, and product licensing. Profit calculations based on these numbers would project Hollywood's annual revenue at a much higher number.

24. Wade Steel, "Halo Film Planned for 2007: Fox and Universal to bring Master Chief to the silver screen," *IGN.Com* (August 23, 2005). Available online at http://xbox360.ign.com/articles/644/644458p1.html.

25. Stuart Roch, "The New Studio Model," *Game Developer Magazine* (October 2004): 6.

26. At the time of writing, *The Wheelman* is scheduled for release in 2008. In the interest of full disclosure, it should be noted that the author of this essay is an employee of Midway Games at the time of writing, but works for a different development studio on a different IP.

27. Rebecca Murray, "*The Wheelman* to be Both a Video Game and Feature Film," *ABOUT.com* (February 28, 2006). Available online at <http://movies.about.com/od/dieselvin/a/wheelman022606.htm>.

28.   This essay is a revised version of papers I delivered at the 2005 Future Play Conference and at the 2006 SCMS conference. The Future Play version is available as "How a Salad Bowl Can Improve Transmedia Storytelling: Integration and Convergence in Film and Game Development." Available online at <http://www.futureplay.org/docs/papers/2005/paper-176_elkington.pdf>.

CHAPTER **12**

Fear of Failing?
The Many Meanings of Difficulty in Video Games

JESPER JUUL

Winning Isn't Everything

It is quite simple: When you play a game, you want to win. Winning makes you happy, losing makes you unhappy. If this seems self-evident, there is nonetheless a contradictory viewpoint, according to which games should be "neither too easy nor too hard," implying that players also want *not* to win, at least part of the time. This is a contradiction I will try to resolve in this essay.

• Question 1: What is the role of failure in video games?
The simplest theory of failure states that failing serves as a contrast to winning, that failure thereby makes winning all the more enjoyable. There is, however, much more to failure. The study of players discussed in this essay indicates that failure serves the deeper function of making players readjust their perception of a game. In effect, *failure adds content* by making the player see new nuances in the game. Correspondingly, the study shows that players have quite elaborate theories of failure as a source of enjoyment in games.

Even so, given the negative connotations of failing, would a game be better received if players did not feel responsible for failing, but rather blamed failures on the game or on bad luck?

• Question 2: Do players *prefer* games where they do *not* feel responsible for failing?

This study strongly indicates that this is *not* the case. Players clearly prefer feeling responsible for failing in a game; not feeling responsible is tied to a negative perception of a game.

In effect, this sharpens the contradiction between players wanting to win and players wanting games to be challenging: failing, and feeling responsible for failing, make players enjoy a game *more*, not less. Closer examination reveals that the apparent contradiction originates from two separate perspectives on games: a goal-oriented perspective wherein the players want to win, and an aesthetic perspective wherein players prefer games with the right amount of challenge and variation. Nevertheless, these two perspectives still present opposing considerations—the goal-oriented perspective suggests that games should be as easy as possible; the aesthetic perspective suggests that games should not be too easy.

To examine this, I will look at the role of failure and punishment. I am writing here about single-player games.[1]

Failure and Punishment

Failure means being unsuccessful in some task or interdiction that the game has set up, and punishment is what happens to the player as a result. We can distinguish between different types of punishment for player failure[2]:

- *Energy punishment*: Loss of energy, bringing the player closer to life punishment
- *Life punishment*: Loss of a *life* (or "retry"), bringing the player closer to game termination
- *Game termination punishment*: Game over
- *Setback punishment*: Having to start a level over and losing abilities.

Losing energy brings the player closer to losing a life, and losing a life often leads to some type of setback. In this perspective, all failures eventually translate into setbacks, and the player's use of time and energy is the most fundamental currency of games.

Whereas early video games in the arcade, on the home console, or for personal computers, tended to force the player to replay the entire game after failing, many home games from the mid-1980s and later became much more lenient by dispersing save points, allowing the player to save the game, or letting the player restart at the latest level played even after game over. As a recent example of this design principle, after reaching game over in *Super Mario Galaxy* (Nintendo EAD Tokyo, 2007), the player loses of coins and collectables, but not overall progress in the game.

In the new area of downloadable casual games,[3] there is a movement from life punishment to energy punishment, with many games featuring energy bars, timers, or other types of soft evaluations of player performance as with the timer in *Big City Adventure: San Francisco* (Jolly Bear Games, 2007) (see Figure 12.1).

The psychological *attribution theory* provides a framework for examining different types of failure and punishment in games. According to attribution theory, for any event, people tend to attribute that event to certain causes. Harold K. Kelley distinguishes between three types of attributions that people can make in an event involving a person and an entity:

- *Person*: The event was caused by personal traits, such as skill or disposition
- *Entity*: The event was caused by characteristics of the entity
- *Circumstances*: The event was based on transient causes such as luck, chance, or an extraordinary effort from the person.[4]

Figure 12.1 *Big City Adventure: San Francisco*—a timer gradually runs out. (Jolly Bear Games, 2007).

In the case of receiving a low-grade for a school test, a person may decide that this was due to the (a) person—personal disposition such as lack of skill; (b) entity—an unfair test; or (c) circumstance—having slept badly, having not studied enough. This maps quite well to many common exclamations in video gaming: a player who loses a game can claim that "I am terrible at video games," "This is an unfair game," or "I will win next time."

During the research for this essay, I developed the hypothesis that energy punishment is being more widely used because it makes the cause of failure less obvious: If the game is over due to a single, identifiable mistake, it is straightforward for the player to attribute failure to his or her own performance or skill (circumstance or person), but if the game is over due to an accumulation of small mistakes, the player is less likely to feel responsible for failing, and the player should be less likely to experience failing as an emotionally negative event. This is the second question mentioned in the introduction: do players *prefer* feeling less responsible for failing?

Video Game Theory through Game Prototypes

To elaborate this discussion, a game prototype study was conducted. This is not without precedent. In a study made 25 years ago, Thomas W. Malone explored the question "Why are computer games so captivating?" by creating a number of game prototypes with the same core game, but with different features (music, scorekeeping, fantasy, types of feedback).[5] In order to explore the attraction of the variations of the game, he let some children play these prototypes and examined how long each prototype was able to keep the attention of young players. From this, he deduced a number of guidelines for developing games and interfaces.

Following Malone, the questions in this essay can be approached as empirical questions—*What do players prefer?* They can, however, also be approached as aesthetic questions—*What is a good game?* These are two historically separate approaches that I nevertheless believe can inform each other in the following.

In collaboration with the game company Gamelab, I developed a game prototype specifically designed to gather data on how players perceive failure. The custom game could be described as a combination of *Pac-Man* (Namco, 1980) and *Snake* (Gremlin, 1977): using the mouse, the player controls a snake that grows as the player collects pills; the player must avoid opponents; and a special power pill allows the player to attack opponents for a short while (see Figure 12.2).

The game was designed with two game modes, an *energy punishment* mode where the player would lose a tail part when hit by opponents, and a

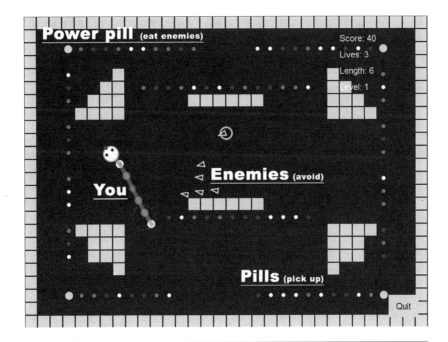

Figure 12.2 Game prototype for the test.

life punishment mode where the player could make only a single mistake before losing a life. In both games, the player has three lives, and the game consists of four levels. We attempted to balance the two games so that they were equally hard (as measured in the number of levels that players would complete). Another reason for developing a new game was that this would give insight to the players' initial experience of learning a new game, and be less a reflection of their previous experience with that game.

First Test, Offline

A preliminary test was conducted offline. Five males and four females from Gamelab's tester base participated. All participants had some experience with and interest in games, and came to the Gamelab offices (see Appendix 1 at the end of this essay for a description of the test procedure). Players were asked how they would rate the game had they found it on the Internet. The rating scale went from 1 to 10, with 10 being the best rating. Additionally, players were asked open questions about their views on failure in games.

Contrary to expectations, this small sample gave no indication that players preferred the energy punishment version of the game. On the other hand, there were indications that the players' ratings were closely tied to their performance in the game, such that a player performing badly would dislike the game, a player performing fairly well would like the game, but a player performing very well would *also dislike the game*. Given the interesting implications of this result, it was decided to focus on only one version of the game (energy punishment), and run a new test online with a bigger sample.

Second Test, Online

A total of 85 players were recruited online[6] and asked to play the game and answer a questionnaire (see Appendix 2 for a description of the test procedure). The players recruited were overwhelmingly male (73 out of 85), and the majority had a game console in their home (also 73 out of 85). Players were generally avid game players (see Figure 12.3).

Game Rating vs. Performance

Based on automated registration of player performances, player responses were placed into three categories, from a bad performance to a good performance:

1. Players that did not complete the game
2. Players that completed the game, losing some lives
3. Players that completed the game without losing any lives.

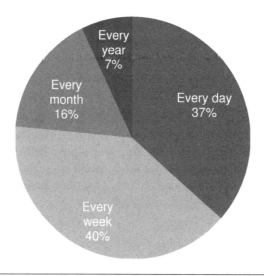

Figure 12.3 Game-playing frequency.

By comparing the average game ratings with the performance of the players (Figure 12.4), we can see an indication that *winning isn't everything*: the most positive players were the ones that *failed* some, and then completed the game. Completing the game without failing was followed by a *lower* rating of the game (the statistical significance was the slightly weak $p<0.06$ for all three categories of player performance combined).

This runs counter to the simple idea that players enjoy a game more the better they do, but it vindicates the game design imperative that a game must be neither too hard nor too easy as argued by, for example, Fullerton *et al.*[7] This returns us to the second question, of whether feeling responsible for failing in a game will make players like the game less. In the test, players were asked why they failed or succeeded. Categories were based on attribution theory, but expanded into smaller subcategories:

- *Person* was split into "I am bad at this kind of game" and "I am bad at games in general" to capture difference between general player skills and player knowledge of specific genres
- *Entity* was asked via "The game was too hard"
- *Circumstance* was split into "I was unlucky" and "I made a mistake" in order to distinguish between the experience of losing due to chance and losing due to a strategic mistake.

As can be seen in Figures 12.5 and 12.6, players were slightly more likely to report being responsible for success ("figured out how to play right") than being responsible for failure ("made a mistake"). This is well-known phenomenon called *attribution asymmetry*, whereby individuals are more

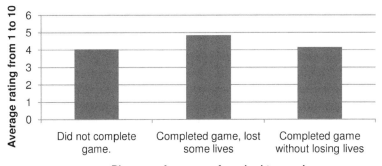

Figure 12.4 Player rating of game as function of performance.

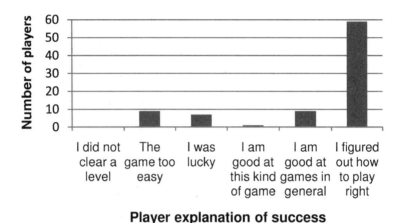

Player explanation of success

Figure 12.5 Player attribution of success.

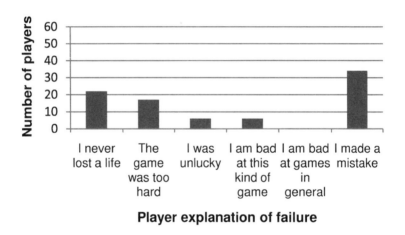

Player explanation of failure

Figure 12.6 Player attribution of failure.

likely to attribute success to personal factors, and failure to external factors (Försterling 87–91).

Do players prefer games where they do not feel responsible for failing? This seems not to be the case. On the contrary, even though players presumably on some level disliked being personally responsible for failing, the feeling of being responsible for failing was nevertheless tied to a *positive* rating of the game (see Figure 12.7).

Since players who never lost a life are not relevant, and too few players answered "I was unlucky" or "I am bad at this kind of game" for the results to be meaningful, we can see how players who answered "The game was too

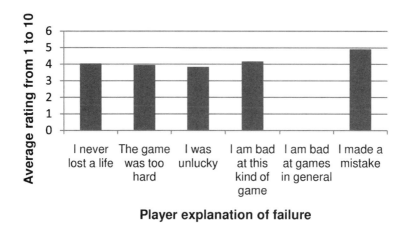

Figure 12.7 Rating as function of failure attribution.

hard" rated the game compared with those who answered "I made a mistake." In this case, there is a clearer significance of $p<0.016$. In effect, this answers the second question of this essay—players *prefer feeling responsible* for their own failure. Or at least the negative emotions from failing are more than cancelled out by other factors. This result is parallel to a study of players playing the bowling mini-game in *Super Monkey Ball 2* (Amusement Vision, Ltd., 2002), in which players exhibited positive reactions when falling off the edge of the playing field, but negative reactions of watching the replay of the same event.[8] Although players do not want to fail, they may nevertheless enjoy it when feeling responsible for it.[9]

Players Reactions When Not Failing

Do players have theories of the function of failure, and in that case, how do they frame them? To find out, players were asked if they had ever experienced a game that was too easy, and *"How do you know if a game is too easy?"* Answers were seen as falling into four categories based on their primary content. These are listed in Table 12.1 with example answers and percentages.

The first response type, "lack of challenge," is somewhat tautological. Response (4) gives room for more interpretation: if a game being too easy is experienced as the game being shallow and uninteresting, it means that the role of failure is much more than a contrast to winning—failure pushes the player into reconsidering strategy, and failure thereby subjectively *adds content* to the game. The game appears deeper when the player fails; failure makes the game more strategic.

Table 12.1 Example answers and percentages

Answer type	Examples
1. Too easy, as lack of a challenge (36%)	"Not challenging enough." "Boring . . . doesn't provide further challenges." "I don't feel challenged. Of course that's a pretty predictable answer, but it's hard to put it any other way." "I get bored."
2. Too easy, as not failing (6%)	"When you never die. And beat it in a day." "It doesn't seem to challenge me—I never lose."
3. Too easy, as not being measured on performance (5%)	"I can do things I know are 'wrong' and don't get punished." "A game is too easy when you are progressing through the game automatically no matter how good you are playing."
4. Too easy, as not having to rethink strategy (27%)	"When I know exactly what to do and I can do it optimizing the result without (big) effort." "No challenge, going through the motions to complete it without any thought." "If the challenge and thought required to complete its objectives become second nature quickly or there is no need for such contemplation." "If the method for solving it is obvious and never fails."

The next question is to what extent the results from this experiment map to players of published commercial games. In a discussion of the initial disappointing reception of the game *Shopmania* (Gamelab, 2006), Catherine Herdlick and Eric Zimmerman discuss how much of the criticism of the game came from the fact that it was perceived as too easy:

> In the original version of *Shopmania*, we approached the first several levels of the game as a gradual tutorial that introduced the player to the basic game elements and the core gameplay. This approach was based on the generally held casual game wisdom that downloadable games should be very easy to play, and that the frustration of losing a level should be minimized. However, the problem with going too far in this direction is that the game ends up feeling like interactive muzak: you can play forever and not really lose, and the essential tension and challenge of a good game are lost. From our analysis, players were telling us that the first seven or eight levels felt like a tutorial. By the third or fourth level, we had playtesters exclaiming out loud, "I get this game. Can I skip the tutorial?"[10]

One of the negative comments on *Shopmania* was about having seen the whole game too early:

> "After 20 minutes, I felt like I saw the whole game . . ." (*Redesigning*)

The "saw" here probably does not refer directly to concrete graphics or level layouts, as much as it ties into some of the player comments in my experiment: The players complain about the game not pressuring them, not threatening with failure. Again, while players may dislike failure, *not failing can be as bad as never succeeding.*

Flow: The Standard Theory of Failure and Challenge

The standard psychological explanation for game failure and challenge is Mihaly Csikszentmihalyi's theory of *Flow* (see Figure 12.8), according to which the challenge of a given activity forms a narrow channel in which the player is in the attractive *flow* state.[11]

While flow theory does suggest that the player may oscillate between anxiety and boredom, it poses the banal problem that the standard *illustration* suggests a smooth increase in difficulty over time. Noah Falstein[12] has refined this to say that game difficulty should vary in waves—sometimes the game should be a little easy, sometimes a little hard, and that irregularity leads to enjoyment, as illustrated in Figure 12.9. An irregular increase in difficulty makes the player more likely to experience both failure and successes.

Conclusions: The Contradictory Desires of Players

I initially discussed a contradiction between the observation that players want to win and the observation that players prefer games where they lose

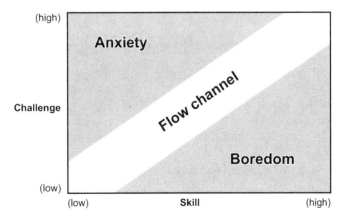

Figure 12.8 The flow channel. (Based on Csikszentmihalyi, 1990, 74).

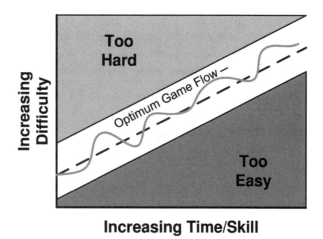

Figure 12.9 *A better flow.* (©2004 Noah Falstein).

some, then win some. This leaves us with several opposing considerations indicating that games should be both easier and harder than they are:

1. The player does not want to fail (makes player sad, feel inadequate).
2. Failing makes the player reconsider his/her strategy (which makes the game more interesting).
3. Winning provides gratification.
4. Winning without failing leads to dissatisfaction.

Points (1) and (3) suggest that games should be very easy, whereas points (2) and (4) suggest that games should not be *too* easy. The actual relationship of game design and game playing is probably not as antagonistic as this seems. A more productive view is that games derive their interest from the interaction between these different considerations, and that the apparent contradiction comes from the fact that games can be viewed from two distinct frames of reference (see Figure 12.10). Playing a game entails (a) a goal-orientation as part of the activity, but a player also has (b) an outside view of the game that entails an aesthetic evaluation of game balance. This is the source of the contradiction discussed in the introduction, between players wanting to win, and players wanting not just to win.

The second question at the start of this essay is whether players would prefer *not* feeling responsible for failing, and whether the success of casual games consequently could be attributed to the fact that they tend to have energy punishment rather than life punishment, making failure seem

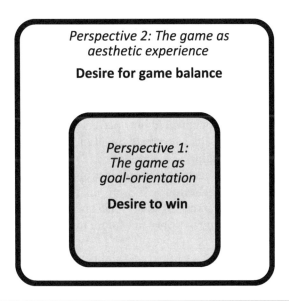

Figure 12.10 Goal-oriented and aesthetic perspectives on a game.

less of a direct consequence of player actions. This idea seems to be largely disproved—player appreciation of the game was tied positively to feeling responsible for failure. This suggests that I had been focusing on the wrong part of the punishment system, and that the attraction of casual games is better explained as sparing use of *setback punishment*: failing in casual games is rarely tied to any substantial setback, and never to having to mechanically replay a game sequence.[13] Players still feel responsible for failing, but they are less likely to feel stuck in the game, being forced to replay a part of the game.

Finally, this research points to another layer of complexity in player behavior. That failure and difficulty is important to the enjoyment of games correlates well with Michael J. Apter's *reversal theory*, according to which people seek low arousal in normal goal-directed activities such as work, but high arousal, and hence challenge and danger, in activities performed for their intrinsic enjoyment, such as games.[14] This yields an extra complication in relation to the game *Shopmania* discussed previously: if the role of failure is to force players to discover new strategies in a game, why is this even necessary? Given that players enjoy a challenge, why do players not simply challenge themselves by finding new ways to play the game? Game designer David Jaffe goes as far as asserting that players are basically lazy and "WILL NOT use ANY mechanic they do not need to use. They will take the path of least resistance to get from A TO B."[15]

The conclusion must still be that players want to fail as well as win, but that players of the *single-player* games discussed here do *not* seek out additional challenge or depth if they do not have to. Perhaps single player games are perceived as designed experiences that players expect to be correctly balanced without having to seek additional challenges themselves?

Conversely, although the focus here has been on single player games, Jonas Heide Smith has documented how players of multiplayer games frequently handicap themselves to create an even playing field, effectively opening themselves to failure (Heide Smith 217–227). Multiplayer games and more open sandbox games seem to encourage players to undertake more challenge-seeking behavior.

The study raises a number of additional questions, but I believe the following are the most obvious ones to explore further:

- Is the relation between game rating and performance also consistent if the game is made easier or harder?
- How do players perceive difficulty in games without time pressure or failure states, such as "endless" mode in *Bejeweled 2* (PopCap Games, 2004) or *Sudoku*?
- In game development experience, it is certain that small changes to game designs *do* matter to players. To what extent can individual elements of a game design be isolated?
- To what extent can we extrapolate from one game to all games?
- Will the results of the test be different with a more "casual" audience?

I have argued that failure is central to player enjoyment of games. This is not that surprising, given conventional wisdom that a game should be balanced to match the skills of players. However, it is notable that failure is more than a contrast to winning—rather failure is central to the experience of *depth* in a game, to the experience of improving skills. The study supports the idea that that *growth*, the experience of learning, of adjusting strategies, of trying something new, is a core attraction of video games.[16] Hence the desire for game balance, losing some, winning some—the experience of variation in the challenge and difficulty of the game. *Failure adds content.*

If the classic tenet of storytelling is Aristotle's, that a story should have a beginning, a middle, and an end, the core tenet of games must be this: *a game should be neither too easy nor too hard*. This is more than the simple truism it sounds like. It reveals much deeper and more complicated facts about games, and players.

Acknowledgments

This research was done in collaboration with Gamelab in New York City, who provided facilities, discussion, feedback, and playtesting. Thanks to T. L. Taylor, Jonas Heide Smith, Eric Zimmerman, Nick Fortugno, Chris Bateman, and Matthew Weise for comments. Thanks also to Svend Juul for statistical expertise.

Appendix 1: Offline Test Procedure

Participants were tested one at a time, and did not see or talk to other participants. Participants were informed that "We are working on a game, and we would like to hear your input. This is not a test of your skill; we would simply like to know what you think about the game."

Each player was asked to play the game until the game was over. It was noted on what levels players lost lives.

Each player was asked "Why did you fail?" and "Why did you complete the level?" The explanations were coded as being either due to *ability* (personal factor), *performance* (circumstance), or the *game* (entity).

After one game had been played, the player was interviewed.

Each player was asked to rate the game as follows: "If this was a game you found on the web, how would you rate it on a scale from 1 to 10, with 1 being the worst and 10 being the best?"[17]

Each player was asked to explain if he or she had ever played a game that was too easy.

Each player was asked how he or she could tell if a game is too easy.

Participants were not paid, but as game testing is often described as a way of entering the game industry, testers may have strong motivation for pleasing the company. This affects the confidence in the absolute judgments of the players, but since the testers' interest in pleasing the company will be statistically uniform, the data can be used relatively in correlation with other data from the test.

Appendix 2: Online Test Procedure

Players were recruited via the author's blog.

Players were told that "This is *not* a test of your skills, but a test of how you feel about playing a little game experiment"; players were not aware that the test concerned failure.

Players were directed to a page with instructions, as can be seen online at http://www.jesperjuul.net/test/rpt2/.

Players were directed to the game. The game consisted of four levels. The player had three lives.

When a player reached Game Over, either by completing all four levels or by losing all three lives, the player was directed to an online questionnaire. In the questionnaire, the player was asked to rate the game as follows: "Say you found this game on the Internet. On a scale from 1 to 10, with 1 being the worst game ever, and 10 being the best game ever, how would you rate this game?"

Only players who completed the entire questionnaire were included.

Notes

1. For studies of players in multiplayer settings, see Jonas Heide Smith, "Plans and Purposes: How Video Games Shape Player Behavior," PhD dissertation, IT University of Copenhagen, 2006, hereafter cited as Heide Smith; and Nicole Lazzaro, "Why We Play Games: Four Keys to More Emotion in Player Experiences," paper presented at the *Game Developers Conference*, San José, 2004. Abstract available online at <http://www.xeodesign.com/whyweplay games/xeodesign_whyweplaygames.pdf>.

2. Not all failure is punished in games—many smaller types of failure go unpunished, such as bumping into a wall.

3. Casual games are understood here as downloadable games that the player can play freely for typically 60 minutes, after which the game must be purchased to continue playing.

4. F. Försterling, *Attribution: An Introduction to Theories, Research and Applications* (London: Psychology Press, 2001), 46–47, hereafter cited as Försterling.

5. Thomas W. Malone, "Heuristics for Designing Enjoyable User Interfaces: Lessons From Computer Games," in *Proceedings of the 1982 conference on Human factors in computing systems* (Gaithersburg, MD: ACM, 1982), 63–68.

6. Via the *Ludologist* blog. Available online at <http://www.jesperjuul.net/ludologist>.

7. Tracy Fullerton, Chris Swain, and Steven Hoffman, *Game Design Workshop: Designing, Prototyping, and Playtesting Games* (San Francisco: CMP Books, 2004), 249.

8. Niklas Ravaja, Timo Saari, Jari Laarni, Kari Kallinen, Mikko Salminen, Jussi Holopainen, and Aki Järvinen "The Psychophysiology of Video Gaming: Phasic Emotional Responses to Game Events," in *Changing Views: Worlds in Play. Proceedings of DiGRA 2005 Conference*, Vancouver, 2005. Available online at <http://www.digra.org/dl/db/06278.36196.pdf>.

9. The conclusions from the *Super Monkey Ball* study may not map to questions discussed in this essay, as *Super Monkey Ball 2* has rewarding audiovisual feedback when the player fails compared to the more basic representation in the game prototype used here.

10. Catherine Herdlick and Eric Zimmerman, "Redesigning Shopmania: A Design Process Case Study," *IGDA Casual Games Quarterly* 2, no. 1 (2006), available online at <http://www.igda.org/casual/quarterly/2_1/index.php?id=6>; hereafter cited as *Redesigning*.

11. Mihaly Csikszentmihalyi, *Flow: The Psychology of Optimal Experience* (New York: Harper & Row, 1990).

12. Noah Falstein, "Understanding Fun—The Theory of Natural Funativity," in *Introduction to Game Development*, ed. Steve Rabin, 1 (Boston, MA: Charles River Media, 2005), 71–98.

13. This is also due to the fact that casual games tend to contain much randomness, making every replay of a single level is a bit different from the previous.

14. J. H Kerr and Michael J. Apter, *Adult Play: A Reversal Theory Approach* (Amsterdam: Swets & Zeitlinger, 1991), 17.

15. David Jaffe, "Aaaaaaaaannnnnnnndddddd Scene!," *Jaffe's Game Design*, November 25, 2007, available online at <http://criminalcrackdown.blogspot.com/2007_11_25_ archive. html>.

16. This is close to what Nicole Lazzaro calls "hard fun" (2004).

17. Since there is no universal scale for rating games, little can be deduced from the individual rating, but ratings can be used comparatively to examine player perceptions of game quality.

CHAPTER 13

Between Theory and Practice
The GAMBIT Experience

CLARA FERNÁNDEZ-VARA
NEAL GRIGSBY
EITAN GLINERT
PHILIP TAN
HENRY JENKINS

In the first *Video Game Theory Reader*, Walter Holland, Henry Jenkins, and Kurt Squire described how the Comparative Media Studies (CMS) program at MIT was beginning to integrate game design into its humanities curriculum. The program had embarked on a resource-restricted journey to the frontier of video game theory: "Our students are working through games on paper, examining existing games, brainstorming future directions, and through this process, trying to address central issues about games and education."[1] The essay drew an analogy to the work by Lev Kuleshov and his students in the early days of film studies; without any experience or access to film-making equipment, they produced thought experiments and insights that came to influence a generation of Soviet film makers. Through the *Games-to-Teach* research project, CMS students generated game designs as a form of theory through practice. The program sought to supplement academic theories of games with more "vernacular" theories, asking its students to think through real-world challenges facing practitioners. The essay also anticipated a near future in which CMS and other academic programs would build the resources and expertise needed to turn prototypes into polished games, training its students to become game designers, much as Kuleshov's training paved the way for Pudovkin and Eisenstein.

The Games-to-Teach program evolved into The Education Arcade in 2003. Student researchers developed *Revolution,*[2] an ambitious modification of the *Neverwinter Nights* (Bioware Corporation, 2002) engine that transported players to Colonial Williamsburg on the eve of the American Revolution. More recently, a partnership with Maryland Public Television began collaboration between students and professional development studios on a game designed to teach math and literacy to middle school students.

For CMS, the establishment of the Singapore-MIT GAMBIT Game Lab in 2006 marked the next leap in its continuing exploration between game theory and practice. Jointly created by CMS and the Media Development Authority of Singapore, GAMBIT is a five-year project to research video games, develop new and innovative games, and prepare students from Singapore's universities and polytechnic for entering the games industry. The GAMBIT name describes the project's many axes of inquiry: Gamers, Aesthetics, Mechanics, Business, Innovation, and Technology. Adhering to the principles of "applied humanism," the conceptual core of the Comparative Media Studies program, GAMBIT translates research into practical application, testing theoretical precepts in contexts outside of academia. GAMBIT sought ways to move students from writing and studying games towards developing and testing playable games.

In the run-up to development, Jenkins described the laboratory as "a space where we can move swiftly from pure research into compelling applications and then partner with the games industry to bring the best ideas to market."[3] What follows is an analysis of the methods used by student and faculty researchers to build games in the academic context. This is also, in the spirit of video games, an attempt to hit a moving target. The pilot year saw tremendous experimentation with new methodologies, with continual testing, revision, and radical rewrites of design and development procedures. Embracing change, GAMBIT continually refines every process used in the lab. This essay does *not* have a universal recommendation for university-based games research. Rather, it is a snapshot of our own navigation through the unique challenges facing academic game developers.

Across Countries and Cultures: Singapore and MIT

The games of the Singapore-MIT GAMBIT Game Lab are merely its public face. Internally, the lab has the mission of furthering the strong research relationships between Singaporean institutions and MIT. MIT has a sterling international reputation as a producer of scientific research, invention, and entrepreneurship. It is also both a proven incubator for new ideas and a proving ground for individuals who are encouraged to think differently. For MIT, Singapore is a partner that understands the importance of education and research for economic development, willing to take calculated risks for potential rewards.

On the other side of the world, Singapore is a modern and technologically forward-thinking nation that has made substantial investments in education in order to position itself as a hub for technological industries in South-east Asia. Singapore students and researchers are methodical, technically proficient, and driven with a relentless work ethic that rivals the tireless reputation of the MIT student body. For Singapore, MIT is a gateway to high-level faculty and research conducted throughout the USA. For both parties, the partnership presents an opportunity for international cultural exchange.

The GAMBIT partnership is an initiative of Singapore's National Research Foundation (NRF), tasked with the mission of identifying new economic opportunities for the country.[4] Traditionally dominated by manufacturing and trade, the Singaporean economy has faced declining manufacturing numbers in recent years. Singapore's neighbors in South-east Asia have also created significant competition for international trade routes. As a result, the government of Singapore set aside public funds for research and development aimed at identifying and exploiting new economic strategies. An earlier research program centered on biotechnology had proven to be successful, encouraging Singapore to launch new initiatives in other areas of research, with the NRF inviting proposals from universities across the world to fund collaborative work with Singapore.

By 2006, Singapore had clear, recognizable strengths in environmental and biological technologies. Both fields were highlighted for expanded research and funding. Interactive and Digital Media (IDM), however, was a significantly different challenge for Singapore. The past decade had seen several Asian countries carve out successful and lucrative niches across a variety of digital media forms such as animation and games. Japan, Korea, China, and India had all identified distinctive niches for themselves within global media flows, developing content that reflected their unique aesthetic and cultural traditions. However, despite having a competent and modern IT infrastructure, creative industries in Singapore were struggling to develop a coherent global strategy.

Despite the emergence of new digital distribution channels that presented new opportunities, Singapore's nascent game industry had yet to understand how to leverage and market its strengths. The government of

Singapore hoped that a solid funding push in IDM research and development would allow Singapore to identify competitive advantages and attract strategic partners needed to push this industry to the next level. With a history of successful educational collaborations such as the Singapore-MIT Alliance (SMA), Singapore approached MIT with a cross-section of its national research challenges. The faculty of MIT responded with hundreds of proposals for collaboration, including one proposing a "games innovation lab," authored by Henry Jenkins and William Uricchio, the co-directors of CMS. The proposal reasoned that it would be impractical for Singapore's game developers to compete head-to-head against market leaders in the production of mainstream games. Growing Singapore's game industry would require a different approach, one that took advantage of Singapore's educational, cultural, and technological strengths.

The Media Development Authority of Singapore (MDA) expressed interest, working with CMS to expand the document into a detailed five-year plan. By the middle of 2006, the IDM Steering Committee of the NRF approved the funding of the Singapore and MIT components of the game lab. However, the success of the lab would clearly hinge on its relevance to the Singaporean game industry and to the rest of the world. Public money was about to be spent on academic research instead of direct industry subsidies. To prove its value to Singapore, the lab could not just write about game theory or suggest abstract recommendations. GAMBIT would have to provide concrete examples of innovation that will help make Singapore successful in an international market. As Jenkins explained, "The next generation of game designers will need to be able to communicate in a global context and appreciate the cultural diversity that characterizes current game production" (Kohler).

Lost in Translation: Video Game Theory and Practice

As GAMBIT forges its links between East and West, it also seeks to bridge the gulf between video game theory and practice. Despite the growth of game studies as an emerging academic field of research, commercial game companies have generally remained disinterested in what academics have to say about the medium. In a widely circulated editorial, Microsoft researcher John Hopson posited several explanations for this disconnect, providing recommendations for academics who wished to get their ideas through to game makers.[5] His most forcefully expressed point was the imperative: *Prove it.* He challenged researchers to come down from the ivory tower and demonstrate the value of their theories through the building of actual games. In a similar response to Janet Murray, Mark Barrett describes his frustration, "I need to know how to make things, and that means I need practical solutions and reliable techniques to draw from."[6]

Some academics, such as Torill Mortensen, responded to subsequent talks on the same topic by pointing to the high barrier of entry for academic researchers.[7] Commercial video games can have production budgets of millions of dollars and require years of work by large, highly skilled professional teams of developers. Most educational institutions are not on the same playing field with such multinational media corporations. Hopson stated that academics had to implement their ideas to gain the attention of the game industry; academics argued that they lacked communication and credibility with the very practitioners whom they needed to implement new ideas (Hopson).

Furthermore, if academia limited all research to that which could be implemented and tested in a commercial project, it would throttle the richness of game scholarship. The giant development budgets in the game industry enable the creation of massive virtual worlds and astonishing visual effects but the studio mode of production currently dominating the game industry requires sure-fire blockbusters within genres already recognized and valued by the hardcore consumers. Helen Kennedy comments, "[Academic researchers] contribute a great deal to the potential meanings, issues, and frameworks which might be applied to the medium . . . thus opening up a field which might appear quite closed, autonomous, and potentially rather self-determining."[8] In short, academic research was valuable because it was not commercially driven, because it could point towards and could explore roads not taken by the mainstream industry, thus holding open alternatives for the future of the emerging medium.

Both perspectives reflected the realities of academic and industrial environments. However, both perspectives also grew from an earnest desire to explore the breadth and depth of the medium of video games. At best, game companies want academia to blaze a trail that they can follow, allowing them to colonize, populate, and profit from new possibilities. Chris Crawford describes the worst case scenario: "the academics are rushing to study games, and the industry doesn't much care."[9] If academics wish for their research findings to influence the industry, researchers need to acknowledge and work within the limitations of the practice. They need to make games.

However, academics can be strategic about how they approach their goals. Instead of relying on professional developers to demonstrate their ideas, they can take advantage of the industry's own inventions to make very different types of games. In 2007, new inexpensive commercial technologies and prototyping practices became widely accessible to the independent, low-cost game developer. New platforms and online distribution methods allowed small games with great ideas to reach new audiences. This presents academic and independent video game developers with a similar opportunity to that exploited by the first generation of independent filmmakers, many of whom had emerged from film production programs in universities. Rather than beat Hollywood at its own game, they identified and filled gaps in the marketplace ignored by the bloated studio films.[10]

Key to GAMBIT's ongoing success would be its ability to articulate academic research questions and execute modestly budgeted game development projects, strategically positioned to avoid having the smaller games directly compete against industry products. However, as with all educational initiatives, GAMBIT has another avenue to influence the industry: the MIT and Singapore students, who will become the game designers, programmers, and artists of the future. GAMBIT research fuels the development of video-game-related classes within the MIT curriculum, enabling new partnerships between the Comparative Media Studies Program and the Computer Science Department. Based on the framework developed by the Education Special Interest Group of the International Game Developers Association,[11] every research question and development project sponsored by GAMBIT needs the support of curriculum and coursework necessary for students to develop their own understanding of games. Even though the long-term effect may only be felt after students graduate and enter the industry, education, development, and research may still enable effective dialogue between academia and industry.

Attempting to bridge the gap between industry and academia is no particular accomplishment in itself; it is a common approach in other disciplines such as engineering. However, the video game industry itself is young: it is constantly adapting to new business models and production schemes. Furthermore, video game scholarship is still in the process of defining itself as an academic discipline, formulating its relationship to other areas of study. Any bridge built between industry and academia would likely be a little unstable for the near future. However, GAMBIT is not facing this challenge alone. To name some other efforts, the Game Innovation Lab at USC, the Entertainment Technology Center at Carnegie Mellon, and the Experimental Game Lab at the Georgia Institute of Technology, all have similar gaming research projects.

GAMBIT's goal of establishing relationships at an international level adds a unique layer of complexity to the whole project. To illustrate this complicated process and the benefits and drawbacks of GAMBIT's early execution, an instructive example would be the story of *AudiOdyssey*, one of the games developed during the first year of GAMBIT.[12] *AudiOdyssey* represents an early attempt by the project to create these bridges—between theory and practice, between education and industry, and between Singapore and the USA. Analyzing the production of the prototype game sheds light on how industrial methods influenced the academic paradigm and vice-versa. In embracing change, unexpected success went hand in hand with informative failures.

Defining Hard Questions: Audio Games Research

Experiments test hypotheses: the results of well-designed experiments will shed light on their hypotheses, and both failure and success can be equally illuminating. Thus, the choice of the hypothesis often has greater bearing on the relevance of the experiment than the outcome. Even with a successful experiment, a poorly chosen hypothesis will fail to address the concerns of practitioners in the field. In the game industry, many practitioners already conflate experimentation with "blue sky" speculation, the exploration of game design possibilities unencumbered by the technological and market constraints of the real world.

To build the bridge between research and practice, GAMBIT needed to adopt an attitude of innovation to guide its experimentation. Innovators speak the language of the industry and desire to improve the experiences of the end-user through the creation of products. Innovators build on what has come before, acknowledge the real world challenges, and help move industry forward in iterative cycles. Innovators aim to stay for the long haul, allowing the reality of practice and the results of experiments to inform their exploration and the future development of the medium.

At GAMBIT, innovation begins with the selection of the right research question, trying to find the "sweet spot" where an academic endeavor can have the most impact. For its first year of operation, GAMBIT culled game research concepts over a semester, engaging CMS students and faculty in a process of conversation, investigation, background research, collaboration with other academic departments, and finally, the submission of written proposals. As required by the terms of collaboration, the lab would only support proposals that attracted mutual interest from faculty at MIT and the consortium of Singaporean institutions. However, the final selection criteria proved to be the most stringent: which proposals would be viable within the harsh timeline of three-month development cycles? How could GAMBIT translate the research questions into quickly and inexpensively produced games, using gameplay to communicate the ideas to the industry, receiving feedback from practitioners and players, and allowing those results to inform multiple iterations?

During a brainstorming session with several CMS-affiliated researchers in the beginning of 2007, GAMBIT collaborators from MIT noted the challenges facing the Singapore game industry, identifying the risks involved in building console and PC games given the competitive advantage enjoyed by the well-established game industries in the USA, Japan, China, and Korea. However, Singapore's wireless infrastructure and good relationships with regional markets gave it an edge in the development of games for mobile phones, particularly games with multiplayer capabilities. Since mobile phones had technological limitations in terms of computational capability and graphical power—good mobile games distinguished themselves with simple gameplay and elegant design instead of photo-realistic 3D graphics—the mobile platform presented a level playing field for market newcomers, independent game designers, and academic research projects.

Further examination of the capabilities of mobile phones noted that they generally had more sophisticated audio features than visual processing power due to their telephone ancestry. Games that stressed sonic artistry over visual detail presented a further opportunity for Singapore to sidestep the graphical arms race and to access a different audience. Music and rhythm games like *Guitar Hero* (Harmonix Music Systems, Inc., 2005) and *Dance Dance Revolution* (Konami Corporation, 1998) were already proving to be popular products among mainstream gamers despite their modest visuals.[13] Conventional industry wisdom assumed that music games represented a niche genre; fans of *Guitar Hero* and its sequels proved otherwise. Yet, the mainstream game industry was not actively exploring other potential forms of audio entertainment, such as radio drama and comedy. Even within existing audio game genres, few designers had fully explored the expressive capacities of the soundtrack.

There was a second motivation for exploring audio game entertainment. The global game industry had noted Nintendo's great success in expanding the market beyond the "hardcore gamer" demographic.[14] Confronting declining games sales in Japan, Nintendo and its competitors had spent significant time and money on games designed to appeal to women and the elderly. Casual games, simpler control schemes, and inclusive marketing were all becoming increasingly visible in mainstream publications such as *Time* and *Newsweek*.[15] However, blind users were not included in this expanded games market. Game industry research over the preceding decade had focused heavily on improving visual sophistication, such as high-definition displays and 3-D acceleration, or on designing new interfaces that were reliant on visual feedback, such as touch screens and wireless pointing devices. The global game industry had showed little interest in courting visually-impaired players.

A huge percentage of Americans (18.6 percent of Americans aged 16–64, according to the 2000 US census) have some form of disability, ranging from mental, motor, or sensory challenges.[16] Small but vocal groups of disabled gamers have been clamoring for accessible games and accessible controllers on websites such as AudioGames.net, eagerly sharing detailed reviews of the few examples that exist. Few of these games were engaging to both sighted and visually-impaired players. Some games designed to be accessible to the blind became *inaccessible* to sighted players.

For example, the primary challenge in first-person shooter games is to shoot an opponent before being shot, often combined with the challenges of navigating a complex environment of cover and traps. The audio-only alternatives were largely limited to basic movement and navigation, where finding and successfully walking through a door based on stereo cues would be a great achievement. Such games do not match the level of challenge presented by similar games designed for sighted gamers. As another example, a generic racing game would have players driving rapidly through twisting courses and exotic locales to edge out the competition. Blind-accessible versions simply offered a variation on "Simon Says," with the player dodging objects rendered as stereo sounds, receiving little feedback about their vehicle's speed or their surrounding environment.

Most creators of blind-accessible games were independent developers and hobbyists working with limited budgets, yet even so, these few titles were in high demand among a group of consumers that had embraced high technology, such as *Shades of Doom* by GMA Games, who wished to participate in experiences taken for granted by their sighted counterparts. The professional industry generally ignored the potentially large market, underestimating and under-serving the growing population of visually impaired gamers.

Through this process of identifying the strengths of Singapore developers (mobile phones), examining how those strengths could be extended (audio games), and describing the market opportunities to be explored (accessible games for the blind), GAMBIT constructed a research proposal that was firmly grounded in reality and could help to expand the understanding of games as a medium. Singaporean researchers were eager to collaborate on an "Audio Games" project. Game developers visiting GAMBIT quickly understood the potentials and challenges that such a project represented. Such a project might be too "risky" for most companies to undertake; yet practitioners indicated that they would be interested in seeing the results, particularly in the form of a playable game.

Exploratory interviews with the blind community in Boston and other developers for blind-accessible games identified unexplored opportunities that enabled the team to refine guidelines, serving as a basis for a prototype. Such a game needed to allow visually-impaired and sighted users to share a common gaming experience. The game had to be accessible to both sighted and visually-impaired users, regardless of the severity of their impairment. An online multiplayer component would allow the sighted and blind to play together without being aware of the visual status of their fellow gamers. The game would aim to make alternative spatial control schemes accessible to blind gamers. On top of all that, the game needed to be fun, challenging, and engaging, relying more on audio than visuals to produce an exciting experience.[17]

Adopting Industry Practices: Agile Game Development

For the Summer of 2007, GAMBIT selected over 30 students from Singapore based on the strength of their academic records, portfolios, and their demonstrated passion for video games to travel to Cambridge, Massachusetts for a nine-week internship, working with MIT graduates and undergraduates to develop six new games. The summer program was an experiment in itself. GAMBIT staff sought to address Hopson's challenge and Mortensen's worries: How could an academic project create polished video games within an environment of extreme limitations of time and development expertise? Academic theorists and researchers had very few examples of finishing and releasing complete games. Released games from academia historically lacked in documentation, stability, and usability. The short development cycle and sheer variety of projects in GAMBIT put organization and management of teams at the highest priority. GAMBIT needed a process that facilitated polish and testing for student-developed games, one that drew a high level of commitment from students without burning them out before the end of the summer. Top-down supervision of the six summer teams was out of the question; each team needed to be relatively self sufficient and able to respond to their projects' unique challenges with extreme flexibility and competent crisis management.

GAMBIT chose not to solve this problem in a vacuum. Instead, by researching evolving management practices among practitioners, GAMBIT identified the "Scrum" project management model as an increasingly popular industrial solution for similar problems in commercial software development.[18] The model presented a strategy for scoping and executing projects that required agile product development on complex tasks that required teams to act on new findings, unexpected outcomes, and user feedback. It seemed ideal for game prototyping and game developers across the world were beginning to take note.[19] GAMBIT thus embraced the "Scrum" model to structure its first summer of game development.

The GAMBIT summer teams were small by game industry standards. Each team had seven members: two programmers, two artists, a game designer, a test lead, and a project manager. In addition, a two-person sound and music team provided services to all of the development teams. After a week of brainstorming and lectures, the teams subsequently adhered to an iterative cycle, dividing work into four fortnightly sprints and demonstrating a playable build of their games every two weeks. This allowed teams to periodically gather user feedback and honestly examine their progress.

Each team worked with one or two researchers to design and build a game to demonstrate a single research idea. The team and researcher would collaborate to produce a list of design and technical features. The researcher would prioritize the list according to the relevance of each feature to the research question. The team would select a few top-priority features to implement over the following two weeks, breaking them down into individual tasks and development strategies. After each fortnight, the team would demonstrate new functionality in a single software build to the researcher. Such an approach pushed team members not just to produce assets (code, concept art, music, design documents) but to also integrate these features into a working prototype every other week.

Before embarking on another sprint, the team and researcher would discuss which methods and strategies worked best and which failed to serve their specific needs. Like their commercial counterparts, teams needed to strategically scale back projects that were too ambitious to meet the deadlines printed on their return airline tickets. Rather than releasing unfinished games with a lot of potential, this process allowed students to focus on the most feasible and engaging ideas. As a fully funded educational research project, GAMBIT students and researchers would share their games without charge. Unlike commercial games that are regularly compared against their competition feature by feature, free games are generally just reviewed on their implemented functionality. Thus, the students had the space to polish their existing features to perfection instead of worrying about the ones that are missing.

Part of the GAMBIT experiment in project management included the minimization of "crunch time," when developers are subjected to weeks or months of perpetual overtime. Crunch time is a source of great discontent among professional game developers. Conventional industrial wisdom considers it unavoidable. Crunch time causes premature burnout in employees, decreases their average quality of life and work, and tends to drive experienced practitioners from the game industry into other fields. Crunch conditions may also reinforce the homogeneity of game development workplaces, driving out all but the young "rock star" developers who have few aspirations outside of their professional lives.[20] GAMBIT staff consistently discouraged overtime to engender a healthy workplace environment and test a model of sustainable development.

Teams were required to freeze all new feature development in the last two weeks, reserving the last sprint for polishing or cutting existing features. In this manner, GAMBIT staff emphasized the importance of competent project management, in the hopes of demonstrating that it would be possible to complete a game development project with minimal crunch.

The creative ability of each team to design gameplay and solve problems was crucial for fulfilling the goals of each researcher. For many students, this was their first experience in a comprehensive production environment. Alongside the efforts to turn theory into practice, GAMBIT also aimed to enhance the education of practitioner-theorists. The summer program periodically featured lectures about game design, usability, animation, and technical issues. Local Boston game industry professionals visited the students to share insider perspectives on design challenges and commercial work. These sessions aimed to expand the intellectual and professional horizons of the students while helping the game development teams refine their designs and techniques.

An academic environment should be more tolerant of mistakes than in industry; GAMBIT assumed that teams would make many mistakes as they ventured into unexplored territories of game research. At the same time, the academy must provide the scaffolding for students and researchers to learn from their mistakes, and this challenge is not unique to education. In practice, while a game designer may envision a beautifully complex game, the expertise, time, and resources of the development team limits its ability to fulfill that vision. Many commercial projects are stillborn because of the inability of team leaders and members to reach compromises that reflect the realities of their production context and to adapt to new information once a plan is set into motion.

From Challenge to Reality: *AudiOdyssey*

The progress of the Audio Games project from research through development illustrates our process of translating theory into practice. Ambitious experimental hypotheses quickly gave way to reality. The original concept of the project straddled mobile platforms, audio-based gameplay, novel control schemes, and accessibility for blind gamers. Despite the considerable audio capabilities of mobile phones, however, the limited system memory of such devices in 2007 made them unsuitable for storing and playing back multiple sound channels. GAMBIT staff decided to dedicate a separate student team to exploring online gameplay on mobile phones with *Backflow*.[21] This freed the Audio Games team from the constraints of mobile platforms to develop *AudiOdyssey*, a music rhythm game that runs on Windows PCs.

Figure 13.1 *AudiOdyssey.* (Copyright 2007, MIT.)

The player takes on the role of a club DJ. Each level in the game is a different song. The player matches sounds in the music with the arrow keys on the keyboard or by moving a motion-sensitive controller for the Nintendo Wii. Successful matches with the music adds layers of instruments, rewarding the player with a richer musical composition, the cheers of an appreciative dance crowd, and a new rhythmic challenge to meet. Completing all the challenges results in a "freestyle" mode, where the player can improvise without constraints. Inevitably, the overexcited crowd accidentally bumps the DJ's turntables, requiring the player to build up tracks for the next freestyle.

The two-person sound team delivered high quality music that the *AudiOdyssey* team worked hard to integrate. Testing proved the game to be fun for both sighted and blind players, satisfying the primary goal for the project. However, an online multiplayer component proved too difficult and time-consuming to implement. Furthermore, while the motion-sensitive Wii controller provided a new experience for blind gamers, the minimal familiarity with the Nintendo Wii also meant that blind testers needed coaching in the use of the motion controller. The keyboard controls were generally easier for all players to understand.

Scrum aimed to reduce crunch time by basing project management decisions on realistic expectations. However, by giving the students ownership over the game design, the increased commitment still resulted in students putting in more hours than were required. Motivated students found it difficult to sacrifice ideas for the sake of personal health, and many only discovered the need for polish time at the end of the project. For instance, once the *AudiOdyssey* team completed a fully functional game with an automated installer, a functioning menu system, and well-implemented gameplay, the team decided to add a new song to the game at the last minute. Despite having made a working game that met all of the GAMBIT standards of quality, they chose to end their development cycle with an extremely difficult level that was practically impossible to play. Recovering the earlier version for public release required an unnecessary amount of unanticipated work by members of the team.

Although the resulting game did not address every design challenge, the careful selection of the core hypotheses allowed failures to provide valuable information about the limits and possibilities of future audio games. The realities of production and the risks of venturing into new design territory informed the translation of theoretical concepts into a complete game. The academic participants better understood the challenges of creating something truly new and the need to balance novelty against the prior expectations and experiences of the audience. What design paradigms would offer similar experiences to sighted and blind players? What control schemes do blind players prefer? How would menus work? Instead of theory and speculation, GAMBIT responded to the challenge by providing concrete examples that the industry could easily understand and adopt.

AudiOdyssey became an effective research tool and an artifact for communicating new ideas in accessible gameplay. As a playable game, *AudiOdyssey* increased the visibility of the core research in both the industry and the press. Demonstrated at the Games Convention Asia 2007 in Singapore, industry professionals were able to pick up a controller and interact with a research concept that, three months earlier, only existed in academic writing. Though imperfect, *AudiOdyssey* provided the team of students and the researchers with valuable educational insight, and the game successfully represents the unique constraints of the research question and the personalities of its development team.

Learning from Students: From *Narbacular Drop* to *Portal*

GAMBIT's student designers benefited greatly from adopting industry methods and confronting high professional standards. It demonstrated that academics could translate their research into a form called for by industry leaders. However, how will the industry respond? Will game companies in Singapore and around the world be willing to adopt fresh ideas from students in their pursuit of mainstream audiences? The advantages of industry acceptance could be huge: professional game companies could observe new kinds of play, expand on them with better production values, deploy them with stable and sophisticated internal tools and engines, and leverage existing distribution networks to bring them to market.

This is precisely what happened in 2007 with the game *Portal* (Valve Corporation, 2007). In 2005, students from the DigiPen Institute of Technology released a game named *Narbacular Drop*,[22] developed as a school project. The player must navigate a series of environmental puzzles by manipulating a portal between two exits in space. To get the character to a high ledge, one could place a portal exit above the ledge and another on a wall close to the character. The player then directs the character to walk through the portal to the previously inaccessible location. The effect is thrilling and uncanny, representing a brand new way of moving through a game space. The above description does the game little justice—one needs to see the game in action to understand its twisted physics, and one needs to play the game to understand its appeal.

Even though *Narbacular Drop* suffers from coarse graphics, buggy

Figure 13.2 *Narbacular Drop.* (Copyright 2005, Nuclear Monkey Software.)

gameplay, and unexceptional sound effects, the core innovation shines through in a functional game that made the rounds at conferences, won awards at independent game festivals, and found its audience through free online distribution. It quickly caught the attention of Valve Corporation, the developer of the popular *Half-Life* (Valve L.L.C, 1998) series of first-person shooters. The students demonstrated the game to company executives, who hired them on the spot to work on a new game, *Portal*, combining the concept of *Narbacular Drop* with Valve's advanced 3-D technologies and substantial professional resources.[23]

In high-profile games such as *Grand Theft Auto III* (DMA Design Limited, 2001) and *Jak and Daxter* (Naughty Dog, Inc., 2001), the industry has shown a tendency to take a kitchen sink approach to game design, stuffing as many features and mechanics into as large a virtual world as possible. While the game industry is largely supported by profits derived from sequels of popular game series, this process begins by the creation of hit games based on new intellectual property. Most games meet with commercial failure and smaller innovative games suggest smaller amounts of financial risk.

If for no other reason other than necessity, academic and independent game developers are comfortable with identifying and honing a single concept to perfection. With both *Portal* and *Narbacular Drop*, the designers started with a core innovation and built their entire game around it. Game producer Kim Swift notes that an established studio risks tarnishing their

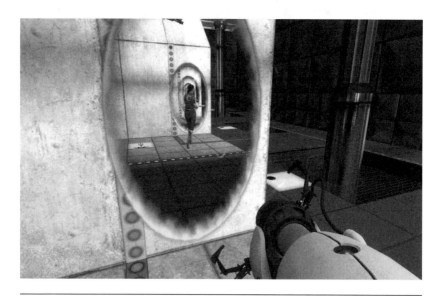

Figure 13.3 *Portal.* (Copyright 2007, Valve Corporation.)

reputation if they release an insufficiently polished product. In contrast, the expectations for an independent or student game are low, allowing players to forgive the rough edges and focus on the ideas.[24] With online distribution, independent video game companies and research projects such as GAMBIT can affordably produce and share playable prototypes that explore new creative territory, knowing that word-of-mouth advertising will allow the most interesting concepts to find their audiences.

So far, no game developed by GAMBIT has yet achieved the visibility of *Narbacular Drop*. As we write, the program is less than one year old. We will learn through successive years of experimentation and innovation. In the meantime, *AudiOdyssey* unearths strategies for designing satisfying game experiences that can be shared by blind gamers and their sighted friends. With this approach, GAMBIT will continue to explore issues and possibilities that exist just off the industry's radar screen.

Post-mortem

The first summer of game development laid the ground for the iterative development process at the Singapore-MIT GAMBIT Game Laboratory. In adopting industry practices, GAMBIT also adopted the convention of the professional "post-mortem." When a developer finishes a new title, the team meets with others in the business to discuss what they learned from the process, highlighting both their successes and their failures. Each of the GAMBIT teams prepared post-mortem presentations, listing the five things they did right and the five things that could have been improved. Like the student teams, the GAMBIT staff also prepared a post-mortem to identify process improvements. Some mistakes were technological, such as a poor software setup for student laptops. Others were methodological: the formation of the teams was rushed and resulted in some poor matches between student abilities and project requirements. More time was also needed for early brainstorming. The role of the test lead needed more definition. However, despite the hiccups in the process, most teams succeeded in designing and implementing a playable game around an innovative core idea.

In the post-mortem, the GAMBIT staff applied the same transparency, reflexivity, and adaptability that was required from the students to the operations of the lab itself, extending the same welcoming embrace of change that resulted in the successful development of the game prototypes. In this manner, the Singapore-MIT GAMBIT Game Laboratory will continue to respond to changing circumstances and new challenges to build bridges between academic research and industry practice, negotiate different priorities and cultures, and contribute to the global growth of the medium of games.

Notes

1. Walter Holland, Henry Jenkins, and Kurt Squire, "Theory by design," in *The Video Game Theory Reader*, eds, Mark J. P. Wolf and B. Perron (New York: Routledge, 2003), 29.
2. Philip Tan, Matthew Weise, Brett Camper, Nicholas Hunter and Henry Jenkins III, *Revolution* (The Education Arcade, 2005).
3. Chris Kohler, "Today's Homework: Make Good Games," *Wired Magazine* (February 13, 2007); hereafter cited as Kohler.
4. Government of Singapore, "About Us," *National Research Foundation of Singapore*, available online at <http://www.nrf.gov.sg/nrf/aboutus.aspx?id=92> (November 28, 2007)
5. John Hopson, "We're Not Listening: An Open Letter to Academic Game Researchers," *Gamasutra.com* (November 10, 2006), available online at <http://gamasutra.com/features/20061110/hopson_01.shtml,2006>; hereafter cited as Hopson.
6. Mark Barrett, "First Person: Academic Intent," *Electronic Book Review* (July 26, 2005), available online at <http://www.electronicbookreview.com/thread/firstperson>.
7. Torill Mortensen, "There's Jargon, and There's What I Understand," *Thinking With My Fingers* (October 8, 2007), available online at <http://torillsin.blogspot.com/2007/10/theres-jargon-and-theres-what-i.html>.
8. Jurie Horneman, "On Academia," *Intelligent Artifice* (December 12, 2004), available online at <http://www.intelligent-artifice.com/2004/12/on_academia.html>.
9. Kevin Delaney, "Are Videogames Ready To Be Taken Seriously By Media Reviewers?" *Wall Street Journal* (New York: November 3, 2003).
10. D. K. Holm, *Independent Cinema*. (New York: Oldcastle Books, 2007).
11. Susan Gold, Tracy Fullerton, Magy Seif-El Nasr, Yusuf Pisan, Darius Kazemi, and Darren Torpey. *IGDA Curriculum Framework: The Study of Games and Game Development*, IGDA Game Education Special Interest Group, 2008. Available online at <http://www.igda.org/wiki/images/e/ee/Igda2008cf.pdf>.
12. Eitan Glinert, Lonce Wyse, Yeo Jingying, Dominic Chai, Bruce Chia, Jim Wilberger, Paviter Singh, Mark Sullivan, Edwin Toh, Fezz Hoo Shuyi, and Guo Yuan, *AudiOdyssey* (Singapore-MIT GAMBIT Game Lab, 2007); hereafter cited as *AudiOdyssey*.
13. Evelyn M. Rusli, "Guitar Hero Rocks Activision," *Forbes.com* (November 27, 2007), available online at <http://www.forbes.com/markets/2007/11/27/activision-guitar-hero-markets-equity-cx_er_1127markets13.html>.
14. James Dobson, "IDC: Wii To Outship & Outsell Xbox 360, PS3 Through 2008," *Gamasutra.com* (March 1, 2007), available online at <http://www.gamasutra.com/php-bin/news_index.php?story=12956>.
15. DFC Intelligence, "The Secret of Nintendo's Success," *Next Generation* (February 26, 2007), available online at <http://www.next-gen.biz/index.php?option=com_content&task=view&id=4822&Itemid=2>.
16. Judith Waldrop, Sharon M. Stern, and US Census Bureau, *Disability Status, 2000* (US Dept. of Commerce, Economics and Statistics Administration, 2003).
17. Eitan Glinert and Lonce Wyse, "AudiOdyssey: An Accessible Video Game for Both Sighted and Non-Sighted Gamers," *ACM Future Play 2007*, ACM Digital Library, 2007, available online at <http://portal.acm.org/>.
18. Ken Schwaber, *Agile Project Management with Scrum* (Redmond: Microsoft Press, 2004).
19. Clinton Keith, "Agile Methodology and Scrum in Game Development," paper presented at *Game Developer Conference 2005*, San Francisco, 2005.
20. Lisa Laughy, "I am a Game School Dropout," *Game Career Guide* (October 4, 2007), available online at <http://www.gamecareerguide.com/features/435/i_am_a_game_ school_.php>.
21. Neal Grigsby, Brett Camper, Alex Chisholm, Henry Jenkins, Eric Klopfer, Scot Osterweil, Judy Perry, Philip Tan, Teo Chor Guan, and Matthew Weise, "From Serious Games to Serious Gaming," *Serious Games: Learning, Development and Change*, eds. P. Vorderer, M. Cody, and U. Ritterfeld (New Jersey: Routledge/LEA, 2008).
22. Kim Swift, Dave Kircher, Realm Lovejoy, Garret Rickey, Scott Klintworth, Eric Brown, Jeep Barnett, and Paul Graham, *Narbacular Drop* (USA: Nuclear Monkey Software, 2005); hereafter cited as *Narbacular Drop*.

23. Douglass C. Perry, "The Portal Interview," *IGN.com* (July 27, 2006), available online at <http://pc.ign.com/articles/721/721723p1.html>.
24. Kim Swift, "From *Narbacular Drop* to *Portal*," paper presented at *Game Developer Conference 2007*, San Francisco, 2007.

CHAPTER 14

Synthetic Worlds as Experimental Instruments

EDWARD CASTRONOVA
MARK W. BELL
ROBERT CORNELL
JAMES J. CUMMINGS
MATTHEW FALK
TRAVIS ROSS
SARAH B. ROBBINS-BELL
ALIDA FIELD

Science, Simulation, and Instruments

In this essay, we argue that *synthetic worlds would be very useful for social scientific experiments*. In stating our argument this way, we are implicitly putting some very restrictive stakes in the ground, stakes that strongly define the claims we are making.

Science

When we say "scientific," we are referring to a certain kind of knowledge. In some schools of thought, we might get away with saying that we are talking about facts, or truth, or reality. Other schools do not admit that such things even exist. At best, they say, we can have agreement about a proposition (though no amount of agreeing, it is said, ever makes a proposition absolutely true). We accept this more limited vision of science, that it is about the pursuit of intersubjective reality, that is, truth claims that many people agree with. We say that virtual worlds can be used to establish this sort of claim.

274 · Edward Castronova *et al.*

The reasoning is simple: a virtual world can be used to replicate research. It is like a Petri dish. It can be made the same way by anybody. If I build a virtual world and run it on a computer, then send you the code and the machine, you can run the same world. You may have different people in yours, but (a) it is easy to determine whether that matters, and (b) there are methods for reducing differences. It is easy to measure differences across people in things that matter—sex, race, family origin, even culture and politics. And since these things can be measured, it is easy to pre-screen participants and make sure that you have the same mix in your experiment as I had in mine.

Thus, if I use a virtual world to establish a truth claim, and you do not believe it, you can simply make the same virtual world and conduct the test yourself. Anything said to be generally true should be true in all replicated experimental environments. Thus if you come to different results, you may feel free to disbelieve my claim. But if your results match mine, you ought to agree with my conclusions. In agreeing, you share a truth claim with me. This is the minimal standard of truth-making by which natural science has advanced so far. Virtual worlds enable the same simple intersubjective persuasion tests to be applied to macro-level social phenomena. The domain of the tests is new, but the method is very old, and very successful.

Experiment

When we say "experiment," we refer to a particular way of establishing an intersubjective truth claim. An experiment is an exercise in the real world in which some proposition of the mind is tested. Virtual worlds, you might say, are not in the real world—how could they be used to conduct an experiment?

But the premise that virtual worlds are not real is utterly false. Virtual worlds are in the real world: they are populated by real people. The inter-actions between people are real, wherever they happen. Two people kissing on a steel ship in the Caribbean are no less in love than two people kissing on a papier-mâché boat in an Indiana cornfield. While mediation does affect things—kissing with a mask on is certainly different from kissing without one—those affects are not enough *a priori* to reject the potential reality of all possible mediated interactions. Many human interactions while wearing masks are completely comparable with ones without them. It resolves to an empirical question: for some, not all, human interactions, the presence of masks creates significant issues of generality, and the question is simply: When do masks matter? However, such questions do not affect our claim.

Our claim is not "activities in the virtual world are always generalizable to the real world." That is the simulationist's claim, and our claim is not a simulationist claim. Our claim is a scientific methodology claim:

> "Events can be induced among humans in virtual worlds that bear relevance for broad truth claims regarding human society."

Consider the same claim made in natural science:

> "Events can be induced among bacteria in Petri dishes that bear relevance for broad truth claims regarding bacterial cultures."

That proposition is beyond all arguing. Now consider this one:

> "All bacterial events in Petri dishes are simulations of bacterial events outside Petri dishes."

This second claim is absurd. It is used to criticize the idea of using virtual worlds for experiments, because, it is said, virtual worlds are not good copies of the real social world. But by examining this case when applied to natural science, we see that the claim is not only absurd, but its simulationist objectives are actually an impediment to scientific progress. If we were to accept this claim, we would be *less*, not more, successful at doing science. The simulationist objection says that the Petri dish does not contain anything like that which is on the outside. Well, of course, that is the whole point! The purpose of the Petri dish is not to recreate conditions on the lab's countertops. On the contrary: *the purpose is to purge the experiment of those conditions.* Recreating the conditions on the countertop is not only a waste of time, it is bad science. The word people use is "contaminated." The Petri dish must contain bacterial cultures that are different from the real world, in very special, controlled, observable ways.

Similarly, the purpose of a virtual world deployed for an experiment would be to differ from reality in very special, controlled, observable ways. Once we understand this, the objection that virtual worlds are not perfect simulations of the real world reveals itself as the product of a mind that grossly misunderstands what science is all about.

Science is an attempt to establish the truth of propositions. An experiment is a test of a proposition. A Petri dish is a tool for performing the test. To make claims about the validity of any one of these elements by themselves is a logic error. Again, consider:

> "You cannot use a glass dish for natural science experiments."

Rubbish. But many people respect, ponder, and weigh the analog:

"You cannot use a virtual world for social science experiments."

Rubbish. It makes no sense to reject any experimental implement *a priori*. The validity of an implement depends on both the nature of the implement and the nature of the proposition. Does the implement allow you to isolate the causal effects of interest? Is it reasonably secure from outside interferences? Do the initial conditions in the implement match those of your theoretical assumptions? Will you affect things by observing?

We accept that many virtual world environments would fail these tests, just as many glass dishes would be perfectly unsuitable for a rigorous examination of bacterial phenomena. But we are puzzled that anyone would deduce from the unsuitability of some or even many potential implements, the conclusion that there can be no suitable implements whatsoever.

Yet the simulationist objection is the one most commonly voiced to the idea of using virtual worlds for research. "But those places just aren't real!" Our claims, however, are not about realness, and realness in the experimental environment is not a good thing. From the perspective of sound scientific method, the simulationist objection is hard to understand.

Very Useful

We are not claiming that all virtual worlds are right for experiments, but rather that it is possible to deploy virtual worlds usefully, indeed, very usefully, for tests of social scientific propositions. Here we are open to objections of practicality. Virtual worlds might be theoretically useful, but not in practice.

Virtual worlds are expensive and hard to build. They are complex. That much is true; the human societies we would study in them are also complex. This leads some to say that there is no point in pursuing controlled experiments in virtual worlds. Human society is so complicated that there is no possibility of controlling the right factors. There is no hope of observing the right things. It is too expensive to replicate an experiment. The project might be theoretically allowable, but practically impossible. Human society is so varied, so manifold, so changing, so bizarre, that it is not possible to study it the way one studies the natural world.

This also strikes us as an odd objection. Cultures of bacteria are complex, as are the tools one uses to observe their subcellular elements. So are collections of subatomic particles, and the supercolliders one needs to study them properly. The complexity of virtual world societies and the difficulties one might have in isolating and observing effects are no more severe than in these cases from the natural sciences. Yet, much has indeed been learned about bacteria and subatomic particles.

Moreover, the relative return to experimenting in social science is extremely high at time of writing. The social impact and scientific value of Galileo dropping his weights was massive compared to the impact of someone ramming muons together today. But, that is only because Galileo was establishing the first set of facts. By the law of diminishing marginal utility, the value of the first fact is immense compared to the value of the 10 billionth fact. When humanity knows nothing at all, the value of learning even one thing—fire!—is huge. And when it comes to social science we are very close to being at a "first facts" stage. Social science is stuck in 1600: lots of conjecture, some observations, and some experiments at the micro level, none at the macro level. In this light, we have deep and renewed respect for the many small-scale experiments that have been done in social science by game theorists, political scientists, economists, and others.[1] These typically involve 2–20 students at a university, working through simple interactive situations over the course of an hour or two. Such experiments speak well to micro-level issues, questions of human motivation, communication, and information processing. What we seek to add are the macro-level experiments. And as far as macro-level studies, we are very much at a first-facts stage.

Thus the value of conducting research in virtual worlds, which present entire societies for study over many months or years, under controlled conditions, is unquestionably high. True, it is costly and complex. But is everything interesting in society so complex that it cannot possibly be studied using experimental methods? Or, rather, are there not simple first facts of extremely high value? Boyle's pneumatical engine, made in 1659, did nothing more than produce a vacuum. At the time, it was considered a costly and complex thing to do. Yet the value of the vacuum as an experimental environment is beyond calculation. Similarly, the value of a virtual world that, say, simply controlled the conditions under which people talk, is almost certainly beyond calculation.

It Has Not Been Tried Before

In the end, we are merely repeating Francis Bacon, "There are two ways of seeking and finding truth. The one method (A) leaps from sense and particulars to the most general axioms and from these principles invents all intermediate axioms. The other method (B) collects axioms from sense and particulars gained by various experiments, so that in the end it arrives at the most general axioms. This latter is the only true one, but it has not been tried before."[2]

The general axioms to which macro-level social experiments lead—on the progress of disease, the management of conflict, the encouragement of human well-being—are of great significance. And they have not been tried before.

In the remainder of this essay, we sketch out protocols and affordances for this new method. The reader will note changes in voice, tone, and direction. This is because the team writing this essay comes from an incredibly diverse array of fields: anthropology, new media, library science, psychology, economics, informatics, and communication. We considered writing and rewriting the essay until it had a single voice. We decided instead to leave the different voices as they are. Our diversity signals to the reader two very important things. First, it shows how many disparate fields stand to gain from using synthetic worlds for experiments. Second, it points to a certain kind of model for social science research, one in which large teams of scholars work together on large projects. That model is comparatively rare in social science today. Our diversity sends the signal that this research tool will require more social scientists to work together.

Why do we not just run an experiment in the real world? We begin by examining current limitations on social science experimental research. Let us imagine that we face some sort of practical research question—how does information about a disease propagate? How many people choose to vote under a given set of political institutions? How do people regulate competition over a scarce resource? Our task is to find some way to run an experiment about that question.

Islands Apart

Our first step might be to use an accepted experimental environment, such as a Petri dish, in which to run our experiment. While Petri dishes are handy, they cannot hold people. Therefore, let us move to something that can—an island. The task is to create an experiment. The first step is to furnish the island with a diverse array of inhabitants. Although this would in itself be a chore, we will assume the logistics of this endeavor are well-handled, and a sizeable group of random individuals are found to populate the island, the first time around.

At the end of the project there would be a definitive answer to our question, assuming guidelines had been followed, but little else of use. Our observations would only speak to this particular island and its people. This is the first hurdle, creating external validity, the ability to generalize and apply results to a host of other situations. So of course, we would have concurrent experiments running.

Now we shall introduce a pair of beachfront properties instead, bringing a nearby island into the fold of our project. But that island does not possess as many game animals or domesticable plants as our initial island. Here is the issue of ecological validity. Without replicating the circumstances and conditions in each portion of the experiment, results concerning external validity are once again threatened. There is room here to perform comparison and contrasts about the activities of our islands in these slightly different scenarios. There could certainly be large differences in what we find on each island concerning the outcomes—there would only be correlation, unless we expand further.

We will upgrade to an archipelago.

A chain of islands, all with a random assortment of participants at each location is now before us. This greater population increases the possibility of external validity—that the information garnered will have applicability to more situations and populations. But the ecological problem from before persists even more now. Some islands continue to have less wildlife and horticultural opportunities than others. Land mass and shelter from storms also vary from one location to the next. Not only are the dissimilar islands breaking the ecological validity of the project—the sameness of the experimental conditions, they in turn threaten the internal validity as well—that what is supposed to be measured is done so accurately and without interference or bias.

Realizing they have neighbors, some groups of islanders feel the need to "outdo" others in a competitive manner, reminiscent of the Hawthorne effect—a change in attitude due to the nature of being under scrutiny. The storms endanger the lives of other islanders, threatening the issue of mortality, and now that may strongly effect the end results. Death tends to cast a pall over even the most committed of participants. Then, some crafty persons fashion a canoe to visit nearby residents and taint both groups with knowledge of the happenings on their islands. Things have deteriorated quickly.

How were we going to answer our question?

The out-of-the-way nature of the islands is supposed to be a boon of non-interference to the research, but the peril here is one from within—us, the researchers—our presence affecting the internal validity by unconsciously influencing the subjects. There is the solution of dropping everyone off after pre-testing and subjecting all the participants to a barrage of surveys, interviews and questionnaires upon the completion of a time period, but several dangers lurk here as well.

Conditions may have at first been unbearable upon the island, but after a time when the situation improved, the latter stages may weigh more heavily upon the mind of our islanders. This maturation of the subjects is often troublesome concerning maintaining internal validity—it also allows for a "rewriting of history,"[3] the memory of bad times, such as struggling over resources at the beginning of the stay may be slowly eroded by recollections of better times when goods were plentiful near the end. Anthropologist Clyde Kluckhohn,[4] who warned against relying too much on "snapshots" of events, encouraged thinking about a larger temporal picture. All the information that goes missing in the interim is of great import. In order to have the whole picture, the project should follow a more procedural current, which again puts pressure on the need to maintain internal validity by not having researchers unwittingly influencing outcomes. A smaller number or a single researcher would be more suitable, but would not have the benefit of verification from others—*Quis custodiet ipsos custodes?*

While this scenario borders on the fantastic, it does illuminate the problems of validity facing social science experiments. It is difficult to replicate conditions, especially the more groups and instances occur. The power to manipulate the environment for control groups or to answer particular questions has its own barriers. And, the way in which information is gathered is left wanting in many areas—so much can interfere with trying to take proper measurements from the subjects, researchers, and the environment. While many of these problems are addressed through various and clever means in the current, divergent paradigm of social science, it is a heavy task.

Given that that a chain of islands would invariably produce so many problems with an experiment involving social science, why use it as an example? Simply that if all the problems, variables and obstructions could be cleared away, it would make for a splendid blueprint for research . . . if we could but encapsulate these remote places into a laboratory, with all the benefits and few of the encumbrances of logistics involving such a huge undertaking—then we might find something new.

The Example: Common-property Resources on a Better Island

It turns out that social scientists have devoted much thought to the difficulties of conducting experiments, not on islands, but in small social-interaction labs. Our proposal is, in effect, to use synthetic worlds to elevate these small-scale experiments to true macro-level experiments: island-sized. If we make this move, issues of external and internal validity arise. While it is tempting to discuss all this in the abstract, we feel it would be better to keep a particular case in mind as well. Therefore in the following section, we consider how these problems play out in a specific case: what if common-pool resource problems, which are heavily tested in small laboratories, were tested in a synthetic world?

Validity

First, let us discuss in general what "validity" means in an experimental context. There are two primary concerns subsidiary to external validity. These are: the ability to generalize results based upon the experimental environment (ecological validity) and the population used for the experiment (population validity). Internal validity, on the other hand, involves accurate control of measurement. In order to preserve internal validity, or accurate measurement, a researcher must simplify and regulate the experimental environment. There is thus a trade-off between these two forms of validity: when an experimental environment is simplified and contrived, things are easier to measure (internal validity), it becomes difficult for the researcher to generalize the results outside of the experimental setting (external validity).

In the next few sections, we will argue that synthetic worlds provide a very handy tool for dealing with the dilemmas of external and internal validity in social science research: they greatly enhance external validity at no cost to internal validity. They are controlled environments with far more complexity, scale, and persistence than is possible in a small lab. In order to ground the discussion, consider the following example, an experiment that is fairly typical in small-scale social science labs today.

The Example: Common-pool Resource Problems

Let us suppose that we would like to create an experiment for the following question: "Does cooperation increase when a common-pool resource is managed by the resource stakeholders as opposed to a central authority?" This is a fairly unspecific question, which actually makes it better suited for a traditional experimental environment but at the same time difficult to generalize to, for example, forest users in Brazil. Before we can attempt to develop an experiment to answer this question, it is appropriate to first define some of the key terms. A common-pool resource will be defined as a resource from which it is difficult to prevent or limit access by users.[5] In a common-pool resource situation, the game-theoretic outcome or Nash equilibrium[6] of the game is for players to descend into what is called "the tragedy of the commons."[7] This is often an unfortunate result. In a "tragedy of the commons" situation, players will act in a self-interested fashion and maximize short term gain even if it means long term loss and the degradation of the common-pool resource. Understanding the game-theoretic result provides two ways to measure cooperation. First, by the player's ability to avoid the Nash equilibrium (player payoff) and also by the health (based on units) of the common-pool resource.

The Traditional Laboratory Experiment

Before we can begin to forge our experiment from the example above, perhaps it would be best to layout the setting and tools available. The experiment will be conducted within a typical university research lab. Here we have access to networked computers and the means to provide our players with anonymity. Through a research grant, we have been provided with a few thousand dollars to provide participants (university students) with monetary incentives to play the game; with enough left over to provide a reasonable stipend to a programmer who will develop the computer interface. Finally, a trained experimental researcher must be present to manage the environment and conduct data analysis. Assuming the pretest is completed with satisfactory results, participants can be brought into the laboratory and provided with the instructions based upon the following game:

> 10 players share a common-pool resource. This resource holds 120 tokens that do not replenish. Play proceeds in rounds and during a round each player has the opportunity to extract between zero and four tokens from the resource. Additionally, each player's actions are hidden from the other players; a player learns only the amount left in the pool at the end of the round. The order in which players are allowed to extract resources from the pool is determined randomly and the game is played until the resource pool is depleted. At the end of each round players must exchange the tokens which they extracted for a monetary payout as follows: 1 token = $1.00 dollar, 2 tokens = $3.50 dollars, 3 tokens = $4.50, 4 tokens = $5.00.

As we have said before, cooperation can be monitored by the ability of the players to avoid the Nash equilibrium and the health of the resource. In this situation, the resource does not replenish itself and therefore we only need to monitor each individual player's ability to avoid the Nash equilibrium. In this situation, like in many common-pool resource situations, the Nash equilibrium is for players to act in a self-interested fashion. This means extracting the highest amount of resources per round to effectively "get them while they can." If each player harvests four resources in each round the maximum payoff per player is $15.00 (3 rounds × 4 tokens). In a situation where players cooperate fully and no players defect, the players will gain $21.00 (6 rounds × 2 tokens). With these payouts one has to wonder, "Why don't the players cooperate all the time, since it is clearly to their advantage to do so?" To answer this question, imagine that you are one of the players within the game. It is the first round of play and you are the first player to choose. You know, based on the payouts, that it is best for each player to take only two tokens, but you know that there is a possibility that another player might defect and take four, leaving you with only $3.50, the other player with $5.00 and two less resources in the pool for subsequent rounds. Based upon this train of thought, it is easy to understand why a player would resign himself to taking 4 tokens per round.

Next, the two forms of governmental control must be added to the game. To begin, the central authority; to simulate many common-pool resource situations in the field, such as forest resources, we shall assume that our central authority does not have the ability to perfectly monitor the resource boundaries and that the odds of catching a perpetrator are around one in eight. We will use one in eight as an arbitrary decision because the resource has large boundaries and the central government is not adequately funded, making it difficult to monitor the resource. Each time a player takes more than the allotted amount of resources, an eight-sided dice will be rolled; if the roll comes up 1, the player is punished and loses one-half of the resources they took that round. What is important to keep in mind is different numbers can be used by researchers in an attempt to understand different situations. A lower or higher possibility of being detected could be used as well as a lower or higher penalty.

To simulate a situation in which players can monitor each other, we can enact a situation in which a player may pay a fee to find out the moves of the other players for example, a fee of $0.10. Players would also be given the ability to sanction one another. For a fee of $1.00, a player would be able sanction another player for half of their earnings. Once again, it is important to remember that these values can be adjusted depending on the situation the researcher wishes to examine.

As we have seen, the above question was set up to be conducted in a laboratory environment. This environment requires that a researcher sacrifices some of the ability to generalize from the experiment into the real world in order to preserve internal validity. It would be difficult to make any predictions, such as how villagers in India might treat a forest common-pool resource under the same situation. Of course, this example only skims the surface of contemporary experimental methods. For a more detailed report of a similar common-pool resource problem, the reader is encouraged to read the work of Elinor Ostrom.[8] The reader could query this sort of experiment in all sorts of ways, but criticizing this kind of research is not our goal. Rather, with this example in mind, let us consider what synthetic worlds could add. First, we consider the tools synthetic worlds provide and then give a brief how-to. We follow that with caveats and concessions, and then point to the future.

Synthetic Worlds and Aggregate Behavior

Suppose we were considering a common-pool resource problem in a synthetic world. What kind of tools are available? How do the tools in a synthetic world work to perform these kinds of experiments?

When attempting to establish macro-level behavioral trends in social institutions, contemporary social science research averages the data of individuals. Individual behavior tendencies are averaged in order to describe aggregate trends, which are then used in depicting the behavior of larger social bodies. For example, in macroeconomics, practitioners average rates of inflation and unemployment. These variables, along with others, are then applied to describe macro-level institutions, such as the national economy. Further, the strength of such an approach to knowledge production is directly related to the precision and accuracy of the data collected—indeed, the validity of any claims on a national census is lost when only a third of all citizens are polled.

By their nature, synthetic worlds are ideal tools for this research method. In order to allow for vast, persistent worlds, the servers on which such environments are stored must keep track of an innumerable amount of data. Among many other variables, this data includes player ability statistics and assets, auction inventory and market prices, resource depletion, and the randomized appearances of rare goods. Additionally, besides tracking information on the state of the world and players, databases may also be used to monitor nearly all of the socially interactive content of the synthetic world. This includes components such as chat logs and player emotes (commands for the visual display of emotive avatar animations). All of this information can be stored, and later, mined for aggregate trends in player behavior.

Thus, the massive databases and monitoring capabilities of synthetic worlds offer the possibility of rich, in-depth data. This includes information on player interactions with the environment (such as resource harvesting, migration, and exchange with non-player character merchants), as well as information on player interactions with one another (including conversations, bartering, and structured alliances). By establishing trends in the data, just as is done with data extracted within laboratory experiments, conclusions can be drawn about the behavioral tendencies of larger populations and social institutions.

In addition to tracking and storing vast amounts of behavioral data, synthetic worlds also permit the experimenter a great deal of control. All manner of methods by which players interact with the environment and each other (including exchange rates, rates of resource renewal, communication channels, and market locations) may be manipulated, allowing for a wide range of potential experimental variables. In controlling for world conditions, experimenters may then observe the dependent effect on participant behavior. We argue that these observations are significant because of the inherent complexity of the social environments in which they occur.

Complexity

When people who are unacquainted with the technology think of synthetic worlds, what usually comes to mind is a relatively simple video game. However, your average online first-person shooter, for example, consists of a basic combat system and a map of terrain over which to engage the enemy. This is a relatively bare-bones form of sociality. The social environments found within synthetic worlds, on the other hand, are much more complicated. Elements of game play include not only a persistent terrain, but rules for the creation and maintenance of assets, as well as avatar-based communication systems. These spaces exist as places for people to meet, engage one another, and interact. Therein, users may generate intricate and meaningful relationships, and social institutions may emerge. Further, the societies that develop in these worlds are almost entirely left to the users to regulate and shape for themselves. Research into such socially-oriented worlds tends to be ethnographic, with significant conclusions being drawn about user behavior through observation.

However, for researchers desiring a more experimental approach, there also exist synthetic worlds that offer a greater deal of designer control. These types of environments may be more achievement-based in their structuring. Specific user objectives, dangers, and lore may be coded into the world from its beginning. In these environments, even more complex social institutions emerge, including standardized player markets and elaborate political alliances. Unlike the more socially-oriented worlds, designers of these environments rely heavily on predetermined content to shape the societies that are formed. And they do this through specific tools.

Control Mechanisms

Depending on the extent to which a designer wishes to guide and control for user behaviors (vs allowing for those behaviors to emerge on their own), he may make use of a number of different elements common to these environments. Specific tools for the creation of social institutions include:

- *Social Roles*—the mechanics of role-playing allow an entire community to mutually validate itself as a society of people who serve functions defined by the world.

- *Advancement Systems*—through regulated achievement and rewards (including prestige, alliance, power, and wealth), players can be induced to invest in a number of different types of action.
- *Status*—though often starting on equal footing, player status disparity results as players take differential paths of advancement.
- *Risk and Danger*—upon failing in a given task, a player may be at risk of losing previously acquired advancement or status, while danger further validates any accomplishment.
- *Scarcity and Forced Cooperation*—by making specific resources and activities scarce, designers can provide incentives for players to either cooperate or come into conflict over them.
- *Messaging*—designers can subtly embed messages to players through the very structure of the world, implicitly suggestive of specific community norms.
- *Personalized Content*—even perfectly-crafted societies leave people wanting something special to do or have for their own, and thus designers often include content which can validate them as individuals within a group context.[9]

Through these mechanisms, designers can motivate and guide player behavior patterns. Let us consider the common-pool resources problem. It would be trivial for the designer to establish an advancement system that rewards players for monitoring and controlling access to the common-pool resource. Moreover, it would be easy to alter the monitoring and incentive system in various ways. By dividing the players among servers, it would be easy to contrast how different incentive systems affect the health of the common-pool. And all of this could be done on a population and time scale that is much greater than available in a small-scale lab. The lab offers perhaps 100 people in interactions lasting a few minutes or hours (sometimes days). The synthetic world offers potentially millions of people interactions lasting years. The two situations are equally controlled, but one is simply larger.

It should be understood that these tools did not just spring from the ground, nor are they the contention of the authors alone. These tools are the product of a gradual development in games and synthetic worlds over the past few decades. Today, the combination of these innovations allows for environments that are Earth-like in their richness and complexity.

Social Institutions

The available mechanisms in synthetic worlds extend beyond simple reward systems. Because of their time and population scale, synthetic worlds are amenable to alterations in social institutions. Social institutions certainly do arise within these environments. Many of them, some explicitly designed so by their world-builders, support player cooperation rather than conflict. These worlds allow for, and sometimes even require, the formation of bodies such as crafting guilds, social clubs, and political alliances in order to achieve certain objectives. Further, since everything is not free, players must behave appropriately with others in order to cooperatively get what they want. To this extent, reputation is key.

Interestingly, though many synthetic worlds are filled with these sorts of explicit grouping mechanisms, the majority of them do not have explicit justice systems or governmental structures. It would seem that most developers prefer to leave such social institutions uncoded, so as to place emphasis on, and drive the need for, reputation systems and the informal norms they support (Castronova). That is, players use the conditions of the world to establish their own cultural conventions and institutions.

This survey of structures available to synthetic world researchers indicates that the individual shards or servers, acting like society-sized Petri dishes, can be subjected to an incredibly wide variety of useful interventions. In manipulating a given variable through the tools described above, experimenters may account for distinct patterns of player action and even differential emergence of social institutions. As is the case with bacteria, control and experimental conditions may yield alternate forms of culture. Indeed, to this extent, researchers constructing and studying synthetic worlds are able to design for and test hypotheses regarding the emergence of specific social behaviors.

The Experimental Process

Given the state of synthetic worlds today, and their likely future evolution, what exactly are the protocols for conducting an experiment using this tool? The tools provide the building blocks of experiments but do not provide a model of the process of how to perform the experimentation. Once again, returning to the laboratory, you need to prepare your experimental environment, duplicate that environment, and then conduct the experimentation. This process can be replicated in synthetic worlds.

In a microbiology laboratory environment, agar (a gelatinous organic medium) is added to each glass or plastic Petri dish. The agar that sits in a Petri dish acts as a controlled medium. Added to this medium is a microbial agent and then it is heated, cooled, or otherwise experimented on. Unlike the laboratory table, the contents of the Petri dish are controlled so that the factors of causation can be determined. The biological agent is then added to multiple Petri dishes. These create experimental instances.

These instances should be as exact matches as possible. The control instance is then left alone, and any number of experimental instances are experimented on. The results are then compared with the control and conclusions generated.

Synthetic worlds provide an analogous model to this. With the tools mentioned above, it is possible to create multiple experimental instances of controlled exact duplication. The word exact can be used here because unlike multiple Petri dishes (prepared by humans) the data that replicates a synthetic world environment, stored in a database, can be perfectly replicated as many times as you have memory space. Then you also have great control of what any objects in the world can and cannot do. So, like the biologist, you can load your virtual Petri dish with the exact same content. You can also control the data gathered and how it is stored in automated and systematic ways. Observation, through databases, can be done in a systematic, automated way. Finally, then, the results can be viewed from that date in real time or in a longitudinal view.

For example, consider the common-pool resource problem, performed in a synthetic world as a game. Build an environment in which the players become emotionally engaged in some kind of quest or adventure. Perhaps they need to go kill a dragon. In order to kill the dragon, they need weapons and armor. To make weapons and armor, they need metal and wood. Metal they can get from a nearby mine. It is a perishable, non-renewing resource, but you design it so that they will never run out. Wood, on the other hand, comes from a small forest: a perishable, renewing resource. You design the forest so that anyone can go in and execute the command "LOG." That command places some wood in the player's inventory, but it also reduces the amount of wood belonging to the Forest object. The Forest object is programmed to grow at a rate that depends on how much wood is still in it. In particular, if all the players go in and log the forest, the amount of remaining wood gets too low, and the forest does not replenish at all but rather dies. Then the dragon cannot be defeated. Indeed, you should probably set it up so the dragon eventually comes and eats the whole village if the wood runs out.

You have given the villagers a common-pool resource problem. You have set up the incentives so that they care about it indirectly. That is, nobody is explicitly playing the game because they want to manipulate common-pool resource problems, they are playing because they like killing dragons. To them, as to people in the real world, the common resource is just an input to other things that we want to do. We need to manage it so as to make our lives, which are focused elsewhere, happy.

What will the villagers do? Well, you can give them a voting power such that whoever they elect to the office of "Forest Ranger" can control who gets to log, and when. Or you could do nothing. Or you could put a fence around the forest and make anyone who enters pay a fee, in gold pieces, to use the forest. Any of these options allow endless variations. You could post information, or post no information. You could "seed" the community with people who talk endlessly about how shameful it is that some people log so often, and try to create social norms. You could allow players to attack and kill one another, or impose a small sanction of one gold piece on any violators they see. All of these mechanisms will matter to the players, because they have become immersed in a world where killing the dragon is of most significance. Because of that, they will want to solve the forest problem. And at that point, we can expect them to deploy whatever tricks and stratagems real people would deploy, given the institutional framework you have created (such as voting, not voting, sanctions, etc.).

For outcomes, you measure a number of things. First, record the time when the dragon is killed—that is a measure of how rapidly the forest problem was managed effectively. Second, record the forest's health over time—see whether there was a risk of the forest dying. Third, record the *per-capita* wood harvest and its distribution—did you create wood inequality? Finally, record some measure of interpersonal conflict—did you spark battles and hostility, or was the village able to manage the forest peaceably?

All that remains then is to replicate the environment 1, 2, or 100 times. On each version, set out a slightly different set of institutions. Run the experiment, and then tabulate the above measures across shards. From this table, you can make *direct causal inferences*. You can state, unequivocally, that such-and-such an intervention on shard 17 was directly responsible for the rapid death of the dragon (the rapid level of development) on that server.

Limitations and Concessions

In many ways, having such a direct evidence of causation is a lodestone for social science research. Causation at the societal level is extremely hard to establish. But there are limitations. For synthetic worlds to be used effectively, it is important to understand these limitations and evaluate the method for its fit to the research question at hand.

Concessions

Certainly, not every question can be answered in an experimental instance. The method is most powerful for collecting quantitative information, usually exported by the system itself. These data are generated by players' actions in the space and are seldom identified with the individual. Thus, collecting qualitative information regarding in-world actions may not be possible for some questions and in some systems. The questions best answered in these digital spaces are ones informed by theories, which can be answered in quantitative ways. Data which requires qualitative explanations may not be interpreted from the pure system data for multiple reasons (lack of an actor's identity, environmental mechanics which do not facilitate textual reporting, etc.). By implementing sometimes-used techniques, such as questionnaires at the log-in screen, it may be possible to draw some modicum of qualitative data from the player base.

Experimental instances must be used to conduct studies with covariant variables. For example, if we want to answer whether or not changing the price of an item in a virtual economy will influence how often the item is purchased, we cannot also change the amount of money dropped by mobile object block[10] (mobs) in the space, at the same time we must also make sure that the rate at which currency enters the system remains constant. In this way we can make sure to control for the co-variation between price and amount of currency so that the results are not skewed. Changes in the frequency of purchase could be influenced by mob drops but also by other secondary mechanical factors or virtual cultural factors. Experimental instances are most effective for isolating the direct outcome of a variable change when the experiment is conducted in this limiting way. This is not to say that the variable can only be adjusted or altered in one way. Running parallel mirror instances, with a different variation of a variable in each one, will be valuable as well, and will allow for mass reproduction of experiments simultaneously.

It must also be noted that this experimental model is not intended to extract data about participants. Rather, we should see these experimental instances as opportunities to observe changes in the system, the system in which the avatars merely function as actors. The "digital Petri dish" functions as a system which can be manipulated to measure outcomes of that system, but not the personality or attributes of the actors in the dish. The outcomes of the system may be generalized to be applied outside the environment (inflation, for example) but the specific behaviors are the acts of avatars, and thus cannot be generalized to describe behaviors of people outside the virtual space.

Limitations

Virtual worlds used as experimental instances must allow for: manipulation of variables, data export, and parallel spaces (that is, a control and an experiment). For example, studies of proxemics (personal social space) in virtual worlds have shown that avatars demand similar amounts of personal space as their human counterpoints.[11] However, these studies seldom include the limitations created by the environment's mechanics—How difficult is it to navigate an avatar to be near another? Do the avatars have attachments such as large weapons which might inhibit physical proximity? Can avatars collide or can they walk through one another? How do users manipulate their camera angles to view other users?—A deep understanding of the social mores and conventions of the space, as well as the ways in which the mechanics of the space might influence actions, are critical to the researcher's choice of environment as well as the construction of the experiment.

In addition to mechanics, one must also be conversant with what variables are available for testing. Questions of economics cannot be tested in spaces where no economy exists. Numbers of male or female avatars cannot be counted if the avatar's gender is not declared as a data element (or if gender is malleable). Of course, if the environment is being custom-made to conduct the experiment, then the desirable factors may be built into the system.

Then there is the issue of attracting a population. Designing and attracting players to games is in and of itself a complicated venture. Players must want to play the games used for experiments or the experiment will fail. The design and creation of the game will take time and a large amount of financial resources. Without proper funding, the creation of a world may stall indefinitely and therefore experiments may never come to fruition.

Player populations in massively multiplayer online game (MMOG) environments are fickle, and will move from game to game if unhappy, disengaged, or otherwise discouraged. The MMOG market is a highly competitive and financially large area in which to exist. For these reasons, extra care must be taken when designing and developing virtual worlds meant to be used solely for research purposes. The worlds must be fun and engaging enough to maintain at least the minimum population required for the experiments. Care must also be taken to engage a variety of player types, from achievers who prefer to gain levels, points, and other status symbols, to killers who desire to gain satisfaction through Player vs Player interaction.[12]

In this same vein, there must be enough content created to allow the player base to explore, and if so desired, create groups and participate in coordinated events such as raids. Natively attracted populations (users who are attracted to virtual worlds and games due to their own personal interest) may only be considered a limited random sample, that is, a random sample from the demographic of interest for the experiment. While random assignment of individuals to shards makes cross-shard inferences valid, if the samples are all drawn from a limited population—college students, for example—the ability to generalize results comes into question.

Some research questions will be affected by this more than others of course, and a very large body of work already relies on such limited populations—indeed, college students—without engendering much criticism. If self-selection remains a problem, selection bias models should be used to correct for the direction of biased effects.

Warnings

There are a few final warnings that must be presented, when considering using virtual worlds as social science research tools. These are not specifically prohibitive, but they are nonetheless vital to mention.

The first of these cautions is this: to truly be able to understand the results of the experiments, the researcher must understand the culture created within, and surrounding the synthetic environment. This includes both the in-game and meta-game elements. If using a pre-existing world, extra time must be spent to learn the ways in which users interact with both the environment and each other. Most of the limitations we just mentioned may or may not be significant, depending on the nature of the population, the nature of the research question, and the nature of the world. A deep understanding of the research tool is necessary for making judgments about validity. You have to understand both the Petri dish, and the bugs, and the counter-top, and the air in the lab, as well as the question you are studying, in order to decide whether you are really learning anything at all.

In the same vein, some players choose to role-play while online. Does this matter? Sometimes it will, sometimes it will not. Taking on a persona and acting in a different way may still provide valid research results; however, for some questions they will not be representative of a sample population (if a specific sample is required for the study), rather, they will represent the population that the role-player puts themselves into via choices in persona, play, and communication. A person role-playing an elf is probably going to have the same reaction to a rise in the price of swords as anyone else. His reaction to a Bible reading is likely to be different, though, if he is role-playing.

Another warning involves fun. The synthetic world has to retain a large population in order to deliver on its promise. Clearly, commercial competition in the MMOG genre, and in games in general, is fierce. A major concern for all game developers (academic and commercial) is that of enjoyment. The player base must desire to play the game (explore the environment, participate in the world's action, etc.), and be motivated to engage with it. If this requirement is not met, the fickle population will move on to other games. Therefore, the researcher must strive, when building or selecting a world to work in, to find an environment that will hold, at the very least, enough interest to fulfill the goals of the research to be committed. Any experimentation can be rendered meaningless if a valid sample population cannot be achieved or maintained.

The final warning to be presented is a caution on the subject of cheating. As Consalvo has identified, there are many categories of cheating and feelings on the subject of cheating.[13] Regardless of the rule system or game structure that is built, there will always be some form, in some amount, of cheating. This will range from finding exploits and abusing the game system (with potentially disastrous economic or social effects), to spending enough time to find an extremely efficient way to achieve a goal (such as killing monsters) that some consider cheating. In its most extreme form, cheating can ruin an entire set of data; in its least offensive form, it will be seen as no more than power gaming. When cheating matters, and when it does not, will, again, depend on the experiment.

Future

Even as we write this, the number of experiments using virtual worlds is growing rapidly. None of this is published research yet, but we are aware of experiments in virtual worlds going on at Cornell, Emory, Georgia Tech, Stanford, USC, Harvard, and University of South Florida. Agencies that have funded, are funding, or seem likely to fund virtual worlds experiments include the National Science Foundation, the MacArthur Foundation, the Department of Defense, the Department of Homeland Security, the Department of Education, the Corporation for Public Broadcasting, the NASB, and the Federal Reserve. Major companies getting involved in virtual world experiments include Cisco, IBM, Intel, Google, and Sony. We are certain that there are also others.

It is a natural step for a graduate student in the social sciences to think about using a virtual world to conduct an experiment. We predict that within five years, papers will be published in mainstream academic journals that were born as virtual worlds experiments in PhD dissertations. Within five years, virtual worlds' experiments will have become a mainstream method in many fields of social science.

There are numerous scenarios in which this future would not happen, of course. Perhaps academic hierarchies will not accept reasonably valid results, simply because of the association between virtual worlds and video games. Perhaps the world-building middleware industry, that seems to be on the road toward bringing down the cost of virtual world creation to a very modest level, will not deliver on this promise. More likely, it may be the case that the most valuable scale for a virtual world experiment will be very, very large, requiring populations in the tens of thousands, worlds so big as to break the budget of even the largest of funders. In that case, progress will depend critically on the formation of consortia of researchers, groups large enough to come together and share large virtual worlds in the same way that physicists share supercolliders.

With this in mind, a good direction for future research is to continue to ponder and critique the uses and affordances of synthetic worlds as research tools, while making simple worlds by which one can test the ideas in this essay.

Notes

1. See the individual work of H. Ostram, J. Walker, R. Goldstone, R. Axelrod, and A. Lang.
2. Adapted from Lisa Jardine and Michael Silverthorne eds. *Francis Bacon: The New Organon* (Cambridge: Cambridge University Press, 2000), 36.
3. H. Garfinkel, *Studies in Ethnomethodology* (Englewood Cliffs, NJ: Prentice-Hall, 1967).
4. C. Kluckhohn, *Mirror for Man* (New York: McGraw-Hill, 1949).
5. E. Ostrom, *Rules, Games, and Common-Pool Resources* (Ann Arbor: University of Michigan Press, 1994).
6. In game theory, the Nash equilibrium (named after John Forbes Nash, who proposed it) is a solution concept of a game involving two or more players, in which no player has anything to gain by changing only his or her own strategy unilaterally.
7. Garrett Hardin, "The Tragedy of the Commons," *Science* 162, no. 3859 (December 13, 1968): 1243–1248.
8. E. Ostrom, B. Guha-Khasnobis, and R. Kanbur, eds. *Linking the Formal and Informal Economy: Concepts and Policies* (New York: Oxford University Press, 2006).
9. Edward Castronova, *Synthetic Worlds: The Business and Culture of Online Games* (Chicago: University of Chicago Press, 2005); hereinafter cited as Castronova.
10. Computer controlled entities in the game.
11. Studies such as N. H. Nassiri, N. J. Powell, and D. J. Moore, "Protecting Personal Space Intelligently in Collaborative Virtual Environments," *IEE Seminar on Intelligent Building Environments* (2005): 2–230.
12. For more about player types, see Richard Bartle, "Hearts, Clubs, Diamonds, Spades: Players Who Suit MUDs (1996)," in *The Game Design Reader: A Rules of Play Anthology*, eds. K. Salen and E. Zimmerman (Cambridge, MA: MIT Press, 2006, 754–787). Available online at <http://www.mud.co.uk/richard/hcds.htm>. For an inside view of player motivations, see B. Sawyer, *Monster Gaming: The Complete How-to Guide for Becoming a Hardcore Gamer* (Scottsdale, AZ: Paraglyph, 2003).
13. Mia Consalvo, *Cheating: Gaining Advantage in Video Games* (Cambridge, MA: MIT Press, 2007).

CHAPTER 15

Lag, Language, and Lingo
Theorizing Noise in Online Game Spaces

MIA CONSALVO

About once a week in Vana' diel,[1] the world stops spinning. I am in a group with five other people (based around the USA, or the world) killing monsters; I am casting my spells, and with little warning, the action stops. My avatar is standing there, my party members are standing there, and sure enough, the monster is still there. We are not frozen like a paused Tivo image, but the battle has stopped, and so has the text stream on the bottom of my screen. And I know, with certainty, that the battle is continuing *somewhere*, just not in front of me. My computer is disconnecting from its Internet connection, and I am going to have to reboot my game before I can rejoin my party, hopefully before they either all die, or (worse) replace me.

Most often I get back into Vana' diel, wave with my avatar and say "I'm sorry" and am allowed to rejoin the party. It happens to everyone, and is considered an unremarkable event. At such times, one or more party members will usually point to a member who appears to be disconnecting (there is a status icon that flashes next to your avatar name to indicate connection problems) and note (usually without alarm) "the white mage is d/cing [disconnecting]. Wait to fight, please." Likewise, players often note the presence of lag in busy zones or during peak play times, their difficulties in logging into the game world on particular days, confusing use of the auto-translate system by other players, and similar communication challenges. Such mundane problems are often seen as minor (occasionally becoming a big deal) and not worthy of extended discussion by players. Researchers tend to take the same approach. But should we? How do communication difficulties and challenges shape the game space and the resulting game experience? And how can we best theorize these activities?

From text-based non-commercial MUDs to 3-D, globe-spanning virtual worlds, game studies scholars have entered such spaces to study the communities and cultures that have been built, how aspects of identity like gender and race are negotiated and played with, as well as the changing terrains of the "lands" themselves (among many other inquiries).[2] One of the principal ways that has been done is through the study of communication—including interactions between players, between players and game administrators, and also interactions between players and NPCs (non-player-characters) and/or bots. While work has been done to analyze the structure and legal status of such worlds,[3] as well as graphical representations and interaction options available,[4] communication structures those interactions, and helps players makes sense of such spaces.

But although communication is used as a lens, it is rarely the focal point of study itself. And particularly when communication breaks down, we are obligated to look more deeply at *how* we are studying communication in game spaces, not simply the events themselves.

Structural and Post-structural Approaches in Game Studies

In developing the field of game studies, many scholars have argued for a ludological approach, which sees games as distinct from other media and technology forms.[5] Such an approach is necessary, they believe, to account for the distinctiveness of digital games—their interactivity, their reliance on rules, their formal structures. While this approach is useful to a certain extent, we can also draw from, while carefully adapting, other theoretical lenses from established fields and disciplines in order to better understand the multifaceted nature of games, and their production and reception. For example, philosophical theories have much to contribute to debates about the magic circle concept as applied to games,[6] while work in audience studies and fan cultures in particular can help us better understand elements of the game playing public.[7]

As communication scholars have also shown,[8] wholesale transfer of a model or theory from one discipline to another can result in complete misapplication, or misunderstanding of key elements of the theory or model. Yet, just as we should not unquestioningly cut and paste theories from one area to another, neither should we completely abandon them in the search for the entirely new. Likewise, as the appendix of this book shows, game studies has already proven to be interdisciplinary in scope, asking questions of games and game cultures that draw from economics, law, sociology, and psychology, to name just a few areas.

In response to the growth of structural approaches, other game studies scholars have argued for looking beyond the rules or construction of games to the context surrounding them. Scholars such as Taylor, Steinkuehler and Williams, and Malaby[9] advocate study of the communities, cultures, and play found within and around game structures and rules as better ways to understand the play situation. Special issues of journals such as *Games & Culture*'s 2006 examination of the MMOG *World of Warcraft* (Blizzard, 2004) also point to the many ways we can analyze games, game players, and game culture.

Through such efforts, we have successfully challenged the belief that online/offline distinctions can easily be drawn,[10] and have pointed to the many ways that game players have utilized in-game and out-of-game communication methods and channels to blend those worlds into satisfying experiences. However, we need to go further in examining how we understand and study "game communication" and the omissions and elisions we unknowingly ignore or smooth over, which can indicate potentially troublesome communication issues.

This essay addresses theory and practice related to how we study communication and how commonly overlooked issues or features must be taken into better account to understand game communication. So although we now draw distinctions between various types of servers for MMOGs (such as Player vs. Environment or Player vs. Player) and the different types of play styles that can emerge in those places, we have done little to examine such things as the use of out-of-game communication methods to enhance in-game play or communication, such as Instant Messaging, Ventrilo, e-mail, and forum browsing. Likewise, issues such as ping time and lag challenge our understandings of how synchronously or not players are communicating with each other. Finally, systems of auto-translation bring to the fore notions of culture and how it is interwoven with game code and player communication to allow as well as inhibit particular types of expression.

This essay takes on several of those issues, delineating important challenges to game communication, and exploring how we can theoretically account for them in order to better understand communication online. In doing so, it points to how theories and methods must continually adapt to changing technologies of communication, as well as different uses by participants. It identifies some key questions to explore, and it also reminds us that communication is not transparent, and our attempts to understand what is "really being said or done" online are likely to only ever be partial and incomplete, but are still demanding of investigation and theorization.

Communication Theory, Origins, Extensions

One theoretical area that should be integrated into games studies is communication theory, which is concerned with the field of human as well as computer-mediated communication. In particular I want to draw on a fairly old (and even somewhat discredited) theory of communication to illustrate how such modification can work, and still allow for meaningful transfer of a theory's ideas and concepts.

In 1948, Claude Shannon conceived of a general "theory of communication" which approached communication from an engineering, or mathematical, perspective. Shannon wrote that "the fundamental problem of communication is that of reproducing at one point either exactly or approximately a message selected at another point."[11] Shannon, an engineer for Bell Laboratories, created a mathematical theory that accounted for the transmission of signals along a communication system, which included an information source, a transmitter, the channel, the receiver, and the destination. He was particularly interested in reducing or eliminating the problem of noise, which led to signal degradation and inaccurate reproduction of messages. It is important to note, however, that for Shannon, "semantic aspects of communication are irrelevant to the engineering problem" (Shannon 1948, 623).

A year later, Warren Weaver attempted to broaden the scope of Shannon's theory, arguing there were three levels of communication problems, including "how accurately can the symbols of communication be transmitted (the technical problem) . . . How precisely do the transmitted symbols convey the desired meaning? (The semantic problem) . . . [and] How effectively does the received meaning affect conduct in the desired way? (The effectiveness problem)."[12]

Through his introduction to Shannon's work, Weaver re-deployed an engineer's mathematical theory into a much broader theory for use by social scientists. No longer just a question of transmitters and signals relaying information, Weaver wanted the theory to address issues of semantics, therefore of meaning. He believed the theory had "deep significance" which could apply to multiple levels of communication (Weaver). He was particularly interested in concepts such as entropy, which he saw as more than the statistical distribution of symbols within a system, and instead advocated for the study of messages for their level of entropy, which later researchers did, showing how similar many mass media sources are in their messages presented to the public (Ritchie).

Other communication theorists such as Lasswell developed similar theories of communication, including his famous model "Who said what to whom in what channel with what effect." That framework further tasked communication researchers with investigating various parts of the system of communication. Those efforts led to a generation of communication researchers studying gatekeepers of news ("who"), the content of messages ("said what") and most frequently the effects of such messages on audiences ("with what effect"), or rather, they investigated how well the signals had been transferred.[13] Although the original Shannon-Weaver theory has fallen largely into disuse since then, the effects tradition it led to still remains strong in the field (Finn and Roberts 1984; Ritchie).

Weaver's original model of communication emphasized a system that was linear and could be interrupted, disrupted, blocked, or (perhaps) was completely successful. It emphasized the structural features of communication systems, much as some ludological theories point to the importance of the structures of game systems, for defining them as games and understanding their operation.

Responding to the dominance of transmission-based views of communication, theorists such as James Carey and Stuart Hall called for competing paradigms for understanding communication—including understanding how communication can function in ritualistic ways and how the meaning-making process of communication is never fixed, and can never completely close off potential meanings in particular messages.[14]

While my past work follows more closely the lines of Carey and Hall, I believe there is value in re-visiting the work of early communication theory, particularly for its attention to the concept of noise. While Hall, for example, has argued that meanings can never be fixed in messages, either in the encoding or decoding process, there has been little in the field of communication studies, or in game studies, which seriously addresses issues pertaining to noise. Slow Internet connections or cable modems, electrical storms, language fluency problems, wording abbreviations, and software and hardware bugs could add noise—all play a role in how we think about and theorize, as well as study, games, and game players. Therefore, we must theorize noise in the game situation.

Therefore, I want to again re-visit and re-interpret the Shannon-Weaver theory and see how it can help us better understand communication as it occurs in online games, and to do so I invoke and re-deploy their concept of noise—as both a technical and semantic challenge to communication. At the same time, I will investigate how the theory can live alongside competing approaches and paradigms, perhaps even complementing them. To do this, the essay draws examples from past research, and builds a more integrative theory of digital game communication from those various understandings.

Game Studies Meets Communication Studies

The little research done that has studied communication in digital games has found that players often have difficulty using tools that developers give them. Stromer-Galley and Martey found that in *The Sims Online* (Maxis, 2002), players rarely used avatar gestures or movements to indicate meaning, relying on textual address to communicate their intentions.[15] Likewise, gamers using an early iteration of the Xbox Live Voice System expressed frustration with certain elements of the medium, often developing workarounds on the fly to communicate with their friends and teammates more effectively.[16] When such systems are better implemented, as found in Williams, Caplan, and Xiong's work with the MMOG *World of Warcraft*, it was found that trust and liking increased among player groups, in particular for participants who could use both text and voice during gameplay.[17]

Lori Kendall has explored communication in the virtual spaces of MUDs and conducted an online ethnography of one space, BlueSky, which is a text-based, persistent world (Kendall). In her study of the space and discussions of her methodology, she argues that such research is more than a textual analysis of a chat/text log. Instead, context is key to understanding how actors relate to each other in particular (specific) virtual spaces, and not knowing their conventions can lead to misunderstandings and miscommunications.

More widely, Rasmussen suggests that the study of communication has become critically important to understanding society, and one way to understand that system is by seeing "the Internet structure as a theoretical idea or model of society."[18] He argues this because both society and the Internet recognize the "importance of communication in the self-production of societal function systems" (Rasmussen 2003, 445). Rasmussen acknowledges the work of Warren Weaver in popularizing Claude Shannon's work and stresses the focal point of that model as "whether or not a message that has been transmitted reaches its destination" (Rasmussen, 447). He uses that insight to argue for the redundant functioning of the Internet, and its distributed nature. For the Internet, communication is too important to suppose that everything is working perfectly—instead, noise and trouble must be expected, and therefore redundant systems and workarounds are requirements for the system. Additionally, communication is conceptualized as always in danger of breaking down, always at risk of being overwhelmed by noise.

And to back up redundant structures or help with the understanding of what is irretrievably lost, "support for communication is supplied from the environment in the shape of media, culture, and a number of other social phenomena that society invents to keep itself going. In such a perspective, sociology should not hide in idealized versions of communication but should assume noise. . . . In this way, sociology may uncover how communication takes place in spite of its improbability" (Rasmussen, 449).

Communication theories, and the transmission model of communication, have much to say to game studies and ludology. For the most part, game researchers have focused on communication as a linear process, perhaps conveying more than information (we look for evidence of community formation, of identity play, and of teamwork) but seeing it still as something transparently understood. And critically, we have largely ignored the "noise" that gets in our way. Lag (by which I mean slow-downs in the performance of Internet-based activities, due to technical factors) is written off or ignored. Language difficulties may be noted in passing, but not studied systematically. Lingo (here defined as the use of terminology specific to a medium or space) may be evidence of community formation, but is not studied as a challenge to communication and gameplay itself. To do so I wish to expand our conceptualization of noise, perhaps creating a definition of noise that is overly broad (certainly in relation to prior communication theorists), at least for present purposes. But in focusing on various phenomena, both technical and cultural, that might be considered as noise in the process of communication, we can in turn gain an even better understanding of the rich cultures, contexts, communities, and spaces that have been and are still in the process of being formed in online games. From there, the concept of noise can be redefined, yet initially it can serve as a test case, pointing to areas that are now not well explored or even questioned.

A General Note on Theory

A final problem to be faced is the role that theory is supposed to play for game studies. As Jay David Bolter argues so convincingly, the purpose of theory changes as we move among disciplines, approaches, and paradigms.[19] In the field of mass communication, for example, theory can be used to predict and explain behavior if one takes a social scientific perspective, or it can be used to explain or critique, when approached with a critical, humanistic lens. Likewise, in areas such as visual or graphic design, theory is a set of design principles, used to aid creators in shaping better (more user-friendly) products and designs. Bolter (2003) argues such shifts in meaning are particularly troublesome in new media studies, where academic critics can also serve as creators, attempting to critique through production—what happens then to theory? He argues that "what we need is a hybrid, a fusion of the critical stance of cultural theory with the constructive attitude of the visual designer" (Bolter, 30). That would seem to result in hybrid practices, as well as hybrid theories and theorists.

In game studies, we have seen a variance in approaches to theory, with only a few of Bolter's proposed hybrids. More usually we find effects scholars who are interested in predicting and controlling behavior in relation to violent video games, and are thus focused on building a very particular type of theory.[20] Likewise, humanists such as Henry Jenkins see theoretical concepts such as knowledge communities, fan cultures, and poaching as guides for explaining how individuals use media, as well as how to understand those practices as part of a larger system of media culture. Writers such as Kline, Dyer-Witheford, and De Peuter take a different approach, using more traditional political economy theories to critique game production systems they see as exploitative.[21] All take different approaches, use different theories, and find different answers.

As such, theory can both help us understand player behavior and perhaps provide a critique of systems, practices, or designs. To that end, this essay draws on communication theory to better understand one more corner of gaming activity, as well as critique current systems and question limitations or options perhaps not fully explored.

To do so, this essay takes its point of departure (and data) from an extended virtual ethnography of *Final Fantasy XI Online*, a Massively Multiplayer Online Game (MMOG) released by Square Enix in 2002, which currently claims over 600,000 players in Japan, North America, Europe, and Australia (Consalvo, *Cheating*). The initial study focused on daily life in the game's fictional world of Vana 'diel, but this essay refocuses its findings and critiques on the systems of communication used by gamers within and across this virtual and the physical world. More specifically, it problematizes our often-unstated assumptions that such systems of communication are transparent or easily understood, and that they do not have particular constraints that can impact what we know about how gamers communicate online.

In the next sections, I explore three types of noise that emerged through extended gameplay and experience with the player community of *Final Fantasy XI Online*. They are different in origin (one is technical, two are cultural or social), yet all factor in the daily life of a Vana' diel inhabitant, in some way or another. Players have attempted various workarounds to the challenges of these types of noise, which I also detail. Their practices, and the original noise itself, demonstrate how both structure and context co-construct successful and problematic game experiences.

Three Types of Noise

Lag Kills . . . Don't Let Lag Happen to You

Lag, or temporal disturbances in the flow of communication, can create minor to significant challenges for players in battle, in chats, in community building, and other venues. Noise can be conceptualized here as a lack of information being received, its untimely arrival, or its disruption of the normal flow of text chat and game information as it scrolls up or down a screen. Lag is a technical problem encountered in any networked play environment which players experience and manage on a regular basis. While often not noticed or encountered, players can experience temporal disturbances shared (or not) by their fellow players, due to slow graphics cards, inadequate RAM, clogged cable modem lines, DDOS attacks, or other factors. Noise here relates to problems with information transfer, for which players must create workarounds, or simply deal with on a (more to less) regular basis.

Players understand the potentially serious problems engendered by lag, as seen in regular posts to message boards such as those found at Allakhazam. Regular readers of the site invariably encounter posts by new or potentially new players, asking if their home Internet connection, which is either a satellite modem or a dialup connection, will be too slow for enjoyable (or even functional) play. Posters are concerned that they will not be able to take part in regular game activities, or that lag will disrupt parties and other group actions at levels unacceptable to both the individual player as well as other players.

Such regular, yet under-theorized problems can result in changing temporal mechanics which impact the gameplay experience. While players have long complained about the unfortunate effects of lag (like the death of your avatar) when playing games like *Counter-Strike* or *Halo* online, lag can also play an important role in shaping perceptions and misperceptions about social communication in virtual worlds. In worlds built with text-based interaction, for example, the ability to write and respond, and to receive communications from the game and other players in a timely manner is vital to building and maintaining communities, from the temporary pickup group or alliance, to longer-term groups of friends, family, and acquaintances.

It is quite common, for example, for players to chat simultaneously with the party members they are grouped with, their Linkshell (guild) friends, and perhaps one or two individual friends within a game, along with listening to the general public conversation in a busy zone. At times, such conversations can be difficult to keep up with, even when the text is flowing smoothly. Yet add lag for a player, and things can quickly turn challenging or even overwhelming. Large chunks of text can fly up and past the cutoff buffer, followed by long moments of seeming inactivity, when communication fails to materialize. If a player is engaged in battle she likely will not stop the activity to open the larger text window and see what went past, but instead wait until a rest period to catch up.

While lag causes problems during battles, it also interferes with less obviously time-sensitive situations, such as when a group is traversing a difficult zone. Players who do not receive warnings or directions at the right time, due to lag, may put a party in needless danger. Likewise, players who get messages late during a battle may miss their timing for executing a special attack, either from a delay in receiving the directive or from their own lagged response to one. Repeated lag can make players feel incompetent, as if they are hurting group progress, and their actions may be judged that way by other members who are not experiencing such disruptions. Such actions do not even need to be fatal to a party or group to cause frustration and less-than-optimal fighting, with too many such episodes leading some players to log off from a game for the night or perhaps even suffer a reputation as a poor player.

While it may seem trivial or annoying to the non-gamer, such experiences can cause deep frustration and anger in players heavily invested in a game, or in a certain event or experience within the game. Such disruptions may knock an individual out of a flow state they may have been in, where they were experiencing an optimal form of gameplay.[22] While game studies scholars have not (yet) extensively studied the entrance and exit conditions, as well as re-entry requirements to gain access to a flow state, lag would certainly be a key inhibitor to achieving such a state.

Yet even in more casual situations, where battles are not raging and the player is not engaged in any critical activity, lag can cause frustration and potential dissention among players. Lag can lead to the loss of opportunities for input into discussions and exchanges. A player may find, when lagged communication finally appears on the screen, that conversation has moved to a different topic. Or her witty remark has been ignored because it appeared after several other Linkshell members' similar responses, or appeared after a new topic has been introduced. Players can begin to self-censor (and remain silent) when lag is bad, to avoid the appearance of always being too late with conversational remarks or out of step with a quickly moving discussion.

For such players, the technical barriers to entry (like the noise of lag) of the online conversation have risen to bothersome or perhaps unscaleable levels. Beyond negotiating language competency, typing skill, and in-game lingo, the flow (or lack of proper flow) of the conversation prohibits or discourages easy participation. Players often express frustration at such times when they are temporally out of step with their fellow gamers. But we do not really know yet what the tipping point is for various gamers, relative to their tolerance for such environments. Do younger or older players accept lag in better stride? Men or women? Are there differences at all? Do such problems inhibit the creation of communities in game spaces, for individuals who experience severe lag regularly? Can lag be a contributing factor in disputes, or the dissolution of groups? If so, with what frequency? These are questions we need to consider in more depth.

As we can see, lag, even when constructed by players as a regular, inescapable (yet annoying) part of gameplay, is an important component of that gameplay to consider when studying how game-players make sense of their gameplay, how it impacts their communication and miscommunication, and leads to fractures in the cohesiveness of the game world.

JP Onry? Cross-Cultural Communication and the Auto-Translator System

Language differences can also create noise when individuals who speak different languages are situated on the same servers, and translators either fail or are not present. Players can create workarounds to this form of noise by developing language guides, by relying on bilingual friends, or learning rudimentary foreign language skills, yet problems (and noise) usually remain.[23]

Such fluency problems could be characterized as cultural noise. Here, noise mutates from the technical to the cultural/social. It is not the system's method of information transfer that is problematic, but rather the grouping of individuals with little to no way to compensate for cultural barriers to communication.

While most MMOGs have servers segregated by region (North America, Asia, Europe), Square Enix chose to have all players log in to the same server spaces, regardless of player language. Given the globalizing nature of gameplay and the variances now even within countries for language preferences and abilities, language could play a vital role in game success, community formation, and general game world atmosphere. While many developers limit such interactions (as in Blizzard's *World of Warcraft*) a few others such as Linden Lab's *Second Life* embrace a global community. And while no virtual worlds I have found require game communication to be conducted in any specific language, some games encourage particular languages and some players see rules where none actually exist.[24]

So for a game like *Final Fantasy XI Online*, the use of both Japanese and English is common and unremarkable for its players. Players in Japan buy a version of the game that allows them to write with kanji, kana, and roman letters, and which has an "auto-translate" system (ATS) built-in. In North America, players receive a version of the game without the Japanese character sets enabled, but with the ATS as well. The ATS allows for translation between English and Japanese, with players starting to type a word, hitting the Tab key, and then having the word or phrase finished for them, or several choices for finishing appear. The player, to signal acceptance of a choice, hits enter to choose that term, and then hits enter again to send the communication into the game world. Players tend to use the system in two ways—as an instrumental tool, when grouping with players who do not speak their language, to exchange vital battle information or request help; and to play with the limits of the translator.

One form of noise that players often face is the fairly limited range of the ATS. It offers a pretty extensive list of terms, phrases, questions, and answers for player to choose from, but most choices are instrumental, rather than social or interpersonal. So, a Japanese player can ask an English-speaking player if she wishes to join an experience points party in the Valkurm Dunes, but cannot offer comments about her difficult day at work, or enquire as to why the English-speaking player decided to play this particular MMOG. The ATS thus allows some types of communication, yet not others.

Likewise, the ATS can also introduce conflicts and confusion—another possible type of noise—into the system, rather than reduce it. For example, English-speaking players often use the ATS for the word "Reward" in shouts to the general player community to indicate they are offering payment for an item or service. However, the direct Japanese translation of Reward using the ATS is actually "Pet food."[25] Other confusing translations also exist, but some have been acknowledged and worked around. Rather than "Pulling" for example, the person charged with bringing a monster to fight back to a party's camp goes "Fishing."

In response to such problems and challenges, some players have attempted workarounds of varying complexities. Some English-speaking players who play on a PC have figured out how to enable the use of Japanese characters in their game interface, allowing them to switch back and forth, using both roman and kanji/kana words as they wish. This of course presupposes some knowledge of the Japanese language. The majority of English-speaking players do not possess this skill, but a certain minority group does. Those bilingual players can be called upon to translate for their friends and family, when others have communication difficulties for which the ATS fails them.

Likewise, for those players who are not fluent in Japanese but wish to go beyond the ATS, there are guides to useful Japanese using romaji characters available thanks to dedicated fans of the game. The website Shigemo.com, for example, has a "FFXI Japanese Language (Nihongo) Guide" listing basic greetings, simple phrases, grammatical tips, and Japanese translations for virtually every job class, race, item, and ability, as well as very specific gameplay phrases (Do you want to level together? = Isshoni level age-masuka?; I'm going to my mog house = mogurimasu) to help players more successfully interact.[26]

Yet for other players, such communication challenges prove to be too much, and they decide to group only with those players who can speak their language. This has led to (specific) charges of racism in game forums, such as when North American players encountered Japanese players who indicated, either directly or through a search comment they have attached to their "seek party" message, that they wish to group with "JP Only" (JP Onry) or "English Party: No Thanks" (which, ironically, they use the ATS to spell out). Likewise, some North American players have written and talked extensively on game boards as well as in-game about their own preferences for grouping with English-speaking players, as it makes parties (they feel) more efficient as well as more enjoyable, due to the ability to make small talk with the other players. Such activities might at first blush seem to revolve around language, yet when they persist, they often draw on racist discourses in those forums.

What such practices suggest is that language will always be a challenge and a potential form of noise, and players will have different thresholds of comfort and ability for interacting with those who do not speak their particular language. While some players may go to great lengths to learn to communicate with others, some may feel no such drive, and actively seek to stay with those of their own language group. While I have not touched here on the cultural differences that have also arisen in gameplay styles, I think this is an important area to consider in the construction of online communities in games. With the global blending of crowds, trouble as well as cross-cultural exchanges can occur.

Thus, cultural noise (read as bias) adds another layer of complexity with which to grapple for communication and game studies scholars. Although technical communication may be successful, culturally meaning can break down, introducing variable levels of noise into the system.

In-Game Lingo, or How I PWNed Dark Spark to Get My RSE Gloves

LOL. Phat Lewt. PWN. Train to zone! Help . . . aggro! W00t—finally got my RSE pants, which give me +32 MP. Yeah, but ur a lvl 60 BLM and you don't have your AF hat—totally gimped. Can I get a tele? A D2? Why don't you just OP? But Ose's timer is up soon—last ToD was 18 hours ago. Whatever—gotta log to use w/c. Wtf???

Finally, game lingo may be noise to the new, casual, or returning MMOG player. It can serve as a shortcut or a marker of status or signal community membership. It goes beyond basic gameplay terms to encompass game-specific terminology, slang, and emerging forms of expression. "Leet speak" is one variant, but each MMOG has its own highly specific, arcane, evolving version of lingo. That lingo can come from both game developers as well as game players, making it another cultural or semantic form of noise found in game systems. Too much lingo can create unacceptable levels of noise for the newbie, or the infrequent player, but player facility in learning lingo is crucial to becoming a part of a particular MMOG community.

For example, in learning the job of Black Mage, a player must learn the names and functions of dozens of spells, from the obvious ("Sleep", "Stun") to the arcane ("Elemental Seal", "Tractor"). Additionally, players have created shortcut names for some spells, such as "D2" for "Warp 2" (the ability to send other party members directly to their home location). The origins of the term "D2" are player-based, yet players still debate if it was a Japanese abbreviation, or North American, and how "Warp" came to be associated with "D." That confusion is regularly reflected in new Black Mages (or "BLMs") frequently asking others why strangers are requesting a "D2" from them, when they have no such spell in their ability list. Additionally, aspiring Black Mages need to learn which stats they should boost or enhance for optimal efficiency, including "INT" or Intelligence, which increases magical spells' damage, and "MP" or Magic Points, which are their supply of magical power. The list goes on, and many formal lists of such lingo exist to help the aspiring BLM.

To overcome that noise and become an active participant in a virtual world like *Final Fantasy XI Online*, individuals must master levels of game fluency that can seem endless, non-intuitive, and deeply frustrating. While Internet language conventions are growing more familiar to the general public (in certain parts of the world, at least), the terms and communication style employed in MMOGs is another magnitude of complexity entirely. Beyond even job specific lingo such as that mentioned above, the world of Vana 'diel bombards new inhabitants with more new vocabularies to assimilate in order to function successfully: multiple areas or zones which are each individually named, various additional races and jobs, armor sets, weapons, racial abilities, NPCs/bots/mobs of varying levels of importance to gameplay or game narratives, a history of the game world, various types of battles, events, holidays, days of the week, and activities like crafting, fishing, and mining.

Add to all of that the experience occurring in real-time, with various developer and player abbreviations, players of various languages and writing abilities, and it is a wonder anything at all is accomplished or shared. Yet we have not truly explored the lingo of game worlds, and how its complexity (or relative simplicity) may play a part in creating enjoyable experiences, group solidarity, and outsider confusion in various players. My own experiences suggest the joys as well as frustrations involved in knowing or not knowing how to "talk the talk" of a particular virtual world.

In response, many players have created guides for various forms of not just gameplay or game activities, but of game lingo. Such products are similar to Shigemo's language guide, but instead serve to translate game world lingo into a physical world vocabulary. The regular production of such guides by players has become a ritualistic part of game community formation. Linkshells (such as ClanBEB) become famous for their detailed maps and careful walkthroughs, as well as explanations of the game world to new or returning players. So while players may participate in contributing to the noise of lingo, they also help other players see through the noise with sophisticated, detailed translations.

This form of noise and players' work to overcome it should make us pause and consider many things—how does such language help create and sustain communities? For who is that fluency level too high? Are there different levels of game fluency, and are those differences significant in any way? Does the presence or absence of "interpreters" (helpful game friends) make a difference, or play a role in lingo acquisition? Does crossover fluency (dialects) exist between the various MMOGs, and are those dialects becoming more similar, or more distinct, over time?

This final level or type of noise is dynamically co-constructed by game developers and players, shifting and changing over time to meet the demands of gameplay as well as the idiosyncratic preferences of players. In global games such as *Final Fantasy*, that lingo is also cross-cultural, created through the interface of three separate languages—Japanese, English, and the vocabulary of Vana 'diel. Players often work diligently to overcome this form of noise, and if they have prior experience with other MMOGs, there may be some transfer of knowledge. However, there will always be particular terms, abilities, and kinks in specific games to learn, and if such learning fails to occur, noise is the result.

Conclusions

The three types of noise I have talked about include a technical form (lag) and two cultural/semantic forms (language and lingo). I have discussed how these types of noise function in one MMOG, how players and developers have created workarounds where possible, and questions for further research and theorizing that they bring up. These likely are not the only types of noise, but they demonstrate how noise gets constructed, or deployed, in different contexts. They also show how the concept of noise can be thought of in technical as well as non-technical ways, and how it can impede both linear communication (the physical disruption of Internet signals, for example) and ritual communication (such as when veteran players use extensive lingo, and newer players feel left out, and confused). Noise can also demonstrate how players can come together to overcome its limitations, or perhaps feel a shared sense of community in understanding its limitations. Noise thus can function to both connect as well as separate players from one another in the game space.

I have argued elsewhere for the importance of considering context in gameplay (Consalvo, *Cheating*; Consalvo, *Circle*). Yet context is never divorced from the structures of the game itself. And context can develop to compensate for deficiencies in game structure. Structural problems that are too serious can also hinder and perhaps destroy meaningful contexts for gameplay.

Games allow players to create those meanings and contexts. Players develop communities and cultures, and discover emergent aspects of gameplay. Some of those elements are in direct relation to the game design, and some are in direct relation to structural problems, here identified as noise.

We must see noise as a regular part of gameplay, and interrogate how gameplay can workaround or deal with that limitation. By doing so, we can add to the field of game studies. While the Shannon-Weaver model is linear, this essay argues that the concept of noise, as distinct from the model, can suggest ritualistic functions as well, in varied cultural and semantic contexts. Noise also raises methodological issues that theories must account for. We cannot see communication in MMOGs as a straightforward linear model. It is reciprocal, redundant, contextual, and imperfect. Compensation is mandatory, and ritual elements of gameplay can emerge to respond to such challenges. The Shannon-Weaver model and communication theory are thus valuable additions to our theorization about games and the field of game studies, by reminding us of the imperfections in our chosen forums of study. And those imperfections are valuable components of study in their own right.

Notes

1. Vana 'diel is the virtual world that players explore in *Final Fantasy XI Online*.
2. Edward Castronova, *Synthetic Worlds: The Business and Culture of Online Games* (Chicago: University of Chicago Press, 2005); Lori Kendall, *Hanging Out in the Virtual Pub: Masculinities and Relationships Online* (Berkeley, CA: University of California Press, 2002);

hereafter cited as Kendall; T. L. Taylor, *Play Between Worlds: Exploring Online Game Culture* (Cambridge, MA: The MIT Press, 2006); hereafter cited as Taylor, *Worlds.*

3. Gregory F. Lastowka and Dan Hunter, "The Laws of Virtual Worlds," *California Law Review* (2003).

4. Mia Consalvo and Nathan Dutton, "Game Analysis: Developing a Methodological Toolkit for the Qualitative Study of Digital Games," *Game Studies* 6, no. 1 (2006). Available online at <http://gamestudies.org/0601/articles/consalvo_dutton>.

5. Espen Aarseth, *Cybertext: Perspectives on Ergodic Literature* (Baltimore, MD: Johns Hopkins University Press, 1997); Gonzalo Frasca, "Simulation Versus Narrative: Introduction to Ludology," in *The Video Game Theory Reader*, eds. Mark J. P. Wolf and B. Perron (New York: Routledge, 2003); Jesper Juul, *Half-real: Video Games Between Real Rules and Fictional Worlds* (Cambridge, MA: The MIT Press, 2005).

6. Mia Consalvo, "There Is No Magic Circle," *Games & Culture* (forthcoming); hereafter cited as Consalvo, *Circle*; Ren Reynolds, "Playing a 'Good' Game: A Philosophical Approach to Understanding the Morality of Games," *IGDA.com* (2002). Available online at <http://www.igda.org/articles/rreynolds_ethics.php>.

7. Henry Jenkins, *Convergence Culture* (New York: New York University Press, 2006); hereafter cited as Jenkins.

8. Seth Finn and Donald Roberts, "Source, Destination, and Entropy: Reassessing the Role of Information Theory in Communication Research," *Communication Research* 11 (1984): 453–476; hereafter cited as Finn and Roberts; David Ritchie, "Shannon and Weaver: Unraveling the Paradox of Information," *Communication Research* 13 (1986): 278–298; hereafter cited as Ritchie.

9. Taylor, *Worlds*; Constance Steinkuehler, and Dmitri Williams, "Where Everybody Knows Your (Screen) Name: Online Games as 'Third Places'," *Journal of Computer-mediated Communication* 11 (2006); Thomas Malaby, "Beyond Play: A New Approach to Games," *Games & Culture* (forthcoming).

10. Taylor, *Worlds*; Mia Consalvo, *Cheating: Gaining Advantage in Videogames* (Cambridge, MA: The MIT Press, 2007); hereafter cited as Consalvo, *Cheating.*

11. Claude Shannon, "A Mathematical Theory of Communication," *The Bell System Technical Journal* 27 (1948): 623; hereafter cited as Shannon.

12. Warren Weaver, "Recent Contributions to the Mathematical Theory of Communication," (1949), available online at <http://grace.evergreen.edu/~arunc/texts/cybernetics/weaver.pdf>; hereafter cited as Weaver.

13. Harold Lasswell, "The Structure and Function of Communication in Society," in *The Communication of Ideas*, L. Bryson, ed. (New York: Institute of Religious and Social Studies, 1948).

14. James Carey, *Communication as Culture: Essays on Media and Society* (Boston: Unwin Hyman, 1988); Stuart Hall, "Encoding/decoding," in *Culture, Media, Language: Working Papers in Cultural Studies, 1972–1979* Stuart Hall, ed. (London: Hutchinson, 1980).

15. Jennifer Stromer-Galley and Rosa Mikeal Martey, "The Digital Dollhouse: Context and Social Norms in *The Sims Online,*" *Games & Culture* 2, no. 4 (2007): 314–334.

16. K. Hew, M. Gibbs, and G. Wadley, "Usability and Sociability of the Xbox Live Voice Channel," paper presented at the *Australian Workshop on Interactive Entertainment*, Sydney, Australia, February, 2004.

17. Dmitri Williams, Scott Caplan, and Li Xiong, "Can You Hear Me Now? The Social Impact of Voice in Online Communities," *Human Communication Research* 33 (2007): 427–449.

18. Terje Rasmussen, "On Distributed Society: the Internet As a Guide to a Sociological Understanding of Communication," in *Digital Media Revisited*, eds. Gunnar Liestol, Andrew Morrison and Terje Rasmussen (Cambridge, MA: MIT Press, 2003): 444; hereafter cited as Rasmussen.

19. Jay David Bolter, "Theory and Practice in New Media Studies," in *Digital Media Revisited*, eds. Gunnar Liestol, Andrew Morrison, and Terje Rasmussen (Cambridge, MA: The MIT Press, 2003): 15–34; hereafter cited as Bolter.

20. Craig Anderson and K. E. Dill, "Video Games and Aggressive Thoughts, Feelings, and Behavior in the Laboratory and in Life," *Journal of Personality and Social Psychology* 78 (2000): 772–790; John Sherry, "The Effects of Violent Video Games on Aggression: a Meta-Analysis," *Human Communication Research* 27 (2001): 409–431.

21. Stephen Kline, Nick Dyer-Witheford, and Greig De Peuter, *Digital Play: the Interaction of Technology, Culture and Marketing* (Montreal: McGill-Queen's University Press, 2003).
22. Mihaly Csikszentmihalyi, *Flow: The Psychology of Optimal Experiences* (New York: Harper Perennial, 1991).
23. Language-specific servers are also a potential workaround.
24. T. L. Taylor, "Does WoW Change Everything? How a PvP Server, Multinational Player Base and Surveillance Mod Scene Caused Me Pause," *Games & Culture* 1, no. 4 (2006): 318–337.
25. Beastmasters, one job class in the game, use pet food to maintain the health of the pets they have fight for them.
26. Shigemo, "FFXI Japanese Language (Nihongo) Guide," (2004), available online at <http://shigemo.com/FFXI/nihongo_guide.html>.

CHAPTER 16

Getting into the Game
Doing Multidisciplinary Game Studies

FRANS MÄYRÄ

This essay will focus on interdisciplinary dialogue and multi-methodology research as an inherent characteristic of game studies. Drawing from the author's experience as the leader or partner in numerous research projects in games and digital culture, it is pieced together as a travelogue of an ongoing trip into conducting game studies within the contemporary, highly competitive and often project-based academic environment. In practical terms, it aims to provide some advice on how to avoid the pitfalls waiting for those venturing into interdisciplinary games research, as well as to point out some of the benefits that can be obtained from such approaches. The essay will conclude by providing some recent examples from interdisciplinary game studies, highlighting the associated methodological challenges and their solutions, followed by summaries of the key findings.

The highly interdisciplinary character of game studies can partly be seen to be born out of necessity: since there is not yet very long history of game studies as an independent discipline, much of the current academic work needs to rely on approaches and findings provided by and rooted in other academic fields. The situation is now quickly changing as the academic communities are starting to provide game studies with a conceptual, theoretical, and methodological corpus of its own, but still for many years most of the academics working in this field will be graduates from other disciplines.

Studies in the sociology of knowledge as well as scholars working in science and technology studies (STS) have long focused on the social, political, and discursive aspects apparent in different academic practices. Doing academic research in games and play is no exception in this sense; researchers who have their background in different disciplines will also most probably carry with them the explicit and implicit assumptions about the nature of knowledge, the proper research questions or subject matters for study and the overall goals of academic enterprise, that are typical to their native disciplinary communities. Particularly when left unspoken, these kinds of differences can produce confusion and conflict among various partners or stakeholders in game research.

I have long been a firm believer in the value of interdisciplinary dialogue in game studies, and in this essay, I will ground the need for such academic boundary-crossing to the fundamental character of games and play themselves. As I have also argued in a textbook (*An Introduction to Game Studies: Games in Culture*), games are best conceived as multiple-layered systems and processes of signification that mix representational and performative, rule-based and improvisational modes in their cultural character. In methodological terms, for most uses and purposes, the analysis of a game as an abstract structure without any consideration of its playing practices would be deemed insufficient, as would a study of game players not informed by some systems-oriented analysis and understanding of the ludic nature of this particular game and its gameplay.

In addition to the application of social sciences and humanities approaches in interdisciplinary game studies, this essay will also briefly discuss some methods derived from the field of design research, and emphasize the potential of game studies as a radical, transformative form of scholarly practice. Encouraging active interchange with different player communities, involvement in experimental game design practices, as well as critical participation into discussions about the role of games in culture and society, interdisciplinary game studies can make manifest its impact on the future direction of games cultures. My final conclusions will nevertheless also modify and set certain preconditions for the interdisciplinary operation of game studies.

Interdisciplinarity: Benefits and Pitfalls

The current wave of academic interest in and discussion of interdisciplinarity reaches at least back to the 1960s, when Thomas Kuhn published his influential study *The Structure of Scientific Revolutions* (1962).[1] An early OECD-commissioned report found five main reasons for the increasing rise of interdisciplinarity during the late 1960s: the development of science, the needs of students, new demands set by professional training, new kinds of needs by society, and challenges faced by contemporary universities in economic and administrative levels.[2] Academic institutions faced an increasingly complex world with new challenges and requirements for their core activities.

The disciplinary nature of academia itself is rooted in antiquity. While Plato had been a proponent of unified science, his pupil Aristotle had tried to establish clearly delineated areas of inquiry, such as "Poetics," "Politics," and "Metaphysics." The modern university system evolved from medieval cathedral schools, where both letters and sciences were traditionally taught, under the customary divisions of the *trivium* (grammar, logic and rhetoric) and *quadrivium* (music, geometry, arithmetic and astronomy). Already ancient Romans had been concerned about the dangers of over-specialization, but the classical educational ideal considered the integration of knowledge to take place through both a community of disciplines of knowledge (*Universitas Scientiarum*) and a community of teachers and students (*universitas magistrorum et scholarium*—the original root for our word "university").[3]

The disciplinary organization of learning, and interdisciplinary or counter-disciplinary tendencies can be seen as embodiments of two main forces shaping the academic world. On one hand, reality rarely keeps within the domain of any single discipline, and advanced study into any subject will soon uncover various potentially significant connections to other phenomena, processes, or ideas that are currently discussed within some other discipline. On the other hand, intellectual continuity and pedagogical clarity generally tend to reinforce disciplinary structures. Even while today many universities feature interdisciplinary research centers, most undergraduate and graduate education continues to be offered within established disciplinary structures like subjects organized into degree programs, departments, and different faculties.

Thomas Kuhn called "normal science" the form of operation among a scientific community which is based on shared assumptions about what the world is like. Normal science is likely to suppress fundamental novelties in thought, because such innovations threaten the very fundamentals of those forms of learning which are committed to disciplinary convention and organization (Kuhn, 5). The emphasis on original innovation in the increasingly competitive research world has led to putting more weight on novel work that would be boundary-breaking or otherwise transformative to the existing state-of-the-art. Within such rapidly-inflated discourses of science policies, "paradigm shifting" innovations are often considered an added value for national competitiveness and therefore also rewarded in public calls for research grants in government-funded research programs.

Work in emerging areas of knowledge is often situated in boundary areas between established disciplines, leading some innovation-oriented thinkers to call for rejection of traditional disciplines altogether. Often termed "transdisciplinarity", this approach to scholarship would involve working more or less permanently in the stage "beyond disciplinary boundaries."[4]

This is the context in which contemporary game studies emerged in the late 1990s and early 2000s. An entire generation of scholars with fresh interest moved to study digital games for multiple reasons, which have already been discussed elsewhere.[5] One fundamental factor has been the personal experience gained while playing digital games; in what constitutes a qualitatively major step beyond most classic board or card games, many digital games provide players with sense of entering an alternate, game-related world, while being engaged in various challenges, often in high speed action in which the player is immersed in simulation that is often audiovisually spectacular.[6] The impact of games in culture or society, for technology or economics, could no longer be ignored. It still remained a major issue, though, what form and content the study of games would adopt when entering academia.

Games as Inherently Interdisciplinary Objects of Study

Games appear as deceptively simple objects for analysis, perhaps explaining why art and cultural studies, social sciences, and many other fields took it so long to address them in a proper manner. This is also an issue of public perception; during the 1970s, 1980s, and 1990s when digital games spread out from the mainframe computers and research laboratories, first into gaming arcades and then into people's homes as television games, console video games, and home computer games, critical awareness of games as an art form remained rather limited. Games like *PONG* (Atari, 1972) or *Pac-Man* (Namco, 1980) may have appeared too trivial and considered "low" forms of commercial electronic entertainment not worthy of thorough artistic analyses. Some mathematicians and economists made use of mathematical game theory, and some anthropologists and historians paid attention to the rich cultural history of games and play, but apart from them, the full potential of games was left untouched by most disciplines.[7] This might also be due to the fact that in addition to being stigmatized as "low" cultural forms and being discussed (mostly in public forums) in relation to violence and harmful media effects, games are also rather difficult and complex objects for study.

Looking at the case of *Pac-Man* for a moment, the surface or representational level of the game is simple enough: a colorful maze is drawn electronically on the screen, inside of which a rather rudimentary drama is acted out between a player-controlled yellow blob (the *Pac-Man* figure, constantly devouring the dots that initially fill the maze) and four ghost figures chasing it. It is possible to look at a session of *Pac-Man* gameplay recorded in video, and proceed to analyze the game on that basis—a storyline focused on the theme of eating and survival would emerge, and a rather stereotypical narrative or cultural analysis would continue from that to discuss this game as a metaphor for consumer society or predatory qualities of capitalism. But when actually played by the researcher personally, the game as an object suddenly gains a different kind of character. The "drama" taking place at the representational level of the maze, ghosts, and hunt does not necessarily vanish, but it is displaced or superseded by the dominance of gameplay—all those feelings, considerations, and actions that come along when accepting the challenge of trying to navigate a maze while eating dots and avoiding ghosts. The prominent structures in the game are no longer the precise shapes in which its graphical surface appears, but rather the underlying dynamic system of forces and counterforces in which player actions are opposed to programmed challenges, or (as in multiplayer versions of games) the actions of other players. When gamers discuss games, they generally acknowledge both of these aspects, critiquing the story-world, graphics, and audio of the game, but often they are most focused on how the game actually plays out—its dynamic gameplay core.

I have named this totality the dual structure of games; as ludic simulations coupled with a digital audiovisual medium, digital games provide players access to both a "shell" (representational layers) as well as the "core" (the gameplay).[8] This is also where the inherent interdisciplinarity of game studies is rooted. As both representational shell and core gameplay contribute to player's experience with the game, neither cannot be ignored while researching and analyzing games. In a sense, games do not exist in separation from their players—except possibly as gameplay video displays shown while in an "attract mode" or during similar non-interactive demonstrations; games *as games* are something that happen only during the interplay, when a player takes actions within a game, and the playful performance brings a pile of dead code alive, transforming it into what we recognize as a digital game. This is a rather obvious philosophical point, but one that is worth discussing here: games are inherently and principally events and processes, not static objects. A game is inseparable from its playing. In conceptual terms this line of thinking has its foundation on both hermeneutical and phenomenological traditions of thought, including the work of Edmund Husserl, Martin Heidegger, Hans-Georg Gadamer, Wolfgang Iser, and Maurice Merleau-Ponty, to mention some key figures.

Gadamer, for example, argued in his major work *Truth and Method* that the mode of being of the work of art is rooted in the concept of play. "The mode of being of play does not allow the player to behave towards play as if towards an object," Gadamer writes.[9] But it should be noted that, even if one agrees with the basic ontological claim that games' existence as works of art (or even the existence of works of art in general) is based on the phenomenon of their play, there are multiple conclusions one can draw from it. Scholars involved in hermeneutics and phenomenology have held differing views regarding what is the right the level of abstraction that scholars should derive from experience of phenomena, and regarding the need for immersion for the understanding of people in their lifeworlds.[10]

One approach would be to adopt the critical gesture called "hermeneutic reduction"; rather than aiming to study all kinds of empirical actualizations that games become when they are played out, a researcher would instead focus on some "typical" or "ideal" form, derived in expert analysis. Espen Aarseth has spoken in favor of such approach. In his DiGRA 2007 conference paper, Aarseth takes as his starting point the concept of the "implied reader" that Wolfgang Iser introduced to the field of literary studies and calls for critical attention to its ludological counterpart, the "implied player." Rather than a historical, flesh-and-blood person, the implied player is a "role made for the player of the game, a set of expectations that the player must fulfill for the game to 'exercise its effect.' "[11] Aarseth also pays attention to the "methodological divide" between formal and informal methods, and notes how humanities and social sciences differ in their conception of the player when applied to game studies. Being a social scientist means, according to Aarseth (131–132), being focused on the player as historical, situated, and flesh and blood, while being a humanist game scholar involves seeing the player as "a necessary but uncontrollable part of the process of creating ludic meaning, a function that is created by the gameplay as well as cocreator of it." Within this broader divide, both humanists and social scientists are then further divided as to whether they adopt formal methods (statistics in social sciences, game ontologies in the humanities) or case-study-based informal methods (field work in social sciences, close playing/reading in the humanities).

I basically agree with much of Aarseth's analysis, but rather than seeing alternative approaches as oppositional and mutually exclusive, I perceive much more room for collaboration. This is mostly based on my personal experience of doing much of my games research within multidisciplinary teams, rather than on some *a priori* preference for interdisciplinarity. In terms of theoretical underpinnings, there is nothing stopping us from using approaches derived from multiple philosophical, scientific, or scholarly traditions together in our work. Often termed "methodological triangulation," the multi-perspectival practice of combining different research approaches is generally considered to be one of the key ways of increasing the reliability and applicability of findings. In addition to using several methods to study a single phenomenon, there also exist the options of data triangulation (researching the same phenomenon at different times or in different locations), and investigator triangulation (using multiple observers of the same phenomenon). For the fourth type of triangulation, multiple theory triangulation, it is hard to come up with examples without leaving the field of single disciplines and venturing into the complex, truly interdisciplinary regions of study.[12]

The main argument in this essay is that since games involve both representations and actions, both variously coded structures and their actual instantiation during the performance of play, there is an inherent need for multi- and interdisciplinary collaboration in the area of game studies. Dipping into the terminology pool, one could put this in terms of the *semiosis*, or meaning attached to games as sign systems, and *ludosis*, or games' meanings experienced as dynamic processes of play, being inseparable, and therefore multiple approaches being inherently important for the study of games. Some disciplines are, because of their intellectual history and key focus, more strongly equipped to study particular aspects or dimensions of games as multi-layered complexes, but no single discipline yet exists that would cover them all. I will next highlight some forms that this interdisciplinary work within game studies can take in practice, even while I will readily admit that there exist many dimensions of interdisciplinarity in game studies that will not be discussed here.

Doing Game Studies in Practice

Practical realities in academia are conditioned by the surrounding world, as are practices in many other areas of life. It is difficult to maintain the idea of totally isolated or ivory-tower-style academic practice, particularly in these days as universities are under increasing pressure to explicitly prove the value of their work to the surrounding society. On the other hand, academic research continues to enjoy relative autonomy and in principle it should be primarily rooted in the free pursuit of knowledge—a central principle in most European universities who follow the "Humboldtian model." Established in institutional form by Wilhelm von Humboldt, founder of the Berlin University, this freedom of students and staff has its strong ideological roots in German philosophical idealism.[13] In many countries there have been various challenges to academic freedom, with many of them arising today from economic concerns. The "impact" of research, for example, may be evaluated in terms of benefits to industry or economical competitiveness, rather than solely on scientific terms. Interdisciplinary game studies can be one way to navigate through these troubled waters of academic inquiry.

I will briefly discuss here three examples of games research projects that we have carried out at the University of Tampere, focusing mostly on methodological solutions and how interdisciplinary collaboration benefited or otherwise affected this work.

Starting the Interdisciplinary Study of Games and Play

The first case study featured here is a research project entitled "Children as Actors of Games Cultures"—here abbreviated as "PeTo" (shorthand derived from the original Finnish name). Carried out in the years 2003–2004, this work had its basis in the study of games cultures which our group had initiated already in the 1990s, and more immediately in work related to such areas as mobile communication, interactive television, the Internet, and gambling, which had been in the focus of our work during the years 2000–2002. The work in 1990s had been institutionally located in the Department of Literature and the Arts, and most of our work was decidedly humanistic scholarship in nature, even if those early approaches to games as hyper- or cybertextuality were already seasoned with a touch of cultural studies. The institutional change at our university around the turn of the century involved several key people moving from their original home base of literary studies into the Hypermedia Laboratory, the new media department, which had a much more interdisciplinary profile. This combination of contexts might be considered typical for contemporary game studies; particularly many European games scholars have been trained in established humanist disciplines, above all within literary studies, and then have moved to focus on game studies in their own terms. The establishment of new research centers to address particularly the promising interdisciplinary areas falling in between classic disciplinary formations is also typical of the wider institutional changes touching contemporary universities.[14]

In the case of the PeTo study, we wanted to understand how digital games are currently played, what the particular holding power factors are that make digital play such an engaging experience, and also to situate such an inquiry within a concrete context of daily life. The initial research topic and focus of this study thus consisted of an entire constellation of interrelated elements that we wanted to learn to know better: what kind of objects or phenomena games are, how game players perceive them, what we can learn about gameplay experiences, and how games are situated in real life contexts. In institutional and practical terms, we had a history of several rejected research grant applications behind us—it had proved exceedingly difficult to attract funding for doing basic research in theoretically-oriented subjects related to games. It was impossible to gain support for a study which would had situated games within digital cultures and explored them in terms of their artistic and aesthetic qualities or structures—possibly considered a paradoxically "highbrow" or serious way of approaching such a "low" subject matter. On the other hand, there were already established research groups within our university working on themes such as information society and children. The research plan for PeTo was thus born half out of necessity, as our interest of doing game studies was faced with academic and financial structures that necessitated working within socially-sanctioned research themes. But it was possible to turn necessity into virtue; our research proved to be beneficial and was strengthened, both methodically and in terms of the value of our findings, through the interdisciplinary collaboration in which we became involved.

The consortium in which we carried out our PeTo study was entitled "Children and Information Society" and it consisted of several research groups working on interrelated subjects. The central partners for our study were researchers coming from the fields of Early Childhood Education, Social Psychology, Computer Science, and Work Research. The entire consortium was coordinated by a new, interdisciplinary center, the Information Society Institute. Early on, an internal research seminar was established as a forum to discuss the methodologies, findings, and coordination of collaborative efforts within this broad-ranging group. The close interdisciplinary relationship was not without its challenges, and early on two partners left the consortium, due to fundamental differences of opinion regarding the practical goals and theoretical starting points of research.

The movement between humanities-based interest in game aesthetics and structural analysis on the one hand, and the social sciences related interest in the real contexts of gameplay on the other, formed the underlying basis of this study. It also contributed to the dynamic tension which proved important for its success; rather than being happy with our initial conceptions of games and digital play, we were constantly challenged by contact and discussions with our informants, as well as by our colleagues from other fields who with their questions particularly raised our interest towards the wider societal changes which surround and define the role of digital gaming today. Finding a way to address all these directions in our inquiry, we played a wide range of different games ourselves, discussed them among our team, and used them to test various models we derived from game studies literature. In the next step, our research dialectic involved social sciences methodologies, and we launched a moderately sized survey study, followed by a smaller selection of in-depth interviews. This negotiation between perspectives offered by multiple disciplinary approaches was effectively engaging us in a circular or spiraling process, which is essential for any true hermeneutic inquiry, as we only later realized. The movement from our preconceived notions to interpretation and then to a revised understanding can even be considered essential for our entire existence in the world, as Martin Heidegger has pointed out.[15] Hermeneutic inquiry has a certain playful and experimental character built into it, which is one more reason to adopt it while doing game studies. The term "hermeneutics" relates back to Hermes, the famously mischievous trickster spirit, carrying with also it associations of complication, multiplicity, jokes and puzzles (Moules). In our case, the joke or trick perhaps was us managing to smuggle fundamental theoretical game studies work into an applied project done under the information society research banner.

The multiple findings of our research were directed to many different audiences, a logical consequence of our multiple starting points. We were able to gain a better understanding of the key holding power factors in digital games and play through this dialogue between humanities-oriented theory and different kinds of player-informants—we interviewed both children and their parents, who were typically middle-aged Finnish women and men. The full range of concepts like "action", "exploration", or "building" that emerged from interviews were organized into a conceptual map during analysis, clustered with the help of factor analysis, and the ensuing categories were then synthesized back into an integrated model of game-play experience. We then moved on to compare the findings with earlier published studies that were coming from the fields of ludology, the psychology of virtual environments, and human-computer interaction (HCI), to mention the key ones, and clarified our conceptual terminology so that while publicizing the results we could properly address relevant ongoing scholarly discussions. An extensive research report focusing on games and digital play was finally produced, including entire chapters dedicated to such issues as digital play in social contexts, learning in games, games as engagement in fantasy, gameplay immersion, game violence, and issues related to the control of game playing within the context of everyday family life.[16] As a joint effort with our interdisciplinary research consortium, we also produced a book which soon was referenced in public discussions as a source of information on children, games, and information society alike.[17]

The Pitfalls and Benefits in Doing Interdisciplinary Game Design Studies

Looking back at this first exploration into doing interdisciplinary game studies, we remain rather encouraged by the results. We were both able to contribute to the theory formation and scholarly discussions within game studies as a specific field of inquiry, while also being engaged in a more wide-reaching form of academic collaboration. We were also able to address several issues that had received ample attention among the general audience, such as game violence, socialization, and learning effects discussions. We also gained some experience about the pitfalls waiting in this road. First of all, for interdisciplinary collaboration to be truly successful, all involved parties need to be genuinely interested in learning new things, new ways of speaking, and looking at issues they already thought they knew very well, and also willing to change themselves during the process. I might be wrong about this, but young researchers appear more inclined to make such jumps across conceptual and paradigmatic chasms rather than those already well established in their careers; exceptions, of course, exist, but mostly they just prove the rule.

A more specific catch waits for those who bravely combine socio-cultural game studies with technical or engineering-oriented research work. This can be immensely rewarding, as will be described below in more detail, but a certain mutual mixing of horizons is a precondition for starting such inquiry. Our team has been involved in joint research efforts where all parties have set off with high ambitions, but the results have been disappointing. Often this has been due to original technical research being set up as the prerequisite for human-oriented researchers starting their work. A typical dependency might be that a novel software or hardware solution is planned to provide totally new kinds of game experiences, interaction modalities, or other features which then become required for the more game- or player-focused part of study to move forward. According to my experience, these kind of development and implementation efforts very rarely conclude with anything functional within the available timeframe, or if a functional technical prototype is successfully implemented, it comes too late to be actually useful in any actual game design or player studies. This is a paradox caused by competitive research funding schemes: in order to be ranked at the top in evaluations, the research grant application needs to include such a level of ambition in all areas of its interdisciplinary spectrum, that all its promises can be considered as "significant contributions" or "original innovations" by the evaluating experts, technical and non-technical alike. A more realistic starting point is to use off-the-shelf, available and reliable technologies while implementing any design experiments or player interaction studies that are to be carried out during research. Of course, close collaboration with cutting edge technical research can be mutually beneficial, and particularly effective it can be used for attracting funding in an environment increasingly supportive of interdisciplinary research activities. Openness to interdisciplinarity can thus be seen as a survival tactic for game studies within an "impact driven" research policy environment. However, for the realities of research practice, no functional "future technology" is needed to gain an adequate sense or experience of future technology. To take one example, it is perfectly possible to simulate interaction with an intelligent computer system with the help of a hidden, real person remotely playing the role of computer—an arrangement known as the "Wizard of Oz experiment."[18]

There are several benefits also to be gained by the joining of forces between software or hardware engineers, game designers, and game scholars. I will highlight these next by discussing several interdisciplinary, game design oriented research projects our team carried out from 2003 to 2006. By now, we had established a research group focused on digital games within our department, but I still remained as its only member who was counted among the (more or less) regular faculty of the university. There were no new job openings, as the Finnish government continued to cut its basic funding from universities, and to move the available resources into competitive research funds. Our group proved to be successful in applying for such grants, concluding with a situation in which our team of young game researchers was the single largest group within the department and one of the largest within the Faculty of Information Sciences, but the overall agenda for carrying out research on issues essential for our understanding of digital games and play continued to be strongly affected by accidents of funding, rather than be solely based on a consistent vision or autonomic evaluations by the academic researchers themselves.

In some cases the research funding programs may also provide lucky accidents. From our perspective one of those was the large-scale effort within European Union to focus research resources on ubiquitous, mobile, pervasive, or ambient media and technology. From our earlier history, which included collaboration with Nokia, the Finnish mobile phone giant, we gained some understanding of these fields. With the trickster Hermes again as our guide, we rephrased some of our ongoing research concerns within such topics as game analysis, player studies, and gameplay experience in terms of future game design. The nature of gameplay experience and fundamental research into games' interactive ontology (that is, their way of existing as interactive events) could now be pursued under the heading of "user experience evaluation" for next generation mobile and pervasive media, and reverse-engineering some of the work carried out in game analysis provided us with fresh starting points for doing game design research. The essential continuity of research interests was thus maintained, but adjusted to fit within the rapidly changing academic landscape.

A highly interesting interdisciplinary collaboration was carried out within a research consortium which the Academy of Finland—the most prestigious sponsor of scholarship in Finland—decided to fund. This involved the concept of "proactive computing" which stands for a future paradigm of information processing, promoted by the microprocessor industry and which is primarily designed to harness the powers of thousands of embedded processors surrounding each individual, supposedly in the rather near future.[19] Our team joined forces with the Tampere University of Technology and the University of Art and Design Helsinki to look into how proactive technology could be implemented in ordinary homes and how to design it in a manner that would empower people rather than leave them at the mercy of some autonomous, semi-intelligent sensor-actuator network. Adopting methods developed within the field of design research, we experimented with a "cultural probes" approach (delivering into people's homes packages of cameras, booklets containing tasks, and other means of self-documentation) to gain a better understanding of how homes and "homeliness" are currently experienced among our informants. On the other hand, drawing from the philosophy of ethics and science fiction studies, we created hypothetical scenarios of future technologies and provisional guidelines for the design and implementation of them. Finally, our engineering team created different "semi-autonomous" objects and environments that we could offer people to live with in their daily lives. Our key findings are reported in a book and a series of articles.[20] In them, we emphasized that a promising direction for the design of future technology was the full exploration of its ludic potential, rather than the more traditional security or health solutions that have been discussed in numerous "smart home" studies. We also observed spontaneous play behaviors that families created around "smart cushions" which we had introduced into their homes. We concluded that ambient, embedded technologies might help in turning everyday environments into places more supportive of spontaneous, playful social interaction and intergenerational play than is common today.

The methodological lessons derived from this collaboration were next applied to a study we did in collaboration with Veikkaus, the company which holds the monopoly for the arranging of lottery and betting games in Finland. Our main focus here was on how the rise of digital games is going to mix with and affect the world of traditional lottery games, but to gain an overview, we launched a new kind of cultural-probes-inspired research approach. This time we designed and delivered to our informants' homes a "game-like cultural probe" package, complete with playing instructions, cards, and other materials. We had effectively turned participation in a sociocultural study of games into the playing of a research game. After our informants had used the cultural probe game for a certain time, the derived materials were analyzed, and the main conclusions were synthesized in light of theoretical literature and used as an inspiration in design concept workshops we organized with professionals of the field.[21] The design concepts, in their turn, were used as starting points for game prototype implementations, in which our goal was to use Adobe Flash to quickly develop small "hybrid" games, meaning that they would draw together elements which would speak to both lottery gamers and video gamers. The interdisciplinary scope thus further expanded to include graphic design, sound design, and interaction design, as we developed and applied the process of iterative game design, testing our earlier work on game design and games' holding power factors. In this study, as well as in some later work we have conducted, the traditional "Lottery culture" has appeared as a major and rather distinctive cultural formation in its own. Only rather recently have similar kinds of hybrid implementations (that we experimented with in our research) appeared commercially, most notably in the field of so-called casual "skill gaming."[22]

A third game-design-focused research initiative I want to discuss here is a large European Union funded project, the Integrated Project on Pervasive Gaming (IPerG for short), which further expanded our scope of interdisciplinary collaboration in doing game studies. Here we joined forces with experimental game art groups like Blast Theory from London and Swedish *larp* (live action role-playing) artists, leading information technology and computer science laboratories from Britain, Germany, and Sweden, as well as the in-house research and development groups of Nokia and Sony. Rather than taking responsibility for any single area in this extensive research collaboration, we were uniquely positioned to be given the overall research lead in game design and evaluation studies through the entire project. Gaining access to many different kinds of experimental games played a major role in broadening the way our team currently thinks about games as an expressive and cultural form. The games designed and evaluated during the project included multiple avant-garde larps, enhanced with sensors and communications technologies, team-based games which spanned across multiple media while making use of both narrative and musical elements, socially adaptable games which were supposed to scale down or up in order to appropriately engage different kinds of people, as well as citywide art games that exploited player movement, emergent behaviors, and social dynamics as parts of the game event.[23]

The main outcomes from this work were organized around a new theoretical model of what defines "pervasive games" (games blended with the environment), and how they expand Huizinga's classic concept of the "magic circle" in multiple ways, including temporal, spatial, and social expansions of gameplay.[24] The specific lessons for interdisciplinary collaboration relate here particularly to the benefits of scale: as dozens of researchers, designers, and experts of various kinds were jointly working with multiple aspects of pervasive games, a joint framework allowed both specialization and theorization to take place. Theoretical contributions from our team were important in providing a shared language and in harmonizing the divergent research goals between different teams. Meanwhile, it was also obvious that a computer scientist, sociologist, or media researcher all today continue to work within their own disciplinary fields and are therefore liable to produce results that are recognized and considered valid scholarship only when evaluated as such using the standards of their particular fields. Doing papers that are "pure ludology" or rooted only in the discussions within the core field of contemporary game studies are not necessarily within the interest of any such established discipline.

Conclusion: The Need for Disciplinary Game Studies

The conclusions I will draw from the above discussion of the role of interdisciplinarity within and around game studies are somewhat mixed and ambiguous. On the one hand, there are obvious benefits to be derived from wide interdisciplinary collaboration. The results and understanding we have been able to reach regarding digital games' ways of existing, of different kinds of players, their experiences, and the social and cultural structures that surround games and play would not have been possible without theoretical and methodological influences, as well as lessons derived from earlier studies originating in the humanities, social sciences, design research, and software engineering, just to name a few. On the other hand, this interdisciplinary activity is at least partly stimulated by the contemporary vogue within the academic funding structures, and not always entirely motivated by reasons derived from the needs or goals of research itself.

As our example hopefully proves, game studies can successfully be carried out within a highly competitive research environment. It is also possible to successfully make contributions to fundamental conceptual and theoretical discussions of game studies while engaged in various interdisciplinary and collaborative efforts. At the same time, interdisciplinarity as a concept is based on dialogue and intermixing of disciplinary formations. As noted above, already within the classical educational ideal a discipline was understood to be based on both a certain unified organization of knowledge, as well as on a community of academics who maintain, renew, and transform such formations through their scholarly practices. If there is no discipline at the heart of game studies, it will remain uncertain what kind of interdisciplinary dialogue it can be involved in. The character of interdisciplinary scholarship has been compared to the figure of web, network, or archipelago (Klein, Interdisciplinarity, 19). A web nevertheless requires certain kinds of holding points as its nodes, or it will quickly become so loose that it will easily appear both immaterial and insignificant.

I will therefore conclude that in order to truly benefit, and be beneficial for others, game studies needs to build up a certain kind of identity of its own. This will consist of concepts, theories, and critical discussions which everyone working within the field of game studies will be expected to know about (even while not necessarily agreeing with them). The busy ongoing activity within publication in the field of game studies, resulting in volumes like the present one, is one key element for such a knowledge-based identity to emerge. The other aspect of disciplinary identity is based on regular venues of communication that are required for the formation of a functional scholarly community. This development is also underway, as is evident in the creation of games-focused scholarly journals, conference series, and academic associations like the Digital Games Research Association, DiGRA.[25] It is perhaps a paradox, but based on my experience, I need to conclude that game studies can best maintain its interdisciplinary role by strengthening its disciplinary self-image. Only that way can games scholars enter into collaborative research efforts on their own terms, and contribute something genuinely new to the broad field of scholarship.

Notes

1. Thomas S. Kuhn, *The Structure of Scientific Revolutions* (Chicago, IL: University Of Chicago Press, 1996).
2. Leo Apostel, G. Berger, A. Briggs, and G. Michaud, eds., *Interdisciplinarity: Problems of Teaching and Research in Universities*, Organization for Economic Cooperation and Development (OECD): Paris, 1972; cit. Julie Thompson Klein, *Crossing Boundaries: Knowledge, Disciplinarities, and Interdisciplinarities* (Charlottesville, VA: University of Virginia Press, 1996), 20.
3. Julie Thompson Klein, *Interdisciplinarity: History, Theory, and Practice* (Newcastle upon Tyne: Bloodaxe Books, 1991), 19–20; hereinafter cited as Klein, Interdisciplinarity.
4. For more on "transdisciplinarity," see Julie Thompson Klein, Walter Grossenbacher-Mansuy, Rudolf Häberli, Alain Bill, Roland W. Scholz, and Myrtha Welti, eds., *Transdisciplinarity: Joint Problem Solving among Science, Technology, and Society—An Effective Way for Managing Complexity* (Basel: Birkhäuser, 2004).
5. See Frans Mäyrä, "A Moment in the Life of a Generation: Why Game Studies Now?" *Games and Culture* 1, no 1 (2006): 103–106.
6. Multiple components can be identified within immersion in gameplay, as has been discussed in Laura Ermi and Frans Mäyrä, "Fundamental Components of the Gameplay Experience: Analysing Immersion," in *Selected Papers Proceedings of DiGRA 2005 Conference: Changing Views—Worlds in Play*. Vancouver: DiGRA and Simon Fraser University, 2005: 15–27. Available online at <http://www.digra.org/dl/db/06276.41516.pdf>.

7. See Stewart Culin, *Games of the North American Indians, Vol. 1: Games of Chance* and *Vol. 2: Games of Skill*. Originally published in 1907 (Lincoln and London: University of Nebraska Press, 1992).
8. See Frans Mäyrä, *Introduction to Game Studies: Games in Culture* (London and New York: Sage Publications, 2008), 17–18.
9. Hans-Georg Gadamer, *Truth and Method* (London and New York: Continuum International, 2004), 103.
10. See Nancy J. Moules, "Hermeneutic Inquiry: Paying Heed to History and Hermes—An Ancestral, Substantive, and Methodological Tale," *International Journal of Qualitative Methods* 1, no 3; hereafter cited as Moules. Available online at <http://www.ualberta.ca/~ijqm/>.
11. Espen Aarseth, "I Fought the Law: Transgressive Play and The Implied Player," in *Situated Play—Proceedings of DiGRA 2007 Conference*, ed. Akira Baba (Tokyo: DiGRA Japan, 2007), 132; hereafter cited as Aarseth. Available online at <http://www.digra.org/dl/db/07313.03489.pdf>.
12. See Norman K. Denzin, *The Research Act: A Theoretical Introduction to Sociological Methods* (Chicago: Aldine, 1970), 297–301.
13. Christophe Charle, "Patterns," in Walter Rüegg, ed. *A History of the University in Europe* (Cambridge: Cambridge University Press, 2004), 48.
14. See also developments discussed in Derek Bok, *Universities in the Marketplace: The Commercialization of Higher Education* (Princeton, NJ: Princeton University Press, 2004).
15. Martin Heidegger, *Being and Time* (Oxford: Blackwell, 1988), 191–195.
16. Laura Ermi, Satu Heliö, and Frans Mäyrä, "The Power of Games and Control of Playing—Children as the Actors of Game Cultures [Finnish language report with an extended English abstract]," *Tampere University Hypermedia Laboratory Net Series* 6 (2004). Available online at <http://tampub.uta.fi/tup/951-44-5939-3.pdf>.
17. Anja Riitta Lahikainen, Pentti Hietala, Tommi Inkinen, Marjatta Kangassalo, Riikka Kivimäki, and Frans Mäyrä, eds. *Lapsuus mediamaailmassa: Näkökulmia lasten tietoyhteiskuntaan* [Childhood in the World of Media: Views into Children's Information Society] (Helsinki: Gaudeamus, 2005).
18. John F. Kelley, "An Iterative Design Methodology for User-Friendly Natural Language Office Information Applications," *ACM Transactions on Office Information Systems* 2, no. 2 (March 1984): 26–41.
19. David Tennenhouse, "Proactive Computing," *Communications of the ACM*, 43, no. 5 (May 2000): 43–50.
20. See particularly: Frans Mäyrä and Ilpo Koskinen, eds. *The Metamorphosis of Home: Research into the Future of Proactive Technologies in Home Environments* (Tampere: Tampere University Press, 2005); Frans Mäyrä, Anne Soronen, Ilpo Koskinen, Kristo Kuusela, Jussi Mikkonen, Jukka Vanhala, and Mari Zakrzewski, "Probing A Proactive Home: Challenges in Researching and Designing Everyday Smart Environments," *Human Technology* 2, no. 22 (October 2006). Available online at <http://www.humantechnology.jyu.fi/archives/abstracts/mayra-et-al06.html>.
21. This approach has been described in Olli Sotamaa, Laura Ermi, Anu Jäppinen, Tero Laukkanen, Frans Mäyrä, and Jani Nummela, "The Role of Players in Game Design: A Methodological Perspective," in *Digital Arts and Culture* DAC 2005 *Conference Proceedings* (IT University of Copenhagen, 2005): 34–42.
22. For examples, go to <http://www.king.com>, <http://www.gameduell.com>, <http://www.worldwinner.com>, and <http://www.bingo.com>.
23. For more on IPerG, its publications and games designed during this research project, see: <http://iperg.sics.se>.
24. See Markus Montola, "Exploring the Edge of the Magic Circle: Defining Pervasive Games," in *Digital Arts and Culture* DAC 2005 *Conference Proceedings* (IT University of Copenhagen, 2005). Markus Montola, Annika Waern and Eva Nieuwdorp, "Domain of Pervasive Gaming." Deliverable D5.3b from the IPerG project, 2006. Available online at <http://iperg.sics.se/Deliverables/D5.3b-Domain-of-Pervasive-Gaming.pdf>. The "magic circle" was first introduced by Johan Huizinga in his work *Homo Ludens: A Study of the Play-Element in Culture*. Boston, MA: Beacon Press (1938), 1955.
25. See <http://www.digra.org>.

Appendix
Video Games through Theories and Disciplines

The interdisciplinary nature of video game studies means that ideas and concepts from a variety of theories and disciplines can be usefully and insightfully applied to the study of video games. What follows is a list (neither comprehensive nor exhaustive) of these areas, each with a brief survey of concepts and how they relate to video game studies. The entries are intended to show the overlap between fields and provide starting points for interdisciplinary research. Together, they provide an overall picture of the way video game studies is positioned among, and interconnected with, a wide range of fields of inquiry. Included in this list are entries for Anthropology, Art and Aesthetics, Artificial Intelligence, Business/Industry (includes Marketing), Communication Theory, Computer Graphics, Computer Programming, Cultural Studies, Design, Economics, Education, Ethnography, Film Studies, Game Theory, Gender Studies (includes Feminism), Genre Studies, History, Human-Computer Interaction, Interdisciplinary Studies, Law, Literary Theory, Ludology, Media Ecology, Medicine, Methodology, Narratology, New Media (includes Interactivity), Phenomenology, Philosophy (includes Morality and Ethics), Politics, Psychoanalysis, Psychology (includes Cognition, Emotion, and Pleasure), Reception Theory, Semiotics, Sociology, Sub-creation Studies, Television Studies, and Theater and Performance Studies.

Aesthetics

(see **Art and Aesthetics**)

Anthropology

As an academic discipline, anthropology came into being in the late nineteenth and early twentieth centuries. In the American tradition it is typically seen to be composed of four subfields: cultural anthropology (also known as sociocultural anthropology, and as "social anthropology" in the British tradition and in many other non-US contexts), linguistic anthropology, archaeology, and biological anthropology (also known as physical anthropology). There are also many focused fields of interest, such as medical anthropology, legal anthropology, economic anthropology, and the anthropology of science and technology.

In its most fundamental sense, anthropology is concerned with the study of anthropos, or human beings. It purposely defines "the human" in very broad terms, because a common theme in most anthropological research is in interest in the cross-cutting domains that define human experience: How is religion political? How is economics shaped by gender? This fascination with the intersectional nature of social life has helped make anthropology a highly interdisciplinary discipline, in constant conversation with a range of other disciplines and strongly motivated to draw techniques and theoretical frameworks from outside anthropology itself. It is for this reason, for instance, that different schools of anthropological work can be classed with the natural sciences, the social sciences, and the humanities. Anthropology also has a longstanding interest in questions of social inequality, and has often helped contribute to activist projects of exposing and redressing forms of injustice.

It is primarily cultural anthropology and linguistic anthropology that have contributed to the study of video games. Video games are created by human beings and thus fall within the purview of anthropology. They are also played by human beings—often in groups, even "massively multiplayer" groups. Even when played alone, video games are still a social phenomenon in that the player is in dialogue with the game's creator and with broader cultural assumptions built into the game itself. What anthropology brings to the table is an interest in how video games can constitute cultural spaces with their own cultural assumptions, and also an interest in how the cultural assumptions created and experienced in video games link up to cultural logics beyond video games themselves, including environments of gameplay.

Methodologically, the primary technique anthropologists have brought to the study of video games is participant observation—the long-term, intensive commitment to engaging in the everyday lives of the persons under study, so as to become as familiar with their cultural perspectives as possible. Anthropologists also make use of a range of other methods, including interviewing, historical and archival research, and textual analysis, but these are usually deployed in the service of participant observation. For instance, few anthropologists would use interviewing in isolation—without pairing such interviewing with participant observation data—because this pairing allows the researcher to investigate the crucial relationship between what people say they do and what they actually do in everyday life. This methodological insight links up to the general anthropological interest in social life as multiply and contextually constituted. Just as humans cannot speak without speaking some language, be it English, German, or Japanese, so humans cannot live except through the experiential prism of one or more cultures. Video games can now help constitute such cultures. And just as English or Japanese is a historical, social product for which no gene could possibly be discovered, so the cultures associated with video games are social phenomena, phenomena that anthropology can help us better understand.

Tom Boellstorff

Art and Aesthetics

An ongoing popular debate regarding the legitimacy of video games concerns the claim of the video game as an art form. As such, video games are often associated with and compared with other media, especially cinema, since both are audiovisual media that rely on similar aesthetic conventions, and often depict diegetic worlds in which narratives take place. Just as cinema struggled to gain legitimacy when it was new, video games now face the same questions regarding their artistic status.

Differences of opinion underlying the debate can be explained by the ambiguity surrounding the notion of art, and the hybrid nature of the video game medium. Examining the medium's aesthetics, we can observe three broad categories of the "artistic" in video games: the video game as a technical craft, as an audiovisual medium, and as an interactive and ludic practice.

First and foremost, the video game is a technical art, as video game creation requires expertise in various domains such as computer science, design, animation, and so on; such skills are often seen as proof of the artistic merit of video games. Great achievements in concept art (seen in the numerous game-art books), character animation, level design, and game physics reveal the creative richness of video games. However, this interpretation of art as a technical prowess departs greatly from the notion of "Art" as understood in Art History and (Philosophical) Aesthetics. Yet, over the twentieth century, popular media like film and video expanded the notion of art in contemporary aesthetics, and succeeded in demonstrating the aesthetic possibilities and expressive potential of the editing of images and sound.

As an audiovisual medium, video games represent their diegetic worlds through graphics and sound. Stories are told by means of character development, plot, and settings. Within this realm of representation, an enormous variety of design possibilities are available. Graphics are the result of many stylistic choices and influences; sounds can be used for different aesthetic and expository ends; and virtual cameras provide a variety of point of views. Level designs can involve disciplines such as architecture and geography.

Video games are also defined by their rules and the interactivity between the game and the player, making them different from traditional arts like cinema or theatre, and requiring new methods of analysis different from those used for traditional media. Video game aesthetics cannot be limited to the way a game looks or sounds, but must take gameplay into account. The player's gameplay experience, both within the diegetic world as well as with non-diegetic features (such as menus, inventories, controllers, and so on) depends on the various design choices made by the game's developers. Bad designs can lead to an unpleasant gameplay experience. Gameplay defines the interactive experience of the video game, and can also contribute to the emergence of aesthetic expressions one expects to find in an art form.

Although this tripartite nature of video games (technical, mediatic, and ludic) is acknowledged in discussions of the artistic nature of the medium, curiously video game aesthetics as such have been underexplored in video game studies. The reason may be due to the aforementioned debate about the legitimacy of video game as a cultural and art form, but also probably because of the low esteem of the "aesthetic" as a dated classical discipline, which in the twentieth century was associated with subjective and obsolete notions of "Beauty" or the "Sublime." Questions about genre, narrative, emotion, space, time, graphics, style, game design, and even gameplay, have all been affiliated with video game aesthetics. These various approaches imply a more profound need in video game theory for a poetics of the video game and a better understanding of the functioning of art and aesthetics within it.

Martin Picard

Artificial Intelligence

Artificial Intelligence (AI) attempts to reduce intelligent reasoning into problem solving. It is therefore not surprising to discover the wealth of applications video games have provided for AI techniques. In most video games, the player controls a character that interacts with and affects a virtual world. Virtual opponents must find ways, within their constraints, to reach the player's character, to follow and anticipate its moves, and even to collaborate between themselves to respond to its actions. The player-character may also be assisted by virtual allies, who can collaborate to reach a common goal, such as in team sport games. It is therefore crucial for the virtual characters, including the player-character, to act with human-like intelligence. They must avoid being too predictable, and adapt to varying strategies. There is also a fine line between challenging and crushing the player-character, therefore maintaining the player in a stimulating game interaction.

AI has also provided a number of standard techniques to cater to the needs in virtual believable intelligence, from the simplest to the most sophisticated ones. Examples include A^* and dynamic A^* algorithms for path planning, flocking and schooling for motions of many opponents, state machines and agents to respond to actions, needs, and constraints, neural networks to learn the behavior of a main character, etc.

In certain types of games, the game itself consists in affecting the evolution of virtual worlds. Evolutionary computation, genetic algorithms, and emergent behaviors are combined to create variations in events and strategies. Similarities with actual evolutions might even hint that these simulation tools could be used to understand and model past and present real world situations.

More than just applying these AI techniques to game situations, new challenges will need to be addressed to respond to the real-time nature of the game actions/reactions, as well as to adapt to the incredible complexity of complete worlds of constraints. Moreover, the notion of stimulating game play and adaptability to the player become crucial notions rarely faced by AI techniques. They must offer good and bad surprises, provide effective attachment to the characters, motivate to surpass oneself, control emotions, etc. All these new challenges need to be recast within effective AI techniques.

Pierre Poulin

Business/Industry

The study of business as practiced in business schools typically comprises several disciplines such as management (including strategy, innovation, entrepreneurship, human resources, and organizational behavior), marketing (including product development—which overlaps with the study of innovation in management), finance, and operations research/operations management. The discipline of management most closely relates to the understanding of the workings of the video game industry. Management has been heavily influenced by the "mother" disciplines of sociology (with institutional theory), economics (with resource theories of the firm), and psychology (in studies of employee behavior in organizations). Generally speaking, most business research, at least as practiced in research business schools, is arcane and aimed at a higher level of theorizing. It is at this level that the research is least focused on specific industries like video games, unless by happenstance, and therefore, least useful. More grounded studies done qualitatively (such as case studies or ethnographies), or more quantitative, applied economics-based studies of how industries evolve or develop, can however offer a useful lens into the workings of video games or creative industries in general. Specific works on creative industries by Richard Caves, or on Hollywood's economics by Arthur De Vany, are good examples (these were written by economists but could have easily come out of researchers in business or public policy schools). The former illustrates how intermediaries act as powerful "gate-keepers" to creative individuals and firms (as would be the case in video games), while the latter offers an example of how the "hits" nature of movies can be quantitatively characterized. Case studies offer another lens into a lower level of phenomena than the industry—one that offers insight into the strategy of a particular firm. An earlier Harvard Business School case on Electronic Arts offers one example of this. In this way, phenomena can be studied at either the firm or organizational level, the industry level, or the product level. At the product level, studies of product development in video games could offer insight into how games can be produced "better," that is, more efficiently. The role of creativity in product development is also broached by research on product development—something that is also of potential value to video game studies.

Feichin Ted Tschang

Cognition

(see **Psychology**)

Communication Theory

Communication theory first developed in the 1940s, in part to understand questions related to wartime propaganda, and the growing influence of the media on society. Theories take into account human communication, mediated communication, and most recently computer-mediated communication. While the field includes theories that study how pairs or groups of individuals interact, the study of mediated and computer-mediated communication is where most work in relation to the study of video games is occurring, with valuable findings.

The richest area in video game studies so far for communication theory has been the study of multi-player communication, particularly communication found in online, persistent games such as massively multiplayer online games (MMOGs). Researchers have successfully employed theories such as social information processing theory and media richness theory to help explain user behavior in games. Information processing theory predicts that computer-mediated communication users adapt to media over time and they work with them strategically to compensate for a potential lack of richness. Relatedly, media richness theory predicts that there is a general ordering of media from rich to poor (with face-to-face communication being the gold standard, and numerical information being the most poor), and that the more cues a medium has, the better suited it is for maintaining relationships. Thus, communication theories can help us see how various additions to online games such as voice chat can enrich the experience for players, as well as how users can strategically choose which type of chat works best in particular situations.

Drawing from the same set of theories, the study of avatars as part of computer-mediated communication has generated provocative findings for game studies research. Research has found that avatars are generally considered to be as rich as audio and video, and further that avatars might be a valuable tool for contextualizing social interaction and relaying non-verbal information, rather than simply providing a high-resolution transmission channel for visual information. Thus, avatars can help us communicate better online by returning some of the non-verbal cues that were initially removed when moving away from face-to-face communication. Research has also found that avatars in online games as well as offline games influence not only how we play games and interact with others in the game, but also how we might be bringing particular expectations into our offline lives as well, based on the avatars we have chosen.

Communication theory also looks at issues related to the context of communication, including social factors such as race, gender, and class. Work in this area has found that such identity markers continue to be important in how individuals perceive games, how they play with others, and how the industry itself constructs its market. Just as with other forms of new media, older power structures often remain, and are only slowly being challenged or changed.

Such a range of theoretical approaches within communication theory suggests the value of this avenue for understanding how gamers interact while playing games, and also how games can help us explore our identities as well as how games can shape our offline selves. As MMOGs continue to grow in popularity globally, such theories will become critical to exploring the interactions that occur in such spaces, as well as how different sorts of spaces, with different affordances and constraints, can offer players richer or poorer sites for communication, community building, and identity exploration.

Mia Consalvo

Computer Graphics

Video games and real-time computer graphics have been closely related since their early days, even though communication between the two communities was not always as strong as one would expect. One reason for this distance is that development on video game consoles involved costly specialized environments and expertise not easily accessible to the academic field. However, the fast evolution of affordable, high performance, and general graphics hardware, supported by common APIs (application programming interfaces), has stirred up synergy between the two communities.

Computer graphics is generally divided into modeling, animation, and rendering, with certain overlaps between these fields in many applications. The challenging real-time requirements of video games have pushed both communities to adapt their techniques and introduce new solutions. The impressive progress of efficient graphics pipelines, combined with faster CPUs and larger memory, have paved the way to new and improved algorithms. On the graphics hardware side, flexible use of texturing and programmable pixel, vertex, and geometry shaders have offered new opportunities to simulate increasingly complex visual effects: sophisticated lighting and shadowing, complex reflections and refractions, skin subsurface scattering, attenuation in participating media, and so forth.

A common method uses pre-rendered textures and various approximations to display visual effects in static environments, and updates only the effects that are critical to the limited movement found in the game. This includes global illumination effects captured by light maps, glossy reflections by environment maps, and other effects.

More than just rendering real-time images, video games also require control of real-time movements. Motion-capture databases for articulated bodies are decomposed and reorganized in motion graphs, interpolated to respond instantly to player actions, and adapted to the surrounding environment with inverse kinematics. Skinning allows games to generate smooth polygonal meshes adapted to the joints between articulated bodies.

To better immerse characters in their environments, real-time collision detection and response is computed between the characters themselves as well as between characters and their environments. Physics-inspired secondary motions are associated with cloth motion, skin deformations, breaking objects, and so forth, as well as inanimate objects falling and breaking, liquids flowing, smoke swirling, and so on.

Typically, game environments are becoming more and more complex, and many strategies have been developed to efficiently stream the necessary data from slower disks and to release memory space from occluded structures. Another important solution to the ever-increasing requirements of memory and disk space consists in generating believable complex worlds, and the behaviors occurring within them, from procedural generative algorithms.

A good understanding of computer graphics, its capabilities and limitations, is crucial to determine what can ultimately contribute to gameplay. The mutual contributions of video games and real-time computer graphics go hand in hand. Efficient simulation of game worlds, illumination, and movement contribute to better immerse the player in believable worlds, and improvements in their quality widens the realm of game design possibilities.

Pierre Poulin

Computer Programming

Video games and computer programming have had a very intimate relationship since their inception, and early computer scientists even used games to test different algorithms and ideas. Computer programming within the context of video games encompasses many varied topics, ranging from low-level, machine-based concerns to more abstract, mathematical pursuits. One cannot understand how video games are developed without knowing basic concepts in three-dimensional mathematics, fundamentals of computer memory, and the role and impact multi-core processing has for games.

Video games involve the placement, rendering, and animation of game objects in a highly interactive fashion. Three-dimensional coordinate systems allow developers to describe the location and orientation of one object relative to other objects, and video game developers typically use a Cartesian coordinate system for their work. This coordinate system allows one to define a location in space through the use of a tuple of coordinates: x, y and z. Each of these values represents the position of an object on each of three orthogonal lines, or axes, that extend from the center of a coordinate system out to infinity. These values define vectors, from which three-dimensional polygonal geometry, and the space of the game world, is constructed. Developers oftentimes refer to several different spaces in which objects reside, depending on how objects relate to one another. For example, "world space" indicates where an object is relative to a central, world coordinate system, whereas "model space" indicates where a part of an object is relative to the object's coordinate system (for instance, a character's mesh has its points defined relative to a central location on the character).

Video games process a lot of information every time they update, ranging from where enemies are relative to the player, to texture-mapped scenery, to how a player should react to being shot. All of these require the use of low-level computer memory. Memory is always limited, and the amount available depends on the gaming platform. For example, the Xbox 360 has 512 MB, the PlayStation 2 has 32 MB, and the Nintendo Wii has 88 MB, while PCs have varying amounts of memory. A game developed for any of these platforms will need a set amount of space for animations, textures, meshes, game data, etc., leading to strict memory budgets.

Because games are real-time, interactive simulations, all of this memory and data must be processed very quickly. For example, a game running at 60 frames/s must complete a new frame every 16.7 ms, with each frame the product of processing input, AI, physics, animation, networking, and graphics. Furthermore, in a given frame, a game might request 400–500 memory allocations of various sizes. For all those allocations to complete in under 1 ms (6 percent of a frame), they would each need to be completed in an average of 0.002 ms. Clearly, memory allocations must be engineered to be efficient for high-performance games.

To engineer efficient memory systems, game software engineers must understand the role of memory alignment and memory caches. All computer processors access memory in chunks of certain sizes. The more aligned a chunk of memory is to the size required by the processor, the more efficiently it can be processed. Memory caches help facilitate more efficient processing of data by proving a relatively small storage space in which to place the most recently accessed data. Cache memory sits between the processor and the main memory. It is a small amount of very fast memory whose job is to store memory recently accessed by the processor. A "cache hit" occurs whenever the processor accesses memory and finds the data in the cache. This is the ideal situation and bodes well for game performance. A "cache miss," on the other hand, is when the processor attempts to access certain data, but it does not reside in the cache. In this case, there is a recognizable performance hit as the system must copy the requested data from main memory into the cache. Taken infrequently, cache misses are not much of a problem, but as more and more game data is processed in a game, cache misses can quickly become a bottleneck to game performance.

A multi-core processor combines two or more independent processing units, or cores, into a single package. Some of the more common multi-core configurations to date are dual-core (containing two processors) and quad-core (containing four processors). Many current generation game consoles and PCs contain multiple cores, and it is the responsibility of game developers to organize their game data and code to use them. At first glance, it may seem that twice the number of processors will speed up the execution of the game by a factor of two. In practice, this is almost never the case. First and foremost, game software must be written to take advantage of multiple processors; if not, there will be no performance gain. Additionally, the performance gained by the use of multi-core processors depends on the type of problem being solved and the algorithms and data used to solve it. Current generation consoles and PCs, with their multiple cores, have introduced a new paradigm in game software development, which has a direct impact on the overall process of game development. Game developers can no longer assume that games will be processed in a serial nature. To fully utilize multi-core processors, all software must be written with parallel processing in mind.

Current generation games also demand high levels of interactivity with the game's world. Game physics plays a central role in providing this immersive experience, and can generally be divided into two major components: collision detection and collision response. Collision detection is the process of determining what objects, if any, intersect with one another. This step uses lightweight data structures to approximate an object's geometry (for example, a character's body can be surrounded with simple capsule versus a complex mesh of triangles). Fast spatial algorithms then use these data structures to check for intersections. If an intersection is found, several pieces of data detailing the intersection are saved for processing in the next phase. Developers must constantly keep in mind that the more complex the geometry used to represent a game object, the more time it takes to process the interaction of this object with other objects.

Collision response is the task of determining what to do to the intersecting objects found in the previous step. It is in this phase that the laws of physics are applied to the rigid bodies that approximate the intersecting game objects. While current generation physics engines can detect and resolve collisions very quickly, there is always a tradeoff between the accuracy and the speed of the simulation. Providing the immersive experience of

a fully interactive game world to the player, without sacrificing performance, is the black art of game physics.

Michael Seare

Computer Science

(see **Computer Graphics, Computer Programming, Human-Computer
Interaction**)

Cultural Studies

Although cultural studies is not a unified field and overlaps with a variety
of fields including media studies, gender studies, political science, philosophy, and anthropology, its central concerns involve such things as ideology, ethnicity, nationality, and social structures, and the way these interact
with cultural values. Cultural studies also looks at processes and issues that
shape these concerns, including power relations and the production of
cultural meaning and identity. Applied to video games, cultural studies
can examine how cultural values are reflected in video games and in their
marketing; how games can be seen as cultural artifacts as well as how they
fit into industry as commercial products, or in the case of experimental
and independent games, how they function outside of the industry.

Used to examine individual games, cultural studies can help reveal the
way games embody ideologies and fit into larger political structures and
projects, and the way that games can train players to think in certain ways
and possibly to accept behavioral rules and procedures, in much the same
way that sojourners into foreign cultures learn and sometimes adapt to
their ways. Because cultures (and cultural stereotypes) are often represented within video games themselves, through characters, artifacts, customs, and game design in general, cultural studies can also be used in form
and content analyses of games and game series as well. How games are
received by different cultures and what this reveals about those cultures
could also be examined. The retrogaming movement, which brings back
old games and their aesthetics, and involves the creation of new games
according to dated aesthetics and technological limitations, is also ripe for
cultural analysis since it underscores the cultural differences of bygone eras.

Cultural studies can also be applied to the surrounding context in which
games appear, including the way people use games, both individually and
socially in fan communities. Different modes of video gaming require
different kinds of study, from the public gaming done in arcades or on
mobile phones or handheld units, to the private gaming on home systems.
In cases of massively multiplayer online games which have hundreds of

thousands or even millions of players, cultural studies maybe even be applied to the cultures that arise within the games' worlds and used to examine their customs, lingo, social groups and classes, and other distinguishing social and cultural features, and also compare them to traditional cultures.

Mark J. P. Wolf

Design

Design, as an area of theory and practice, tries to derive universal or elemental principles that can be usefully applied in any design context, from websites to street signs, corporate logos to public spaces. The field draws from architecture, classic composition, psychology, sociology, engineering, literary theory, and countless other fields, and as such, often presents itself as an eclectic assembly of general rules and best practices to be deployed or disregarded as needed. Nevertheless, design theorists and practitioners point to the tendency of certain principles to appear repeatedly across wide-ranging contexts as evidence that they are universal, or at least nearly so. The overlap between design studies and video games pulls in several directions: the analysis of video games as a way to derive and support general principles of design; the study of specific video games for how well they follow design principles and how that affects their impact; and the application of design principles by game developers to guide and potentially improve their games.

Examples of design principles commonly applied in video games include such basics of classic composition as the rule of thirds, where design spaces are divided into a grid of nine equal blocks, with rules dictating the placement of primary design components resulting in a visually interesting relationship between those elements. The golden ratio, in which the larger part of a whole forms a ratio of 0.618 to the whole itself, is found throughout the natural world and has likewise found its way into world of art, becoming a main principle of classic design. Similar compositional guidelines exist for the ratio of waist to hip, the head to the body, and for the relationship of elements in the human face, with the manipulation of the those ratios thought to have predictable aesthetic results. While these principles have long been understood by artists and are present throughout art and design, more recently derived concepts such as the application of the Fibonacci sequence or the manipulation of figure-ground, also known as figure-field, perception as discussed in Gestalt theory show the ease with which design practitioners engage new areas of thought to their advantage. Originally derived by an Italian economist to discuss distribution of wealth, the 80/20 rule, which contends that 80 percent of the effects generated by any large system are due to 20 percent of the variables in that system, might be used to anticipate how players interact with game interfaces. Similarly, understanding psychological and sociological dynamics such as bias toward faces that are classically attractive or infant-like in appearance, the tendency to look for closure and alignment among related elements in a design, or the tendency to look for confirmation rather than contradiction of previously drawn conclusions when confronting new evidence can all be usefully employed in game design. Similarly, game designers have recently drawn upon disability studies to improve the accessibility of their games. These are just a few examples of design principles that have been effectively borrowed from a wide range of intellectual fields and applied to video games.

Commonly-used design principles might be seen to compete or even contradict in their potential application, and not all design principles are applied equally or in all contexts. The role of the designer is to know which principles to apply and when and how to apply them. Nevertheless, design theorists would argue that many design principles will appear regardless of intent. While it is common in popular game reviews to comment on art and game design and whether it is "good" or "bad," usually to the point of assigning numerical ranks in an attempt at objectivity, less attention is paid to the reasons why that design is more or less pleasing to the viewer. The study of design in a game context would base that appraisal upon an understanding of why game design is effective or not, due to the effective application of design principles and a given game's adherence, variance, and creativity in deploying them. The application of design concepts to game studies then offers the advantage of a common language that draws upon the fruits of many other fields.

Trevor Elkington

Economics

Contemporary mainstream economics is a social science that relies on rigorous argumentation and mathematics to produce formal models of economic phenomena: those relating to the production, distribution, trade and consumption of goods and services. The advantage of the mathematical approach is that it delivers tangible, quantifiable results that can potentially predict future outcomes. The downside is that the models involve a large number of assumptions that may or may not hold true, limiting the applicability of the results in practice.

Taken at face value, many video games involve activities that bear a resemblance to economic phenomena: buying and selling items, using money, consuming, gathering raw materials, etc. Sometimes economic terms are used in the narrative; in other cases the rules of the game make economic analogies apparent. Could economic analysis be applied to video games to yield some useful new understanding about them?

One could analyze the economy of *Super Mario Bros.* as follows: "The factors of production are Mario's labor and boxes. By expending Mario's labor on the boxes, a player can produce goods such as mushrooms and flowers. The goods are perishable and must be consumed immediately. Consumers generally prefer flowers over mushrooms." However, this analysis is not very useful: it does not provide us any new insights beyond what we already know about the mechanics of the game and player behavior.

More complex game economies can be much more difficult to understand and explain. For example, in massively-multiplayer online games, interactions between large numbers of players, goods, production processes and consumption activities can lead to unexpected consequences. Prices can crash or skyrocket, goods can become sparse or overabundant, characters can end up penniless or ridiculously rich, and players can lock into unintended behavior patterns. From a designer's point of view, it may be difficult to anticipate the consequences of a small tweak or a new feature in the economy. In these cases, economic analysis may be useful.

The branch of economics that deals with large-scale aggregate measures such as total production and general price level is called macroeconomics. Existing macroeconomic models can rarely be applied to game economies, because the game economies' resemblance to real national economies is only superficial at the macro level. Instead, macroeconomic analysis of game economies is carried out using models tailored for each game. One notable macroeconomic phenomenon observed in games is called "mudflation": a situation where the aggregate amount of goods in circulation increases faster than the number of consumers. In the real world this is called real economic growth and gladly welcomed, but in a game economy it can spoil everything by making the game too easy.

The other main branch of economics is called microeconomics, and it comprises a variety of theories and approaches for analyzing economic phenomena on the level of markets and individual decision-makers. For example, supply and demand curves explain how equilibrium prices of goods are determined on the market. This can be used to predict how a market reacts to shocks, such as the developer making some raw material twice as hard to obtain.

In addition to the analysis of purely economic phenomena, in recent decades there has been a trend of extending economic analysis to areas that used to be the exclusive domain of disciplines such as sociology or social psychology. For example, rational choice theory and game theory have been used to analyze families and human relationships.

Game theory focuses on situations where the most favorable behavior of a decision maker depends on other decision makers' choices. In video games, game theory can predict typical player behavior, and how that behavior changes if the rules are changed. Applications include analyzing multiplayer rulesets, optimizing AI player behavior and understanding the dynamics of cooperative play in the presence of conflicting incentives.

While this discussion focused on economic analysis of video games conducted with the purpose of understanding, predicting and developing games, an interesting related research strategy is the use of video games to develop economic theory. Rich behavioral data from massively multiplayer games can be used to test and possibly improve the models and assumptions regarding human behavior on which economists so often rely.

Vili Lehdonvirta and **Tuukka Lehtiniemi**

Education

Education can be defined broadly as pedagogy, or an interest in the activities of teaching and learning. Therefore, a pedagogical approach to video games is an attempt to understand the use of video games for teaching and learning across multiple contexts. Although pedagogy is often confined by definition to Elementary and Secondary environments, education and the study of video games involves teaching and learning in both in-school and out-of-school contexts (for example, at home), in K-12 and post-secondary classrooms, and in work and professional training opportunities. There are three important theoretical considerations related to the study of video games from an educational perspective.

First, educational video game researchers look at both direct and indirect instruction of video games. Direct instruction describes learning with games that focus on concrete teaching or learning of concepts, skills, or knowledge. An example of direct instruction would be a student learning math concepts through an educational mathematics game or a business professional learning sales techniques through a sales game. Indirect instruction can be defined as learning concepts, knowledge, or skills with a game where the main goal of the game is something other than learning those particular concepts, skills, or sets of knowledge. An example might be teaching social studies in a commercial-off-the-shelf (COTS) role-playing game or improving surgical dexterity through the use of a hand-held sports game.

A second important pedagogical consideration is the notion of what is actually being taught or learned. Many educational researchers focus on the use of educational or COTS games to teach content; in doing so, they focus on the psychological notion of cognition. The content learned, perceived, or reasoned could be knowledge or skills and the content is applied to a home, school, or work environment. Training future medical doctors, teaching students math and science, and improving students' reading and writing abilities are all examples of content-based pedagogy. The content or skills learned could come from direct or indirect instruction.

Conversely, for other researchers, the "what" being learned relates to psychological features outside of cognition; oftentimes these elements of study relate to social and emotional characteristics. Exploring one's identity, confronting issues of race and gender bias, and investigating happiness, depression, or violence after video game play are all examples of a social and emotional approach to research. Again, this type of learning could be direct or indirect.

A third and final important differentiation in understanding the pedagogical study of video games is to understand the purpose for the game itself. There are three subcategories within this final pedagogical differentiation. First, some educational researchers are interested in educational game design. These researchers often draw on the field of instructional design. Instructional design is the systematic development of instruction drawing on adapted and adopted theories of learning. Educational researchers explore what pedagogical theories can be applied to various gaming environments to create the most effective teaching and learning conditions. For instance, educational game researchers might be interested in the importance of a training level for player motivation, enjoyment, and learning.

A second use of the video game is actual video game play itself. Video game play has become an important pedagogic tool for instruction and research because most theories of learning highlight the importance of play. Current and past pedagogic theories have suggested that play provides a safe and motivational environment for learners to try out knowledge and skills they have gained. Many researchers and theorists have argued that play—and video game play—provides a point of interaction between learning and doing, thus enabling the practical application of concepts, skills, and knowledge. The fact that these gaming environments are enjoyable for users provides continued motivation to support their learning.

A final notion of video game use is video game development. Although much of the educational research focuses on game design and game play, innovative tools allow even young learners to create video games without having to understand complex programming languages. Video game creation is important because it provides learners with authentic opportunities to create artifacts of their learning as well as opportunities for others to learn from their creations. Developers end up having to learn content and skills as they prepare to create a meaningful and engaging environment for teaching and learning.

Richard E. Ferdig

Emotion
(see **Psychology**)

Ethics
(see **Philosophy**)

Ethnography

Ethnography, literally the "writing of culture," is properly speaking not a method but the product of a method. It is a literary form that aims to present a comprehensive understanding of a culture, or at least of some aspect of a culture. Ethnography is strongly linked to a particular discipline, cultural anthropology, but sociologists, cultural studies scholars, political scientists, and others sometimes produce ethnographic work as well. It is also strongly linked to a particular method, participant observation. In participant observation, a researcher strives to involve herself or himself in the everyday lives of the persons whose culture is the subject of inquiry. In doing so, the researcher works to elucidate cultural assumptions and logics that may be implicit or unspoken, and thus cannot be understood through elicitation methodologies like interviews.

As products of a methodology founded in participant observation, ethnographies typically seek to present the reader with a sense of what it is like to live as a member of the culture described. Many ethnographies employ vignettes or first-person narratives in service of this goal. However, most ethnographies also draw upon historical data, textual analysis, and quantitative data to round out their analytical frameworks. Originally, ethnographies often sought to present a complete picture of a culture. But even in the early work of classic researchers like Bronislaw Malinowski, ethnographers have found it necessary to focus their analyses. For instance, while originally aiming to present a complete ethnography of the Trobriand islanders (near Papua New Guinea), Malinowski ended up with a series of ethnographies: one focusing on trade, one focusing on agriculture, one focusing on law, and so on. Cultures are so complex that an ethnography that attempted to cover every aspect of even a small, localized culture would become so large as to be impractical. As a result, contemporary ethnographers almost always focus on particular aspects of a culture, although typically they remain attentive to how other cultural domains impinge upon and shape aspects of the culture under consideration.

Ethnography was a relative latecomer to the study of video games, which early on was dominated by both quantitative and literary approaches. However, ethnography is now a major modality by which researchers present analyses of video games. This can include treating a video game as a culture in its own right, particularly in the case of massively multiplayer online games that persist as virtual places whether or not any particular participant is logged in. Contexts of video game play, from arcades to living rooms, can also be described and analyzed through ethnographies. As the study of video games continues to expand, there will undoubtedly appear whole new genres of ethnographic writing that provide new perspectives on video games, their embeddedness in cultural contexts, and how they can become cultural contexts themselves, with a profound impact on social life.

Tom Boellstorff

Feminism

(see **Gender Studies**)

Film Studies

Film studies is an interdisciplinary field of research which examines films in eclectic ways, exploring their formal, aesthetic, and rhetorical devices toward an understanding of the medium's properties and conventions. As it has developed a variety of conceptual frameworks and useful tools for analyzing how images and sounds function, film studies represents a fertile ground for transmedial approaches which theorize about audio-visual media, including video games. It is even possible to imagine video games as a remediation of many other art forms, including film. As a result, it is primarily on the basis of a comparative analysis that looking at video games through the lens of film studies can prove valuable.

As an audio-visual medium, video games share some common ground with film when it comes to visual and sound design. Shared features such as camera angles, framing and composition, camera movements, lighting, sound, and optical effects are used in creating cohesion, through specific points of view, between the player and the digital spaces and worlds explored in games. Video games also exploit elements of *mise-en-scène* in terms of the arrangement and movement of figures in game space, as well as editing patterns to establish spatial, temporal, and rhythmic relations between virtual "shots." Video games also use filmic sound conventions to build an emotional setting. From the blood-chilling atmosphere of a survival horror game to the action-packed sequences of a first-person shooter, games rely on soundscapes and musical scores resembling those designed for movies. Formal analyses rooted in film theory are not only useful for analyzing and understanding a video game's pre-rendered non-interactive structures such as cut-scenes, but can be used when studying interactive sequences as well since they can highlight key differences between movies and video games.

While video games do not always rely on a narrative structure, many mainstream games have backstories based in elaborate fictional settings, and their depictions often follow cinematic conventions. Since video games can be seen as a new form of storytelling, it is not surprising that they borrow elements from the narrative structures of films, even though such applications may need to be adapted to the non-linear structures found in some games. Likewise, tools from film theory used for the analyses of spectator interpolation, suture, and audiovisual conventions can be used to analyze video games.

The video game industry also has economical and institutional parallels with the film industry, and replicates its modus operandi in the areas of pre-production, production, and post-production, and likewise shares the pressure of release dates. Finally, similar marketing processes are used for promoting films and games. Indeed, both share the same venues, including theatres and rental stores, and compete for the use of the television in the home.

Although some may resist using film theory to study video games due to the differences between film and video games, the cinematic nature of so many games and their borrowing from the film medium, both formally and in terms of content, make film theory a useful approach to study video games that can (and should) be used in conjunction with other approaches.

Guillaume Roux-Girard

Game Theory

How do, or how should, strategic participants in a multi-player game behave? Game theory attempts to answer this question. This is perhaps a more ambitious goal than it at first seems, since the range of games is vast. For example, tic-tac-toe, auctions, economic markets, and trade negotiations are all considered "games," and game theory originated as the mathematical study of such human interactions. Today, massive multiplayer video games belong to the most complex classes of games, and here we will discuss three aspects of game theory that have particular relevance for video games: game design, game dynamics, and complexity theory.

First, let us consider game design. More specifically, we focus on one particular aspect known as *mechanism design*. The central question in mechanism design is how to design a game to ensure desired behaviors or outcomes? For instance, in multi-player games, if players act in a purely self-interested fashion then the resultant outcome may be poor for society as a whole and, perhaps surprisingly, even for every single individual player, too. To see this, consider a fisherman deciding how many fish to catch in a season. It is clearly in his short-term interest to catch as many fish as possible. However, if every fisherman makes such a decision then the fish stock may become depleted or even exhausted. Evidently, this is a poor outcome for the fishermen as well as the fish! A similar issue arises with congestion effects in road networks. Commuters decide whether or not to drive to work, and if so which routes to take; if too many commuter choose to drive along the same roads then the resulting congestion could end up delaying all the drivers (as well as decrease the air quality for everyone).

One goal of mechanism design is to alleviate these problems by changing the rules of the game before it is played. This may be achieved by attempting to change the inherent *incentives* to the players in the game. In our examples this may be achieved via the sale or auction of fishing permits and by introducing road tolls. The additional costs may influence behavior by making certain options relatively less attractive. These examples illustrate that even subtle changes to the game may have drastic effects on behaviors or outcomes. In most social contexts the goal of mechanism design will typically be to try to encourage nice or cooperative behavior. Note, though, that mechanism design can also be used for the opposite effect if that would improve the playability of the video game!

A second important area of research concerns dynamic games, into which category most video games fall. The game situation and the participants may change over time. How does this affect strategic decision making, especially in the context of repeated interactions between players? From a practical perspective, this question is still not at all well understood.

Finally, consider complexity theory, a well studied concept in computer science. For time and/or communication complexity reasons, many game theoretic concepts and prescriptions may not be appropriate in games played over a short time period or in real-time games. Determining what concepts may be applicable to video games therefore requires some understanding of the computational powers of the game participants (be they humans or computers). As an illustration, consider the game of chess. It is known that optimal strategies for the players exist. In fact, chess has a *value*: either white can always force a win or black can always force a win, or both players can always force a draw. However, the sheer number of possibilities involved implies that neither the value of the game nor the optimal strategies are known. Moreover, it is unlikely that they ever will be known, and this is despite the fact that chess is a relatively simple game. This observation has big implications. For example, can we expect players to choose strategies the finding of which may be computationally beyond them? Complexity issues also have major consequences for the other two topics discussed, such as which mechanisms have a realistic chance of being successful. Algorithmic game theory is a field that attempts to address and quantify these issues.

Adrian Vetta

Gender Studies

Video games intricately intersect with gender and represent a compelling arena in which to explore, advance, and contest feminist agendas. Digital games emerged as an obscure, novel form of play for adolescent males and have evolved into a major form of entertainment. Although both girls and boys and adult women and men play games, many game genres remain male-oriented, and the industry male-dominated.

Considerable research has focused on questions of what female players want in a game. In the mid 1990s, female entrepreneurs introduced the first "Pink Games" tailored to ultra feminine girl interests. Some feminists object to games which emphasize stereotypically feminine interests, seeing them as ghettoizing girl games, reinforcing stereotypes and limiting girls' choices. In the current industry context where almost all commercial game designers are male, some feminist research looks at the kinds of games girls create as a way of understanding their preferences and interests.

Feminist theories consider how social structures contribute to gender inequalities. As games become increasingly sophisticated and pervasive, the tendency for boys to spend vastly more time playing games perpetuates a technology gender gap. Games are considered a gateway for young people to technological skill and interested in computer programming. Playing games, particularly complex games, and constructive associated activities such as modding and machinima serve as trajectories to technological expertise. In ways that never happened with television or movies, those who seek to empower girls and women see that goal advanced by playing games, and impeded by lack of gaming experience.

As digital games come to be designed and used for purposes beyond entertainment as games for learning and games for physical and cognitive health, feminist theories motivate and inform studies of whether all players are equally well served by the design of games and the social contexts in which they are played.

Gender studies of the representation of females in games, both as non-player characters and player avatars include content analysis of hypersexualized physical representation, gender-stereotypical roles, and implicit values, overt themes, and game narratives involving violence and sex including violence against women.

Post-structural feminists object to the essentialization of gender, including assumptions of innate and universal differences. Post-structural feminist theorist Judith Butler introduced the notion of "gender play," meaning that both girls and boys, and men and women, experiment with gendered expressions. Class, ethnicity, and other cultural factors influence an individual's developing gender identity. Gender is "performed" in different local contexts. Gaming activities are not neutral or isolated acts, but involve a person's becoming and acting in the world as part of the construction of a complex identity.

Post-feminist theorists study how individual players perform gender within a particular game and within a particular social context. Games permit players to role play, to try on different identities, to choose and customize their avatar. Thus, depending on the game, players can choose to appear to be female, male, or androgynous. Games involve competition, cooperation, (virtual) violence, and (virtual) sex. Game play occurs not in isolation but in a social context with its own gender-related complexities.

Gender differences research looks at essentialist differences between female and males, such as studies of 3-D rotation abilities, functional brain analysis, and competitiveness. An extreme example are evolutionary biology perspectives looking back at presumed gender roles in prehistoric hunter-gatherer societies. Feminist scholars tend to take issue with viewing gender differences as immutable socio-biological imperatives, arguing that such approaches ignore cultural, contextual, and individual differences, reinforce stereotypes and limit possibilities.

Carrie Heeter

Genre Studies

Historically, genre constitutes a key way of understanding a variety of literary and artistic forms. The concept is of importance to video game scholars because genre conceives of the relations between texts as central to the production of meaning. As John Frow points out in his book *Genre* (2006), genre remains "a set of conventional and highly organized constraints on the production and interpretation of meaning." In light of the narratology/ludology debate, video games may no longer be unproblematically analyzed as simply "texts" that produce "meanings," as this is only a part of their operation. Video games complicate ideas of genre that rely on narrative structure (like literary genres) or iconography (like visual genres), by hybridizing narrative and visual iconography, with concerns unique to the video game medium: virtual representation of spaces, movements, and actions, and well as non-representational elements, particularly modes of interaction. Thus, whilst *Halo: Combat Evolved* (Bungie Studios, 2001) and *Sid Meier's Alpha Centauri* (Firaxis, 1999) are both games with a science-fiction narrative and iconography, the two games' spaces, movements, and actions are completely different. Rather than being considered of the same genre, they are more usefully each placed in a genre with other games that share similar game elements; *Halo* with a long series of iterations of first-person shooters going back to *Wolfenstein 3-D* (id Software, 1992), and *Alpha Centauri* with other turn-based strategy games like *Civilization* (Microprose, 1991) and *Master of Orion* (Simtex, 1993).

Much as in other media, genre comes into play in video games in the form of a tacit agreement between video game designers, publishers, and promoters, and the audience or players. Thus genre acts as a notion that cues players to previous experiences of play, and publishers to successful market demographics. However, these categories are not always so neatly delineated that they produce endless imitations. *Mass Effect* (BioWare, 2007), for example, is a role-playing game that draws on elements from the first-person shooter genre. *Mario and Luigi: Partners in Time* (AlphaDream, 2005), also is considered to be a role-playing game, however, it also shares many spatial, and aesthetic similarities with platform games. The parameters of genre are blurry, and the categories themselves are often flexible enough to accommodate games which have substantial differences.

Genre in video games walks a fine line between repetition and innovation. Often, successful games that experiment with genre conventions establish their own genres or subgenres, as the video game industry seeks to capitalize on the initial game. For example, *Grand Theft Auto III* (Rockstar North, 2001)—which is itself one in a series of several sequels—has become a more or less a subgenre into itself, spawning a number of imitators that follow its very successful genre conventions: *True Crime: Streets of LA* (Luxoflux, 2003), *Saints Row* (Volition, 2006), and *The Getaway* (Team SOHO, 2003). The following of generic conventions has become a standard practice in the video game industry, however, the audience will also often criticize games that are perceived as relying on genre conventions without also introducing an innovation or twist.

Thomas H. Apperley

History

At a very basic philosophical level, it is impossible to separate the present and the past. History, then, is the vital discipline of interpreting the ever-present past. Historians sift, sort, select the past (what is available to them anyway) and patch together a story that helps make sense of current conditions. They may also take already-interpreted evidence and re-interpret it.

While historians do not have many formally titled methodologies, certain definitions and techniques are foundational to historical research. All history is based on the analysis of textual evidence: written and printed documents, photographs, videos, film, audio recordings, and interviews with eyewitnesses of historical events or conditions. Historians distinguish between primary and secondary sources: the former are direct records of an event and the latter are either much later accounts or interpretations of primary sources. Naturally, primary sources are of critical importance for developing historical accounts. Historians can also study the work of other historians: this is called historiography. This kind of activity can be very useful for analyzing the ideological bias and cultural blindspots of history writers.

Practically any kind of history can be filtered through any kind of social theory or ideological perspective: gender theory, Marxism, post-modernism, liberalism, post-colonialism, a wide variety of religious world-views, and more. However, the second half of the twentieth century saw a general shift of perspective within the discipline, largely related to the rise of postmodern ways of thinking. This resulted in a number of different emphases, such as a focus on interpretation rather than objectivity and the consideration of human agency rather than deterministic explanations. One of the biggest shifts has been from a top-down account of history—a biography-style narrative of great political, economic, and military leaders—to a bottom-up account, which stresses the experiences of social groups as a whole, with special attention given to so-called ordinary people.

What can the study of history do for the study of video games? In a general sense, it helps to avoid reducing the study of games to simplistic, mechanistic, and deterministic explanations. For example, why are the leading companies so successful? Economic, psychological, and techno-logical explanations go part of the way, but all these forces occur within a particular context. Good history reveals the incredible complexity of any social activity.

What kinds of things are worth historical study? The most obvious is also the most heavily done: biographies of the pioneers of the game industry. But the shift to a bottom-up perspective in history suggests that much more is possible. Social histories of the games industry would emphasize the socioeconomic context of the pioneers, none of which worked in a vacuum. There could be histories of play: games are not just made—they are *used*.

There could be attention to marginalized voices. Progressive scholarship, for example, examines the voices of underprivileged social groups. A feminist history of gaming might be an example. Social Construction of Technology theorists argue that any solid history of technology investigates so-called failures just as much as the successes. Spectacular flame-outs like the *Virtual Boy* or *Daikatana* are widely documented, but game historians could also examine the multitude of unremarkable AAA-budget games with C-level sales or the projects that started and never finished. Another possible avenue is focusing on very local histories of gaming or histories outside of the centers of power in the USA, Europe, and Japan.

Historiography can also contribute to video game studies. Most obviously, this would mean an analysis of the growing field of game history. A little less obviously, this might also mean an intellectual history of scholarship that could give some perspective to the still-establishing field of video game studies.

It is not just video game studies that can benefit from historical theory—the relationship works the other way too. One of the most interesting things that games do to history is they tend to shift attention to historical social systems and historical environments as opposed to an emphasis on events and narrative coherence. And games about history wreak havoc with deterministic conceptualizations of the past—as such, they are an interesting window into the controversial area of study theory called virtual history.

Kevin Schut

Human-Computer Interaction

Human-Computer Interaction (HCI) is an interdisciplinary field focused on the design and evaluation of user interfaces for computational systems. HCI is concerned with methodologies for designing, prototyping, implementing, evaluating, and comparing interfaces; developing new hardware, software, styles, and techniques for interaction; and developing models and theories of interaction, including those concerning the behavior, goals, capacities, and limitations of the human users of interfaces.

A point commonly made is that, from the user's point of view, the interface *is* the (software or hardware) product, since the interface is, in some sense, all the user ever sees. This principle applies at least as much to video games as to office productivity software, since the act of interacting with the game probably contributes more to the user's overall enjoyment than achieving a high score. Given this importance of user interfaces, and the challenges of designing for a variety of users with different backgrounds and skill levels, HCI has adapted or developed several methods to support the stages of an iterative design life cycle. These include: methods for gathering information about current interfaces and requirements for new interfaces, such as observational techniques and task analysis; methods that enable users to directly influence the design process, such as participatory design; methods for quickly prototyping interfaces, using paper or using software that allows interfaces to be quickly "sketched"; and methods for evaluating designs and prototypes, such as usability testing, heuristic evaluation, or cognitive walkthroughs. Most of these methods could be applied to video game design with some adjustment.

HCI also studies traditional and novel input and output hardware devices that could eventually make their way into video games. Examples of input devices include keypads and keyboards for both sitting and mobile use; pointing devices (mice, joysticks, trackballs, touchpads, hand guns, wands, and so on) with 2, 3, or more degrees of freedom; microphones for audio input; and cameras, eye tracking devices, and motion-capture (mocap) devices that could be used in multimodal or perceptual interfaces. Output devices include screens, projectors, stereoscopic displays (involving LCD shutter glasses or head-mounted displays, for example), 3-D volumetric displays, speaker and headphone systems for audio output, and haptic devices for touch output or force feedback. At the time of writing, haptic output is common in gamepad controllers, and the recent Nintendo Wii has been surprisingly successful in popularizing a non-traditional pointing device. At the same time, the mouse stubbornly remains the most common pointing device used in desktop video games, in part because of its pointing performance. Fitts' law predicts the average time required to point at an on-screen target using a pointing device, and can be used to characterize the performance of a pointing device in terms of an index of performance. Studies using Fitts' law have shown that the mouse has an excellent index of performance, outperforming most other pointing devices.

On the software side, HCI investigates many interaction styles and interaction techniques that have been or could be applied to video game interfaces. Topics include natural language interfaces, window management, direct manipulation, gestural interaction, two-handed interaction (for example, with two mice), and techniques for navigating 2-D and 3-D worlds. One interesting example is radial menus (also known as pie menus), which are a non-traditional kind of menu enabling a fast, gestural style of input. Radial menus have been slowly adopted in an increasing number of software applications, and probably achieved the greatest and earliest penetration within video game interfaces. There are, nevertheless, much more sophisticated interaction techniques that remain almost completely unused outside of the HCI research community. HCI also studies new and better ways of rendering visual information on the user's display device, making use of 3-D depth cues, transparency, animation, zooming, and techniques from information visualization for visually depicting large, dynamic sets of abstract data.

An additional area within HCI of increasing relevance for video games studies is Computer Supported Collaborative Work (CSCW), which studies the design and use of interfaces when multiple users collaborate to complete tasks. Video game interfaces increasingly support multiple players who may be co-located or situated remotely over a network. Within a game, players communicate, collaborate, coordinate, and compete. Outside a game, they may share, buy, and sell custom modifications or user-created game content. CSCW has design methodologies, interaction techniques, and theories which could be directly applied to video game design.

Michael McGuffin

Industry

(see **Business/Industry**)

Interactivity

(see **New Media**)

Interdisciplinary Studies

Interdisciplinarity is a wide phenomenon, covering all those multiple forms of research and education that fall between established academic disciplines, or which exploit multiple disciplinary perspectives and methodologies in productive ways. Interdisciplinarity is a natural part of new, emerging fields of science and scholarship, including video game studies.

Interdisciplinary studies of games and play have sometimes included studies of games where the "ludological" analyses of interactive (ludic) structures have been enmeshed with concepts that are originally derived from within literary, film, or television studies. Other fruitful encounters have taken place at the disciplinary borderlands surrounding disciplines such as computer science, psychology, sociology, education research, legal studies, and economics. Given the broad disciplinary range that has been typical for game studies conferences and seminars, it is perhaps indeed more difficult to find some discipline which has *not* been applied to the academic study of games, than to give a comprehensive list of those which have.

The most challenging and overt form of interdisciplinarity involves crossing major academic division lines, like those between natural sciences, social sciences, mathematics, humanities, and the arts. It is easier for a humanist to collaborate with a colleague trained in another humanist discipline, than to write a paper together with a physicist, for example. Yet, such a striking combination of disciplinary perspectives might actually lead into more original and surprising outcomes.

The main obstacles in doing interdisciplinary game studies are the same as for interdisciplinarity in general: there are cultural barriers between academic disciplines that make it sometimes hard for scholars even to understand what differently trained colleagues are speaking about. The fundamental values as well as practical aims and mindsets of doing research might also be at odds with each other. The discussion and debate necessary to sort out the communicational stumbling blocks take time, and might just lead researchers to realize better their fundamental disagreements, rather than to help them in creating a productive partnership. Operating within one's native discipline is often an easier, quicker, and less risky way of doing research.

Why then, does interdisciplinarity remain one of the buzzwords of twenty-first century academia? To start with, the multi-perspective processes that are involved in doing interdisciplinary research will result in more information being collected about the subject of study. Next, as the researchers are comparing their results, the knowledge they create will also stand in a more solid ground and be more likely to endure the tests of time and critique. Finally, as interdisciplinary work needs to be conversant with multiple theoretical and conceptual dialects and generally free from domain-specific jargon, it is in good position to make an impact beyond the narrow circles of specialists. It is also possible to argue that as parts of our world are becoming increasingly interconnected in many different ways, most research work will eventually need to develop into interdisciplinary directions to keep in pace with the change. As everything is (or could be) connected with everything else, only an interdisciplinary team or researcher is able to make sense of it.

Doing interdisciplinary game studies is typically teamwork, but it is also possible for a single person to develop competencies in multiple fields. The danger of eclecticism is, however, something that needs to be taken into account; a dilettante who dabbles in multiple research traditions, without really understanding the core fundamentals from any of them, is only a caricature of truly interdisciplinary research. It is advisable to consider carefully whether some genuine research problem or shared interest makes it necessary to bring multiple theories, methodologies or discourses into a single study, or if satisfactory results can be perfectly well be achieved within some single, established approach.

It is difficult, then, to set limits as to how innovative and productive interdisciplinary video game studies can be; if game researchers, for example, combine approaches from sociology, geography, and computer science, they might find interesting ways of studying situated play in mixed reality multiplayer games. The combination of perspectives and research traditions derived from anthropology and game design research might inspire researchers to address the potentials of game engines for preserving the art and traditions of native storytelling. Other innovative applications of interdisciplinary (or even transdisciplinary) approaches to doing game studies can easily be found from the proceedings of recent games conferences. Interdisciplinarity currently appears to be a key part of studying digital games and play.

Frans Mäyrä

Law

The framework of law, in particular law and society, is an important area for future video game research. The video gaming industry is economically massive and continues to grow in earnings capacity. Furthermore, with advancements in technology, games are increasingly becoming realistic and interactive. While law is a relatively new academic lens in the study of video games, it holds a key vantage point given the intersection of law in many areas of our everyday life.

There are also many ways to approach the study of law and video games. Adopting the traditional legal approach, one might examine case law on video games. Here a video game researcher will enter the realm of free speech, copyright, anti-trust, game violence, criminal liability, and even personal injury (whereby some claim that specific games cause epileptic seizures). In case law, however, one will find debates about probability and "evidence" to be qualitatively different from discussions of probability and "statistical strength" in other disciplines. In the traditional approach to legal research, individual cases are treated as data, which differs from the conceptualization of research data found in other areas, such as the aggression literature on individual dispositions towards violence.

While case law is the classic approach, and a worthy avenue to pursue, there are many different ways to conceptualize the intersection of law and video games in everyday life. One approach taken previously by this author was to examine issues of governance and self-regulation in the video game industry (see Gray and Nikolakos 2007, *Canadian Journal of Law and*

Society). The self-regulation of video games, and issues of voluntary compliance by game companies, is an important but so far relatively untapped area of video game research. More research is still needed on the everyday compliance aspects of the system of self-regulation in the video game industry (which is governed by the ESRB—Entertainment Software Rating Board).

There are also many high-profile cases involving specific video games (such as the banning of the game *Manhunt* in several nations) which could form interesting socio-legal studies. Indeed, there is a host of issues just waiting to be pursued by the next generation of game researchers. Overall, future research should begin to pay special attention to how video games are increasingly being legislatively debated, governed, and regulated across and within various nations.

Garry C. Gray

Linguistics

(see **Semiotics**)

Literary Theory

A common feature shared by narratology and ludology is a tendency towards formalism. If according to Jesper Juul, games "are formal systems that provide informal experiences," certain trends in recent literary theory can be insightful in the elaboration of non-formal approaches to video games, players, and gameplay.

Upon the influence of both European semiology and American pragmatism, and modern hermeneutics, literary theory has radically unfurled the classical definitions of its main object, the text, making it applicable not only to a body of written discourse, but to any cultural object that produces meaning through interpretation. Such a generous paradigm has already welcomed manifestations as diverse as dance choreographies, *in situ* performances, TV shows, and video games. Textual analysis, in the broadest sense, could be defined as a way to view a piece of work as the expression of certain tensions, hence the classical opposition between spoken language and its mechanical inscription through writing and print, the hermeneutic circle going back and forth between the global comprehension of a work and the local interpretation of its parts, or Derrida's deconstruction of great philosophical oppositions present in a given text.

Analyzing video games as texts, one could observe how some feature tension between game and narrative, emphasized in sandbox games, which offer large-scale virtual worlds as well as intricate plots embedded in them, therefore offering the player the dual possibility of free-roaming at will in a digital playground and casting himself as a character in a Byzantine criminal fantasy. One could also observe tension between thematic elements in games, as in the example of the already familiar juxtaposition of ancient gothic figures and postmodern technological nightmares in horror series.

Possible and fictional worlds theories, which were shaped by the application of modal logic to literary works, can also be applied to video games. Game worlds themselves stand as challenges to these theories, for, albeit fictional, they are not purely logical and imaginary constructions built by authors and readers, but dynamic environments that players can explore, interact with, and, in the case of MMOG and Internet-based virtual worlds like *Second Life*, even alter.

Perhaps the most vital contribution of literary theory to video game studies comes from the willingness of scholars from the past fifty years to include the reader in the analysis of texts, thereby construing literary works through the process that breathe life into them. Applied to video games, literary theory invites a kind of *player-response criticism*, which would never allow players to be insulated from gameplay. That means never forgetting, while observing game dynamics, that gameplay isn't solely about what games make the player do, but about how and why he does it, what it does to him, and what he makes of it retrospectively. The opposition between heuristic and hermeneutic readings drawn by Michael Riffaterre in his 1983 book, *Text Production*, translates appropriately to gameplay, and clarifies the fundamental interplay of actions undertaken by the player while following the strictly logical nature of the game as a formal structure, and of actions informed by the player's thoughts and sensibilities about the game world, which he enters with his own set of ideas, values, and beliefs. This dynamic speaks for itself in recent games in which a player's actions, *ethically measured*, can modify gameplay settings and plot evolution.

All in all, literary theory represents a standpoint—not the only one, but a *good* one—upon which players can be seen as thinking as well as acting subjects, and video games can be studied as meaningful cultural objects.

Samuel Archibald

Ludology

In the context of video games, *ludology* was first coined by Gonzalo Frasca, and initially meant "the study of games." Around the year 2000, ludology was the idea that the interesting phenomenon in digital culture was not interactive television or virtual reality (many people really did think that), but *video games*; that video games were important enough to be their own field of study, with their own vocabularies, theories, observations, and questions to be asked.

Part of that initial movement was hence to deny video games studies as being simply a subcategory of media studies, film studies, narrative studies, or new media studies. This led to many of the first ludological texts (Frasca, Eskelinen, Juul) being vehemently anti-narrative, as narrative was the default concept being applied to video games at the time. This gives ludology its two different meanings today:

1. *Ludology.* The study of games as such; the study of games as a separate field with its own theories that are sensitive to the specifics of the medium and the game-playing activity.
2. *Ludology.* The study of games as distinct from narratives.

The second definition became part of what was known as the conflict between *ludology and narratology*. Ludology was here typically contrasted with the works of Janet Murray or Henry Jenkins, even if the contrast was simplistic and somewhat ironic as all early ludological texts used narrative theory to demonstrate that games were distinct from narratives. Three simple observations illustrate this distinctiveness:

- Stories are predetermined sequences; games are not determined (otherwise they would not be games).
- There are games without stories.
- There are great games with terrible stories and bad games with great stories.

These were points often emphasized by ludology early on: how far *did* narrative theory extend in the description of games? What were, not just the similarities, but the *differences*? To be fair, a more practical version of that discussion had already been played out in game development circles some years before (Crawford, Costikyan, and others), and the ludology-narratology front was quickly softened. Still, the importance of that discussion was to format the field of video game studies, and to force those working with narrative and games to take a step back and reconsider their assumptions.

The next step for ludology has been to describe games positively rather than in contrast to other cultural forms. What *is* a game—is it an amorphous cultural category or can anything more detailed be said about what games are? How does time work in games? What is it like to play a game? How are games structured? Is there a specific attitude that a player has towards a game? What is the "magic circle" around a game—to what extent is a game a separate world? What are game rules and how are they made? What does a game mean? What emotions do players experience? How have games changed over time? In what way are video games games? What is a *good* game? How and when do players understand games? How are games developed? Are there different player types or playing styles?

These are the types of questions that ludology asks. This makes ludology intensely interdisciplinary since no discipline is irrelevant for ludological inquiry, while ludology at the same time tries to build a unique field in which games can be discussed.

The first meaning of ludology is probably the most important today: ludology is the continuous reminder that video games are to be taken seriously and that one cannot do wholesale applications of theories from other fields onto games. If early ludology was against broad applications of narrative theory onto games, ludology today should be wary of simplistic applications of the next field that tries to colonize video games. Ludology is about being observant and unprejudiced, taking things seriously, players and games.

Jesper Juul

Marketing

(see **Business/Industry**)

Mathematics

(see **Game Theory, Computer Science**)

Media Ecology

In 1964, Marshall McLuhan released *Understanding Media*, still famous for pithy and cryptic aphorisms like "the medium is the message." As much as this is a ground-breaking and well-known work, however, other publications around the same time, like Eric Havelock's *Preface to Plato* and Jack Goody and Ian Watt's article "The Consequences of Literacy" were actually propounding similar theoretical views. In fact, earlier authors, such as Harold Innis, Edward Hall and Lewis Mumford had already published ideas along the same lines. Today, this significant body of theoretical literature and many subsequent publications have coalesced into a school of thought called Media Ecology (or, in some quarters, "medium theory").

The unifying theoretical point that winds throughout this work is that the tools of communication, by their very structure—as opposed to the messages they carry—shape communication and culture. Media are the environment in which human symbolic interaction plays out. Just as a tropical climate and an arctic climate lead to fundamentally different ways of material lifestyle, a society with photography and a society without will have powerfully different ways of communicating, and those differences will shape culture, and perhaps even individual patterns of thought. Neil Postman, for example, argues that an image-saturated culture prefers associative, emotional discourse over the linear, expository discourse common to print culture.

Note that this perspective does not require a belief in technological determinism, even though that is a frequent charge. The best Media Ecology scholarship recognizes that media are not static, and are not independent of human activity. In fact, media are more than technology: they are the entire set of physical and cultural tools that we use to communicate. Thus, to say that media are a symbolic environment or a stage upon which our cultural acts out social drama is not the same thing as saying that media brainwash or program cultures. In fact, McLuhan's dictum aside, a medium can communicate multiple messages, so its power is not a dictatorial one. Rather, individual media—and a society's overall collection of media and their interplay—encourage certain possibilities and discourage others. Creators and users are free to fight against these tendencies, meaning that at best, we can call this a soft determinism. Perhaps the term that captures this idea best is Innis' term "media bias." An angle or slope can be conquered, given sufficient effort—just as the construction of a medium does not lock down a culture and its communicative possibilities.

Media Ecology has a natural fit with the study of video games. Specifically, it can contribute a focus on the medium itself, as opposed to game-making and game-playing. These latter two foci are, of course, absolutely crucial. But making a game is different than, say, making a movie, and playing game is not reading a book. Nor, for that matter, is playing a game on a computer the same as playing on a physical board. If we study production and interpretation or use while pretending the medium is completely neutral or malleable, we get a very incomplete picture of communication. A media ecology analysis of the structure of digital games gives us a better idea of what kind of interaction is possible and likely.

This kind of analysis will be crucial in helping us understand our culture's evolving digital landscape, as computer and video games are key components of computer-mediated culture. McLuhan argued that print society was linear and rational in nature, while television culture was more associative and free-flowing. Whether he was right or not, a similar analysis of games has profound implications. What is the nature of video game interactivity, and what kind of cultural implications does that character-istic have? What about the systematic nature of the rules systems that even the most abstract of games have? While narratives are clearly not a *necessary* part of games, many incorporate them; how does the medium transform deployment and understanding of story? How are the fictional-world-building capabilities of a video game different from how other media create imaginary places? How does computer networking and the Internet transform the possibilities of game-player interaction? This is just a small sampling of the questions raised by Media Ecology theory.

Kevin Schut

Medicine

The field of Medicine is concerned with people's physical health and well-being and its restoration (the term "medicine" comes from the Latin *medicina*, meaning "healing"). The overlap between medicine and video games, then, mainly concerns the use of games and their interfaces, and the effects this can have on a person's health.

As early as the 1980s, writings appeared on repetitive stress injuries (RSI) caused by video games, such as "Space Invader wrist" and "Gamer's thumb," which were the result of repeated joystick use and button-pushing. More recently, the term "Wii elbow" has already been used to describe pain or numbness caused by excessive use of the Wiimote controller.

Ever since their earliest days, video games have also been accused of promoting a sedentary lifestyle and taking players away from other more vigorous activities, such as sports. Some games have challenged these assumptions, including Konami's *Dance Dance Revolution* game series (which have been used in physical education classes), and especially those made for the Nintendo Wii. While its *Wii Sports* and *Wii Play* games are making players move around (and even giving players warnings suggest-ing they take a break after the system has been in use for awhile), the new *Wii Fit* game, with its Balance Board, aims at combining exercise and entertainment. Video games have already been used to help people overcome phobias, and now hospitals are beginning to use the Wii as a therapeutic tool in rehabilitation and physical therapy routines for patients recovering from illnesses, strokes, accidents, and combat injuries. Besides encouraging exercise, video games can also help players question unhealthy eating habits, like Ian Bogost's online game *Fatworld* (2007) which examines America's obesity epidemic.

Thus a knowledge of medicine will be useful to video game studies researchers studying such things as ergonomics, the player's posture, and possible effects of video gaming including headaches, eyestrain, epileptic seizures due to flashing screens, carpal tunnel, nerve damage caused by vibrating haptic controllers (like Nintendo's *Rumble Pak*), fatigue and lack of sleep due to excessive online activity, and the use of video games in therapy or exercise regimens. As more of these aspects are addressed by video game hardware designers and as newer games and game systems continue to incorporate new types of interfaces, the overlap between medicine and video games will continue to be a fruitful area of research, and one which may find ways to improve the health and well-being of video game players. Projects like Games for Health (www.gamesforhealth.org), which wants to help foster and support the community that uses video games and game technologies, and encourage game development talent to find new ways to improve the management, quality, and provision of healthcare worldwide, are already working in this direction.

Mark J. P. Wolf and **Bernard Perron**

Methodology

Research into video games is continuously expanding and evolving, providing opportunities for the development of original and innovative research methodologies. Two factors, multidisciplinarity and interdisciplinarity, afford both challenge and opportunity to researchers as a nascent field struggles to define its own overarching methodology. Due to both of these factors, there are ongoing debates within the field of games studies as to the nature of the paramount methodology for the study of video games. The questions raised in game studies research often bridge disciplinary boundaries merging issues of effects, meaning, context, and structures. As a result, disciplinary boundaries are not always easily maintained in applied research circumstances. An interdisciplinary lens may be best suited to the field of games studies.

As this appendix shows, video games provide an object of study for a variety of disciplines. This poses a variety of challenges in researching video games given that scholars typically employ unique methodologies specific to their field of study. Individual researchers approach the video game not only through their disciplines but also through theoretical positions. Video games can be viewed in a variety of forms, as spaces, encounters, relationships, a set of mechanics, or as artifacts. Therefore the position of the researcher will often inform the methodological framework which then influences the research methods that are chosen. It may be argued that no single research method is the most appropriate for the discipline of game studies because each method offers advantages contingent upon the research question and approach. There is a wide range of criteria to consider when deciding which method to employ.

A variety of approaches are employed in games studies. Three common approaches are positivistic, interpretive, and critical theory. Positivistic research focuses on testing theories of human behavior by establishing hypothesis about relationships, measuring variables, and then analyzing the data, typically employing methods that are quantitative in nature. Interpretive research is often underpinned by philosophical traditions such as phenomenology or hermeneutics. Usually interpretive research is qualitative in nature; for instance, ethnography, ethnomethodology, and semiotics. Understanding video games through a critical theory approach would look at how some groups might attempt to enhance their interests at the expense of other less powerful groups. Critical theorists often work with historical material, comparative studies, and analysis of secondary data.

Both qualitative and quantitative methods are employed in the study of video games. The ways that data are collected varies according to the methodological framework. Qualitative research does not privilege a single methodology but employs multiple methods. Some ways in which qualitative research data is gathered is through participant observation, direct observation, interviewing, case studies, focus groups, discourse analysis, narrative analysis, and psychoanalysis; while quantitative methods employ statistical content analysis, questionnaires, surveys, and experiments.

It has been argued that answering many of the questions that are relevant to game studies requires multiple methods. Quantitative methods are appropriate for examining broad trends in groups of people. For example, research obtaining statistical data can show that particular genres of video games are played by particular demographics of gamers. However, qualitative research can be used to explore nuanced, contextual issues seeking to understand individual responses to particular games in specific situations. Accordingly, qualitative researchers deploy a wide range of interconnected methods in an attempt to achieve a deeper understanding of the subject they are researching. Researching video games demands particularly innovative methodologies as researchers are often in the unique position of endeavoring to capture both online and offline data. Researchers often blend multiple research methodologies and research methods into the design of their research project in order to capture the richest data.

Shanly Dixon

Morality

(see **Philosophy**)

Narratology

Narratology has been a contested territory of inquiry in video game studies (see "Ludology"). The narratological study of video games typically tackles two topics. In the wake of the Russian formalists led by Vladimir Propp and the French structuralists Claude Bremond and Algirdas Julien Greimas, a first branch of narratology can be called narrative semiotics, and seeks to understand the combinatorial mechanics and underlying structures of stories. This can take various forms, from symbolic interpretation or traditional character and plot analyses to the elaboration of game-specific models (such as branching trees, networks, rhizomes, etc.) charting the structure of their events.

A second approach is concerned with the video game as a medium, and attempts to uncover its specificity among the larger narratological landscape. This is not unlike Gérard Genette's study of literature or David Bordwell's analysis of narration in the fiction film. The question to be resolved here is not whether video games conform to the various definitions of narrative, narration, story, or plot—all devised in reference to other media—but rather in what ways they are narrative or contain narrative features, what they share with other narrative objects, how they differ from them and how they can still be understood as stories. In this view, video games are not a simple extension of other media, but form a unique new narrative proposition.

In both of these cases, the task for researchers is to see the possibilities for adapting the notions and theories of narratology to video games without losing sight of their specificity. While ludology rightly pointed out that one should not blindly apply concepts from other disciplines in an act of "theoretical imperialism," one should also avoid the other extreme that would end up throwing the baby out with the bath water. Though video games with extensive dialogue and engaging storylines are undoubtedly more than simple transpositions or adaptations of pre-digital gaming principles on a new (graphical and computerized) medium, they are nevertheless games first and foremost, and any study cannot ignore this essential duality.

Consequently, the study of game mechanics as narrative devices constitutes a possible area of inquiry. Much as the narratological study of cinema revolves around the usage of the filmic apparatus, game narratives are bound to be delivered in certain ways by the expressive potential of simulations. The temporal operations on order, frequency and duration, for instance, are bound to differ from non-interactive narrative forms, just as the unique relationship between a player and her avatar undoubtedly adds to or modifies the existing narrative points of view used in novels and movies. How do game mechanics contribute to the unfolding of the game's story? Do they tell something different from the scripted (non-interactive) cut-scenes or dialogues? What of the various distinctions between *sjuzhet* and *fabula*, story and discourse, or story, plot, and narrative? How do narrative elements influence the player's understanding of the game? Are video game narratives closer to literature, drama, film, or role-playing games, and which of their unique affordances do they share? What can we learn from comparing and contrasting them to these other forms of storytelling? All of these questions represent the interests of narratology in video games.

Dominic Arsenault

New Media

While a variety of definitions of "new media" exists, one can define them as software-based simulations of previously existing physical and electronic media plus a number of previously non-existent media which are also implemented in software. This definition follows the formulation which Alan Kay, the key person responsible for inventing new media, provided in a September, 1984 *Scientific American* article: "It [a computer] is a medium that can dynamically simulate the details of any other medium, including media that cannot exist physically. It is not a tool, though it can act like many tools. It is the first metamedium, and as such it has degrees of freedom for representation and expression never before encountered and as yet barely investigated."

How do you know if you are dealing with new media or not? If you are creating or interacting with cultural objects and situations via a computer which is running some software, the answer is yes. In other words, if you are in the presence of running software, you deal with new media. Following this definition, interacting with a website, experiencing an interactive installation, and playing a video game all qualify as new media experiences. For instance, when you play a first-person shooter, the software generates a virtual world, directs non-player characters, keeps track on your weapons and "health," and controls every other aspect of your experience. Essentially, you are playing against the software.

The switch from physical and electronic media to media implemented in software has many fundamental consequences. One of the most important is something which I call "Permanent Extendibility." In the 1960s and 1970s, Ivan Sutherland, Ted Nelson, Douglas Englebart, Alan Kay, and other pioneers of computational computing added many previously non-existent properties to media they simulated in a computer (which included writing and editing text, the creating and editing of images, animations, paint programs, and so forth). For instance, in the case of text, you can search for particular phrases, change fonts and colors, change formatting of pages, and so on. Subsequent generations of computer scientists, hackers, and designers added many more properties, but this process is far from finished. And there is no logical or material reason why it will ever be finished. It is the "nature" of computational media that it is open-ended, and new techniques are continuously being invented.

To add new properties to physical media requires modifying their physical substance. But since computational media exists as software, we can add new properties or even invent new types of media by simply changing existing software, writing new software, adding plug-ins and extensions, or by putting existing software together (for instance, people are daily extending capacities of mapping media by creating software mashups which combine the services and data provided by Google Maps, Flickr, Amazon, and other sites, and media uploaded by users).

In short, "new media" is "new" because new properties (that is, new software techniques) can always be easily added to them. In industrial (mass-produced) media technologies, "hardware" and "software" were one and the same thing. For example, book pages were bound in a particular way that fixed the order of pages. The reader could change neither this order nor the level of detail being displayed. Similarly, film projectors combined hardware and what we now call a "media player" software program into a single machine. In the same way, the controls built into a twentieth-century mass-produced camera could not be modified at the user's will. And although today the user of a digital camera similarly cannot easily modify camera hardware, the transferring of pictures into a computer gives the user access to endless number of controls and options for modifying pictures via software.

In the nineteenth and twentieth century there were two types of situations in which a normally fixed industrial medium was more fluid. The first type of situation is when a new medium was being first developed: for instance, the invention of photography in the 1820s–1840s. The second type of situation is when artists would systematically experiment with and "open up" already-industrialized media, such as the experiments with film and video during the 1960s, which came to be called "Expanded Cinema."

What used to be separate moments of experimentation with media during the industrial era became the norm in a software society. In other words, the computer legitimizes experimentation with media. In its very structure, new media is "avant-garde" since it is constantly being extended and thus redefined. If in modern culture "experimental" and "avant-garde" were opposed to "normalized" and "stable," this opposition largely disappears in software culture. And the role of the media avant-garde is performed no longer by individual artists in their studios but by a variety of players, from very big to very small—from companies such as Microsoft, Adobe, and Apple to independent programmers, hackers, and designers.

Lev Manovich

Pedagogy

(see **Education**)

Performance Studies

(see **Theater and Performance Studies**)

Phenomenology

As a theory of subjectivity and intersubjectivity, phenomenology should figure among the many fields and practices that can be used to study video games, especially immersive and first-person ones. Moreover, in using phenomenology, one could use its offspring: Heideggerian existentialism and philosophy of language, and Gadamerian hermeneutics (for example, the work of Paul Ricoeur). In drawing theoretical insights from phenomenology, one could also consider Maurice Merleau-Ponty's views on ontology and politics—for instance, in theorizing online multiplayer first-person video games.

Phenomenology was begun by German philosopher and mathematician Edmund Husserl. At the dawn of the twentieth century, many philosophers and mathematicians (such as Russell, Frege, Cantor, and Wittgenstein) were looking for a theory or a system that would insure the foundations of knowledge, and especially scientific knowledge, including mathematics. Husserl tried to theorize the mind's very basic structures in a Cartesian way (*Cogito ergo sum*, "I think, therefore I am"), and was led to propose the notion of a "transcendental ego," that is, a universal structure of consciousness or a faculty, the subjective faculty. The mind and its knowledge would then depend on such a universal subjective faculty intrinsic to everyone. Thus, it can be said that Husserl's works are laid upon Kant's epistemological magnum opus, *Critique of Pure Reason*. This has in turn inspired Paul Ricoeur in his description of selfhood as "ipseity" (from the Latin *ipse*, "oneself"), that is, a pure and universal faculty of self-personalization.

In regard to video game theory, the notions of ipseity and of transcendental ego can be used to think of the pronoun "I" outside of the boundaries of grammar and linguistics, and to add another, if not a greater, extension to the immersive "first person" represented in many video games. The very structure of a transcendental ego or of the ipseity suggests that there would exist in everyone a universal faculty to be a subject, almost pronoun-like, and this would in turn imply a necessary network of other selves within which oneself can thrive as a self, just like the grammatical first person solely exists in relation with the other grammatical persons, and with language as a whole.

If selfhood stems from a network of subjectivities, a universal structure fulfilled by each individual (as a phenomenological view would put it), then video games can be envisioned as the ludic mediation and embodiment of universal and ontological structures. Not only would video games be rooted in an anthropological soil (see Caillois and Huizinga), but they would also connect with a human necessity to be a self in relation to a network of selves, just like a pronoun exists only with a grammatical backdrop. This in turn could be connected with views about democracies, but with a strong humanistic content (since phenomenological positions can be reduced to worldviews created in and with a book culture).

To think about immersive structures and first-person shooters with a phenomenological apparatus would lead to reflections about culture, individuality, and community, and might shed new light on first-person shooting games. If subjectivity and intersubjectivity are universal faculties, then first-person shooting games should be envisioned as the representation of a suicidal destruction of selfhood. But then, why play them? To address this question using phenomenology might expose and explain many paradoxes and theoretical dead ends. Moreover, phenomenology could then be used to bind a new electronic culture to the humanistic book culture.

Patrick Poulin

Philosophy

The philosophical tradition of systematically comprehending human nature in terms of game and play is of relatively recent origin. In the late eighteenth century Friedrich Schiller said that *Man only plays when he is in the fullest sense of the word a human being, and he is only fully a Man when he plays*. More than a century later, Johan Huizinga suggested that human culture originally has been played out and still to this day develops through games. This position was picked up by Roger Caillois and Hans-Georg Gadamer for their respective concepts of culture and aesthetics.

Roger Caillois unconvincingly tried to prove that pre-modern culture was based on role-playing and vertigo games while the modern world is based on competition and games of chance. It must be added that Jean

Baudrillard used Callois' approach to pre-modern and modern society in his notion of the hypermodern society, which according to Baudrillard is based on role-playing and vertigo games as in the pre-modern era. Hans-Georg Gadamer on the other hand made it clear that since culture is based on game and play then aesthetics must be based on game and play as well. Consequently, art ought to be realized as works of game and play.

These various positions on the subject may help as a conception of how games work as aesthetics and culture. However, in order to understand philosophical game design we have to move a step further. The philosophical game designer must not only know about game aesthetics and culture but morality and ethics as well. When designing a philosophical game, the designer has to create an ethical game system. This does not necessarily have to be an ethical system that is true to the real world (even though this may in fact be appreciated), but at least it must be internally consistent to its own reality. The ethical system should represent the ethics of the fictional world in question.

By delving into Aristotelian ethics and comparing this with Aristotelian poetics, the designer has a starting point from which to begin his journey into philosophical game design. He may look into any philosophical system of ethics and morality from Augustine and Boethius to Kierkegaard and Gadamer, figuring out how to construct them as game systems. In an attempt to accomplish a philosophical game system, it could be fruitful for the game designer to think of ethics and morality in terms of cybernetics as presented by Norbert Wiener and second order cybernetics as it is formulated by Gregory Bateson who is in addition known for his theory of play and fantasy. Philosophy can also be use to analyze the ideology within a game through the way it links actions and consequences, the player's point of view and the requirements of play, and what behavioral aspects of a game have the potential to spill over into the rest of the player's life.

Finally, game theory by John von Neumann and Oskar Morgenstern ought to be mentioned. Here we find a theory that is capable of simulating decision-making in games. It is necessary to say that even though this theory may indeed simulate ethical decisions, it is certainly not a theory of ethics and should not be used as such. Still, game theory could be valuable when creating philosophical game design because it may assist the designer apprehending the decision-making process in games, thereby comprehending ethical consequences.

Lars Konzack

Pleasure

(see **Psychology**)

Politics

Political theory offers us a well-integrated and mature field which mixes multiple disciplines, from its treatment of organizational structure, to psychological motivation, to ethical philosophy; such multi-modality provides a unique vantage point from which to view game design and analysis. In the study of political form, perhaps the most straightforward example is the founding notion of checks and balances in democratic government. At heart, both political apparatuses and games (analog and digital) are rule-driven structures which guide human behavior, intentionally limiting the possible states of a system and the actions available to the actors within it. These restrictions create negative feedback loops, preventing any single entity—whether politician, government agency, or human or computer game player—from consolidating power too quickly or repeatedly. In the well known example of the US government, the executive, legislative, and judicial branches have unique blocking capabilities amongst themselves: the president may veto a bill passed by congress, which in response may override this maneuver with a two-thirds majority of its own members; the Supreme Court may later nullify the law by determining it to be unconstitutional. Such balance similarly underpins the genres of strategy, puzzle, and role-playing games, among others, in which possible actions, counteractions, and resources are divided up across a finite set of abstracted "types"—characters, vehicles, materials, etc. The relationships within political models are both hierarchical (as in consolidation and direction of power), as well as lateral, necessitating power sharing through cooperation and competition. Political structures provide a rich set of models that are particularly applicable to the low-level game design task of "tuning," in which the numeric properties and potential actions of these entities are iteratively adjusted. From a perspective of comparative analysis and design, politically-derived examples are often more attractive than those from related fields: more tangible and representational than purely statistical or economic models, and more holistic and systemic than specific scenarios from game theory.

While humanistic disciplines such as literary studies and film studies are often most useful for examining modes of representation in games—particularly the ways in which we receive and make meaning of a game's audiovisual and narrative elements—political theory is naturally oriented towards the non-linear, combinatorial aspects of game action, yet also strives to incorporate representational context. In this way, political models can be likened to the "half-real" notion of games offered by game researcher Jesper Juul, the foundation of logical rules grafted with and interdependent upon fictional assignments. Political checks and balances promote and often ensure that there is no single course of action for achieving an end, yet also no open-ended, undirected process: widely considered a desirable game design trait which facilitates replayability and stimulates individual strategies of play. Rather than modeling an abstract decision-making process, political science is also centrally concerned with the mental state of actors both direct (politicians) and indirect (the governed populace). Most important are the factors which motivate action and gauge governmental stability, such as the distribution of wealth, and peace both internally and with other political entities. The consideration of these structurally "external" influences and their psychological effects is by contrast underserved in game studies, which by and large has not yet developed a significant theoretical approach to player motivation. Political science's integration of formal rule structures with psychological factors (also offered in different flavors by philosophy and game theory, among others) can provide helpful scaffolding for future game analysis and design. Finally, political science has a long history (at least from Plato's *Republic* onwards) of considering the ethical ramifications and responsibilities of individuals and societies. In the charged public debate over game violence and media effects, the application of philosophical ethics within the context of a rule-driven structure may offer new perspectives that go beyond binary claims of individual player action and reaction.

Brett Camper

Psychoanalysis

Psychoanalysis provides a theoretical and conceptual framework to study video games in relation to players as a mediated experience, independent from or within clinical practice. As a framework, psychoanalysis focuses on the mental functions operating and affecting individuals, cultures, and societies. For game studies, psychoanalytic approaches study the relationship of players and games. This includes relationships of multiple players to each other, players and game interfaces, players and game narratives, and players and game displays.

Psychoanalysis grows out of the tradition of psychoanalytic therapy pioneered by Sigmund Freud and Jacques Lacan, which focused heavily on language and representational structures as a means of uncovering and explaining psychological phenomenon. Psychoanalytic phenomenon includes the relationship of the conscious to the subconscious, and areas of interconnection as with repressed conscious memories which are driven to the subconscious and then may erupt as the return of the repressed. In this formulation, tension between the conscious and the subconscious can lead to the return of the repressed in a manner like Dr. Jekyll's Mr. Hyde returns—unbidden and uncontrollable. The tension between the known and the unknown and the controlled and the uncontrolled underlies many video game narratives with characters who must recover lost or repressed memories; many gameplay sequences where players lose control to a cinematic sequence or another component of the game; and the overall tension in gameplay control, because the full sense of control is attainable only when the risk of a loss of control is possible. In addition to internal phenomenon, psychoanalysis also studies the external representations and communication of those phenomena.

Psychoanalytic research focuses on language, representation, and communication to explain the symbolic operations and their processing for specific relationships, thereby showing how mental functions operate in individuals and in larger groups. Literary and film criticism expanded psychoanalysis to include the study of particular works and forms in relation to readers and viewers. This includes film studies' work to explain the relationship of the viewer to the characters on screen. The underlying power dynamics framed through psychoanalysis helps to explain issues of identification and control from film viewers over film characters as subjects-objects within the view of their "gaze." For game studies, psychoanalysis thus provides a language for studying the relationship of a player or all of a particular set of players to a single game, a set of games, or gaming as a whole.

Psychoanalysis affords the framework by which to model and explain game narratives, game visual representations, and high-level constructs in gameplay as well as the complex relationship of the player to games. The relationships between the player and the game includes those between the player and the game interface; between the player and the game world as a phenomenological space that the player experiences through the game representation; between the player and the game world as a looked-upon representational space; and between the player and actual gameplay. As a mediated experience, the player's relationship to gameplay includes the relationship of the player to the player's avatar (the graphical representation of the player in the game) as well as the player to the player's actions in the game. Each of these relationships complexly affects the others during gameplay just as the game interface, visual representation, and narrative all operate together to form the game as a construct in operation during gameplay.

Psychoanalysis can also be used to create games that properly model or react to psychological factors, thereby helping to design, for instance, games tailored to specific applications, such as games for therapeutic uses. Because of their ability to model complex situations as simulations and to then combine that with objectives through meaningful play, games grow increasingly popular as psychological training devices, often for training under stress as is the case for many military and disaster training games, and as tools for creating simulated environments for therapy, as in the use of games used to treat phobias through exposure therapy which gradually desensitizes phobic patients to their phobias through the safety of a simulated environment.

As gaming becomes ever more varied in terms of players (player interests, ages, backgrounds, and communities) and game types (causal games, massively multiplayer games, etc.) and complexity (visual representations leaning toward realism and other artistic styles; game interfaces with voice, motion, buttons, and other controls), psychoanalysis provides an essential cornerstone for any area of video game studies by providing a means to study the importance of the player-game relationship. Further, psychoanalysis's emphasis on the importance of language and representation provides a critical vocabulary for studying all areas of game representation, including image, sound, narrative, and code, all of which are increasingly important for the larger concerns of digital media studies and software or code studies.

Laurie N. Taylor

Psychology

Psychology is a science concerned with the human mind and behavior, thus its relevance to game studies is paramount. Psychological theories and concepts can help game scholars in studying motivations for gameplay. They can also be applied to the development of psychologically-oriented game design methods.

In contemporary psychology, we find many approaches for possible application to video game studies. Early efforts in adapting psychological concepts for understanding the nature of video games include Loftus and Loftus's *Mind at Play: The Psychology of Video Games* (1983), but this book as well as others highlight an approach in which psychologists try to understand games, rather than approaches in which game scholars, with their particular expertise in games, try to apply ideas from the discipline of psychology. Now that game studies has emerged as a discipline of its own, there are many opportunities for producing player-centered studies that focus on the psychology of games and play.

The premise for psychological investigations into games is that gameplay is experiential in nature; that is, playing games engages the human mind and produces behavior: individual instances of play are instances of particular psychological behavior in which players plan actions, perform them, make use of their cognitive abilities, and experience emotions.

During such behavior, players use various means, such as perception, to gather information from their surroundings. In addition, players process the information by making inferences and deductions, which lead to actions in hope of completing the game's goals and competing with others. Consequently, analysis into the experiential nature of games and play covers their psychological, cognitive, and emotional aspects.

A game scholar adopting such an approach can formulate research questions of the following kinds: What is it that motivates players to engage themselves in a game, submitting oneself and one's behavior to rules, and what kind of pleasures do players seek from playing games? What can game studies and game design learn from the psychology of goals and plans? Do games, by and large, privilege some cognitive abilities over others? What kinds of emotion categories are there, and how do they relate to categories of games? Finally, how does the psychology of our everyday goals differ from the one in the "magic circle" of games?

The answers to such questions can be sought, for example, by looking into research on the psychology of entertainment, where the work of scholars such as Dolf Zillman on concepts of "selective exposure" and "mood management" can be used in order to understand why players prefer one game genre over others, or what prerequisites there are for a player to enjoy a session with a game in the first place. Work on so-called reversal theory and psychology of excitement by Michael Apter is another possible approach for these kinds of investigations.

Cognitive scientists and psychology scholars have constructed many theories about human emotions and pleasures. Such research has produced understanding concerning the process of experiencing emotions, and various categorizations of emotions. These findings and formulations can help game scholars and designers in making nuanced distinctions regarding the emotional experience that a particular game, or a game genre, elicits. According to emotion theorists, the human affective realm can be divided into three causally linked domains: Emotions lead to moods that lead to dispositions. This opens up a psychological perspective towards the concept of genre: player tastes regarding specific game genres can be conceptualized and studied as emotional dispositions.

It has been argued that the main question of cognitive science is essentially a design challenge: How to design a mind. This includes charting out and anticipating the potential problems the mind would have to face, what kind of considerations it would have to do, etc. Thus, when embarking into studying psychology, cognition, and emotion in terms of games, game scholars are exploring questions central to game design: How players would behave while interacting with the game design. From a psychological standpoint, the design goal for a new game would, then, be the experience of the player, rather than a design of rules and their visual embodiments as such. Psychologically, cognitively, and emotionally orientated video game studies that focus on the above issues can produce results that inform game design practices towards methods increasingly sensitive to players and their aspirations.

Aki Järvinen

Reception Studies

At the very foundation of reception studies, lies the refutation of the eternal nature of beauty and its potential manifestation through art, a common conception inherited from Platonism. The traditional function of art associated with this essentialist conception—the production of a good mimesis leading to the contemplation of beauty—was violently rejected by modernist thinkers and artists such as Valéry and Cézanne. However, modernity's concern with reception was limited to revealing the illusionist deception and perceptive alienation of mimetic art, related to bourgeois society. It is under the influence of phenomenology that the aesthetic object was defined not as the work of art in itself, but as the encounter between the work and its user (*The Act of Reading* by Wolfgang Iser [1974]). Hans Robert Jauss, also throughout the course of the 1970s, defined most clearly and precisely the theoretical framework of reception studies.

In *Toward an Aesthetic of Reception* ([1976] 1982), Jauss proclaimed that the work of art is not the expression of a timeless essence, and that its meaning is not fixed and immutable; rather, it is the accumulation of consecutive reinterpretations (or chain of reception) that constitutes the work's meaning. That is not to say, however, that reception studies conceive the work of art as a completely open meaning system, on the contrary: Jauss insists on the determination exerted by the context of reception. Stanley Fish's notion of "interpretative communities," composed of readers with similar skills and references, similarly sought to integrate clear boundaries to the conception of meaning-making in reception studies. The aesthetic of reception is not only a plea for the exhaustive study of the interaction between art and its audience, but a very strong case for the reformation of literary history and art history. For Jauss, the historical approach should focus on the chains of reception associated with different works instead of simply listing and organizing bodies of work in a chronological manner; the rehabilitation of rejected material at a specific period of time is a fact infinitely more significant than those accumulated under the influence of positivistic methodology. Jauss's aesthetic of reception can be summarized through the key concept of the "horizon of expectations," the frame of experience interiorized by readers/viewers at a given time, which can be formulated in accordance with three aspects: preliminary experience with the norms of artistic forms/genres; implicit relationship of the work with other works in the reception context; comparison between the poetic and pragmatic uses of language (and therefore between the imaginary world and real life). This last aspect stresses that the work can be received not only against the limited backdrop of art, but also against the extended horizon of real life. Thus, the aesthetic of reception acknowledges the potential creative social power of art, a function that was ignored by previous historical paradigms in favor of simple world reflection (transcendent for neoclassicism, socio-historical for Marxism) or autonomous production (formalism).

In the realm of video game studies, the novelty of interactivity contributed to a general interest toward the user's activity. The aesthetic of reception can be associated broadly to research focusing on the psychological involvement of the player, such as cognitive approaches. Literature that focuses on the relationship between text and player, the semantic and cultural context of reception, and the effects and consequences of games relate directly to reception studies. On the other hand, the historical reform proposed by Jauss has not yet been embraced by major publications.

Carl Therrien

Semiotics

Semiotics can be considered either a "science" (according to Ferdinand de Saussure), "doctrine" (according to Charles Sanders Peirce), or "discipline" (according to Umberto Eco) governing the study of signs and symbols. At its core, semiotics involves an analysis of representationalism and intentionality as fundamental components of human activity and expression and, potentially, as more general features of the natural world.

Semiotics as a science would attempt to uncover laws of representationalism governing human consciousness, self-awareness, and, in broader contexts, the organics of cognition. Biosemiotics represents well the aspirations of semiotics as a science. Culturalists who regard signs and symbols as artifacts of human culture rather than expositions of human nature also apply the methods and terminology of semiotics to their own ends. The use of semiotics in cultural studies, however, is distinct from its use as a science.

The distinction between semiotics as a science and semiotics as a methodological tool is usefully analogous to Saussure's well-known distinction between *langue* (abstract, systematic principles of language) and *parole* (actual speech). While *parole* remains a vital component of language studies, many linguists have expectations of more fundamental structures (such as Noam Chomsky's posited "deep structure") guiding the construction and maintenance of human language, which is known as *langue*. Emphasizing language as embodied form, then, marks a division between formal linguists and sociolinguists and between the study of signs and symbols as a mechanic of nature and their study as a negotiable feature of human society. It is the benefits of the first, more formal approach to video game semiotics that I wish to emphasize here.

The primary goal of a science of signs and symbols of video games is to locate and highlight similarities among video games and other formal mechanisms governing human communications and play. These similarities can then be considered evidence of some objective form that might either produce or explicate (or both) the subjective experience of play. If this goal were achieved, the origin of such a form—and the play it evokes—would be more fully and properly understood in the context of natural history than cultural exchange. This result—a reprioritization of hermeneutical interpretations of social play in favor of a more thorough consideration of the biomechanics of individual play—could then more clearly delineate the broader area of study of which video game scholarship is some smaller part: that is, phenomenology and the nature of representation.

Video games in particular offer opportunities to pursue a science of semiotics. The mechanics and algorithms of video game design and play—their hardware and software—are procedurally more evident and empirically more accessible than those of previous game forms. That is, regardless of their mediated and malleable social functions, video games are digitally-coded mechanical devices and lend themselves to scrutiny as such.

The mechanical properties of video games beg examination in a manner similar to that of David Marr's investigation of the mechanics of vision and Philip N. Johnson-Laird's analysis of the mechanics of thought. Indeed, procedural structures of video game design and play can be considered homologous to the cognitive structures that enable and interpret them. Thus, the study of video games—particularly mapping the interactive and transformative properties of gameplay—has the capacity to reproduce the representational qualities of the human mind in form and, perhaps, in function.

From the perspective of semiotics as a science, video games are most essentially *semiotic machines* that generate and transform meanings through the coded manipulation of signs and symbols. The more precisely we are able to replicate the evocative qualities of games, the more likely we are to gain insight into some of the more problematic areas of cognitive science. These include a variety of data management, categorization, and contextualization issues plaguing artificial intelligence as well as the more compelling and recurring mysteries of human consciousness and self-awareness.

David Myers

Sociology

Sociology comprises the examination and analysis of social life and social relations. Sociologists develop theories explaining the continuously evolving nature of social behavior. Particular fields focus on the study of media and its political, social, and cultural impact. In researching video games, sociologists empirically examine a variety of questions surrounding games. They view game spaces as arenas where people explore a range of sociological issues such as: the ways in which social groups might form through games; the significance of video games within particular social and cultural contexts; and how games might reflect or influence constructions of identity, embodiment, race, gender, sexuality, and spatiality.

Sociologists employ quantitative and qualitative methods in the study of video games. Quantitative sociological studies of video games provide the possibilities for examining the increasing pervasiveness of gaming, gathering data regarding issues such as the types of video games people play, or the amount of time spent on particular video games. The data is gathered through widespread surveys, questionnaires, or interviews. This type of data can provide the foundation for more nuanced qualitative research projects. Qualitative research is engaged in order to understand the player experience as contextualized in particular cultural environments. Data is typically gathered through ethnography. For instance, ethnographic research of a player's gameplay might involve participant observation or open-ended interviews, providing insight into how play fits into the context of daily life. Qualitative research attempts to capture the changeability of the long-term play experience, for example, the variability of game content, cultural circumstances, and personal taste.

Unlike many other disciplines which approach video games as media texts, a sociological approach would view games as situated in the practice of everyday life. For sociologists, games might serve as bounded spaces in which social interactions occur. Sociologists do not generally approach games as texts or artifacts but rather as encounters. They are typically most interested in multiplayer and online games or when video games are played in social situations.

A sociological perspective towards the field of games studies might use some of the basic theories employed by sociologists as a lens through which to examine video games. From a sociological standpoint, a feminist approach to analyzing video games could examine the ways in which female avatars are portrayed within the space of the game as well as through the experience of the female player. A Marxist approach might look at the consumption and production aspect of games, viewing players as both producers of content and consumers of the play experience. Some topics that may be explored from this perspective would be players as producers, issues of alienation, and intellectual property rights. A phenomenological approach would seek to understand and describe the meaning of the experience of video game play from the perspective of the player enabling the researcher to understand more fully the social significance of play. A postmodern approach to game studies from a socio-logical perspective might explore theoretical issues such as simulation, hyper-reality, and the social construction of space within the game. A symbolic interactionist approach to the study of video games would focus on the interactions amongst players, use of symbols in communications, interpretation as an aspect of interaction with the self, or identity as fluidly constructed through interaction with others. A micro-interactionist approach would examine everyday social interactions on a small scale looking at social co-ordination and micro-organization (for instance, a conversational analysis of shooting games would be a paradigm case for interaction analysis), while a macro-interactionist approach would be broader in focus, researching communities such as cyber communities or fan communities. A functionalism focus might examine social problems with a sociological approach to media effects.

Sociological research on video games could potentially inform policy makers, administrators, educators, game developers, the industry, and the general public.

Shanly Dixon

Subcreation Studies

The nascent field of Subcreation Studies examines the building of imaginary diegetic worlds within and across a variety of media, and considers these worlds as distinct objects which are often transmedia and transnarrative in their construction. Originally coined by J. R. R. Tolkien, the term "subcreation" is used to distinguish human creation from God's *ex nihilo* creation, as well as to indicate its reliance on the latter through the use of the "sub" designation (the term literally means "creating under"). "Subcreation" also refers both to the process and product of world-building, while avoiding philosophically slippery terminology like "real" and "imaginary," which tend to be seen as mutually exclusive domains. Unlike other approaches which are medium specific or narrative specific, subcreation studies is concerned with the world itself, in which multiple narratives can occur and which can be viewed through a variety of media windows (such as film, television, comic books, novels, or video games). This approach is particularly well-suited to video games, whose diegetic worlds, unlike those of other media like film, television, or print, contain an interactive element that often allows for navigation and exploration of the world under the player's control. Some video games are also part of larger, transmedia worlds, and thus must be considered with the rest of the world in mind, while others are self-contained and exist on their own within a single game.

Subcreation studies looks at each world as a whole, and is concerned with the world's inner consistency, as well as its global structures, and the way in which they relate to the local smaller-scale structures within the world. Global structures include those of space (maps, layouts, connections between places), time (chronologies, histories, the timing of events), the genealogies, languages, and cultures of the world's inhabitants, and narratives that incorporate all of these. The worlds of video games, which range from simple single screens of flat graphics to elaborate three-dimension online worlds populated by millions of characters, can also contain various ontologies and rules by which they operate, which players must learn when they vicariously inhabit these worlds through the use of avatars. Examining video games through a subcreative approach produces a more holistic view of its diegetic world, and one which is not limited by medium or narrative or by the player's experience. As the diegetic worlds of video games grow larger and more detailed and complex, such an approach grows in relevance and provides a way to discuss the design of the world in such a way as to make it distinct from the design of the game, as well as to discuss it in comparison to other subcreated worlds.

Mark J. P. Wolf

Television Studies

As a field, television studies has much to offer to students and scholars of video and computer games. Like other modes of critical theory and fields informed by the changes in literary studies during the latter half of the twentieth century, television studies is informed by questions of medium/form, class, race, gender, and industrial analysis. Television studies proceeds with questions first raised by film theory: How does the medium's apparatus function? How do spectatorship and reception operate? Television studies analyzes televisual form through models like Raymond Williams's key scholarship on television as flow, sound, or schedule, and televisual audiences through the lenses of fan studies, gendered viewing, or as quantifiable, measured groups.

Marshall McLuhan's early work on television as a global village facilitator and an electronic medium continue to have influence upon the field. Williams's theory of flow, which describes how television programs and advertising become for viewers an undifferentiated flow of images, can be seen as a starting point for academic inquiry into television and the current online television journal *Flow* (www.flowtv.org) takes its name from Williams's work. As a critical and theoretical field, television studies is informed by British cultural studies, in particular the work of Stuart Hall on encoding/decoding and subcultural studies by Dick Hebdige; Frankfurt School analysis of culture industries; and theorists as diverse as Foucault, de Certeau, Althusser, and Fredric Jameson. Because of its diffuse formal structure as an ongoing stream of media content, television has lent itself to a wide range of approaches and methods. Recent academic work on television has addressed its role in space, as global technology, and as a new media technology and home theater system.

Television studies also approaches the medium through quantitative methodologies, historical and textual analysis, and industry discourse. In the USA, television studies emerged alongside cultural studies and gender studies in the late 1970s. At the same time, Birmingham School cultural critics in Great Britain wrote on the dynamics of cultural reception and class, generating interest in popular culture forms and audiences, including television. Today television scholars continue to engage with questions of history, the discursive form of TV, textuality, class, race, gender, and the medium's industrial structure while also addressing how new technologies, including video games and the Internet, continue to transform television as a global medium.

Scholars of video and computer games might utilize the field of television studies in several ways. Television studies provides a deep understanding of television technologies situated inside and outside of the home. The field also provides a framework for understanding the culture of home video entertainments like gaming, as well as critical models for approaching interactivity and fandom.

Sheila C. Murphy

Theater and Performance Studies

Classic definitions of play and games often describe a close relation between games and theatrical practices. In Roger Caillois's seminal categorization of game types in *Les Jeux et Les Hommes* (*Man, Play and Games*, 1958), for instance, theatre and spectacles are included as examples of the category *mimicry*. Several instances of overlap between the phenomena play, games, theatre, and performance art make the disciplines of theater and performance studies a repository of perspectives and theories relevant to the study of games.

Since the publication of Brenda Laurel's influential study *Computers as Theatre* in 1991, drama theory based on the principles of Aristotle's *Poetics* has inspired an increasing number of software designers to create dramatically compelling interactive entertainment. However, in order to design so-called "serious games"—that is, games with a political, educational or otherwise serious purpose besides entertainment—non-Aristotelian dramatic principles have been put forward. The progression of events in Aristotelian drama is based on a cause-effect relationship, providing the audience with the illusion that every action on stage happens by necessity. According to the German dramatist Bertolt Brecht, this makes Aristotelian theater conservative and bourgeois, actively preventing social progress in society. In non-Aristotelian Brechtian theater, the illusion is continuously broken, reminding the audience that what they see is fiction, and provoking them to relate it to their own social reality. The Brazilian theater director, writer, and politician Augusto Boal's *Theatre of the Oppressed* is another example of a non-Aristotelian dramatic system that has influenced the thinking on how to design games with a serious purpose. In Boal's theatre, a participating audience (*spect-actors*) is invited to contribute possible solutions to conflicts presented on stage that are acted out one after the other until an agreeable solution is reached. Often, the conflicts presented are also actual conflicts contributed by the audience. The *Theatre of the Oppressed* thus provides a place for people to rehearse solutions to real life conflicts, based on the belief that by doing a previously unthinkable action on stage, the blocks that prevent us from doing similar actions in real life are removed and we are free to act differently in the future.

As a result of the so-called performative turn in the humanities, heavily influenced by the works of anthropologists such as Victor Turner, Erving Goffmann, and Clifford Geertz, many theatre studies departments have expanded their research area into the broader field of performance studies, in which a range of human activities are studied including games, rituals, and sports. Another branch of the performative turn dates back to the philosopher J. L. Austin and his 1962 book *How to Do Things with Words*. Here Austin introduces a type of utterances he calls *performatives*, different from mere descriptive statements in that they do not describe anything but rather execute an action: Betting is one example, promising another. Austin's theory has been used to analyze text-based games where every command is linguistically triggered, and every action is described in words, demonstrating that these should be treated as performative rather than descriptive or narrative types of texts. The distinction between performative and descriptive utterances may be a useful analytical tool also in the analyses of role-play in graphic multi-player game environments, where the character performs mainly through the use of words.

Dedicated role-play in multi-player environments is often based in traditional techniques for character personification, drawing on principles developed by the Russian actor and theatre director Constantin Stanislavski at the beginning of the twentieth century. These principles describe how to become the character through deep physical and psychological identification with it, in which one asks oneself a series of questions concerning how the character would think, feel, and react in various situations. The more casual role-play most players perform in a multi-player game, executed with simple commands such as <greet>, <dance>, and <cheer>, has on the other hand been compared with earlier theatre forms such as the commedia dell'Arte. The stock characters of commedia dell'Arte all had a fixed repertoire of typical gestures and actions, which they performed in their specific, characteristic way. Likewise, character types in massively multiplayer games such as *World of Warcraft* have their own characteristic way of performing the various actions available, depending on their race and gender.

The emerging phenomenon of pervasive games, ubiquitous games, and flashmobs is one of the most intriguing links between games and performance studies at the moment. Already in the 1960s American and European performance artists experimented with concepts that blurred the distinctions between gameplay and performance. Most notably Allan Kaprow's *Happenings* were an attempt to replace the exclusiveness surrounding Performance Art—in which art is performed in front of an audience— with a participatory concept of play that included everyone attending. In a series of articles entitled "The Education of the Un-Artist, Parts I–III" (1971–1974), he recommends that artists abandon the art concept altogether and start teaching people how to play instead. Interesting experiments in which performance is mixed with elements of gaming today include works by the Britain-based performance groups Blast Theory and Forced Entertainment.

Ragnhild Tronstad

Bibliography

Aarseth, Espen. *Cybertext. Perspectives on Ergodic Literature.* Baltimore: The Johns Hopkins University Press, 1997.
_____. "Computer Games Studies, Year One." *Game Studies* 1, no. 1 (July 2001). Available online at <http://www.gamestudies.org/0101/editorial.html>.
_____. "Playing research: Methodological Approaches to Game Analysis." In *Proceedings of the Digital Arts and Culture Conference*, Melbourne, Australia, 2003. Available online at <http://www.spilforskning.dk/gameapproaches/GameApproaches2.pdf>.
_____. "I Fought the Law: Transgressive Play and The Implied Player." In *Situated Play—Proceedings of DiGRA 2007 Conference*, edited by Akira Baba (Tokyo: DiGRA Japan, 2007, 130–133). Available online at <http://www.digra.org/dl/db/07313.03489.pdf>.
ActionButton.net. Review of *La-Mulana* (GR3 Project). Available online at <http://www.actionbutton.net/?p=193>.
Adams, Ernest and Andrew Rollings. *Fundamentals of Game Design.* Upper Saddle River: Prentice Hall, 2007.
Alexander, Leigh. "M-Rated Games Sell Best." *Game Developer* (October 2007): 5.
Anderson, C. and K. E Dill. "Video games and aggressive thoughts, feelings, and behavior in the laboratory and in life." *Journal of Personality and Social Psychology* 78 (2000): 772–790.
Arsenault, Dominic, Bernard Perron, Martin Picard, and Carl Therrien. "Methodological Questions in "*Interactive* Film Studies." *New Review of Film & Television Studies*, forthcoming in 2008.
_____. "Dark Waters: Spotlight on Immersion." In *Game On North America 2005 International Conference Proceedings*, Ghent: Eurosis-ETI, 2005: 50–52. Available online at <http://www.le-ludophile.com/Files/Arsenault%20-%20Dark%20Waters.pdf>
Bandura, Albert. "Toward a Psychology of Human Agency." *Perspectives on Psychological Science* 1, no. 2 (2006): 164–180.
_____. *Self-Efficacy: The Exercise of Control.* New York: W. H. Freeman; 1997.
Baron-Cohen, Simon, and John E. Harrison, eds. *Synaesthesia.* Cambridge, MA: Blackwell, 1997.
Barrett, Mark. "First Person: Academic Intent." *Electronic Book Review* (July 26, 2005). Available online at <http://www.electronicbookreview.com/thread/firstperson/transient>.
Bartle, Richard. "Hearts, Clubs, Diamonds, Spades: Players Who Suit MUDs (1996)." In *The Game Design Reader: A Rules of Play anthology*, edited by K. Salen and E. Zimmerman

(Cambridge, MA: MIT Press, 2006, 754–787). Available online at <http://www.mud.co.uk/ richard/hcds.htm>.

Bateson, Gregory. *Steps to an Ecology of Mind*. New York: Balantine Books [1955] (1972).

Bekoff, Marc and John Alexander Byers, eds. *Animal Play: Evolutionary, Comparative, and Ecological Perspectives*. Cambridge: Cambridge University Press, 1998.

Benzies, Leslie, Dan Houser, Jamie King, Renaud Sebbane *et al. Grand Theft Auto III*. UK: DMA Design Limited, 2001.

Bernstein, Charles. "Play It Again, Pac-Man," In *Postmodern Culture* 2, no. 1 (September, 1991). Reprinted in Mark J. P. Wolf, ed. *The Medium of the Video Game*. Austin: Texas University Press, 2001, 155–168

Bluestien, Greg. "Creators Put Politics into Video Games." In *The Associated Press* (January 21, 2007). Available online at <http://www.sfgate.com/cgi-bin/article.cgi?file=/n/a/2007/01/20/ entertainment/e115220S54.DTL>

Bogost, Ian. *Persuasive Games: The Expressive Power of Videogames*. Cambridge, MA: MIT Press, 2007.

Bok, Derek. *Universities in the Marketplace: The Commercialization of Higher Education*. Princeton, NJ: Princeton University Press, 2004.

Bolter, J. "Theory and Practice in New Media Studies." In *Digital Media Revisited*, edited by Gunnar Liestol, Andrew Morrison, and Terje Rasmussen. Cambridge, MA: MIT Press, 2003, 15–34.

Bolter, J. David and Richard Grusin. *Remediation: Understanding New Media*. Cambridge, MA: MIT Press, 1999.

Bordwell, David. *Making Meaning. Inference and Rhetoric in the Interpretation of Cinema*. Cambridge, MA: Harvard University Press, 1989.

Boyer, Brandon. "Top 2007 Xbox Live Games Show Retro Success." *Gamasutra.com* (January 7, 2008). Available online at <http://www.gamasutra.com/php-bin/news_index.php? story=16051>.

Boyer, Pascal. "Cognitive Constraints on Cultural Representations: Natural Ontologies and Religious Ideas." In *Mapping the Mind: Domain Specificity in Cognition and Culture*, edited by Lawrence A. Hirschfeld and Susan A. Gelman. Cambridge: Cambridge University Press, 1994, 391–411.

Branigan, Edward. *Point of View in the Cinema. A Theory of Narration and Subjectivity in Classical Film*. Berlin: Mouton Publishers, 1984

Bryce, Jo and Jason Rutter. "An Introduction to Understanding Digital Games." In *Understanding Digital Games*, edited by Jo Bryce and Jason Rutter. London: Sage, 2006, 1–17.

Caillois, Roger. *Des jeux et des hommes*. Paris: Gallimard, 1958.

Carey, James. *Communication as Culture: Essays on Media and Society*. Boston: Unwin Hyman, 1998.

Carr, Diane, Andrew Burn, Gareth Schott, and David Buckingham. *Computer Games. Text, Narrative and Play*. Cambridge: Polity, 2006.

Casetti, Franceso. *Theories of Cinema, 1945–1995*. Translated by Francesca Chiostri and Elizabeth Gard Bartolini-Salimbeni, with Thomas Kelso. Austin, TX: University of Texas Press, 1999.

Castronova, Edward. *Synthetic Worlds: The Business and Culture of Online Games*. Chicago: The University of Chicago Press, 2005.

Caune, Jean. "La médiation culturelle : une construction du lien social." In *Les enjeux de l'information et de la communicaiton* (2000). Available online at: <http://w3.u-grenoble3.fr/les_ enjeux/2000/Caune/index.php>.

Charle, Christophe. "Patterns." In *A History of the University in Europe*, edited by Walter Rüegg. Cambridge: Cambridge University Press, 2004, 33–82.

Clark, Andy. *Being There. Putting Brain, Body, and World Together Again*. Cambridge, MA: MIT Press, 1997.

Cole, Jonathan, Oliver Sacks, and Ian Waterman. "On the Immunity Principle: A View from a Robot." *Trends in Cognitive Sciences* 4, no. 5 (2000): 167.

Consalvo, Mia. "There is No Magic Circle." *Games & Culture*, forthcoming.

––––––. *Cheating: Gaining Advantage in Videogames*. Cambridge, MA: The MIT Press, 2007.

Consalvo, Mia and Dutton, Nathan. "Game Analysis: Developing a Methodological Toolkit for the Qualitative Study of Digital Games." *Game Studies* 6 no. 1 (2006). Available online at <http://gamestudies.org/0601/articles/consalvo_dutton>.

Cook, Daniel. "The Chemistry of Game Design." *Gamasutra.com* (July 19, 2007). Available online at <http://www.gamasutra.com/view/feature/1524/the_chemistry_of_game_design.php>.

Courtés, Joseph. *La sémiotique narrative et discursive: méthodologie et application.* Preface by A. J. Greimas. Paris: Hachette supérieur, 1993.

Crawford, Chris. *The Art of Computer Game Design.* (Electronic Version, 1984). Available online at <http://www.vancouver.wsu.edu/fac/peabody/game-book/Coverpage.html>.

_____. "Interactive Storytelling." In *The Video Game Theory Reader,* edited by Mark J. P. Wolf and Bernard Perron. New York: Routledge, 2003: 259–273.

Csikszentmihalyi, Mihaly. *Flow: The Psychology of Optimal Experience.* New York: Harper & Row, 1990.

Culin, Stewart. *Games of the North American Indians, Vol. 1: Games of Chance. Vol. 2: Games of Skill.* Originally published in 1907. Lincoln and London: University of Nebraska Press, 1992.

Cupchick Gerald C. "Emotion in Aesthetics: Reactive and Reflective Models." *Poetics* 23: X (1994): 177–188.

_____. "Aesthetics and Emotion in Entertainment Media." *Media Psychology* 3 (2001): 69–89.

Davidson, Donald. *Essays on Actions and Events.* Oxford: Oxford University Press, 1980.

Delaney, Kevin. "Are Videogames Ready To Be Taken Seriously By Media Reviewers?" *Wall Street Journal,* November 3, 2003.

Delwiche, Aaron. "From *The Green Berets* to *America's Army*: Video Games as a Vehicle for Political Propaganda." In *The Player's Realm: Studies on the Culture of Video Games and Gaming,* eds. P. Williams and J. H. Smith. Jefferson NC: McFarland 2007: 91–109.

Demaine, Erik D., Hohenberger, Susan, and Liben-Nowell, David. "Tetris is hard, even to approximate." In *Proceedings of COCOON'2003* (2002). Available online at: <http://www.lcs.mit.edu/publications/pubs/pdf/MIT-LCS-TR-865.pdf>.

DeMaria, Rusel and Johnny L. Wilson. *High Score!: The Illustrated History of Video Games,* 2nd edn. New York: McGraw Hill, 2003.

Denzin, Norman K. *The Research Act: A Theoretical Introduction to Sociological Methods.* Chicago: Aldine, 1970.

DFC Intelligence. "The Secret of Nintendo's Success." *Next Generation* February 26, 2007. Available online at <http://www.next-gen.biz/index.php?option=com_content&task=view&id=4822&Itemid=2>,

Dienst, Richard. *Still Life in Real Time: Theory After Television.* Durham, NC: Duke University Press, 1994.

Dobson, James. "IDC: Wii To Outship & Outsell Xbox 360, PS3 Through 2008." *Gamasutra.com* (March 1, 2007). Available online at <http://www.gamasutra.com/php-bin/news_index.php?story=12956>.

Dodson, Joe. "Review: *Van Helsing.*" *Game Revolution.* Available online at <http://gr.bolt.com/games/ps2/action/van_helsing.htm>.

Ebert, Roger. "Review: *The Matrix Revolutions.*" *Chicago Sun-Times* (November 5, 2003). Available online at <http://rogerebert.suntimes.com/apps/pbcs.dll/article?AID=/20031105/REVIEWS/311050301/1023>.

Eco, Umberto. *The Role of the Reader: Explorations in the Semiotics of Texts.* Bloomington: University of Indiana Press, 1979.

Eco, Umberto. "Interpretation and Overinterpretation: World, History, Texts." In *Tanner Lectures.* Cambridge, 1990. Available online at <http://www.tannerlectures.utah.edu/lectures/Eco_91.pdf>.

_____. *The Role of the Reader: Explorations in the Semiotics of Texts.* Bloomington: Indiana University Press, 1979.

Egenfeldt-Nielsen, Simon, Jonas Heide Smith, and Susana Pajares Tosca. *Understanding Video Games.* New York: Routledge, 2008.

Epstein, Brian Jay. *The Big Picture: The New Logic of Money and Power in Hollywood.* New York: Random House, 2005.

Ermi, Laura and Frans Mäyrä. "Fundamental Components of the Gameplay Experience: Analysing Immersion." In *Selected Papers Proceedings of DiGRA 2005 Conference: Changing Views— Worlds in Play* (Vancouver: DiGRA & Simon Fraser University, 2005: 15–27). Available online at <http://www.digra.org/dl/db/06276.41516.pdf>.

Ermi, Laura, Satu Heliö, and Frans Mäyrä. "The Power of Games and Control of Playing—

Children as the Actors of Game Cultures [Finnish language report with an extended English abstract]." *Tampere University Hypermedia Laboratory Net Series* 6 (2004). Available online at <http://tampub.uta.fi/tup/951-44-5939-3.pdf>.

Eskelinen, Markku. "The Gaming Situation." *Game Studies* 1 (July 2001). Available online at <http://www.gamestudies.org/0101/eskelinen/>

Fahey, Rob. "Warner Bros Plans Penalties For Poor Quality Licensed Titles." *GamesIndustry.biz* (May 26, 2004). Available online at <http://www.gamesindustry.biz/content_page.php?section_name=pub&aid=352>.

Falstein, Noah. "Understanding Fun—The Theory of Natural Funativity." In *Introduction to Game Development*, edited by Steve Rabin. Boston: Charles River Media, 2005, 71–98.

Finn, Seth and Donald Roberts. "Source, Destination, and Entropy: Reassessing the Role of Information Theory in Communication Research." *Communication Research* 11. no. 4 (1984): 453–476.

Fish, Phil. Interview. *Arthouse Games*. Available online at <http://northcountrynotes.org/jason-rohrer/arthouseGames/seedBlogs.php?action=display_post&post_id=jcr13_1196041006_0&show_author=1&show_date=1>.

Foo, C. Y. "Redefining Grief Play." Paper presented at *the Other Players conference*, Center of Computer Games Research, IT University of Copenhagen, December 6–8, 2004. Available online at <http://www.itu.dk/op/papers/yang_foo.pdf>.

Försterling, F. *Attribution: An Introduction to Theories, Research and Applications*. 1. London: Psychology Press, 2001.

Fowler, Alastair. *Kinds of Literature. An Introduction to the Theory of Genres and Modes*. Cambridge, MA: Harvard University Press, 1982.

Frasca, Gonzalo, "The Sims: Grandmothers are Cooler than Trolls." In *Game Studies* 1, no. 1 (July 2001). Available online at <http://www.gamestudies.org/0101/frasca/>

———. "Simulation versus narrative: Introduction to ludology." In *The Video Game Theory Teader*, edited by Mark J. P. Wolf and Bernard Perron. New York: Routledge, 2003, 221–235.

Freeman, David. *Creating Emotion in Games. The Craft and Art of Emotioneering*. New Riders Publishing, 2003.

Frow, John. *Genre*. New York: Routledge, 2006.

Fullerton, Tracy. *Game Design Workshop. A Playcentric Approach to Creating Innovative Games*, 2nd edn. San Francisco: Morgan Kaufmann, 2008.

Fullerton, Tracy, Chris Swain, and Steven Hoffman. *Game Design Workshop: Designing, Prototyping, and Playtesting Games*. San Francisco: CMP Books, 2004.

Gadamer, Hans-Georg. *Truth and Method*. London and New York: Continuum International, 2004. In French: *Vérité et méthode*. Paris: Éditions du Seuil, 1976.

———. *The Relevance of the Beautiful and Other Essays*. Cambridge: Cambridge University Press, 1986.

Gallagher, Shaun. *How the Body Shapes the Mind*. Oxford. Clarendon, 2005.

Gallagher, Shaun and Dan Zahavi. *The Phenomenological Mind. An Introduction to Philosophy of Mind and Cognitive Science*. Oxon: Routledge, 2008.

Gantayat, Anoop. "Virtual Console Numbers Revealed." *IGN Entertainment* (November 28, 2007). Available online at <http://wii.ign.com/articles/838/838286p1.html>.

Garcia Landa, José Ángel. "Retroactive Thematization, Interaction, and Interpretation: The Hermeneutic Spiral from Schleiermacher to Goffman." *BELL* (*Belgian Journal of English Language and Literatures*) 2 (2004): 155–166. Available online at <http://www.unizar.es/departamentos/filologia_inglesa/ garciala/publicaciones/spiral.pdf>

Garfinkel, H. *Studies in Ethnomethodology*. Englewood Cliffs, NJ: Prentice-Hall, 1967.

Gassée, Jean-Louis and Howard Rheingold. "The Evolution of Thinking Tools." In *The Art of Human-Computer Interface Design*, edited by Brenda Laurel. Reading, MA: Addison-Wesley, 1990.

Gerstmann, Jeff. "Enter the Matrix Review." *Gamespot.com* (May 20, 2003). Available online at <http://www.gamespot.com/ps2/action/enterthematrix/review.html>.

Gervais, Bertrand. *À l'écoute de la lecture*. Montréal: VLB Éditeur, 1993.

Gibbs, Raymond W. *Embodiment and Cognitive Science*. New York: Cambridge University Press, 2006.

Gibson, James J. *The Ecological Approach to Visual Perception*. Boston: Houghton Mifflin, 1979.

Glinert, Eitan and Lonce Wyse. "AudiOdyssey: An Accessible Video Game for Both Sighted and

Non-Sighted Gamers." In *ACM Future Play 2007*. ACM Digital Library, 2007. Available online at <http://portal.acm.org/>.

Gold, Susan, Tracy Fullerton, Magy Seif-El Nasr, Yusuf Pisan, Darius Kazemi, and Darren Torpey. *IGDA Curriculum Framework: The Study of Games and Game Development*. IGDA Game Education Special Interest Group, February 2008. Available online at <http://www.igda.org/wiki/images/e/ee/Igda2008cf.pdf>.

Government of Singapore. "About Us." *National Research Foundation of Singapore*, November 28, 2007. Available online at <http://www.nrf.gov.sg/nrf/aboutus.aspx?id=92>.

Greenfield, Patricia. "Les jeux vidéo comme instruments de socialisation cognitive," *Réseaux*, 67 (September–October 1994): 33–56.

Greimas, Algirdas Julien. *Du sens : essais sémiotiques*. Paris: Ed. du Seuil, 1992.

Grigsby, Neal, Brett Camper, Alex Chisholm, Henry Jenkins, Eric Klopfer, Scot Osterweil, Judy Perry, Philip Tan, Teo Chor Guan, and Matthew Weise. "From Serious Games to Serious Gaming." In *Serious Games: Learning, Development and Change*, edited by P. Vorderer, M. Cody, and U. Ritterfeld. New Jersey: Routledge/LEA, 2008.

Grodal, Torben. "Stories for Eye, Ear, and Muscles: Video Games, Media, and Embodied Experiences." In *The Video Game Theory Reader*, edited by Mark J. P. Wolf and Bernard Perron. New York: Routledge, 2003, 129–155.

———. "Video Games and the Pleasures of Control." In *Media Entertainment: The Psychology of Its Appeal*, edited by Dolf Zillmann and Peter Vorderer. Mahwah, NJ: Lawrence Erlbaum Associates, 2000, 197–213.

———. *Embodied Visions*. New York: Oxford University Press, forthcoming.

———. *Moving Pictures. A New Theory of Film Genres, Feelings and Cognition*. Oxford: Clarendon Press, 1997.

Guffey, Elizabeth E. *Retro: The Culture of Revival*. London: Reaktion Books, 2006.

Gunning, Tom. "The Cinema of Attractions: Early Film, Its Spectator and the Avant-Garde." *Wide Angle* 8, no. 3–4 (1986): 63–70.

Gygax, Gary, *Role-Playing Mastery*. Glasgow: Grafton Books, 1989.

Haggard, H. Rider. *King Solomon's Mines*. 1885.

Hall, Stuart. "Encoding/Decoding." In *Culture, Media, Language: Working Papers in Cultural Studies, 1972–1979*, edited by Stuart Hall. London: Hutchinson, 1980.

Hawkins, Matthew. "Interview: Rodney Greenblat, Creator of Sony's Almost Mario." *Gamasutra. com* (July 5, 2005). Available online at <http://www.gamasutra.com/features/20050705/hawkins_01.shtml>.

Heaton, Tom. "A Circular Model of Gameplay." *Gamasutra.com* (February 23, 2006). Available online at <http://www.gamasutra.com/features/20060223/heaton_pfv.htm>

Hébert, Louis. "The Canonical Narrative Schema." In *Signo*, edited Louis Hébert (2006). Available online at <http://www.signosemio.com/greimas/a_schemanarratif.asp>.

Heidegger, Martin. *Being and Time*. Oxford: Blackwell, 1988.

Henriot, Jacques. *Sous couleur de jouer*. Paris: José Corti, 1989.

Herdlick, Catherine and Eric Zimmerman. "Redesigning Shopmania: A Design Process Case Study." *IGDA Casual Games Quarterly* 2, no. 1 (2006). Available online at <http://www.igda.org/casual/quarterly/2_1/index.php?id=6>.

Herman, Leonard. *Phoenix: The Fall & Rise of Videogames*. Springfield, NJ: Rolenta Press, 1994. 2nd edition published in 1997.

Hew, K., M. Gibbs, and G. Wadley. "Usability and Sociability of the Xbox Live Voice Channel," paper presented at the *Australian Workshop on Interactive Entertainment*, Sydney, Australia, February, 2004.

Hirschfeld, Lawrence A., and Susan A. Gelman, eds. *Mapping the Mind: Domain Specificity in Cognition and Culture*. Cambridge: Cambridge University Press, 1994.

Hjort, Mette. "From Epiphanic Culture to Circulation: The Dynamics of Globalization in Nordic Cinema." In *Transnational Cinema in a Global North: Nordic Cinema in Transition*. Detroit, MI: Wayne State University Press, 2005.

Hodges, Nicola J., Janet L. Starkes, and Clare MacMahon. "Expert Performance in Sport: A Cognitive Perspective." In *The Cambridge Handbook of Expertise and Expert Performance*, edited by K. Anders Ericsson, Neil Charness, Paul J. Feltovich, and Robert R. Hoffman. Cambridge: Cambridge University Press, 2006, 471–488.

Holland, Walter, Henry Jenkins, and Kurt Squire. "Theory by design." In *The Video Game*

Theory Reader, edited by Mark J. P. Wolf and B. Perron. New York: Routledge, 2003, 25–46.

Holm, D.K. *Independent Cinema*. New York: Oldcastle Books, 2007.

Hopson, John. "We're Not Listening: An Open Letter to Academic Game Researchers." *Gamasutra.com* (November 10, 2006). Available online at <http://gamasutra.com/features/20061110/hopson_01.shtml>.

Horneman, Jurie. "On Academia." *Intelligent Artifice* (December 12, 2004). Available online at <http://www.intelligent-artifice.com/2004/12/on_academia.html>.

Hornsby, Jennifer. "Agency and Actions." In *Agency and Action*, ed. John Hyman and Helen Steward. Cambridge: Cambridge University Press, 2004, 1–23.

_____. *Actions, International Library of Philosophy*. London: Routledge & Kegan Paul, 1980.

Hu, Y. and M. A. Goodale. "Grasping after a Delay Shifts Size-Scaling from Absolute to Relative Metrics." *Journal of Cognitive Neuroscience* 12, no. 5 (2000): 856–868.

Huizinga, Johan. *Homo Ludens: A Study of the Play-Element in Culture*. Boston: Beacon Press, (1938) 1955. Other edition New York: Roy, 1950.

Hunicke, Robin, Marc LeBlanc, and Robert Zubek. "MDA: A Formal Approach to Game Design and Game Research." 2004. Available online at <http://www.cs.northwestern.edu/~hunicke/MDA.pdf>.

Hurley, Susan. "Active Perception and Perceiving Action: The Shared Circuits Model." In *Perceptual Experience*, edited by Tamar Szabó Gendler and John Hawthorne. Oxford: Oxford University Press, 2006, 205–259.

Isbister, Katherine. *Better Game Characters by Design. A Psychological Approach*. San Francisco: Morgan Kaufmann, 2006.

Jacob, Pierre and Marc Jeannerod. *Ways of Seeing. The Scope and Limits of Visual Cognition*. Oxford: Oxford University Press, 2003.

Jaffe, David. "Aaaaaaaaannnnnnnnddddddd Scene!" *Jaffe's Game Design*, November 25, 2007. Available online at <http://criminalcrackdown.blogspot.com/2007_11_25_archive.html>.

Jameson, Fredric. *Postmodernism, Or, the Cultural Logic of Late Capitalism*. Durham: Duke University Press, 1991.

Jardine, Lisa and Michael Silverthorne eds. *Francis Bacon: The New Organon*. Cambridge: Cambridge University Press, 2000.

Järvinen, Aki. *Games without Frontiers. Theories and Methods for Game Studies and Design*. PhD dissertation, University of Tampere, 2008. Available online at <http://acta.uta.fi/english/teos.phtml?11046>.

Jauss, Hans Robert. *Toward an Aesthetic of Reception*. Minneapolis: University of Minnesota Press, 1982.

Jenkins, Henry. *Convergence Culture: Where Old and New Media Collide*. New York: New York University Press, 2006.

_____. *Fans, Bloggers, and Gamers: Exploring Participatory Culture*. New York: New York University Press, 2006.

Johnson, Mark. *The Body in the Mind: The Bodily Basis of Meaning, Imagination and Reason*. Chicago, IL: University of Chicago Press, 1987.

Johnson, Steven. *Everything Bad is Good for You : How's Today's Popular Culture is Actually Making Us Smarter*. New York: Riverhead Books, 2005.

Juul, Jesper. "The Open and the Closed: Games of Emergence and Games of Progression." In *Computer Games and Digital Cultures Conference Proceedings*, ed. Frans Mäyrä. Tampere: Tampere University Press, 2002: 323–329. Available online at <http://www.jesperjuul.net/text/openandtheclosed.html>

_____. *Half-Real: Video Games between Real Rules and Fictional Worlds*. Cambridge, MA: MIT Press, 2005.

_____. "A Certain Level of Abstraction." In *Situated Play—Proceedings of DiGRA 2007 Conference*, edited by Akira Baba (Tokyo: DiGRA Japan, 2007). Available online at <http://www.digra.org/dl/db/07312.29390.pdf>

_____. "Swap Adjacent Gems to Make Sets of Three: A History of Matching Tile Games." *Artifact Journal* (London: Routledge, 2007). Available online at <http://www.jesperjuul.net/text/swapadjacent/>.

Kasavin, Greg. "The Chronicles of Riddick: Escape From Butcher Bay—Developer's Cut Review."

GameSpot.com (December 10, 2004). Available online at <http://www.gamespot.com/pc/action/chroniclesofriddick/review.html>.

Kay, Alan. "Computer Software." *Scientific American* 251, no. 4 (September 1984): 52–59.

Keith, Clinton. "Agile Methodology and Scrum in Game Development," paper presented at *Game Developer Conference 2005*, San Francisco, 2005.

Kelley, John F. "An Iterative Design Methodology for User-Friendly Natural Language Office Information Applications." *ACM Transactions on Office Information Systems* 2, no. 1, (March 1984): 26–41.

Kendall, Lori. *Hanging out in the Virtual Pub: Masculinities and Relationships Online.* Berkeley: University of California Press, 2002.

Kent, Steve L. *The Ultimate History of Video Games: From Pong to Pokemon and Beyond. The Story Behind the Craze that Touched our Lives and Changed the World.* Roseville, CA: Prima, 2001.

Kerr, J. H. and Michael J Apter. *Adult Play: A Reversal Theory Approach.* Amsterdam: Swets and Zeitlinger, 1991.

Kilner, J. M., Y. Paulignan, and S. J. Blakemore. "An Interference Effect of Observed Biological Movement on Action." *Current Biology* 13, no. 6 (2003): 522–525.

Kilner, James, Antonia F. de C. Hamilton, and Sarah-Jayne Blakemore. "Interference Effect of Observed Human Movement on Action is Due to Velocity Profile of Biological Motion." *Social Neuroscience* 2, no. 3 (2007): 158–166.

Kinder, Marsha. *Playing with Power in Movies, Television, and Video Games: FromMuppet Babies to Teenage Mutant Ninja Turtles.* Berkeley: University of California Press, 1991.

King, Geoff. *Spectacular Narratives: Hollywood in the Age of the Blockbuster.* London: I. B. Tauris, 2000.

King, Geoff and Tanya Krzywinska. *Tomb Raiders and Space Invaders: Videogame Forms & Contexts.* London: I. B. Tauris, 2006.

Klein, Julie Thompson. *Crossing Boundaries: Knowledge, Disciplinarities, and Interdisciplinarities.* Charlottesville, VA: University of Virginia Press, 1996.

———. *Interdisciplinarity: History, Theory, and Practice.* Newcastle upon Tyne: Bloodaxe Books, 1991.

Klein, Julie Thompson, Walter Grossenbacher-Mansuy, Rudolf Häberli, Alain Bill, Roland W. Scholz, and Myrtha Welti, eds. *Transdisciplinarity: Joint Problem Solving among Science, Technology, and Society—An Effective Way for Managing Complexity.* Basel: Birkhäuser, 2004.

Kline, Stephen, Nick Dyer-Witheford, and Greig De Peuter, eds. *Digital play: The Interaction of Technology, Culture and Marketing.* Montreal. McGill-Queen's University Press, 2003.

Kluckhohn, C. *Mirror for Man.* New York: McGraw-Hill, 1949.

Kohler, Chris. "A Tour Through *Game Center CX*'s Faux Retrogames." *Wired* (November 16, 2007). Available online at <http://blog.wired.com/games/2007/11/a-tour-through.html>.

———. "Today's Homework: Make Good Games." *Wired Magazine*, February 13, 2007.

Konzack, Lars. "Computer Game Criticism: A Method for Computer Game Analysis." In *CGDC Conference Proceedings*, edited by Frans Mäyrä. Tampere: Tampere University Press, 2002, 89–100. Available online at <http://www.digra.org/dl/db/05164.32231>.

Konzack, Lars and Thessa Lindof, "How Multiplayer Games Create New Media Politics." In *Changing Views: Worlds in Play. Proceedings of DiGRA 2005 Conference*, Vancouver, 2005. Available online at <http://www.digra.org/dl/db/06278.06580.pdf>.

Krzywinska, Tanya. "The Pleasures and Dangers of the Game. Up Close and Personal." *Games and Culture* 1, no. 1 (January 2006): 119–122.

Kubovy, Michael. "On Pleasures of the Mind." In *Well-Being: The Foundations of Hedonic Psychology*, edited by Daniel Kahneman, Ed Diener, and Norbert Schwarz. New York: Russell Sage Foundation, 1999, 134–154.

Kuhn, Thomas S. *The Structure of Scientific Revolutions.* Chicago: University of Chicago Press, 1996.

Lahikainen, Anja Riitta, Pentti Hietala, Tommi Inkinen, Marjatta Kangassalo, Riikka Kivimäki, and Frans Mäyrä, eds. *Lapsuus mediamaailmassa: Näkökulmia lasten tietoyhteiskuntaan.* [Childhood in the World of Media: Views into Children's Information Society.] Helsinki: Gaudeamus, 2005.

Lakoff, George. *Women, Fire, and Dangerous Things: What Categories Reveal About the Mind.* Chicago: University of Chicago Press, 1987.

Lakoff, George and Mark Johnson. *Metaphors We Live By*. Chicago: University of Chicago Press, 1980.

Lasswell, Harold. "The Structure and Function of Communication in Society." In *The Communication of Ideas*, edited by L. Bryson. New York: Institute of religious and social studies, 1948.

Lastowka, Gregory F. and Dan Hunter. "The Laws of Virtual Worlds." *California Law Review*, 2003. Available online at <http://ssrn.com/abstract=402860>.

Lattuca, Lisa R. *Creating Interdisciplinarity: Interdisciplinary Research and Teaching among College and University Faculty*. Nashville, TN: Vanderbilt University Press, 2001.

———. *I am a Game School Dropout*. Game Career Guide, October 4, 2007. Available online at <http://www.gamecareerguide.com/features/435/i_am_a_game_school_.php>.

Lazzaro, Nicole. "Why We Play Games: Four Keys to More Emotion in Player Experiences." Paper presented at the *Game Developers Conference*, San José, 2004. Abstract available online at <http://www.xeodesign.com/whyweplaygames/xeodesign_whyweplaygames.pdf>.

Lentz, Kirsten. "Quality vs. Relevance: Feminism, Race and the Politics of the Sign in 1970s Television." *Camera Obscura* 15 (May 2000): 45–93.

Lin, H. and Sun, C-T. "The 'White-Eyed' Player Culture: Grief Play and Construction of Deviance in MMORPGs." In *Changing Views: Worlds in Play. Proceedings of DiGRA 2005 Conference*, Vancouver, 2005. Available online at <http://ir.lib.sfu.ca/retrieve/1609/5922543c8cba0a282491dbfdfb17.doc>.

Lombard, Matthew and Theresa Ditton. "At the Heart of It All: The Concept of Presence," *Journal of Computer-Mediated Communication*, no. 2 (1997).

Lowenstein, Douglas. "E3Expo 2005 State of the Industry Address." *Entertainment Software Association Archive* (May 18, 2005). Available online at <http://www.theesa.com/archives/2005/05/e3expo_2005_sta.php>.

Malaby, Thomas. "Beyond Play: A New Approach to Games." *Games & Culture*, forthcoming.

Malone, Thomas W. "Heuristics for Designing Enjoyable User Interfaces: Lessons From Computer Games." In *Proceedings of the 1982 Conference on Human Factors in Computing systems*. Gaithersburg, MD: ACM, 1982, 63–68.

Manovich, Lev. *The Language of New Media*. Cambridge, MA: MIT Press, 2001.

Maravita, Angelo, and Atsushi Iriki. "Tools for the Body (Schema)." *Trends in Cognitive Sciences* 8, no. 2 (2004): 79–86.

Massimilla, Bethany. "The Lord of the Rings, The Third Age Review." *Gamespot.com* (November 4, 2004). Available online at <http://www.gamespot.com/ps2/rpg/tlotrthethirdage/review.html>.

Mayer, J. D. and Y. N. Gaschke. "The Experience and Meta-experience of Mood." *Journal of Personality and Social Psychology* 55 (1988): 102–111.

Mäyrä, Frans. *Introduction to Game Studies: Games in Culture*. London: Sage, 2008.

———. "A Moment in the Life of a Generation: Why Game Studies Now?" *Games and Culture* 1, no. 1 (2006): 103–106.

———. "The Quiet Revolution: Three Theses for the Future of Game Studies (Hard Core Columns 4)." *DiGRA.org* (2005). Available online at <http://www.digra.org/hardcore/hc4/>.

Mäyrä, Frans and Koskinen Ilpo, eds. *The Metamorphosis of Home: Research into the Future of Proactive Technologies in Home Environments*. Tampere: Tampere University Press, 2005.

Mäyrä, Frans, Anne Soronen, Ilpo Koskinen, Kristo Kuusela, Jussi Mikkonen, Jukka Vanhala, and Mari Zakrzewski. "Probing a Proactive Home: Challenges in Researching and Designing Everyday Smart Environments." *Human Technology* 2, no. 2 (October 2006). Available online at <http://www.humantechnology.jyu.fi/archives/abstracts/mayra-et-al06.html>.

McCarthy, Anna. *Ambient Television: Visual Culture and Public Space*. Durham, NC: Duke University Press, 2001.

McLuhan, Marshall. *Understanding Media: The Extensions of Man*. New York: McGraw-Hill, 1964.

Merleau-Ponty, Maurice. *Phenomenology of Perception*. London: Routledge & Kegan Paul, 1962.

Microsoft. "*Jetpac Refuelled*." Product description. Available online at <http://www.xbox.com/en-US/games/j/jetpacrefuelledxboxlivearcade/>.

Microsoft. "*Prince of Persia Classic*." Product description. Available online at <http://www.xbox.com/en-US/games/p/princeofpersia xboxlivearcade/>

———. "*Yie Ar Kung Fu*." Product description. Available online at <http://www.xbox.com/en-US/games/y/yiearkungfuxboxlivearcade/>.

Miller, Stephen Paul. *The Seventies Now: Culture as Surveillance*. Durham: Duke University Press, 1999.

Miller, Toby. *Television Studies*. London: BFI, 2002.

Milner, Arthur David and Melvyn A. Goodale. *The Visual Brain in Action, Oxford Psychology Series No. 27*. Oxford: Oxford University Press, 1996.

Montfort, Nick and Ian Bogost. *Video Computer System: The Atari 2600 Platform*. Cambridge, MA: MIT Press, forthcoming.

Montola, Markus. "Exploring the Edge of the Magic Circle: Defining Pervasive Games." In *DAC 2005 Conference Proceedings*. Copenhagen: IT University of Copenhagen, 2005.

Montola, Markus, Annika Waern, and Eva Nieuwdorp. "Domain of Pervasive Gaming." Deliverable D5.3b from the IPerG project, 2006. Available online at <http://iperg.sics.se/Deliverables/D5.3b-Domain-of-Pervasive-Gaming.pdf>.

Moran, Joe. *Interdisciplinarity. The New Critical Idiom*. New York: Routledge, 2001.

Moreau, René. *The Computer Comes of Age: The People, the Hardware, and the Software*. Trans. J. Howlett. Cambridge, MA: MIT Press, 1984.

Mortensen, Torill. "There's Jargon, and There's What I Understand." *Thinking With My Fingers*, October 8, 2007. Available online at <http://torillsin.blogspot.com/2007/10/theres-jargon-and-theres-what-i.html>.

Moules, Nancy J. "Hermeneutic Inquiry: Paying Heed to History and Hermes—An Ancestral, Substantive, and Methodological Tale." *International Journal of Qualitative Methods* 1, no. 3 (2002). Available online at <http://www.ualberta.ca/~ijqm/>.

Msxnet. "Konami SCC Sound Chip." Technical reference. Available online at <http://bifi.msxnet.org/msxnet/tech/scc.html>.

Murray, Janet H. *Hamlet on the Holodeck: The Future of Narrative in Cyberspace*. New York: Free Press, 1997.

Murray, Rebecca. " 'The Wheelman' to be Both a Video Game and Feature Film." *ABOUT.com* (February 28 2006). Available online at <http://movies.about.com/od/dieselvin/a/wheelman022606.htm>.

Myers, David. "Self and Selfishness in Online Social Play." In *Situated Play—Proceedings of DiGRA 2007 Conference*, edited by Akira Baba. Tokyo: DiGRA Japan, 2007. Available online at <http://www.digra.org/dl/db/07312.58121.pdf>.

———. "The Aesthetics of the Anti-Aesthetics." In *Aesthetics of Play Conference Proceedings*, ed.Rune Klevjer. Bergen, Norway: University of Bergen, 2005. Available online at <http://www.aestheticsofplay.org/myers.php>.

———. "Comments on Media Aesthetics and Media Policy," paper presented at the *State of Play II: Reloaded conference*, New York Law School, New York, New York. October 28–30, 2004. Available online at <http://www.loyno.edu/%7Edmyers/F99%20classes/Myers_SoPII_discpaper.rtf>.

———. *The Nature of Computer Games: Play as Semiosis*. New York: Peter Lang, 2003.

Nassiri, N., J. Powell, and D. Moore. "Protecting Personal Space Intelligently in Collaborative Virtual Environments," *IEE Seminar on Intelligent Building Environments* 2 (2005): 230.

New London Group (The), "A Pedagogy of Multiliteracies: Designing Social Futures," *Harvard Educational Review* 66, no.1 (Spring 1996): 60–92.

Noë, Alva. *Action in Perception*. Cambridge, MA: MIT Press, 2004.

Norman, Donald A. *The Design of Everyday Things*. New York: Basic Books, 2002.

Oatley, Keith. *Best Laid Schemes. The Psychology of Emotions*. Cambridge: Cambridge University Press, 1992.

Oatley, Keith and Jennifer M. Jenkins. *Understanding Emotions*. Malden, MA: Blackwell, 1996.

Orland, Kyle. "GameSpot Denies Eidos Pressured Firing of Gerstmann." *Joystiq* (November 30, 2007). Available online at <http://www.joystiq.com/2007/11/30/gamespot-denies-eidos-pressured-firing-of-gertsmann/>.

———. Review of *Milon's Secret Castle* (Hudson Soft). *Games for Lunch*, (December 13, 2007). Available online at <http://gamesforlunch.blogspot.com/2007/12/milons-secret-castle.html>.

Ostrom, E. *Rules, Games, and Common-Pool Resources*. Ann Arbor: University of Michigan Press, 1994.

Ostrom, E., Guha-Khasnobis, B., and Kanbur, R., eds. *Linking the Formal and Informal Economy: Concepts and Policies*. New York: Oxford University Press, 2006.

Pargman, Daniel and Peter Jakobsson. "The Magic is Gone: A Critical Examination of the Gaming Situation." In *Gaming Realities: A Challenge of Digital Culture*, edited by Manthos Santorineos. Athens: Fournos, 2006, 15–22.

Parish, Jeremy. "Metroidvania Chronicles: Faxanadu." Review of *Faxanadu* (Hudson Soft). Available online at <http://www.gamespite.net/toastywiki/index.php/Site/Metroidvania 09Faxanadu>.

Perron, Bernard. "The Heuristic Circle of Gameplay: the Case of Survival Horror." In *Gaming Realities: A Challenge of Digital Culture*, edited by Manthos Santorineos (Athens: Fournos, 2006, 65–66). Available online at <http://www.ludicine.ca/sites/ludicine.ca/files/Perron%20-%20Heuristic%20Circle%20of%20Gameplay%20-%20Mediaterra%202006 pdf>

_____. "A Cognitive Psychological Approach to Gameplay Emotions." In *Changing Views: Worlds in Play. Proceedings of DiGRA 2005 Conference*, Vancouver, 2005. Available online at <http://www.digra.org/dl/db/06276.58345.pdf>.

_____. "From Gamers to Gameplayers. The Example of Interactive Movies." In *The Video Game Theory Reader*, edited by Mark J. P. Wolf and Bernard Perron. New York: Routledge, 2003: 237–258.

Perry, Douglass C. "The Portal Interview." *IGN.com* (July 27, 2006). Available online at <http://pc.ign.com/articles/721/721723p1.html>.

Peterson, Eric. "A License to Review." *Game Developer* Magazine (October 2007): 64.

Polevoi, Robert, "Lesson 83: 3D E-Commerce With MetaStream- Part 3," from his January 5, 2000 column *3-D Animation Workshop*. Available online at <http://www.webreference.com/3d/lesson83/part3.html>.

Prensky, Marc. "Digital Natives, Digital Immigrants." *On the Horizon* 9, no. 5 (October 2001). Available online at <http://www.marcprensky.com/writing/Prensky%20-%20Digital% 20Natives,%20Digital%20Immigrants%20-%20Part1.pdf>

Raessens, Joost. "Playful Identities, or the Ludification of Culture," *Games and Culture* 1, no. 1, 2006: 52–57.

Raessens, Joost and Jeffrey Goldstein, eds. *Handbook of Computer Games Studies*. Cambridge, MA: MIT Press, 2005.

Rasmussen, Terje. "On Distributed Society: The Internet as a Guide to a Sociological Understanding of Communication." In *Digital Media Revisited*, edited by Gunnar Liestol, Andrew Morrison, and Terje Rasmussen. Cambridge, MA: MIT Press, 2003, 443–468.

Ravaja, Niklas, Timo Saari, Jari Laarni, Kari Kallinen, Mikko Salminen, Jussi Holopainen, *et al.* "The Psychophysiology of Video Gaming: Phasic Emotional Responses to Game Events." In *Changing Views: Worlds in Play. Proceedings of DiGRA 2005 Conference*, Vancouver, 2005. Available online at <http://www.digra.org/dl/db/06278.36196.pdf>.

Reeves, Byron and Clifford Nass. *The Media Equation: How People Treat Computers, Television, and New Media Like Real People and Places*. Stanford: CSLI Publications, 1996.

Reynolds, Ren. "Playing a 'Good' Game: A Philosophical Approach to Understanding the Morality of Games," *IGDA.com* (2002). Available online at <http://www.igda.org/articles/rreynolds_ethics.php>.

Richardson, Daniel C., Michael J. Spivey, Lawrence W. Barsalou, and Ken McRae. "Spatial Representations Activated During Real-Time Comprehension of Verbs." *Cognitive Science* 27, no. 5 (2003): 767–780.

Ritchie, David. "Shannon and Weaver: Unraveling the Paradox of Information." *Communication Research* 13, no. 2 (1986): 278–298.

Rizzolatti, G., L. Fogassi, and V. Gallese. "Mirrors in the Mind." *Scientific American* (November 2006).

Roch, Stuart. "The New Studio Model," *Game Developer Magazine* (October 2004): 6.

Rodriguez, M. Andrea and Max J. Egenhofer. "Image-Schemata-Based Spatial Inferences: the Container-Surface Algebra." In *Lecture Notes in Computer Science*, Vol. 1329, edited by Stephen C. Hirtle and Andrew U. Frank. Springer-Verlag: Berlin, 1997, 35–52. Available online at <http://www.spatial.maine.edu/~max/COSIT-CS.pdf>.

Roessler, Johannes and Naomi Eilan, eds. *Agency and Self-Awareness. Issues in Philosophy and Psychology*. Oxford: Oxford University Press, 2003.

Rollings, Andrew and Dave Morris, *Game Architecture and Design*. Scottsdale, AZ: Coriolis, 2000.

Rollings, Andrew and Adams, Ernest. *On Game Design*. Indianapolis: New Riders, 2003.

Roseman, Ira J., Ann Aliki Antoniou, and Paul E. Jose. "Appraisal Determinants of Emotions: Constructing a More Accurate and Comprehensive Theory." *Cognition and Emotion* 10, no. 3 (1996).

Rusli, Evelyn M. "Guitar Hero Rocks Activision." *Forbes.com*, (November 27, 2007). Available online at <http://www.forbes.com/markets/2007/11/27/activision-guitar-hero-markets-equity-cx_er_1127markets13.html>.

Sale, Katie and Eric Zimmerman. *Rules of Play: Game Design Fundamentals*. Cambridge, MA: MIT Press, 2003.

Salen, Katie and Eric Zimmerman, eds. *The Game Design Reader. A Rules of Play Anthology*, Cambridge, MA: MIT Press, 2005.

Sawyer, B. *Monster Gaming: The Complete How-to Guide for Becoming a Hardcore Gamer*. Scottsdale, AZ: Paraglyph, 2003.

Schaeffer, Jean-Marie. *Pourquoi la fiction?* Paris: Éd. du Seuil, 1999.

Schoback, Kathy. "The Economics of a Next-Gen Game." *Game Developers Conference 2005* (March 9, 2005).

Schwaber, K. *Agile Project Management With Scrum*. Redmond, WA, USA: Microsoft Press, 2004.

Scott, A. O. "Wallowing in Music for the Miserable, Then Splashing Down in a Giant Vat of Beer." Review of *The Saddest Music in the World* (film). *New York Times*, April 30, 2004. Available online at <http://query.nytimes.com/gst/fullpage.html?res=9E02EFDD173DF933A05757C0A9629C8B63>.

Seff, Micah. "Happy Feet Dances Its Way to High Sales." *IGN.com* (January 11, 2007). Available online at <http://wii.ign.com/articles/754/754654p1.html>

Shannon, Claude. "A Mathematical Theory of Communication." *The Bell System Technical Journal* 27 (1948): 623–656.

Sheets-Johnstone, Maxine. *The Roots of Thinking*. Philadelphia: Temple University Press, 1990.

Sherry, John. "The Effects of Violent Video Games on Aggression: A Meta-Analysis." *Human Communication Research* 27 (2001): 409–431.

Shigemo. "FFXI Japanese language (Nihongo) guide," 2004. Available online at <http://shigemo.com/FFXI/nihongo_guide.html>.

Smith, Edward E. and Stephen M. Kosslyn. *Cognitive Psychology: Mind and Brain 1*. Upper Saddle River, NJ: Pearson/Prentice Hall, 2007.

Smith, Jonas Heide. "Plans and Purposes: How Video Games Shape Player Behavior." PhD dissertation, IT University of Copenhagen, 2006.

Smith, Murray. *Engaging Characters: Fiction, Emotion, and the Cinema*. New York: Oxford University Press 1995.

Smith, Peter K., ed. *Play in Animals and Humans*. Oxford: Basil Blackwell, Inc, 1984.

Sotamaa, Olli, Laura Ermi, Anu Jäppinen, Tero Laukkanen, Frans Mäyrä, and Jani Nummela, "The Role of Players in Game Design: A Methodological Perspective." In *Digital Arts and Culture DAC 2005 Conference Proceedings*. IT University of Copenhagen, 2005, 34–42.

Spariosu, Mihai I. *Dionysus Reborn: Play and the Aesthetic Dimension in Modern Philosophical and Scientific Discourse*. Ithaca, NY: Cornell University Press, 1989.

Spelke, Elizabeth S. "Core Knowledge." *American Psychologist* 55, no. 11 (2000): 1230–1233.

Spelke, Elizabeth S. and Katherine D. Kinzler. "Core Knowledge." *Developmental Science* 10, no. 1 (2007): 89–96.

Spencer-Brown, George. *Laws of Form*. New York: The Julian Press, 1972.

Spigel, Lynn. *Make Room for TV: Television and the Family Ideal in Postwar America*. Chicago: University of Chicago Press, 1992.

Steel, Wade. "Halo Film Planned for 2007: Fox and Universal to Bring Master Chief to the Silver Screen." *IGN.Com* (August 23, 2005). Available online at <http://xbox360.ign.com/articles/644/644458p1.html>.

Steinkuehler, C. and Williams, D. "Where Everybody Knows Your (Screen) Name: Online Games as 'Third Places'." *Journal of Computer-Mediated Communication* 11, no. 4 (2006).

Stromer-Galley, Jennifer and Rosa Mikeal Martey. "The digital dollhouse: Context and social norms in The Sims Online." *Games & Culture* 2, no. 4 (2007): 314–334.

Suber, Peter. *The Paradoxes of Self-Amendment: A Study of Logic, Law, Ominipotence, and Change*. New York: Peter Lang, 1990. Available online at <http://www.earlham.edu/~peters/writing/psa/index.htm>.

Suits, Bernard. *The Grasshopper: Games, Life and Utopia*. Toronto: University of Toronto Press, 1978. Other edition: Boston: David R. Godine, 1990.

Sutton-Smith, Brian. *The Ambiguity of Play*. Cambridge, MA: Harvard University Press, 1997.

Swift, Kim. "From Narbacular Drop To Portal." Paper presented at *Game Developer Conference 2007*, San Francisco, 2007.

Takahashi, Dean. *Opening the Xbox*. Roseville, CA: Prima Publishing, 2002.

Tan, Philip, Matthew Wiese, Brett Camper, Nicholas Hunter, Henry Jenkins III, *et al. Revolution*. USA: The Education Arcade, 2005.

Taylor, T. L. *Play between Worlds: Exploring Online Game Culture*. Cambridge, MA: MIT Press. 2006.

———. "Does WoW Change Everything? How a PvP server, Multinational Player Base and Surveillance Mod Scene Caused Me Pause." *Games & Culture* 1, no. 4 (2006): 318–337.

Tennenhouse, David. "Proactive Computing." *Communications of the ACM* 43, no. 5 (May 2000): 43–50.

Texas Instruments. "TMS9918A/TMS9928A/TMS9929A Video Display Processors." Technical reference. Available online at <http://emu-docs.org/VDP%20TMS9918/Datasheets/TMS9918.pdf>.

"The New Games Journalism." *Penny Arcade* (30 November 2007). Available online at <http://www.penny-arcade.com/2007/11/30#1196409660>.

Thomas, David, Kyle Orland, and Scott Steinberg. *The Videogame Style Guide and Reference Manual*. London: Power Play Publishing, 2007. Also available online at <http://www.gamestyleguide.com>.

Tomasello, Michael. *The Cultural Origins of Human Cognition*. Cambridge, MA: Harvard University Press, 1999.

Turner, Victor. *The Ritual Process Structure and Anti-Structure*. Chicago: Aldine Publishing Co., 1969.

Von Wright, Georg Henrik. *Explanation and Understanding*. Ithaca: Cornell University Press, 1971.

Vorderer, Peter, Christoph Klimmt, and Ute Ritterfeld. "Enjoyment: At the Heart of Media Entertainment." *Communication Theory* 14 (2004): 388–408.

Waldrop, Judith, Sharon M. Stern, and US Census Bureau. *Disability Status, 2000*: US Dept. of Commerce, Economics and Statistics Administration, US Census Bureau, 2003.

Weaver, Warren. "Recent Contributions to the Mathematical Theory of Communication," 1949. Available online at <http://grace.evergreen.edu/~arunc/texts/cybernetics/weaver.pdf>.

Wegner, Daniel M. *The Illusion of Conscious Will*. Cambridge, MA: MIT Press, 2002.

Wegner, Daniel M. and Betsy Sparrow. "Authorship Processing." In *The Cognitive Neurosciences*, 3rd edn, edited by Michael S. Gazzaniga. Cambridge, MA: MIT Press, 2004, 1201–1209.

Wikipedia. "Konami SCC." Technical reference. Available online at <http://en.wikipedia.org/wiki/Konami_SCC>.

Williams, Dmitri, Scott Caplan, and Li Xiong. "Can You Hear Me Now? The Social Impact of Voice in Online Communities." *Human Communication Research* 33, no. 4 (2007): 427–449.

Williams, Raymond. *Television; Technology and Cultural Form*. London: Fontana, 1974.

Winnicott, Donald Woods. *Jeu et réalité. L'espace potentiel*. Paris: Gallimard, 1971.

Winston, Brian. *Media Technology and Society: A History from the Telegraph to the Internet*. London: Routledge, 1998.

Wolf, Mark J. P. "Assessing Interactivity in Video Game Design," *Mechademia 1: Emerging Worlds of Anime and Manga*, of the series *Mechademia: An Annual Forum for Anime, Manga and The Fan Arts*, December 2006: 78–86.

Wolf, Mark J. P., ed. *The Video Game Explosion: A History from PONG to PlayStation and Beyond*. Westport: Greenwood Press, 2007.

———. *The Medium of the Video Game*. Austin: University of Texas Press, 2001.

Wolf, Mark J. P. and Bernard Perron, eds. "Introduction." In *The Video Game Theory Reader*, New York: Routledge, 2003, 1–24.

Zielinski, Siegfried. *Audiovisions: Cinema and Television as Entr'Actes in History*. Amsterdam: Amsterdam University Press, 1999.

Zillman, Dolf. "Mechanisms of Emotional Involvement with Drama." *Poetics* 23, no. 1 (1995): 33–51.

About the Contributors

Thomas H. Apperley is a Research Fellow in Literacy Education at Deakin University in Melbourne, Australia. His book *Videogame Audiences: Local Practices, Global Cultures* is forthcoming from Peter Lang. [thomas. apperley@deakin.edu.au]

Samuel Archibald is a postdoctoral fellow at the University of Poitiers, France. He works with the research group *B3: Esthétiques comparées* ("Comparative Aesthetics") under the supervision of Professor Denis Mellier. His current research is devoted to the remediation of print and film fictions through the Internet and its interplay with readers, spectators, and users alike. He has a PhD degree in Semiotics from the University of Quebec in Montreal (UQAM), where in 2007 he defended a thesis entitled "The Text Meets the *Technique*: Reading in a Digital Age". He has published articles on the interplay between narrative textuality and gameplay in video games, digital fictions and fictional identities on the Web, e-poetry, and the overall impact of materiality over the reception of literature, films and digital media. Samuel Archibald is also affiliated with the *Nt2, laboratoire de recherche sur les nouvelles formes de textes et de fictions* (a research unit studying new fictional and textual forms), based in Montreal. [archibald.samuel@gmail.com]

Dominic Arsenault is a PhD student at the University of Montreal's department of Film Studies and Art History, and holds a scholarship from the Social Sciences and Humanities Research Council of Canada. Before entering the academic world, he was employed as a game writer for a start-up studio named Evillusion. Since then he has presented, written, and lectured on narration in the video game, fictional and systemic immersion, design issues, and coherence between game rules and narratives, with a hint of thoughts on music for added flavor. He is currently working on the notions of genre, continuity, and innovation in video games for his thesis, and developing a live multiplayer game/music show/art performance prototype. He enjoys some limited Internet presence on his website. [http://www.le-ludophile.com], [dominic@le-ludophile.com]

Mark W. Bell is a PhD student in the Indiana University Telecommunications Department. He studies virtual worlds and social networking with the Synthetic Worlds Initiative. Previously, he spent 15 years in the software development industry. Mark is highly involved in the Second Life research community, managing the SL Researchers mailing list and presenting at several conferences, including NCA and AoIR. Mark has published on the Web 2.0, Second Life, graphic novels and technical books. [bellmw@indiana.edu]

Tom Boellstorff is Associate Professor in the Department of Anthropology at the University of California, Irvine, and Editor-in-Chief of *American Anthropologist*, the flagship journal of the American Anthropological Association. His research projects have focused on questions of sexuality, globalization, nationalism, HIV/AIDS, and cybersociality. He is the author of *The Gay Archipelago: Sexuality and Nation in Indonesia* (Princeton University Press, 2005), winner of the 2005 Ruth Benedict Award from the Society of Lesbian and Gay Anthropologists; *A Coincidence of Desires: Anthropology, Queer Studies, Indonesia* (Duke University Press, 2007); and *Coming of Age in Second Life: An Anthropologist Explores the Virtually Human* (Princeton University Press, 2008). He is also co-editor of *Speaking in Queer Tongues: Globalization and Gay Language* (University of Illinois Press, 2004), and author of publications in *American Anthropologist, American Ethnologist, Cultural Anthropology, Annual Review of Anthropology, Journal of Asian Studies, Journal of Linguistic Anthropology, Games and Culture, Ethnos*, and *GLQ: A Journal of Lesbian and Gay Studies*. [tboellst@uci.edu]

Brett Camper studies the history and practice of independent media production and distribution, with an emphasis on video games. He has spent the past nine years in digital media and software development in academia and industry, and is currently a product manager designing online media services. Formerly, he was the research manager at MIT's Education Arcade group, where he served as a designer and technical lead for the multiplayer history role-playing game Revolution. Before coming to MIT, he was a program manager for the e-commerce platform of Internet media pioneer RealNetworks. An independent developer himself, he has created games for the PC, Nintendo's Game Boy Advance handheld platform, and Macromedia Flash. He holds an MSc in Comparative Media Studies from MIT. [bcamper@alum.mit.edu]

Edward Castronova holds a PhD in Economics from Wisconsin, 1991. He is an Associate Professor in the Department of Telecommunications at Indiana University, Bloomington. He is an expert on the economies of large-scale online games and has numerous publications on that topic. His latest is a book, *Exodus to the Virtual World: How Online Fun is Changing Reality* (2007). [castro@indiana.edu]

Mia Consalvo is the Associate Director of Graduate Studies and Associate Professor in the School of Media Arts & Studies at Ohio University. She teaches courses in the theory of digital games, digital games and global culture, cultural and critical theory, and textual analysis. She is the author of *Cheating: Gaining Advantage in Video games* (MIT Press, 2007), and was executive editor of the Association of Internet Researchers' *Research Annual* series. She is currently co-editor of *The Blackwell Handbook of Internet Studies* with Charles Ess and Robert Burnett, to be published in 2008. Her research focuses on the hybrid character of the global games industry, as well as gender and sexuality as related to digital gameplay. She has published related work in *The Video Game Theory Reader*, as well as the journals *Game Studies, Games & Culture, Television & New Media*, and *The International Review of Information Ethics*. She currently serves as Vice President of the Association of Internet Researchers, and she serves on the steering committee of Women in Games International. Mia is a regular speaker at the annual Game Developers Conference, and has given more than 60 national and international conference and invited presentations. [consalvo@ohio.edu]

Robert Cornell hails from an anthropology background (BA, Beloit College, 2007) and has participated in numerous ethnographic research projects in virtual worlds (funded by the McNair Scholars Program). In the fall of 2007, he joined the graduate program of telecommunications at Indiana University. Active in the Synthetic Worlds Initiative, his current research interests include application of cultural complexity theory to online domains, and using virtual worlds as social science research spaces. [robcorne@indiana.edu]

James J. Cummings is a graduate student within the Department of Telecommunications at Indiana University. With a background in psychology and anthropology, his research interests pertain to the motivational structure and hedonic value of games and modern media as approached from an evolutionary perspective, as well as the how these technologies may be designed and employed for both learning and advocacy. [cummingj@indiana.edu]

Shanly Dixon is a lecturer and a PhD student in the Humanities Doctoral Interdisciplinary Studies in Society and Culture Program at Concordia University in Montreal. Her disciplines include Sociology, Communication, and Education. She researches young people's engagement with new media and digital technology. She has co-edited the book *Growing Up Online: Young People and Digital Technologies* (2007). [dixons@alcor.concordia.ca]

Trevor Elkington is Senior Associate Producer at Midway's Surreal Software studio in Seattle, Washington. Previously, he worked as a Producer for Sony Computer Entertainment, America (SCEA). Prior to turning to video game development, Trevor was Assistant Professor of Popular Culture at the University of Copenhagen, Denmark, and has taught literature and media studies at the University of Washington. He is the author of numerous articles on media, film, and literature, as well as co-editor of the essay collection *Transnational Cinema in a Global North: Nordic Cinema in Transition*, which positions the film industries of the five Nordic countries in a globalized context. He received his PhD in Comparative Literature from the University of Washington in 2001. [trevorelkington@hotmail.com]

Matthew Falk earned his BSc and MA at Ohio University. He is currently a PhD student in Telecommunications at Indiana University, working with the Synthetic Worlds Initiative. His research is focused on models of gamer behavior and player motivation, and he is interested in the development of virtual worlds for social science research. [mfalk@indiana.edu]

Richard E. Ferdig is an Associate Professor of Educational Technology at the University of Florida's College of Education. His research interests focus on educational gaming, the uses of innovative media for teaching and learning, virtual and online education, and what he calls a "deeper psychology of technology". He graduated from Calvin College with a BA in Psychology and from Michigan State University with an MA in Educational Psychology. He received his PhD from Michigan State University in Educational Psychology. At UF, he co-directs the face-to-face and online graduate programs in Educational Technology. [rferdig@gmail.com]

Clara Fernández-Vara is a Research Associate in Singapore-MIT GAMBIT Game Lab, as well as a PhD candidate in Digital Media from the Georgia Institute of Technology. Her research concentrates on the development of video game theory, focusing on adventure games, and the design of players' experience with the aid of storytelling. She is particularly interested in applying performance theory and textual analysis to the study of video games. [telmah@mit.edu]

Alida Field is a graduate student in the Telecommunications Department at Indiana University. [acfield@indiana.edu]

Sébastien Genvo is Professor in Information and Communication Sciences at the University of Limoges (IUT du Limousin), Centre de recherches sémiotiques (CeReS). A former game designer and author of several publications on video gaming, his research relates to the aesthetic, cultural, economic, and ideological aspects of this medium. He has edited a book entitled *Le game design de jeux vidéo. Approches de l'expression vidéoludique*, published by L'Harmattan in 2006, and has recently edited an issue of the journal *Médiamorphoses* (from the Institut National de l'Audiovisuel) on the history and culture of the medium. [sebastien. genvo@wanadoo.fr], [sebgenvo@yahoo.fr]

Eitan Glinert is a MIT graduate student at the Singapore-MIT GAMBIT game lab whose research centers on highly usable and accessible video game interfaces. He was the project lead on *AudiOdyssey* (2007) an innovative Wiimote rhythm game designed for a mainstream audience yet completely playable by the visually impaired. Before coming to MIT, Eitan worked at the Federation of American Scientists on *Immune Attack* (still in development), an educational video game that teaches immunology to high school students in a fun and engaging way. [glinert@alum.mit.edu]

Garry C. Gray is a Post-Doctoral Fellow at the Institute for Work & Health and he also works with the Canadian SSHRC Community-University Research Action Alliance on the Consequences of Work Injury. He received his PhD in 2008 (Sociology of Law, University of Toronto) and holds a Master's Degree in Criminology. He is a past recipient of the Best Graduate Article Award in the Law & Society Section of the American Sociological Association. His overall research focus is on issues of law, regulation, and risk (with special attention to workplace safety). He has previously published in *Criminal Justice Review* (2007), *British Journal of Criminology* (2006), *Studies in Law, Politics and Society* (2002), and is currently a special guest editor with *Human Relations* (2009). He has also undertaken research on the self-regulation of virtual reality and issues of voluntary compliance and enforcement in the video game industry (*Canadian Journal of Law and Society*, 2007). [garry.gray@utoronto.ca]

Andreas Gregersen is, at the time of this writing, finishing his PhD thesis at the University of Copenhagen's Department of Media, Cognition, and Communication. His thesis is on computer game system structure and core cognitive capacities (i.e., perception and action), embodiment, and play. The general argument is that the framework allows one to connect material and formal structures to functionality. [agr@hum.ku.dk]

Neal Grigsby was the design lead on GAMBIT's mobile phone video game *Backflow* (2007). He earned his Master's degree from the MIT Comparative Media Studies Program in 2007, where he researched youth, games, and media literacy, and wrote his thesis on narratives of adolescence. He is a producer and designer of interactive media who has helped develop websites including Tikatok and Looksmart. Neal also holds a Bachelor's degree in film studies from UC Berkeley, where he met his wife, the artist Rebecca Bird Grigsby. [ngrigsby@alum.mit.edu]

Torben Grodal is professor at the University of Copenhagen in the Department of Media, Cognition, and Communication. Besides books and articles in Danish on literature, he has published *Moving Pictures, a New Theory of Genre, Feelings and Cognition* (1997) and *Filmoplevelser* (2007), an advanced introduction to film theory. He has also edited a book *Visual Authorship: Creativity and Intentionality in Media* (2004) and written a series of articles on film emotions, narrative theory, art films, video games, evolutionary film theory, and intertextuality. He has just finished a new book: *Embodied Visions: Evolution, Emotion, Culture, and Film* that is forthcoming from Oxford University Press. [grodal@hum.ku.dk]

Carrie Heeter is a Professor of Telecommunication, Information Studies, and Media; Principal Investigator in the GEL Lab (Games, Entertainment, and Learning); Creative Director for Virtual University Design and Technology; and Adjunct Professor of Education at Michigan State University. She has studied and designed interactive experiences from the early days of multimedia to the exciting promise of virtual reality and the amazing reach of the Internet. Games bring all of those strands together with remarkable potential. Heeter co-founded the Serious Game Design

M. A. emphasis and teaches graduate classes in Design Research. Her recent game design work focuses on games to adapt to individual players' play style and learning style, games to maintain and improve cognitive performance, and decision-making games. Her research focuses on the intersection of design, interactivity, and player impacts. She is editor in chief of investiGaming.com, an online gateway to research about gender, gaming, and computing and co-editor of the forthcoming book, *Beyond Barbie and Mortal Kombat: New Perspectives in Gender, Gaming, and Computing*. [http://investigaming.com], [http://seriousgames.msu.edu/], [http://commtechlab.msu.edu/principals/carrie.html], [heeter@msu.edu]

Aki Järvinen has been studying and developing games since 1998. He has experience both from academia and the game industry. His doctoral dissertation "Games without Frontiers: Theories and Methods for Game Studies and Design," focused on games and game play from perspectives of psychology and design research. Järvinen works as a lecturer, consultant, and designer in the game and entertainment industries. [aki@gameswithoutfrontiers.net]

Henry Jenkins is the Co-Director of the MIT Comparative Media Studies Program and the Peter de Florez Professor of Humanities. He is the author and/or editor of twelve books on various aspects of media and popular culture, including *The Wow Climax: Tracing the Emotional Impact of Popular Culture* (2006); *Convergence Culture: Where Old and New Media Collide* (2006); *Fans, Bloggers and Gamers: Exploring Participatory Culture* (2006); *Hop on Pop: The Politics and Pleasures of Popular Culture* (2003); *From Barbie to Mortal Kombat: Gender and Computer Games* (1998); and *Textual Poachers: Television Fans and Participatory Culture* (1992). Jenkins writes regularly about media and cultural change at his blog, henryjenkins.org. He is one of the principal investigators for The Education Arcade, a consortium of educators and business leaders working to promote the educational use of computer and video games and of the Knight Center for Future Civic Media, a joint effort with the MIT Media Lab to use new media to enhance how people live in local communities. He is one of the principle investigators for GAMBIT, a lab focused on promoting experimentation through game design, and of Project nml, a MacArthur Foundation funded project that develops curricular materials focused on promoting the social skills and cultural competencies needed to become a full participant in the new media era. Jenkins has an MA in Communication Studies from the University of Iowa and a PhD in Communication Arts from the University of Wisconsin-Madison. [henry3@mit.edu]

Jesper Juul is a video game researcher at the Singapore-MIT GAMBIT game lab in Cambridge, and has worked with video game theory since the late 1990s. Originally trained in literature, his work has included early discussions of games as non-narrative, game structure, game definitions, the interplay of rules and fiction, player perceptions of failure in games, and video game history. Prior to working at MIT, he was an assistant professor in video game theory and design at the Centre for Computer Game Research Copenhagen where he also earned his PhD. His book *Half-Real* on video game theory was published by MIT Press in 2005. Alongside his academic work, he has worked as a game designer and programmer, making CD-ROM titles, multiplayer web-based games, and downloadable games. He is currently working on a book project on the subject of casual games. [http://www.jesperjuul.net/], [j@jesperjuul.net]

Lars Konzack is an assistant professor in multimedia at Aalborg University, Denmark. He has an MA in information science and a PhD in Multimedia. He is working with subjects such as ludology, game analysis and design, geek culture, and sub-creation. He has, among others, published "Computer Game Criticism: A Method for Computer Game Analysis" (2002) and "Rhetorics of Computer and Video Game Research" (2007). [konzack.blogspot.com], [lars@konzack.dk]

Vili Lehdonvirta graduated from Helsinki University of Technology in 2005 with an MSc (Tech.) in Electronic Business, and is currently pursuing a PhD degree in economic sociology at Turku School of Economics, Finland. He works as a researcher at Helsinki Institute for Information Technology HIIT, focusing on virtual consumption and real-money trade of virtual property. [vili.lehdonvirta@hiit.fi]

Tuukka Lehtiniemi received an MSc (Tech) degree from Helsinki University of Technology in 2006 and a MSocSci (Economics) degree from University of Helsinki in 2008. He works as a researcher at Helsinki Institute for Information Technology HIIT, concentrating on applying economics in the study of virtual economies. [tuukka.lehtiniemi@hiit.fi]

Lev Manovich is the author of *Soft Cinema: Navigating the Database* (The MIT Press, 2005), and *The Language of New Media* (The MIT Press, 2001) which was hailed as "the most suggestive and broad ranging media history since Marshall McLuhan". He has also written 90+ articles which have been reprinted over 300 times in many countries, earning him the reputation of "the world's most widely-read new media theorist". Manovich is a Professor in Visual Arts Department, University of California, San

Diego; a Director of the Software Studies Initiative at California Institute
for Telecommunications and Information Technology (CALIT2); and a
Visiting Research Professor at Godsmith College (London) and College
of Fine Arts, University of New South Wales (Sydney). He is much in
demand to speak about digital culture, having conducted 285 lectures
and seminars to date around the world. [www.manovich.net)],
[manovich@ucsd.edu]

Frans Mäyrä has studied the relationship of culture and technology from
the early 1990s. He has specialized in the cultural analysis of technology,
particularly on the ambiguous, conflicting and heterogeneous elements
in this relationship, and has published on topics that range from information technologies, science fiction and fantasy, to the demonic tradition,
the concept of identity and role-playing games. He is currently teaching,
researching, and heading numerous research projects in the study and
development of games, new media, and digital culture. He has also
served as the founding President of the Digital Games Research Association (DiGRA). Publications: *Koneihminen* (Man-Machine; editor, 1997),
Demonic Texts and Textual Demons (1999), *Johdatus digitaaliseen kult-
tuuriin* (Introduction to Digital Culture; editor, 1999), *CGDC Conference
Proceedings* (editor, 2002), *Lapsuus mediamaailmassa* (Childhood in the
World of Media, editor, 2005), *The Metamorphosis of Home* (editor, 2005),
An Introduction to Game Studies (2008). [http://www.uta.fi/~frans.mayra/],
[http://www.unet.fi/fransblog], [frans.mayra@uta.fi]

Michael McGuffin is an Assistant Professor in the Department of Software
and IT Engineering at the École de Technologie Supérieure, an engineering
school within the University of Quebec in Montreal. His research interests
lie in human-computer interaction, information visualization, and interactive computer graphics. He was previously a post-doctoral researcher at
the Ontario Cancer Institute, working on visualization and user interfaces
for bioinformatics, within Dr. Igor Jurisica's lab. He completed a PhD in
Computer Science at the University of Toronto, where his homebase was
the Dynamic Graphics Project (DGP) lab, with Professor Ravin
Balakrishnan as advisor. He has over three years of experience developing
user interfaces at software companies, including the computer graphics
companies Alias|Wavefront in Toronto and Discreet Logic in Montreal
(both companies now part of Autodesk). The first video game he programmed was for a TRS-80 computer with a black-and-white screen, 64 kB
of RAM, and cassette tape storage. During his PhD studies, his productivity
sharply declined after his lab acquired an Xbox game console, and sharply

rose after the console was stolen by an anonymous savior. [http://profs. logti.etsmtl.ca/mjm/], [michael.mcguffin@etsmtl.ca]

Sheila C. Murphy is an Assistant Professor in the Department of Screen Arts and Cultures at the University of Michigan. Her work and teaching are centered around new media theory, video games, Internet media, and cultural reception. She is currently working on a book entitled *iLook: Visuality and Experience in Digital Culture* that examines the relationships between old and new media modes, visualities and objects ranging from television, computers and the Internet to digital games and simulations. She blames her lack of video game skills on the highly gendered dynamic of playing video games with her siblings as a younger person. [scmurphy@umich.edu]

David Myers is Distinguished Professor of Communication within the School of Mass Communication at Loyola University, New Orleans, USA. He was one of the first scholars to extend the study of games and play to include analyses of video games in an article published in *Simulation & Gaming* in 1984. His monograph on the use of signs and symbols in video games, *The Nature of Computer Games: Play as Semiosis* (Peter Lang), appeared in 2003. He continues to write and publish internationally on the formal characteristics of video games and human play. [dmyers@loyno.edu]

Bernard Perron is an Associate Professor of Cinema at the University of Montreal. He has co-edited *The Video Game Theory Reader* (New York: Routledge, 2003). He has written *Silent Hill: il motore del terrore* (Milan: Costa & Nolan, 2006), an analysis of the Silent Hill video game series. He has also edited issues on play for *Intermedialities* (Montreal, 2007), on cinema and cognition for *Cinemas: Journal of Films Studies* (Montreal, 2002), and co-edited one on intermedial practices of montage and configurations of alternation in early cinema for *Cinema & Cie* (Milan, 2007). His research and writings concentrate on editing in early cinema; on narration, cognition, and the ludic dimension of narrative cinema; and on interactive cinema and video games. [<http://www.ludicine.ca/>], [bernard.perron@umontreal.ca]

Martin Picard is a PhD candidate in Comparative Literature and Film Studies and Part-time Lecturer in the History of Art and Film Studies Department at the University of Montreal. His publications and research interests cover film and digital media, video game culture and theory, and

Japanese film and aesthetics. He is currently writing a thesis on the relationship between the aesthetics of video games and cinema. [martinpicard@videotron.ca]

Patrick Poulin is a PhD student in comparative literature at the Université de Montréal. He has completed a Master's degree in comparative literature, with a Master's thesis on the *Silent Hill* video game series. His fields of study include contemporary philosophy (Deleuze, Foucault, Agamben), literature (Joyce, Kafka), contemporary aesthetics, and new media theory. Patrick Poulin published his first fiction book *Morts de Low Bat* in January of 2007 (Quartanier), and he has since participated in several literary events. He is also a regular contributor to *Etc.* contemporary art magazine, *ovni* literary review, and *Esse*, and he works as a coordinative editor for *Intermédialités.* [poulin.patrick@gmail.com]

Pierre Poulin is Professor of Computer Graphics in the Computer Science and Operations Research Department of the University of Montreal. He is interested in realism and the efficiency of images and animations in all kinds of applications. He has developed an internationally recognized expertise on a wide range of computer graphics topics, including reflection models, shadowing algorithms, local and global illumination, image-based automatic and interactive modeling, several natural phenomena, facial animation, fire and fluid animation, hardware real-time rendering, and software visualization. He was co-chair of three international conferences, appeared on program committees of more than 30 international conferences, and is sought as a reviewer for more than 30 papers each year. He currently supervises more than 10 graduate students, and the majority of his 35 graduated students work in the computer graphics industry in Montreal. [http://www.iro.umontreal.ca/~poulin], [Pierre.Poulin@umontreal.ca]

Sarah B. Robbins-Bell (the "Intellagirl") is a PhD candidate in Rhetoric at Ball State University, Muncie, Indiana. She is the co-author of *Second Life for Dummies* and has been teaching university courses using *Second Life* for several years. Sarah's research centers around methods to classify the communication mechanics in virtual worlds as a basis for research methods in the future. [http://www.intellagirl.com], [intellagirl@gmail.com]

Travis Ross holds a Master's of Information Science from Indiana University, and a BSc in Computer Science from Indiana University Southeast. In the past he worked as a software developer for Samtec, Inc.

and Service Net—both relatively small but fast-growing companies in Louisville, Kentucky. More recently, he had the opportunity to serve the United States Peace Corps as an Information Technology/Education Volunteer in Bartica, Guyana. His Peace Corps work allowed him to experience firsthand the promise technology, particularly gaming, holds for literacy and education in the developing world. For the last year he has been involved in the production and management of *Arden: World of William Shakespeare*, a virtual world intended for use as a laboratory for social science experimentation. His general research interests include the effects of ICTs on society, virtual worlds, sustainable computing in the developing world, video game production, and game theory. Specifically, he would like to examine topics such as modeling player behavior in virtual worlds; success and failure in game development teams; online governance; and game technology as a tool for improving existing real world policy or vice-versa. [trlross@indiana.edu]

Guillaume Roux-Girard is a Master's Degree student in Film Studies at the University of Montreal. His research concentrates on sound in horror video games. [guillaume.roux-girard@umontreal.ca]

Kevin Schut is an Assistant Professor in the Department of Communications at Trinity Western University in Langley, BC, Canada. He received his PhD in Communication Studies at the University of Iowa in 2004, with a focus on Media Ecology theory, Social Construction of Technology theory, and critical cultural studies. His research interests are the intersection of culture, technology, faith, and history, and he finds that computer and video games are a perfect place to investigate this. He has published articles and chapters on fantasy role-playing games and masculinity, mythology in computer games, Evangelicals and games, and the presentation of history in strategy games. As of the time of writing, he is in the midst of his first game production project, working with a colleague and multi-disciplinary team of students to produce and market *Label: Rise of Band*, a small, turn-based strategy game. He is pretty sure that *Civilization* is a plot to make him waste time, and he will get around to fixing that after finishing the next turn. [Kevin.Schut@twu.ca]

Michael Seare is a Senior Software Engineer at THQ's Incinerator Studios in San Diego, California. His five-year experience in video games has centered primarily on animation and physics, but he often finds himself writing low-level systems, tools, and user-interface code. Michael started his career in software development in 1999 where he worked in the robotics and defense industries. When Michael is not flipping bits on a computer, he enjoys spending time with his wife and daughter, running along the beach, and playing video games. [michaelseare@yahoo.com]

Tim Skelly is the author of the classic Cinematronics vector-based arcade games *Star Hawk* (1978), *Sundance* (1978), *Warrior* (1979), *Rip-Off* (1980), *Star Castle* (1980) and *Armor Attack* (1981). His non-vector games for D. Gottlieb/Mylstar include *Reactor* (1982), *Insector* (1983) and *Screw Loose* (1984). Today, these games are highly prized by collectors. He is an artist and illustrator of several books and magazine articles and is the author of *Shoot the Robot, Then Shoot Mom* (1983), a book of cartoons about classic arcade games. In 1985, as part of a small group of friends and fellow game veterans, he co-founded Incredible Technologies. While there, he was responsible for the visual aspects of all products. He devised and created the primary screen displays for Virtual Worlds' original *BattleTech Center* (1990) and for that project designed the Mad Cat and other Clan OmniMechs. During his time at Incredible Technologies, he took an interest in human-computer interface issues and, drawing upon his video game experiences, became active in the HCI community. After a stint as Art Director with the SEGA Technical Institute, where he contributed to *Sonic the Hedgehog 2* (1992), he was recruited to be one of the first researchers in the Microsoft User Interface Research Group. While at Microsoft, he lectured often on campus and at conferences on the topic of "Seductive Interfaces" his research into how user interfaces affect the user. Partially because of that work, he was appointed to the 1996 Panel on Human-Computer Interface Technologies by the US Government. He helped found Microsoft's Life-like Computer Character Conference and has contributed to conferences held by the AAAI, ACM SIGGRAPH and ACM SIGCHI, presenting tutorials on interface design. He has been a member of the advisory board and a contributor to Wiley's *Handbook of Interface Design* (1997) and for a number of years was a member of the editorial advisory board for Morgan Kaufmann's series of user interface related books. [tskelly@gmail.com]

Philip Tan is the US Executive Director of the Singapore-MIT GAMBIT Game Lab, a multi-year game innovation initiative hosted at the Massachusetts Institute of Technology. Prior to his current position, he worked closely with game developers in Singapore to launch industry-wide initiatives and administer content development grants. He has produced and designed PC online games at The Education Arcade, a research group at the Massachusetts Institute of Technology that studied and created educational games. He complements a Master's degree in Comparative Media Studies with work in the Media Development Authority of

Singapore, Boston's School of the Museum of Fine Arts, the MIT Media Lab, WMBR 88.1FM, and the MIT Assassins' Guild, the latter awarding him the title of "Master Assassin" for his live-action role-playing game designs. He also headed a live DJ crew at MIT. [philip@mit.edu]

Laurie N. Taylor, PhD, researches digital media and creates digital projects at the University of Florida. Her articles have appeared in various journals and edited collections, including *Game Studies: The International Journal of Computer Game Research* (2003), *Media/Culture* (2004), *Computers and Composition Online* (2004), *Works & Days* (2004), *Videogames and Art: Intersections and Interactions* (2007), and *The Player's Realm: Studies on the Culture of Video Games and Gaming* (2007), and her writings about games and digital media have also appeared in many popular venues. Her current research includes studies of game and digital media interfaces, horror video games, methods of digital representation, and issues of the archive. [Laurien@ufl.edu]

Carl Therrien is currently pursuing a PhD in semiology at Université du Québec in Montreal. His research focuses on the playful and mediated immersion in fictional worlds, in video games and other media. Major publications include two historical contributions in Mark J. P. Wolf's *The Video Game Explosion: A History from PONG to PlayStation and Beyond* (Greenwood Press, 2007), articles on the methodology of interactive film studies (">>Pointez-et-cliquez ici<< Les figures d'interactivité dans le cinéma interactif des premiers temps", in *Film Style*, Forum, 2007), on video game design ("L'appel de la simulation. Deux approches du design vidéoludique", in *Le game design de jeux vidéo*, L'Harmattan, 2005), and on the playful nature of contemporary cinema ("Cinema under the influence of play", in *Narrativity: How Visual Arts, Cinema and Literature are telling the world today*, Dis Voir, 2006). [carl.therrien@gmail.com]

Ragnhild Tronstad is a postdoctorate research fellow at the Department of Media and Communication, University of Oslo. Within the field of game studies, her research has focused mainly on adventure games and MMORPGs, more specifically on the relation between riddles, questing, and seduction; on theatricality and performativity in multi-user games; and on character identification and questions of identity in virtual worlds. Her current research project, financed by The Research Council of Norway, is entitled "Play, Performativity, and Presence: A Study of the Play Concept in New Media Art." [ragnhild.tronstad@media.uio.no]

Feichin Ted Tschang is an Assistant Professor of Management in the Lee

Kong Chian School of Business, Singapore Management University. His research focuses on the growth and development of information technology industries, and he most recently studied the development of the US video game industry. From this, he has written journal articles on the nature of creativity in the design and development process, product development, and studio formation in the industry. He has a PhD in Public Policy Analysis and Management, from Carnegie Mellon University. [tedt@smu.edu.sg]

Adrian Vetta completed a BSc and MSc at the London School of Economics, before studying for a PhD in Mathematics at the Massachusetts Institute of Technology. In 2003, he took up a joint appointment at McGill University in the Department of Mathematics and Statistics, and the School of Computer Science. His research interests concern algorithms, complexity and game theory. [vetta@math.mcgill.ca]

Mark J. P. Wolf is an Associate Professor in the Communication Department at Concordia University Wisconsin. He has a BA (1990) in Film Production and an MA (1992) and PhD (1995) in Critical Studies from the School of Cinema/Television (now re-named The School of Cinematic Arts) at the University of Southern California. His books include *Abstracting Reality: Art, Communication, and Cognition in the Digital Age* (2000); *The Medium of the Video Game* (2001); *Virtual Morality: Morals, Ethics, and New Media* (2003); *The Video Game Theory Reader* (2003); *The World of the D'ni: Myst and Riven* (2006); *The Video Game Explosion: A History from PONG to PlayStation and Beyond* (2007); *J. R. R. Tolkien: Of Words and Worlds* (forthcoming in 2009); and two novels for which he has begun looking for an agent and publisher. He is on the advisory boards of Videotopia, and the *International Journal of Gaming and Computer-Mediated Simulations*, and several editorial boards including those of *Games and Culture*, *The Journal of E-media Studies*, and *Mechademia: An Annual Forum for Anime, Manga and The Fan Arts*. He lives in Wisconsin with his wife Diane and his sons Michael, Christian, and Francis. [mark.wolf@cuw.edu]

Eric Zimmerman has been working in the game industry for fourteen years. He is the co-founder and Chief Design Officer of Gamelab, an independent game development company based in New York City. Gamelab creates and self-publishes innovative singleplayer and multiplayer games that are distributed online, on mobile phones, and through retail, including the hit downloadable games *Jojo's Fashion Show* (2008), *Miss Management* (2007) and *Diner Dash* (2003). Pre-Gamelab titles include *SiSSYFiGHT 2000* (2000) and the PC title *Gearheads* (1996). Eric has taught courses at MIT, New York University, and Parsons School of Design. He has lectured and published extensively about game design and is the co-author with Katie Salen of *Rules of Play: Game Design Fundamentals* (MIT Press, 2004), and *The Game Design Reader: A Rules of Play Anthology* (MIT Press, 2006), as well as the co-editor of *RE:PLAY* (Peter Lang Press, 2004). [www.gamelab.com], [eric@gamelab.com]

Index

Kluchhohn, Clyde 280
Knightmare II (see *Maze of Galious*)
Kristiansson, Johan 225, 226, 227, 229
Krzywinska, Tanya 4, 5
Kubovy, Michael 89, 102, 103, 104, 106, 107
Ku Klux Klan 39
Kuleshov, Lev 253–4
Kuma\War 39–40
Kuhn, Thomas 314–15

Lacan, Jacques 376
lag 301, 303–305, 309–10
    and social communication 303–04
    and time sensitive situations 304
    and flow state 304
    and casual situations 304–05
Laguna Racer 154–55
La-Mulana 17, 169–94
Lakoff, George 56
language 16, 19, 23, 27, 28, 56, 301,
    305–307, 361, 373, 376–77, 381–82
    conventional 51–2
    poetic 51–2
Lantz, Frank 31
Lara Croft Tomb Raider: Anniversary 166
larp (live action role-playing) 326
laserdisc games 161
Laurel, Brenda 387
law 360–61
learning (see also education) 24, 25, 26, 28,
    29, 35, 48, 50, 51, 75, 119, 241, 250, 277,
    308, 309, 315, 322, 323, 352
Lee, Peter 29, 31
Legend of Zelda 179
Legend of Zelda: Twilight Princess, The 79
Legend of Zelda: Phantom Hourglass, The
    144
lens flare 185–86
Levine, Ken 39
licensed video game adaptations 214–15,
    223
    critical reception 215–217, 219–21,
    223–24, 227–28, 231
light mapping 164
liminal 54, 57, 59, 62n19
Lindoff, Thessa 42
lingo 307–09
    and Black Mage job 308
lingusitics (see semiotics)
literacy, traditional 23

literary studies 320
literary theory 361–62
literature 320
Loftus, Geoffrey R. 378
Loftus, Elizabeth F. 378
loot 54, 58
Lord of the Rings, The, film trilogy 213
Lord of the Rings: The Third Age, The 18,
    220–21, 231
lottery 325, 326
Lowenstein, Douglas 228–29, 232
ludic attitude 27, 111, 129n7, 133–34,
    136–40, 142–47
ludic mediation 133–34, 137, 139–40
ludology 34, 296, 139, 301, 318, 322, 327,
    353, 361, 362–64, 369
ludosis, of games 319
ludus 14, 147

M.A.C.H. 3 161
MacArthur Foundation 29, 31
Macintosh TV 209
Maddin, Guy 186, 191
magic circle 16, 24, 26, 28, 48, 95, 111–12,
    113, 296, 326, 364, 379
magic cycle 115–18, 120–27
    hermeneutic Spiral 117, 123
    heuristic Spiral of Gameplay 115–16,
    120–23
    heuristic Spiral of Narrative 116–17,
    122–23
Magic the Gathering 105
Magnavox Odyssey 201, 202, 204
Malinowski, Bronislaw 348
Malone, Thomas W. 240
Manhole, The 161
Manovich, Lev 109–10, 207–08
Marble Madness 159
Mario 157
Mario and Luigi: Partners in Time 354
Mario Bros. 157, 160
mapping, body- 69–73, 75, 79, 80
marketing (see also business and industry)
    190, 215, 225, 227, 233n2, 260
Marr, David 382
Marvel: Ultimate Alliance 122
Mass Effect 354
mass media 43, 139, 202, 298
massively multiplayer online game
    (MMOGs)

Related titles from Routledge

The Video Game Theory Reader

"*The Video Game Theory Reader* is a crucial and timely edited volume which focuses exclusively on the theorization of video games, and thereby makes great strides towards ameliorating a persisting gap in the academic literature..." – *Robert T. Wood, University of Lethbridge, New Media & Society*

"*The Video Game Theory Reader* serves as an excellent introduction to video game studies, the current positions in the field, and the current problems with video game studies..." – *Laurie Taylor, University of Florida, Journal of Film and Video, Winter 2003*

"If anyone has doubts that video games warrant serious reflection and examination as a creative medium, *The Video Game Theory Reader* will dispel them. If anyone involved in the creation of video games is looking for fresh perspectives on their art, they'll find them right here." – *D.B. Weiss, author of Lucky Wander Boy*

In the early days of Pong and Pac Man, video games appeared to be little more than an idle pastime. Today, video games make up a multi-billion dollar industry that rivals television and film.

The Video Game Theory Reader brings together exciting new work on the many ways video games are reshaping the face of entertainment and our relationship with technology. Drawing upon examples from widely popular games ranging from *Space Invaders* to *Final Fantasy IX* and *Combat Flight Simulator 2*, the contributors discuss the relationship between video games and other media; the shift from third- to first-person games; gamers and the gaming community; and the important sociological, cultural, industrial, and economic issues that surround gaming.

The Video Game Theory Reader is the essential introduction to a fascinating and rapidly expanding new field of media studies.

Contributors include: Mia Consalvo, Chris Crawford, Patrick Crogan, Markku Eskelinen, Miroslaw Filiciak, Gonzalo Frasca, Walter Holland, Henry Jenkins, Kurt Squire, Torben Grodal, Alison McMahan, Bernard Perron, Bob Rehak, Ragnhild Tronstad, and Mark J. P. Wolf.

Mark J. P. Wolf is an Associate Professor in the Communication Department at Concordia University Wisconsin.

Bernard Perron is an Associate Professor of Cinema at the University of Montreal.

ISBN 10: 0–415–96578–0 (hbk)
ISBN 10: 0–415–96579–9 (pbk)

ISBN 13: 978–0–415–96578–1 (hbk)
ISBN 13: 978–0–415–96579–8 (pbk)

Available at all good bookshops
For ordering and further information please visit:
www.routledge.com

Related titles from Routledge

Understanding Video Games

"*Understanding Video Games* is required reading for all students of game studies and game design. The text engagingly and comprehensively tackles the exploding field of video game studies, providing the reader with a thorough understanding of the debates, key ideas and history of this fascinating medium." – *Mia Consalvo, author of Cheating: Gaining Advantage in Videogames*

From Pong to PlayStation 3 and beyond, *Understanding Video Games* is the first general introduction to the exciting new field of video game studies. This textbook traces the history of video games, introduces the major theories used to analyze games such as ludology and narratology, reviews the economics of the game industry, examines the aesthetics of game design, surveys the broad range of game genres, explores player culture, and addresses the major debates surrounding the medium, from educational benefits to the effects of violence.

Throughout the book, the authors ask readers to consider larger questions about the medium:

- What defines a video game?
- Who plays games?
- Why do we play games?
- How do games affect the player?

Extensively illustrated, *Understanding Video Games* is an indispensable and comprehensive resource for those interested in the ways video games are reshaping entertainment and society. A companion website (www.routledge.com/textbooks/9780415977210) features student resources including discussion questions for each chapter, a glossary of key terms, a video game timeline, and links to other video game studies resources for further study.

Simon Egenfeldt-Nielsen, **Jonas Heide Smith**, and **Susana Pajares Tosca** are members of the Center for Computer Games Research at the IT University of Copenhagen.

ISBN 10: 0–415–97720–7 (hbk)
ISBN 10: 0–415–97721–5 (pbk)
ISBN 10: 0–203–93074–6 (ebk)

ISBN 13: 978–0–415–97720–3 (hbk)
ISBN 13: 978–0–415–97721–0 (pbk)
ISBN 13: 978–0–203–93074–8 (ebk)

Available at all good bookshops
For ordering and further information please visit:
www.routledge.com

Related titles from Routledge

The Meaning of Video Games:
Gaming and Textual Strategies

"Steven E. Jones rolls his katamari through wonderful terrain, collecting insights about how video games relate to reality TV, otaku culture, British gift-book annuals, and our perspectives on outer space. *The Meaning of Video Games* draws on the methods of textual studies and on a solid understanding of games and how they are played. It is an enjoyable, edifying, next-generation book." – *Nick Montfort, Massachusetts Institute of Technology*

"In *The Meaning of Video Games* Steven E. Jones makes it look easy, effortlessly dissolving distinctions between media studies, game studies, and textual studies. Close readings become 'close playings' (and back again) as the book creates an interdisciplinary convergence culture every bit as mobile and networked as the objects of its study." – *Matthew G. Kirschenbaum, University of Maryland*

"The meaning of video games – suggests Jones – is not intrinsic to the text, but is produced dynamically from the interaction between author and user, code and system, machine and human being. The pleasant digressions on otaku culture, reality TV shows and TV series such as *Lost* (which opens the volume) make reading *The Meaning of Video Games* pleasant, if not essential." – *Matteo Bittanti, Videoludica*

The Meaning of Video Games takes a textual studies approach to an increasingly important form of expression in today's culture. It begins by assuming that video games are meaningful – not just as sociological or economic or cultural evidence, but in their own right, as cultural expressions worthy of scholarly attention. In this way, this book makes a contribution to the study of video games, but it also aims to enrich textual studies.

Early video game studies scholars were quick to point out that a game should never be reduced to merely its "story" or narrative content and they rightly insist on the importance of studying games as games. But here Steven E. Jones demonstrates that textual studies – which grow historically out of ancient questions of textual recension, multiple versions, production, reproduction, and reception – can fruitfully be applied to the study of video games. Citing specific examples such as *Myst* and *Lost*, *Katamari Damacy*, *Halo*, *Façade*, Nintendo's *Wii*, and Will Wright's *Spore*, the book explores the ways in which textual studies concepts – authorial intention, textual variability and performance, the paratext, publishing history, and the social text – can shed light on video games as more than formal systems. It treats video games as cultural forms of expression that are received as they are played, out in the world, where their meanings get made.

Steven E. Jones is Professor of English at Loyola University in Chicago.

ISBN 10: 0–415–96055–X (hbk)
ISBN 10: 0–415–96056–8 (pbk)
ISBN 10: 0–203–92992–6 (ebk)

ISBN 13: 978–0–415–96055–7 (hbk)
ISBN 13: 978–0–415–96056–4 (pbk)
ISBN 13: 978–0–203–92992–6 (ebk)

Available at all good bookshops
For ordering and further information please visit:
www.routledge.com